A WORLD APART

The Will and Testament of the Biala Rabbi

A Guide to Chasidism

The Jewish Literary Treasures of England and America

The Legacy of Polish Jewry

The World of Chasidism

Treasures of Judaica

Chasidism and the State of Israel

Chasidism: The Movement and Its Masters

A Guide to Life

Chasidic Rebbes

Chasidic Story Book

The Prince who turned into a Rooster

Chasidic Encyclopedia (Editor)

A WORLD APART

The Story of the Chasidim in Britain

Harry Rabinowicz

With a Foreword by
RABBI DR JONATHAN SACKS
Chief Rabbi of the United Hebrew
Congregation of the British Commonwealth

VALLENTINE MITCHELL
LONDON • PORTLAND, OR.

First published in 1997 in Great Britain by
VALLENTINE MITCHELL & CO. LTD.
Newbury House, 900 Eastern Avenue
London IG2 7HH, England

and in the United States of America by
VALLENTINE MITCHELL
ISBS, 5804 N.E. Hassalo Street
Portland, Oregon 97213-3644

British Library Cataloguing in Publication data

Rabinowicz, Harry M.
World Apart: Story of the Chasidim
in Britain
I. Title
296.83320941

ISBN 0-85303-261-0 (cloth)
ISBN 0-85303-278-5 (paper)

Library of Congress Cataloging-in-Publication data

Rabinowicz, Tzvi, 1919–
    A world apart: the story of the Chasidim in Britain / Harry
Rabinowicz; with a foreword by Jonathan Sacks.
        p.   cm.
    Includes bibliographical references and index.
    ISBN 0-85303-261-0 (cloth) 0-85303-278-5 (paper)
    1. Hasidism – Great Britain – History – 20th century. 2. Hasidim –
Great Britain – Biography. 3. Judaism – Great Britain – History – 20th
century.   I. Title
BM198.4.G7R33 1996
297.8'332'0941 – dc20   95-5666
                                                            CIP

Typeset by Vitaset, Paddock Wood
Printed in Great Britain by
Bookcraft (Bath) Ltd, Midsomer Norton, Avon

IN MEMORY OF
STELLA AND ALEXANDER MARGULIES

Contents

List of Illustrations

PHOTO CREDITS

The author wishes to thank the individuals and institutions listed below for permission to reproduce some of the photographs in their possession.

Rabbis M Hager, E Halpern, C Jacobs, S Pinter, S Rubin, Rabbi and Mrs C Schlaff, J Shaw, A D Suffrin, S F Vogel.

Messrs Anthony Buckley, I M Cymerman, Henry Jacobs, Motel Schonfeld, M Margulies, Ronen Numa, Mrs Connie Kacenellenbogen, Mrs C M Feldman.

Mr J Groskopf of the *Jewish Tribune*, The Lubavitch Foundation, Mrs D Steinberg of *Beis Yaakov Grammar School for Girls*, the Yesodey Torah Schools.

Special tribute must be paid to the late Valerie Chazan for the two beautiful photographs taken before her tragic death.

Foreword by the Chief Rabbi

In this important and original book, Rabbi Dr Rabinowicz has illuminated a hitherto neglected field of Anglo-Jewish history. If it is true that in the last few years our community has enjoyed a revival of traditional Jewish life, then it is a revival built on the foundations laid by the little-known pioneers described by Rabbi Rabinowicz, who nurtured the seeds of intensive Jewish religious life, often under immensely difficult conditions.

Anglo-Jewry has always been characterised as a formal, seemingly cold community. However, we learn from this latest work from Rabbi Rabinowicz's prolific pen that in numerous small nuclei, *shtieblech* and *chevrot*, key individuals preserved and promoted the vital spirit of Chasidism which they had brought from its source in Eastern Europe. Their influence, as Rabbi Rabinowicz shows, was far beyond their numbers.

We may learn, too, the lesson implicit in the story told in this book. The long-term spiritual history and viability of any community is not necessarily in its great and formal organisations, important and valuable as they undoubtedly are – but in the *mesirat nefesh* of individuals and families, who recognise the needs of a particular community or group, and establish small but vital initiatives to meet them. This was an authentic Jewish response, which we would do well to note today.

Rabbi Rabinowicz has once again placed us all in his debt by his painstaking research and devoted scholarship.

Chief Rabbi Dr Jonathan Sacks
London, 1995

Preface

The Chasidic community in London, especially in Stamford Hill, is an extremely complex universe. Each Chasidic sect has its own customs and rituals, which it maintains meticulously. There are marked differences between Belz and Satmar, between Lubavitch and Ger, and even within the Belz community itself. It is the close allegiance each sect has to its own rebbe that marks the main difference between the various sects. It is a long way geographically from Miedzyboz to Manhattan, from Belz to Bnei Brak, and from Satmar to Stamford Hill, but the links are strong and close. Clearly Chasidism has withstood the test of time for over 200 tormented years.

A casual stroll around Stamford Hill in North London, reveals the unselfconscious Jewishness that prevails there. The Chasidic community is the only section of Anglo-Jewry that is increasing because it has a high birth rate, and it is significant that it has the lowest juvenile delinquency rate in the world. Jewish learning in today's Chasidic world is more vibrant, more intensive, more widespread even than in pre-war Poland.

The successive waves of Jewish immigrants who found refuge in England in the eighteenth and nineteenth centuries, the early Chasidim of the pre-Second World War era, as well as the bulk of the German refugees of the 1930s, somehow integrated into the Anglo-Jewish establishment in the course of one or two generations. The offspring of the Chasidim who came to England before the Second World War left the world of the *shtiebl* behind them, and became involved in the development of the United Synagogue, the Federation of Synagogues and the Union of Orthodox Hebrew Congregations.

In contrast, the post-1945 Chasidic community has remained a sect apart, with its own life-style. Though a minority among its fellow-Jews, it is uninfluenced and unaffected by the world outside. Today's Chasidim wear the same distinctive Chasidic garb as they did in Eastern Europe. Men have beards and sidelocks which are never cut and only rarely trimmed. The fringes of their four-cornered ritual undergarment dangle from their long, sombre-hued silk coats and large black skullcaps peep out from their broad-brimmed black or sable-trimmed hats (*shtreimlech*). Youngsters wear *payot* (side-locks) wound round their ears or else leave them hanging loose. Married women cover their hair with an all-embracing kerchief or wig, and women of all ages wear their dresses long, their arms encased in wrist-length sleeves and their legs covered with opaque dark stockings.

The Chasidim are surrounded by, but almost completely inoculated against, the influence of the Anglo-Jewish society around them. They have erected their own spiritual *eruv* (cordon); they do not subscribe to the nineteenth-century Enlightenment slogan: 'Be a Jew in your house and a human being in the street.' They are totally unwilling to face any *kulturkampf*. They take pride in their otherness in garb and appearance, and their fervent devotion to customs and traditions brooks little compromise. Their *shtieblech* are full of worshippers who pray with the intense intimacy, love, joy and ardour with which their forefathers prayed in the 'old country'. They have established a comprehensive network of educational establishments, from kindergartens to *kollelim*, from *yeshivot* to girls' seminaries.

Education is a fulcrum in Chasidic life. There are about 40 strictly Orthodox educational establishments in the 'sacred square mile' of Stamford Hill. Boys and girls are segregated at a very early age, and the sexes never mix at school or at play. Despite the Chasidic community's relative numerical insignificance – it does not number more than 3,000 families – no other section of Anglo-Jewry spends so much money on educational institutions to ensure its survival. The schools and *yeshivot* are maintained without much State or local authority subsidy, and without financial or even moral support from the general Jewish establishment. Only minimal concessions are made to comply with the legal requirements of secular education.

No other section of Anglo-Jewry devotes such large sums of money to support its own poor brethren. The generous charity of the Chasidim extends to the support of various educational institutions in the Holy Land, and even of Torah institutions in the United States of America.

The Chasidim are completely indifferent to the attitude of some of their fellow-Jews who regard them as 'fanatics', 'primitives', 'the twisted product of Ghetto anti-semitism'. To their opponents, Chasidic theology is tantamount to a *via negativa*, akin to extremism and fundamentalism.

Britain is no longer a homogeneous society; its population represents diverse cultures, religions and orientations. In this pluralistic religious milieu, Chasidism is able to flourish. To the Chasidim their way of life is the only authentic Jewish way of life, and they have nothing in common with secularised and semi-assimilated fellow-Jews.

The almost total absence of archival material and the non-preservation of unpublished sources are major obstacles to the detailed study of Chasidism in this country, as it is in other parts of the world. In the words of the late Abraham Joshua Heschel: 'We remain unsure of thousands of simple facts, biographic data, bibliographic detail . . . Research on Chasidism suffers from a dearth of documents.'[1]

All Chasidic sects, with the excepton of Lubavitch, eschew publicity. It is difficult to obtain the biographies of their rebbes, and the compiler of a *Who's Who* in Chasidism would receive little co-operation.

Many people, Chasidic rebbes and Chasidim, have discussed my work with me. I am grateful to all for their time, patience and wisdom. Gathering material has been a brain-picking operation. Without their help and advice it would have been a less rewarding task. The names of all these individuals are too numerous to mention.

I would like to express my gratitude to many institutions, particularly the Federation of Synagogues, for permitting me access to their archival material. I am grateful to Mr Marcus J Margulies of Time Products plc, Mr A Kramer and the Golda Werner Charitable Trust, Mr Mark Kennedy, Mr and Mrs Keith M Newton, Mrs Mary Kason, the Lord Ashdown Charitable Trust, the Montague Road *Beth Hamidrash* Trust, who gave generously to facilitate my research. Special thanks to my colleagues and friends, Rabbi Joseph Shaw, Rabbi Dr B Susser, Revd S Venitt and Mr David Shepherd who read all or part of the manuscript at one stage or another, all of them offering helpful advice.

My elder son Nathan David read the manuscript in its early stages and made many valuable comments on stylistic matters, and my younger son Jacob Isaac, too, scrutinised the typescript and made a number of perceptive suggestions. I want to express my appreciation to Norma Marson, the editor at Vallentine Mitchell, for her interest and worthwhile comments in preparing the book for publication.

Once again, however, my greatest debt is to my wife Bella. Not only did she participate in the research work, but her wholehearted involvement and constant support have been major factors in making the writing of this book an enjoyable undertaking.

Needless to say, if there are any errors of commission or omission, the fault is mine alone: *autoris culpa est*.

H.R.

London, 29 *Tishri* 5754

1 • The Chasidic Movement

The story of Chasidism, the greatest revivalist movement in the history of Judaism, forms one of the most fascinating and, at the same time, elusive chapters of Jewish history. Many have attempted to describe it. Some, like Peretz, Steinberg, Anski, and, in our days, Buber, Wiesel and Agnon, have done this with great poetic skill; others, like Horodetzky, Dubnow, Weiss and Scholem, with deep historic skill and insight. As yet, only a fringe has been uncovered. For Chasidism, rooted in a world of pure feeling and emotion, eludes the rational grasp of the historian, just as it stubbornly refuses to present itself verbally.

Chasidism is not an ideology to be taught or propagated, but a mode of life; not a theology, but a continually renewed relationship with God. Chasidism brushed away uncertainties and estrangements and revitalised Judaism, not by introducing revolutionary doctrines, but by simply leading the people back to the principles preached by the great prophets and teachers of Israel. To hallow the profane, and to dedicate everything to the service of God, was the Chasidic way to redemption.

Chasidism was born in the mid-eighteenth century, in Eastern Europe, in the southern provinces of Podolia and Volhynia, as testified by the history of the Jews of Eastern Europe which can be traced, period by period, for over one thousand years.

As a result of persecution in eastern Germany in the thirteenth century, there was a mass migration of Jews to Poland, and by the sixteenth century the Jewish population there had increased, and constituted five per cent of the general population. Poland needed middle-class administrators to develop its industries and commerce; it welcomed the Jewish immigrants as being competent in such positions and made them feel at home. As early as 1264, King Boleslas the Pious of Great Poland and Kalish granted the Jews security of person and property. These rights and privileges were confirmed by almost all the subsequent kings of Poland, and became part of Poland's common law.

By the middle of the sixteenth century, Polish Jewry was the most highly organised Jewish community in Europe. Not since the abolition

1

of the Patriarchate and the Exilarchs of Palestine and Babylon, had the Jews enjoyed so full a measure of autonomy. 'The Council of Four Lands', an elaborate organisation amounting to a 'State within a State', gave great help and encouragement to Torah education. Polish Jewry produced a galaxy of distinguished rabbis who made outstanding contributions to the Talmud and Jewish Law. Poland was described as 'heaven for the Jews, paradise for the nobles, and hell for the serfs'. The Jews were not confined to ghettos, nor did they have to wear yellow badges. 'In this country,' writes Rabbi Moses Isserles (1525–72), the foremost rabbi of Polish Jewry, 'there is no fierce hatred against us as in Germany. May it so continue until the advent of the Messiah.'[1]

This golden epoch was of brief duration. The atrocities committed by the raging Cossacks under Bogdan Chmielnicki (1593–1657) were bestial beyond description and added crimson pages to the already overflowing book of Jewish martyrology. In the Ukraine, tens of thousands of Jews were slain, and many communities were all but annihilated. Only one-tenth of the community survived this holocaust. It was a genocidal destruction that is ranked with the devastation of the Second Temple as one of the major disasters in Jewish history, to be surpassed only by the horrors of the Second World War.

As if the cup of suffering were not already brimming over, the rehabilitation of stricken Jewry was impeded by two decades (1648–67) of uprisings, invasions, wars, famines and epidemics in the larger society in which they lived, and the rise of false messiahs in their own ranks. The Jews, particularly those in the villages, suffered from the collapse of law and order.

Intrinsic to Judaism is the belief in the coming of the Messiah, who will fulfil the biblical prophecies and gather together the scattered remnants of the House of Israel. For two thousand years, with a faith that never faltered, and with a yearning that was never stilled, the Jews have believed in and have waited for this promised Redeemer. That conviction rendered them, especially at that time, pathetically vulnerable. Like shooting stars, false messiahs flashed across the skies of Jewish history, inevitably leaving despair and disillusionment in their wake.

In 1648, at the age of 22, Shabbetai Zevi (1626–76), a native of Smyrna, proclaimed himself the long-awaited redeemer. In many communities, Jews sold their possessions and waited for the trumpet of the Messiah. Shabbetai Zevi eventually saved his life from the wrath of the Turks by converting to Islam. He brought despair to the thousands who had believed in his leadership. But the messianic dream would not die. Men arose who again and again created the same illusion. The last and the most harmful of these false messiahs was Jacob Frank (1726–91), the antinomian, a native of Podolia, who preached that the Talmud should be abandoned and that the Deity was a Trinity. Orgies took the place of mystic speculation, and pagan rites became the order of the day. The majority of the Jewish people could only feel relief when Frank and his 600 followers embraced Christianity in 1759.

To political instability and the disappointments over the messianic pretenders were added deteriorating social conditions. In Eastern Europe, class division among the Jews was as clear cut as in the society in which they lived, but the basis of the classes was different. Among the Jews the division was between the scholars and the ignorant. The Jews all worshipped the same God, but the scholars were completely isolated from the ordinary man in the street. Few among the people had the privilege of attending a *yeshiva*, and so the Talmud was a closed book to most. Many scholars pursued fame and honour.[2] Leadership was restricted to a few wealthy oligarchs who were generally unconcerned at the plight of the wretched poor. Jews living outside the towns had no votes in the *kehillot* elections, although they were required to pay communal taxes and observe all regulations. The social status of the common or ignorant person was very low.[3]

Although the eighteenth century is known as the Age of Enlightenment, a period in western civilisation when traditional concepts concerning the nature of man and society were being scrutinised, challenged and reappraised, in Eastern Europe the belief in demons, spirits and the transmigration of the soul was widespread. The Jews of Podolia and Volhynia were, moreover, surrounded by hatred, and their skies were overcast by clouds of medieval superstition. They needed a guide to lead them through the maze of misery, to comfort them and to strengthen them in their spiritual weakness. There was an overwhelming need for such a leader to ensure the survival of the Jewish people and resurrect their faith.

Into that vacuum came the *Besht*, as he became known, the founder of the Chasidic Movement, Rabbi Israel Baal Shem Tov (1700–60), literally, 'Master of the Good Name'. He was born in Okup, a small town in the Province of Podolia, to poor and elderly parents. Orphaned as a child, he became an assistant teacher, and in 1736 he settled in Miedzyboz. Despite a long-time lack of authentic data regarding his parentage, early upbringing and family life, the *Besht* is no longer a shadowy figure. His historical authenticity has recently been established

3

by Mr Roseman's study of contemporary local records.[4] 'I have come into this world,' the *Besht* said, 'to show man how to make the observance of three principles his aim in life, namely, the love of God, the love of Israel and the love of the Torah.' He transformed abstractions into living realities, and spoke directly to the masses in a language they understood. He aimed not to bring man closer to God, but to bring God closer to man. He rejected asceticism and self-affliction. Enthusiasm (*hitlahavut*) and ecstasy took the place of ritual forms of worship. He believed and preached that every individual could help to hasten the advent of the Messiah, and national redemption would be realised only by individual efforts.

Cabbala was originally the jealously kept esotericism of an intellectual elite, who revelled in its mind-intoxicating and mind-illuminating profundities. This was the rich inheritance that the *Besht* wished to share with the masses. He believed that all the children of Israel were entitled to enter this spiritual kingdom, and he threw it open for all to learn its secrets. What had been the privilege of the few became accessible to the many. Chasidism, in its early stages, was, briefly, mysticism for the masses. Though it did not include conjectures and assumptions about the mysteries of the 'Divine Chariot' or the 'Acts of Genesis', it stressed, in the main, the path leading to Godly life on earth. 'I have set the Lord always before me' became the *leitmotif* of the *Besht*. A man has to worship God in all his activities – in eating, in drinking, in his business dealings. The *Besht* wiped away the narrow intellectualism which had estranged the Jewish masses from their heritage. Chasidism focused upon fundamental Judaism, its sublimely simple principles, stressing the joy of life, love of man, sincerity in word and deed – qualities that the common people potentially possessed. Thus, almost miraculously, Chasidism brought comfort, courage and a form of other-worldly ecstasy to Jewish people of all classes and all sections. Chasidism brought back vigour to Judaism, not by introducing revolutionary doctrines, but simply by leading the people back to the original principles preached by the great prophets and teachers of Israel. To hallow the profane and to dedicate everything to the service of God was the Chasidic way to redemption.

Chasidism, confined at first mainly to Podolia, Volhynia and Galicia, expanded widely under the *Besht*'s successor, Rabbi Dov Baer, the Maggid of Mezerich (d. 1773), who was the ideal successor. Trained in rabbinical schools, he was able to influence Jewish classicists. His home town, Mezerich, was nearer to Polish Lithuania than to Podolia. He attracted a number of outstanding followers from the Ukraine, Galicia and Lithuania. Most of his disciples later became famous Chasidic rebbes, founders of great dynasties. His court was the training ground for the *Zaddikim* of the future. Among his disciples were Rabbi Levi Yitzchak of Berdichev (1740–1809), a man who loved God and loved Judaism, but whose love for the Jews exceeded them both. He was Israel's greatest advocate, tempering justice with mercy. Rabbi Nachum of Chernobyl (1730–97), one of the pioneers of Chasidism in the Ukraine, was loud in his praise of charity and his denunciation of the love of money.

While the *Besht* founded Chasidism and Rabbi Dov Baer developed and organised the movement, Rabbi Jacob Joseph Katz of Polonnoye (d. 1784), a leading theoretician, initiated its literature by producing four monumental works, the greatest of which is *Toledot Yaakov Yosef.* Published in 1780, it was the first written manifesto of Chasidism; it was followed by the *Noam Elimelech* of Rabbi Elimelech of Lejask (1717–94). This book discovered the *Zaddik* in his role as God's factotum on earth. It was instantly acclaimed for its power and profundity and became one of the classics of Chasidic literature.

Another of Dov Baer's disciples was Rabbi Shneur Zalman (1745–1813), the author of the *Tanya*, the 'Bible' of *Chabad*, this last word being the acronym of three Hebrew words: *chochmah* (wisdom), *binah* (understanding), and *da'at* (knowledge), three kindred faculties. *Chochmah* is the initial idea, *binah* is the development of this idea and *da'at* is its logical conclusion. The basis of the Chabad movement, which Rabbi Shneur Zalman founded, was that the mind has domination over the heart, that faith must be interwoven with understanding. This movement also became known as Lubavitch, after the small town Lybavichi in Belorussia in which Rabbi Zalman's successor lived. Possessed of the learning of a sage and the emotional temperament of a Chasid, Rabbi Shneur Zalman added flavour to the Chasidic movement.

Like other religious sects throughout the ages, the Chasidim were at first persecuted and their principles distorted and practices maligned. Talmudists put aside their calm deliberations and precipitously condemned the movement. Rabbi Elijah ben Solomon Zalman, the Gaon of Vilna (1720–97), possibly the greatest Halachic authority since Maimonides, became Chasidism's foremost opponent. Though himself a mystic, the Gaon failed to see the value and the potential of Chasidism. He regarded it as having more in common with the false messianism of Shabbetai Zevi and Jacob Frank than with Luria's Cabbala.

5

The establishment of Chasidic houses of worship, he felt, might cause division and confusion in the House of Israel. He found it unpardonable that some Chasidim disregarded the prescribed hours of prayer. To him, the criticism of intensive Torah study – expressed by some of the Chasidic leaders – threatened the very survival of Judaism. The cult of *zaddikim*, too, was foreign to the Gaon, for they constituted a new type of teacher whose powers stemmed from the emotions rather than from knowledge, the heart rather than the head. He could not regard Chasidism as the next phase in the development of Jewish mysticism.

Jewish Lithuania became the stronghold of the opposition to the Chasidic movement and the centre of Chasidic persecution. In 1772, with the approval of the Gaon, the community of Vilna issued a *cherem* (excommunication) against what the Gaon described as the 'Godless sect'. Even this did not satisfy the opposition. They felt that stronger measures were necessary to destroy the movement. To this end, they informed the Russian authorities of the subversive activities of the Chasidim. The Russians acted with practised speed. On two occasions, in 1798 and in 1800, Rabbi Shneur Zalman was imprisoned by the Russian authorities, who brought many charges against him, all of which he successfully refuted. The 'civil war' was finally settled by State intervention after two decades of strife. The *Jewish Statute*, issued by Czar Alexander I on 9 December 1804, granted every Jewish community the right to worship and let others worship as each saw fit. The Chasidim had won the right to exist.

As the movement spread, great *zaddikim* arose who led the people wisely and well in the paths of the Torah. Despite the antagonism shown towards them by the rabbinate of the eighteenth century few Chasidim questioned the validity of the *Halachah*.

During the nineteenth and our own twentieth century, the Chasidic world has produced more outstanding spiritual leaders than has any other period since Talmudic times. Rabbi Nachman of Bratslav (1772–1810), the great-grandson of the *Besht*, was the most gifted story-teller in the annals of Chasidism. His stories rank with the classic tales of Hans Christian Andersen.

Poland, which was the *achsanya shel Torah* (the asylum of the Law), responded to the resurrecting force of Chasidism. The pioneers there were Rabbi Israel Hofstein (1733–1815), the Maggid of Kozienice; Rabbi Jacob Isaac, 'the Seer of Lublin' (1745–1815); and Jacob Isaac, 'the Holy Jew of Przysucha' (1765–1814), who maintained that the study of the Talmud purifies the mind and that it is only through hard work and sincere devotion that one can reach the highest spiritual pinnacle. Rabbi Menachem Mendel Morgenstern of Kotzk (1787–1859) attached no importance to what were popularly called miracles. He believed that the greatest achievement was to transform a Jew into a real Chasid. Religion to him was not something passive, not just a mere pattern, a routine, but a test of a man's spirituality. He did not go out to the masses of Chasidim, but only reached the select few, the spiritual élite.

The nineteenth century was the golden era of the movement. The rebbes were no longer itinerant preachers, but established figures with their own 'courts' and dynasties. Many a remote hamlet in Russia and Poland owes its immortality to a Chasidic rebbe who lived there and adopted its name as his title. So it was with Belz, Ruzhin and Ger. These small towns not only produced unique personalities who moulded and refashioned the lives of Jews but for more than a hundred years were focal centres, cities of refuge for Chasidim in Eastern Europe. In the nineteenth and twentieth centuries, many of the Chasidic rabbis of Poland, Galicia and Hungary were acknowledged princes of the Torah. Rabbi Isaac Meir Alter of Ger, Rabbi Abraham Bornstein of Sochaczew, Rabbi Meir Yechiel Halevi Halstock of Ostrowiec and Rabbi Zevi Hirsch Spiro of Munkacz were renowned Halachic authorities.

The Chasidic sky was composed of many planets, each set in its appointed place, each revolving in its orbit and each contributing to the brilliant light that flooded the Jewish world. The power of the rebbe was far-reaching. His most casual utterances were invested with many layers of mystic meaning and his considered judgements were unquestioned counsels. He wore infallibility like a silken *kapote*, and his endorsement was thought to guarantee the success of any project. A rebbe was a guide to whom followers could turn for advice with their problems, whatever they might be. He was a teacher, counsellor and father confessor to whom the Chasidim could unburden their hearts; a friend in this world and an advocate in the world to come. He was not an official of the community, nor was he elected or appointed. Unlike the rabbi (*rav*) he required no ordination, and unlike the priest (*kohen*) he did not necessarily inherit his office, although a rebbe was often automatically succeeded by a son or grandson.

From the remote and humble villages of Eastern Europe during periods of almost continuous pogroms and persecution, these rebbes, by precept, practice and exhortation, ensured the survival of *Yiddishkeit* leading the people in the paths of the Torah, helping them to live fuller and more meaningful lives.

The personalities and lives of these highly individualistic *zaddikim* varied considerably. Some lived in style, others barely subsisted in abject poverty. Some were known as 'wonder-workers', others were authors, orators and scholars. Entrancing tales were told about them, and they themselves added mystical and marvellous new dimensions to the art of story-telling. Many *zaddikim* maintained large households, receiving and entertaining hundreds of followers. For many-faceted was the role of the rebbe. He was the attorney (*melitz yosher*) who pleaded for his client before the august assembly of the Heavenly Court; he was the *guter Yid* (good Jew), the friendly father-figure, to whom his children could unburden their hearts. Whether they needed spiritual strengthening or *gezunt und parnossa* (health and sustenance), the rebbe's blessing and his assurance that 'The Almighty would help' sounded like music to the ears of the afflicted Jews, sunk in despair. The rebbes established *shtieblech* in the various towns in which their followers resided, and the life of the Chasidim centred upon them. *Zaddikism* never became an instrument of oppression or corruption. Self-seeking practitioners were rare, if they existed at all.

Chasidism brought about a veritable renaissance of Jewish music. 'Serve the Lord with joy' was the vibrant theme that surged through Chasidism. Its music had unique characteristics. Each dynasty had its own favourite melodies, and it was often possible to identify a Chasid by the tune he hummed. Dance, too, was the expression of the highest level of religious fervour, often to the point of complete self-oblivion. Chasidim danced as they prayed and rejoiced as they danced, fired by religious enthusiasm (*hitlahavut*), not by riotous revelry.

Both Kuzmir (Kaziemiersz) and Modzitz occupy important places in the history of Chasidic musicality. What *Chabad* did for the philosophy of Chasidism, Modzitz did for its music. The Modzitzer melodies captivated the Chasidic world. The dynasty of Bobow (Bobowa), too, is renowned for its musical creativity.

Popular misconception puts the Chasidic woman in her place – in the kitchen and in the nursery – assigning to her only the function of producing and serving an ever-increasing family. This is false. The *Chasida*, as she was called, occupied an honoured position in the Chasidic world, and often the wife converted the husband. The emotionalism of the Chasidic movement attracted the women, who brought to it sensitivity and appreciation. They read Chasidic anecdotes (printed in Yiddish) as avidly as their twentieth-century counterparts devour romantic novels.

When it became known that one of the five assassins of Alexander II, the 'Czar liberator', on 1 March 1881 was a Jewess, the cry went up among impoverished peasants and urban poor in Russia that the Jews had killed the Czar. The Jews became convenient scapegoats. By the end of that year, 215 Jewish communities in the Ukraine, White Russia and Bessarabia had been devastated. Hundreds were killed, 20,000 left homeless, 100,000 were financially ruined and property valued at well over half a million pounds destroyed. The pogroms continued for a further three years and there were sporadic outbreaks throughout the next quarter-century.

The Temporary Laws of 3 May 1882, known as the May Laws, prohibited Jews from settling outside the area of the so-called Pale of Settlement, which constituted no more than four per cent of Russian territory. Jews were forbidden to acquire land by purchase or lease. They were required to supply a great number of army recruits, who were excluded from any promotion. Severe numerical limits were imposed on admission to the universities. The Jews, a literate and law-abiding community, were made second-class citizens: a total of 140 statutes were enacted, discriminating against them.

The Jewish position in Russia was graphically described in a memorandum addressed to the Czar by the Lord Mayor of London on 10 December 1890:

> Pent up in narrow bounds within your Majesty's wide Empire, and even within those bounds forced to reside chiefly in towns that reek and overflow with every form of poverty and wretchedness; forbidden all free movement, hedged in every enterprise by restrictive laws; forbidden tenure of land or all concern in land, their means of livelihood have become so cramped as to render life for them well-nigh impossible. Nor are they cramped alone in space and action. The higher education is denied them, except in limits far below the due proportion of their needs and aspirations. They may not freely exercise professions, like other subjects of your Majesty, nor may they gain promotion in the army, however great their merit and their valour.

Throughout the nineteenth century, the links between Chasidism and the land of Israel were well maintained. All Chasidim were passionate lovers of Zion. There were many instances of rabbis giving active expression to their love for the Holy Land. For most of them this was a spiritual passion. They did not, however, support Zionism. In the eyes of Chasidim, the *Haskalah* (Enlightenment) movement was synonymous with assimilation, even with apostasy, and many of the *Maskilim* (Enlightened Ones) carried the flag of Zionism. Moreover, the restoration of Palestine by political means was regarded as tantamount to interference with the Divine order of things. Most of the Chasidim were associated with the *Aguda* or Agudat Yisrael, a world-wide organization of Orthodox Jews, which, in 1923, resolved that the Movement must support the Jewish people spiritually and materially in the Holy Land as elsewhere.

While the Zionists were building the National Home, the *Aguda* was mainly Diaspora-orientated. Its achievements in the Holy Land in the inter-war years were negligible. Though vociferous in politics, it put little effort into contributing to the colonising of the Holy Land. Its vast resources were concentrated in Poland, the main reservoir of its strength, where one-third of the Jewish population were Chasidim. Its influence extended to every sphere of East European Jewish life – political, economic and social. Its representatives sat on parliamentary councils in Poland, Lithuania, Latvia, Hungary and Romania. With one-third of Polish Jewry being Chasidim, Chasidic rabbis, with the exception of Belz and Alexander, were associated with the *Aguda* and participated in the communal, municipal and parliamentary elections. The *Aguda* maintained its own schools and, with its support, Sara Schenierer (1883–1935), the dressmaker turned educationalist, established the *Beth Yaakov* schools for girls. By 1937 there were 250 *Beth Yaakov* schools with 38,000 pupils. There were *Agudist* youth and women's organisations, a daily newspaper and a publishing house.

In the inter-war years Poland was the home of the great *yeshivot*, usually situated in tiny towns which, to the entire Jewish world, became the Cambridges, the Oxfords, the Harvards and the Yales. The trend towards Chasidic *yeshivot* developed when the rebbes began to establish their own religious academies. Though the *Aguda* was anti-Zionist, paradoxically it was passionately pro-Zion. But few of its adherents translated this ancient yearning into practical reality. From 1881 until the outbreak of the First World War in 1914, nearly two million Jews left Eastern Europe. Yet the Chasidim hesitated. They feared the moral dangers of the Godless countries of the West and the possible anti-Jewish influence on their children more than they feared the physical dangers from murderous mobs where they lived. Their rabbis discouraged emigration and only a small number had the courage to withstand this pressure and to leave Eastern Europe before the Holocaust.

During the crucial inter-war years the power of Chasidism increased.

This was a period of political awakening. No longer confined to the *shtiebl*, the Chasidim began to exert their considerable influence on every phase of Jewish life. Warsaw, the capital of Poland, was the home of many Chasidic rebbes, and the Rebbe of Ger, Rabbi Abraham Mordechai Alter, was the dominant figure of Polish Chasidism. There were also sizable Chasidic communities in Hungary, Romania and Czechoslovakia, which were dominated by the dynasties of Sadagora, Boyan, Satmar and Munkacz.

The six years between 1939 and 1945 saw the catastrophic end of a millennium of East European Jewish culture, as Nazi-occupied Poland became the graveyard of six million Jews. World Jewry was diminished by nearly a third of its number. As the Holocaust raged, the lights of Chasidism were dimmed. The Jewish quarters of Warsaw, Lodz and Lublin, once citadels of piety and learning with their hundreds of *shtieblech*, *batei midrash*, Chasidic courts and *yeshivot*, became piles of rubble, with the almost total annihilation of the Jewish communities. Rebbes by the score perished with holy scrolls in their hands and holy words on their lips.

The destruction of East European Jewry and the isolation of Russian Jewry behind the 'Iron Curtain', have given added significance to the Torah institutions of the Western hemisphere. Chasidism refused to die, and out of the ashes it arose again.

Little is generally known about the part Chasidim are playing in the rebuilding of the State of Israel. They are no longer, as they were in the nineteenth century, an unproductive element, depending on *chalukah* (charity), but are, for the most part, integrated into the economy of the country. Often the Chasidim are erroneously identified with the *Neturei Karta*, a tiny but highly vocal group of militant followers of Satmar, but the vast majority of Chasidim reject the ideology of these zealots and are repelled by them. Israel is today a thriving centre of Chasidism. It is the home of many great surviving dynasties. Chasidic courts flourish in Jerusalem, Tel Aviv and Bnei Brak, and new Chasidic *yeshivot* are being established. Nearly 60,000 Chasidim support the *Aguda* and the most numerous Chasidic sect is Ger. Old Chasidic texts are being reprinted and new books written. Whilst most tourists visit the *Mea Shearim* quarter of Jerusalem, many miss the picturesque Chasidic district of Geula. They holiday in the popular resort of Netanya, but few are aware of the existence of *Kiryat Sanz* just outside it. Similarly, few visitors to Tel Aviv visit *Kiryat Vishnitz* in nearby Bnei Brak.

The first Chasidic attempt to establish an agricultural settlement in

Palestine was made by Rabbi Ezekiel Taub of Yablona (Jablonow in Galicia), a descendant of Rabbi Ezekiel Taub of Kazimiersz. In *Adar* 1925, the Rabbi of Yablona arrived in the Land of Israel accompanied by 12 families. The Jewish National Fund allotted these settlers some dunams of land near Nahalal, and soon there were 100 families living there. Their industry and courage aroused general admiration.

In his autobiography, Dr Chaim Weizmann (1874–1952) describes a visit to these unusual Chasidic pioneers.

> On the way to Nahalal, we passed a hill crowned with newly erected barracks, around which clustered a number of people who looked like recently arrived refugees. They made a striking group. We discovered that they were Chasidim who, led by their Rabbi, had landed in Palestine only a few days before. Many of them had since then been compelled to sleep in the open which, despite the light rains still to be expected in April, they were finding a wonderful experience. Balfour [Lord Arthur James, 1848–1930] alighted from the car and went into the barracks to receive the blessings of the Rabbi. I told him that if he would come again in a year or two he would find quite a different picture; he would find these people established on their own land, content and looking like peasants descended from generations of peasants.[5]

A number of Chasidic rebbes and Chasidim settled in the United States before the Second World War and during the war a few more rebbes found refuge in New York. It was only after the end of the war that the Chasidim really began to exert an influence on the Jewish community. Brooklyn, Williamsburg, Crown Heights and Boro Park have become Chasidic centres. Within a radius of 40 blocks, there are more than 30 synagogues of varying sizes and many Chasidic schools for boys and girls, as well as *yeshivot* and *kollelim*.

Today, the Satmar community in Williamsburg alone accounts for 30,000 Chasidim and that of Lubavitch in Crown Heights numbers more than 1,000 families. Other Chasidic groups, such as Bobow, Vishnitz, Stolin and Bratslav have many adherents. Ten per cent of American *yeshivot* are Chasidic.

There are sizable Chasidic groups in Australia, South America and Canada, and over 1,300 Chasidim live in Antwerp,[6] where their spiritual leader until recently was Rabbi Moses Isaac Gewirtzman (1882–1976). Renowned as a miracle-worker, he was the most venerated *zaddik* of post-war Europe and has been succeeded by his son-in-law, Rabbi Leizer.

Chasidism has even overflowed the borders of the Sephardi world, for in Morocco and Tunisia many Jewish children receive a Chasidic education. Chasidism has reached countries and continents which have never before beheld a Chasid. The global activities of Lubavitch span 30 countries on six continents, from Hawaii to Hong Kong, Columbia to Costa Rica, and Venezuela to Vancouver. They represent 'the Mission to Jews by Jews'.

Today there are probably no more than 200,000 Chasidim throughout the world, but the movement's significance cannot be assessed on the basis of numbers alone. Chasidism is receiving the careful attention and research of writers and thinkers of many denominations.

Chasidic philosophy has added a new dimension to daily life, and some 3,000 works of Chasidic literature have enriched the minds of men. Buber made Chasidism and its leaders, its tales, and even the names of tiny Chasidic townlets in Eastern Europe, famous in his writings. The movement is now highly respected and its ideas feature in every religious anthology.

Moreover, Chasidic music has a special quality. It has influenced synagogal liturgy and the songs and dances of modern Israel are greatly indebted to it. The steady output of recordings of Chasidic song and dance is audible evidence of the timelessness of its melodies, which poignantly express the yearnings of the Jewish soul. Today, Chasidism exerts a discernible influence on Jewish writers. Its inspirations can be detected in the poetry of the Nobel Prize winner Nelly Sachs, the stories of Nobel Prize winners Shmuel Yosef Agnon, Isaac Bashevis Singer, Elie Wiesel and the writings of Abraham Joshua Heschel.

In a letter written to his brother-in-law, Rabbi Gershon of Kitev, in the Holy Land, Rabbi Israel Baal Shem Tov made this startling revelation: 'On *Rosh Hashanah* (New Year) 1747, I experienced an uplifting of the soul and asked the Messiah: "When will you come?" and his reply was: "This shall be a sign to you: when your teachings (Chasidism) will become generally known."'[7] Just as the Dutch Rabbi Manasseh Ben Israel (1604–57) had, a century earlier, in 1650, in one of his treatises *Hope of Israel* (*Spes Israelis*), maintained that the final redemption of the world would take place when the scattered children of Israel would extend 'from one end of the earth to another', so Rabbi Israel Baal Shem Tov affirmed that the spread of Chasidism throughout the Jewish world was a prerequisite to redemption.

Hence, the Chasidim today are the defenders of the faith and are reviving the traditions of their fathers in the lands of freedom.

2 • Winds of Change

In the nineteenth century, Chasidism was greatly maligned. The historian Heinrich Graetz (1817–91) had nothing to offer but abuse when he dealt with the movement which was making such headway in his own lifetime. To him 'the new sect, a daughter of darkness, was born in gloom, and even today proceeds stealthily in its mysterious way . . . Ugly as the name, Besht, was the form of the founder and the order that he called into existence.'[1]

He was far from accurate and remarkably inept in his interpretation of this movement. Graetz was no doubt influenced by the philospher Solomon Maimon who wrote: 'The Besht [he named him Yoel instead of Israel] became very celebrated on account of some lucky cures that he effected by means of medical knowledge and his conjuring tricks, and gave out that this was not done by natural means but solely by Cabbala and the use of sacred names.'[2] The *Mithnaggedim*, as the opponents of the Chasidim were called, were not their only enemies. The men of the *Haskalah* regarded Chasidism as a conglomeration of base superstitions and semi-magical and blind fanaticism.

Joseph Perl (1773–1839), the Galician satirist, attacked the Chasidim for what he called their ignorance, crudity and lack of culture. This attitude is reflected by the historians of the nineteenth century. Isaac Marcus Jost (1793–1860) regarded Cabbala as 'superstitious tendencies and vagaries of dreams'.[3]

It is not surprising that the non-Jewish historians followed the example of the Enlightenment. Alexander McCaul (d. 1863) of Trinity College, Dublin, in his *Sketches of Judaism and the Jews*, wrote: 'The Chasidim are a fanatical sect whose fanaticism exceeds the bounds of belief.'[4] Similarly, the American writer, Hannah Adams (1755–1837), in her *History of the Jews*,[5] calls the Besht 'artful Israel', who prohibited his adherents under the most severe spiritual penalties from cultivating and using their intellects. She further stated that 'Melech' (no doubt referring to Rabbi Elimelech of Lejask) 'prohibited the use of medicine for the sick'.[6]

14

Chasidism had a bad press everywhere. As late as 1880 the London *Jewish Chronicle* wrote:

> All these sects, however, have one principle in common: they shun civilisation as a contagious malady, disregard those who do not partici-pate in their doctrines, prohibit the reading of any profane book or news-paper, even when written in Hebrew, and maintain themselves as well as their children in profound ignorance and superstition. They live for the greater part in poverty, sometimes misery, but believe that they are certain to be rewarded in the future life for their studies.[7]

In marked contrast to the attitude of both *Maskilim* and *Mithnaggedim* was that of Sir Moses Montefiore (1784–1885) who was perhaps the most outstanding Jewish personality of the nineteenth century. After retiring from the Stock Exchange at the age of 40, he devoted the rest of his life to fighting for the rights of the Jews throughout the world. Although a Sephardi, he did not discriminate between his fellow-Jews; Sephardim and Ashkenazim, Chasidim and Mithnaggedim; all were his beloved brethren.

The Chasidim in the Holy Land and in Eastern Europe regarded him with great veneration. Sir Moses's first encounter with the Chasidim took place in the Holy Land. Dr Louis Loewe (1809–88), secretary to Sir Moses, described the charismatic Chasidic rebbe, Dov Baer of Ovruch (1760–1841) in these words: 'One of the most rare sages I ever met. Not only was he acting without drawing any salary from communal funds, but he also distributes charity. From five to 15 people would eat at this table every day.'[8] Sir Moses also formed a close association with the Bak family, Chasidim of Ruzhin who became pioneers of Hebrew printing in the Holy Land.[9] In 1843, Sir Moses sent them a new printing press and the printer gratefully acknowledged this 'gift of Sir Moses and Lady Montefiore' in his publications.

In an effort to improve the economic situation of the Jews in Russia, Rabbi Yitzchak of Warka (d. 1848) consulted Rabbi Israel Friedmann of Ruzhin who advised him to contact one of his Chasidim, Israel Binenfeld of Cracow, who would personally carry letters from the Rebbe to Sir Moses. In a letter dated 22 *Elul* 1840 Rabbi Israel appealed to the Baronet to come to Russia and to intervene with the Czarist authorities.[10] Binenfeld came to London in November 1845 and, armed with a letter of recommendation from Chief Rabbi N M Adler, visited Sir Moses at East Cliff Lodge, Ramsgate, on 16 November 1845, and he readily agreed to undertake the journey.[11]

When Sir Moses visited Warsaw on 13 May 1846 the Chasidic leaders, Rabbis Isaac Meir Alter and Yitzchak Kalish of Warka, called upon him. 'The same day,' recorded Dr Loewe, 'a deputation of that pre-eminently conservative class of the Hebrew community, known by the appellation of "Chasidim" paid us a visit. They wore hats, according to European fashion, instead of the Polish *czapka* or the *mycka* which is similar to that worn by the Circassians.'[12]

Writing from Warsaw to Hananel de Castro (d. 1863), a prominent English Sephardi, Sir Moses stated: 'Here I have already received the promise of many of the Chasidim to change their fur hats for German hats and to adopt the German costume generally.'[13]

There are many apocryphal accounts of the intellectual duels between Sir Moses and his secretary on the one side and the Chasidim on the other. 'Behold there is a good case to be made in favour of Enlightenment,' Dr Loewe reasoned. 'Mordechai [the hero of the Book of Esther] understood the dialect of Bigthan and Teresh, two of the king's chamberlains who sought to lay hands on King Ahasuerus.[14] Had not Mordechai been conversant with his native tongue he would not have been able to discern the plot. The salvation of the Jews was cetainly due to Mordechai's linguistic ability.' Rabbi Isaac Meir of Ger with characteristic acumen easily countered this argument.

> From the story of the Book of Esther, you can equally deduce that the Jews were not at all conversant with their native tongue. Had it been generally known that the Jews understood the native tongue, Bigthan and Teresh would not have spoken in Mordechai's hearing. Mordechai, as a member of the Sanhedrin, was certainly a linguist, but this did not apply to the masses.

To the end of his life Sir Moses supported the needs of the Chasidic community in the Holy Land.[15]

Another link between nineteenth-century England and Chasidism was Laurence Oliphant (1829–88), prolific and popular writer, wit, secret agent, war correspondent, mystic, entrepreneur, restless and sagacious traveller. This Victorian gentleman, described by East European Jews as a 'second Cyrus' became a legend in the ghettos of Eastern Europe. In the middle of May 1882 Oliphant expressed his desire to meet the Chasidic rebbe of Sadagora, Rabbi Abraham Jacob Friedmann (1819–83).

The Rebbe and his sons gave Oliphant a warm welcome. Oliphant wanted the Rebbe's help to establish a national fund to purchase the

Holy Land from the Turks,[16] and he gives a graphic description of his momentous visit.

> The Rebbe sent his own carriage for us – a handsome barouche, drawn by a pair of valuable horses, with coachman and groom with kaftan and curls . . . The Rabbiner himself was a man with a white beard, apparently between 60 and 70 years of age who conversed intelligently on the subject of the conditions and projects of the Russian Jews.[17] The Rebbe claimed direct descent from the House of David.[18]

Oliphant's enthusiasm was not shared by the *Jewish Chronicle* which stated, 'Mr Oliphant seems to be much impressed by the sect of Chasidim, which certainly does, at first sight, impress the observer with its strange mysticism.'[19]

In the first hundred years of its existence, the Chasidic movement established no roots in England. The Rebbe of Lubavitch, Joseph Isaac Schneersohn (1880–1950) recalled in his memoirs that his ancestor, Rabbi Moshe, spent some time in London engaged in literary activities.[20] Rabbi Nachman of Bratslav lived the last five months of his life (May to October 1810) in Uman. There he renewed his acquaintance with Hirsch Baer Hurwitz (1785–1857) who later settled in England and changed his name to Hermann Hedwig Bernard. In 1837, Bernard was appointed Preceptor in the Hebrew Language by the University of Cambridge at a stipend of £30 per year. In none of his many writings is there any mention of Rabbi Nachman or his Chasidic acquaintances.[21]

The 'apostate and penitent' Sanislav Hoga forms another tenuous link with Chasidism. Hoga's Hebrew name was Yecheskel or Chaskel. His father Yehuda Arye Leib was the Rabbi of Kuzmir (Kazimiersz) and a devoted Chasid of Rabbi Jacob Isaac Hurwitz of Lublin. Chasidic legend has it that the youthful and unruly Chaskel played practical jokes on the Rebbe of Lublin. On one occasion he placed in the pocket of the Rebbe's kaftan a piece of parchment on which he had inscribed in beautiful Hebrew lettering the words: 'Jacob Isaac is the Messiah', signed with the Tetragrammaton. When the Rebbe found this missive, his spontaneous reaction was: 'This can surely not be genuine. Had the Almighty signed it, He would have used the word *Emet* (Truth) which is God's traditional signature. As it is, no good will come of the writer, he will become an apostate.'

In 1816 Chaskel was appointed assistant to the censor of Jewish publications, and despite his eventual conversion, was at first the spokesman for Chasidism. On 3 August 1824 a disputation took place in

Warsaw between the warring Jewish sects and Hoga appeared as the spokesman and defender of Chasidism.

In 1838 we find him in London where, in the latter part of his life, he engaged in literary and scientific activities. It is not certain whether he returned to Judaism. Though he was buried in Highgate Cemetery, it is said that to atone for his former activities he actually starved himself to death at his lodgings at 98 Charlotte Street, London. He, too, makes no reference to his Chasidic background in his prolific writings.[22]

The first sympathetic interpretation in England of Chasidism was given by Dr Solomon Schechter (1850–1915), of Cairo Geniza fame, although at one time he was very critical of Chasidim and Chasidism. Schechter's father Isaac lived in Foscani, Romania, but came from Lukasch, Volhynia, and was a Chasid of Lubavitch. Schechter himself was named Shneur Zalman after the founder of Chabad, Rabbi Shneur Zalman of Liady. After receiving a rabbinic education in the *yeshivot*, in 1875 he went to study in Vienna, where his tutors were Isaac Hirsch Weiss, Adolf Jellinek and Meir Friedmann, who was himself brought up in a Chasidic milieu. In 1882 Schechter came to England as tutor to Claude G Montefiore (1858–1938) who devoted his life to philanthropy and scholarship and for many years financed and edited the *Jewish Quarterly Review*. Schechter maintained that the blood of generations of Chasidim ran in his veins, and he retained throughout his life the warmth of feeling, the simple faith, and the joy in Jewish observance he had imbibed in his Chasidic home. He believed with the Chasidim that the spark of Divinity is in every person.[23]

On 13 November 1887 Schechter delivered a paper on Chasidism at the new session of the Jews' College Literary Society and Dr Michael Friedlander (1833–1910), the principal of Jews' College, presided. It was at this meeting that Dr Hermann Adler (later Chief Rabbi) stated that 'The Chasidim were not opposed to learning and Talmudism. In fact, to give one example, his own famous relative, Rabbi Nathan Adler, was one of the most learned Talmudists of the day.'[24]

He was referring to Rabbi Nathan ben Simeon HaKohen Adler (1741–1800), a disciple of Rabbi Tevele David Schiff. Adler, the author of Glosses on the Mishnah under the title *Mishnat Rabbi Nathan*, used the Prayer Book of Rabbi Isaac Luria, employing the Sephardi pronunciation. However, strictly speaking, he was a Cabbalist and not a Chasid.

Schechter's paper on Chasidism, his first literary effort in England, was originally written in German and was translated by C G Montefiore.

It was later incorporated and published in his work, *Studies in Judism.*[25] Schechter admitted 'that there was a time when I loved the Chasidim, as there was a time when I hated them'.[26] During the time he spent in Vienna and Berlin, Schechter, under the pseudonym *Chisda ben Chisda*, had published a series of 'Satires on Chasidism' in the Hebrew periodical *HaShachar.*[27] His first satire was an imitation of Joseph Perl's *Megillat Temirim*. In these articles, Schechter ridiculed the Chasidim who 'literally bathed themselves in whisky'.[28] He poked fun at the Rebbe of Lublin who was anxious to hasten the coming of the Messiah. 'He was persuaded to drink a lot of whisky and threw himself out of the window.'[29] Schechter probably alludes here to the fact that, on the night of *Simchat Torah* of 1814, after the *Hakafot*, Rabbi Jacob Isaac Hurwitz, the 'Seer', left his *Beth Midrash* and retired to his room on the first floor of his house. At midnight, a Chasid, Eliezer of Chmelnick, passed the courtyard of the Rebbe and saw a stricken body lying on the ground. This mysterious fall of the 'Seer' has never been explained. The Rebbe died on *Tisha B'Av* 1815 of the injuries sustained in this fall.

In his second satire,[30] under the signature of *Yachaz ben Rahza*, Schechter wrote on Rabbi Baer Friedmann of Leove (1817–66), the son of Rabbi Israel of Ruzhin, who temporarily defected from the Chasidim and lived for a time in Czernowitz at the home of the *Maskil* Dr Juda Leib Reitman.[31] The defection was naturally widely exploited by the *Maskilim* when the erstwhile rebbe declared publicly that he sought to escape from the 'foolish crowd', and wished 'to remove the thorns from the vineyard of the house of Israel and to free Judaism from the irrational customs that have no basis in Jewish law'.

In his 1889 London lecture on Chasidism, however, Schechter donned the mantle of a *Baal Teshuvah* (penitent). He stressed the 'genius of its founder',[32] conceded that 'there can be no real doubt of the Baal Shem's claim to originality', and applauded the three virtues to which Chasidism assigns the highest honours: *shiflut* (humility), *simchah* (cheerfulness),[33] and *hitlahavut* (enthusiasm).[34]

The paper expressed appreciation of the strong bond that Chasidim created among themselves: 'The Chasidim were second to no other sect in their loyalty and affection for one another. No sacrifice was too great for a brother Chasid. They knew no differences of rich and poor, old and young, wise and ignorant.'[35] Schechter admitted that 'the greater number of the Baal Shem's leading disciples as well as Baer's[36] were beyond question men of pure unalloyed piety who would have rejected with scorn any idea of making trade of their sacred profession,'[37] and he fully endorsed that 'several Zaddikim were learned men, and thinkers of no ordinary kind. The works of Solomon Ladier[38] or Mendel Vitebsker,[39] read with attention and without western pre-conception, certainly give the impression of both originality and depth of thought.'[40]

Schechter appreciated the Chasidic past, then, but showed less approval when he discussed contemporary events. He believed that Chasidism ceased to be a force for the regeneration of the Jewish people from the day when *Zaddikism* replaced the original doctrines. He blamed Chasidic leaders for the weakening of the movement. 'Each Zaddik,' he said, 'sought to have a whole little sect to himself, from which to draw an undivided revenue.'[41] In his opinion, the *Zohar* was 'one of the most interesting literary forgeries and is a marvellous mixture of good and evil'.[42]

The subsequent history of Chasidism is almost entirely a record of decay. As formulated by its founder, the new creed amounted to a genuine reformation, pure and lofty in ideal. After his death unhappily it was rapidly corrupted and perverted.[43]

> . . . among the Chasidim of today there is not one in 10,000 who has the faintest conception of those sublime ideas which inspired Baal Shem and his immediate disciples. It is still the interest of the wretched ringleaders of a widely spread delusion to crush and keep down every trace of reflection and thought, so that they may play at will with the consciences and purses of their adherents.[44]

> . . . although the Chasidim have not been wholly ignored by historians or novelists, the references to them have been almost exclusively by men saturated with Western culture and rationalism. To them, the rude and uncouth manifestations of an undisciplined religious spirit could not be other than repellent; to them, Chasidism was a movement to be dismissed as unaesthetic and irrational.[45]

Questioned as to whether the Baal Shem was an impostor, Schechter replied that he was 'altogether unconcerned whether the Baal Shem was or was not an impostor'. All he cared to study was what was the ideal of the people and what they wanted to find in the Baal Shem.[46]

The Reverend Simeon Singer (1846–1906), the translator of the Authorised Daily Prayer Book, said in criticism that he 'missed from Mr Schechter's treatment of the theme a reference to that unselfishness which was so marked a feature of the Baal Shem's character. By his unselfishness he had proved the genuineness of his mission and was therefore no impostor.'[47]

It is noteworthy that the Reform minister and scholar Dr Albert Lowy (1816–1908) pointed out that in the works of Chasidism he found 'many charming things and great gems of imagination'.[48]

Schechter was very pleased with his London lecture. Writing to Richard Gottheil (1862–1936), the orientalist, he stated: 'You will have observed from my paper on the Chasidim . . . I honour and admire every warm and inner faith. Without faith we belong to the Felix Adler[49] religion, and ethical science or the so-called historical Judaism which is no less repugnant to me.'[50]

When Rudyard Kipling's *Kim* was published, Schechter opened a lecture at the Jewish Theological Seminary in New York with these words: 'Gentlemen, have you read *Kim*? Do so at once, for you will find in the portrait a real Chasid.'[51] And while Schechter maintained that Chasidic literature consisted of some '200 volumes', in reality it numbered by then nearly 1,000.[52]

3 • In the Footsteps of the Master

Israel Zangwill (1864–1926) was not only Anglo-Jewry's most celebrated novelist and dramatist, but also a man of action, participating in movements to procure a home for his homeless fellow-Jews of Eastern Europe. He was the first writer in English to represent the Jewish immigrant in fiction. Modern Zionism was born in his London study in Kilburn when Theodor Herzl came to him with an introduction from Max Nordau.[1] He founded and was president of the Jewish Territorial Organisation. Unlike Schechter, Zangwill came from a *Mithnaggedic* background. His father Moses was born in Lithuania and his mother in a village near Brest-Litovsk.

Zangwill was part of the 'Wanderers' or the 'Wandering Jews' – a literary Jewish club, meeting in different homes in London. The membership included Joseph Jacobs; the publicist Lucien Wolf; the joint proprietor of the *Jewish Chronicle*, Asher Isaac Myers; Herbert Bentwich, the founder and first president of the English Zionist Federation; and the painter and Royal Academician Solomon J Solomon.[2]

Zangwill's neighbour was Schechter, who also lived in Kilburn, in Gascony Avenue. Zangwill greatly admired 'his traditional scholarship, his unparalleled erudition, his spiritual insight and his dominating Jewish feeling,'[3] and he always regarded himself as an ardent student of Dr Schechter's ideas.[4] In his Preface to *Dreamers of the Ghetto*, he pays tribute to Schechter: 'I owe the celestial vision of "the Master of the Name" to my friend Dr S Schechter, Reader in Talmudics at Cambridge, to whose luminous essay on the Chasidim – in his *Studies of Judaism* – I have a further indebtedness.'[5]

Even when Schechter left London for Cambridge their friendship continued. In 1891 Schechter wrote to Zangwill: 'Come and stay next Sabbath. We could then have a talk about Shabbetai Zevi, about whom I intend one day to write an essay under the title "The Theological

Bubble".[6] In a lecture entitled 'The Ghetto', delivered in the late 1890s in various places, Zangwill said:

> A century later we have another pair of equally antithetical Movements of Reason versus Mysticism. There arose in Galicia a wonder-working Rabbi called 'The Master of the Name' who protested against the Talmud in the name of emotion and a direct intuition of God – a sort of Quaker and Shaker. Contemporary with him was Mendelssohn, the 'Nathan the Wise' of Lessing's famous play, who strove to reconcile the old Judaism with European culture and to put away all mystical extravagances as well as the hope of Palestine . . . From Mendelssohn practically springs the modern reform movement of Judaism, as from the 'Master of the Name' sprang a sect of 'saints' whose wonder-working powers bring them, in obscure European districts, the income of princes.[7]

Commissioned by Judge M Sulzberger of the Jewish Publication Society of America to write on scenes from Jewish life in the East End of London, Zangwill produced the book *The Children of the Ghetto*, which was hailed by critics on both sides of the Atlantic as a great masterpiece, and he was fêted as the Dickens of the ghetto. In chapter 26 of this masterpiece, Zangwill introduces Meckish who 'was a Chasid which in the vernacular is a saint, but in the actual is a member of the sect of the Chasidim whose centre is Galicia.'[8] Zangwill here follows Schechter's footsteps and gives us an insight into the origin of Chasidism.

> In the eighteenth century Israel Baalshem, 'the Master of the Name', retired to the mountains to meditate on philosophical truths. He arrived at a creed of cheerful and even stoical acceptance of the cosmos in all its aspects, and a conviction that the incense of an enjoyed pipe was grateful to the Creator. But it is the inevitable misfortune of religous founders to work apocryphal miracles, and to raise up an army of disciples who, having squeezed the teaching of their master into their own mental moulds, are ready to die for the resultant distortion. It is only by being misunderstood that a great man can have any influence upon his kind. Baalshem was succeeded by an army of thaumaturgists, and the wonder-working Rabbis of Sadagora who are in touch with all the spirits of the air, enjoy the revenue of princes and the reverence of Popes. To snatch a morsel of such a Rabbi's Sabbath *kugel*, or pudding, is to ensure paradise, and the scramble is a scene to witness. Chasidism is the extreme expression of Jewish optimism. The Chasidim are the Corybantes or salvationists of Judaism.[9]

In his *Ghetto Tragedies*[10] in a story entitled *Bethulah*, Zangwill narrates a romantic encounter between an American Jew and the beautiful daughter of an Eastern European Chasidic Rebbe. The American is unsuccessful in rescuing her from her superstitious background. The concept he puts forward in this story, that the Messiah would be born of Bethulah's 'immaculacy', has greater affinity with Christian dogma and Sabbatean heresy than with Chasidism.[11]

Five years later he wrote *Dreamers of the Ghetto*, a chronicle of the lives of distinguished individuals in various lands and times, individuals who rebelled against convention and broke new paths.[12] Among the *dramatis personae* were Uriel Acosta, Shabbetai Zevi, Benedict Spinoza, Israel Baal Shem Tov, Solomon Maimon, Heinrich Heine, Ferdinand Lassalle and Benjamin Disraeli.

Dealing with Rabbi Israel Baal Shem Tov, Zangwill states that he came 'to teach man true life and true worship'. Zangwill gives the background of Chasidism, which does not know 'the arid wilderness of ceremonial law, the barren hyper-subtleties of talmudic debate, which in my country had then reached the extreme of human sharpness in dividing hairs, the Dead Sea fruit of learning, unquickened by living waters? And who will wonder if my soul turned in silent longing in search of green pastures.'[13] The Baal Shem led his campaign to replace 'the strictness of conscience with spontaneity of conscience by denouncing all teachers as misleading and ungodly.'[14]

Zangwill, like Schechter, admired the Besht's quality of humility.

> The Master lived in the hourly presence of God and of the other prophets of Israel, the *Tannaim* and the *Amoraim*, and all who had sought to bring God's kingdom upon the earth, that God and creation, Heaven and Earth, might be one and the Messiah might come and the divine peace fall upon all the world. And when he prayed and wept for the sins of his people, his spirit ascended to celestial spheres and held converse with the holy ones, but this did not puff him up with vanity.[15]

He has the Baal Shem take part in the following dialogue: 'Is not to pray the greatest of all pleasures?'

'"To pray?" I repeated wonderingly. "Nay, methinks it is a heavy burden to get through our volumes of prayer."

'"A burden?" cried the aged man. "A burden to enter into relation with God, to be reabsorbed into the Divine unity? Nay, 'tis a bliss as of a bridegroom with a bride. Who does not feel this joy of union – this Divine kiss – has not prayed."'[16] The Besht believed that the breath of

God vivified the universe, renewing daily the work of creation, and that hence the world of every day was as inspired as the Torah, the one throwing light on the other.[17]

Dealing with contemporary times, Zangwill echoes Schechter's sentiments and states:

> Now that he [the Baal Shem Tov] is dead and these extravagances are no longer to be checked by his living example, so monstrous are the deeds wrought and the things taught in his name, that the Chasidism he founded is becoming, despite every persecution by the Orthodox Jews, despite the scourging of their bodies and the setting of them in the stocks, despite the excommunication of our order and the closing of our synagogues, and the burning of our books – a mighty sect through the length and breadth of Central Europe.[18]

Similarly he follows Schechter's view of the *Zaddikim*, 'who influence men and govern them and gain of their gold for their further operations',[19] for 'many of them (*Zaddikim*) have only the outward show of Sainthood'.[20] He proceeds in the same vein.

> And I weep the more over this spoliation of my Chasidim, because there is so much perverted goodness among them, so much self-sacrifice for one another in distress, and such faithful obedience to the *Zaddik*, who everywhere monopolizes the service and the worship which should be given to God. Alas! that a movement which began with such pure aspiration which was to the souls of me and many other young students as the shadow of a great rock in a weary land, that a doctrine which opened out to young Israel such spiritual vistas and transcendent splendours of the Godhead, should end in such delusions and distortions.[21]

> . . . since our otherwise great sect is split into thousands of little sects, each boasting its own *Zaddik*, superior to all others, the only true intermediary between God and man, the sole source of blessing and the fount of grace, and each lodging him in a palace (to whom they make pilgrimages at the festivals as of yore to the temple) and paying him tribute of gold and treasure . . . Every day the delusion and impostures of those who use his name multiply and grow.[22]

Zangwill believed that Chasidism might possibly have maintained its potency if its leader had not abandoned the other force that moved mankind, namely Hebraism. Hence the failure of the Master's dream. He was equally scathing of Dov Baer the Maggid of Mezerich:

For Baer made of the Master's living impulse a code and a creed which grew rigid and dead. And he organized his followers by external signs – noisy praying, ablutions, white Sabbath robes and so forth – so that the spirit died and the symbols remained and now of the tens of thousands who call themselves Chasidim and pray the prayers and perform the ceremonies and wear the robes, there are not ten that have the faintest notion of the Master's teachings.[23]

Zangwill in his very last work, *The Voice of Jerusalem*, stated: 'Here arose the important heresy of modern Judaism, the joyous mysticism of the followers of the Master of the Name, the Jewish St Francis.'[24]

Elkan Adler (1861–1946), the third and youngest son of Chief Rabbi Nathan Marcus Adler, and half-brother of Chief Rabbi Hermann Adler, was a solicitor and the founder of the law firm Adler & Perowne, humorously referred to in the City of London as the Old Testament and the New Testament, since Edward Perowne was the son of the Master of Corpus Christi College, Cambridge.[25] On *Simchat Torah* 1888, he paid a visit to the *Minyan* of Rabbi Juda Leib Diskin in Jerusalem and, like Samuel Pepys who described his visit to the London Synagogue on 14 October 1663,[26] Adler too gives his impressions.

Some of the young men of the Yeshiva were dancing around the room in rollicking fun, each a *pas seul*, and one of them with true Oriental hospitality, thought he would honour and gratify me by exchanging his head-covering for mine[27] . . . In fact, I felt somewhat like Gulliver among the Brobdingnagians, when the monkeys patronized him. The style of rejoicing was nonetheless of great interest. The tune to which they danced and which in other *Chasidish Chevras* was evidently the favourite, made a deep impression at the time. A musical friend, the Rev. Francis Cohen, has been good enough to transcribe my now half-faded recollections of the Chasidish howl. He says that the harmonization is not very classical, but 'rather like a Chasid's nightmare after a heavy supper of Beethoven' . . . The manner in which they make the *Hakafot*, or circuits of the synagogue, during the Rejoicing of the Law, is funnier still. Each bearer of a scroll is surrounded by three or four men who dance slowly, but with evident gusto and superabundant gesticulation . . . It was comical and shocking to see venerable grey-beards pirouetting on their toes like some European fairy of the pantomime, but it was highly appreciated, and I had to simulate satisfaction for fear of being rebuked as Michal was when she objected to King David's 'dancing with all his might' . . . There has always been a mystic bent in the Jewish mind, and to this, as Dr Schechter has shown, Chasidism gives full scope. It is a joyful and emotional sort of religion not that which appeals to the cold intellect of the Porch, or even to the more excitable reasoning powers of the Forum. But that it has 'caught on', this need surprise no one who has watched the gigantic march of the Salvation Army.[28]

Moses Gaster (1856–1939), historian, linguist, bibliographer, orator, and folklorist, was the 'grand old man' of Anglo-Jewry. An assiduous and versatile scholar, he ranged the whole world of Judaic knowledge. Gaster's first public reference to Chasidism was at the famous Schechter lecture at Jews' College when he remarked: 'The Chasidim were Jews in form, conception, and development; and it was curious to notice how identical Chasidism was with Buddhism.'[29]

In his presidential address to the Jewish Historical Society of England in London on 19 November 1906, Gaster, dealing with Chacham David Nieto (1654–1728) stated, that 'he [Nieto] joined hands with all the sober-minded and clear-headed rabbis on the continent, and helped to purify Judaism and prevented it from falling into the mystical deadening trances of Chasidism and from turning away into apostasy as Frank and his followers had done'.[30]

Advances in scholarship led to a far more complete picture of Chasidism and 'revisionist' historians, headed by Simon Dubnow, emerged. One of the pioneers was Samuel Abba Horodezky, the historian of Jewish mysticism and author of *HaChasidut VeHaChasidim* (Chasidism and Chasidim) – monographs on great Chasidic leaders from the Besht to Israel Friedmann of Ruzhin.[31] Horodezky saw in Chasidism a revolt against the severe legalism of the rabbinate. He exalts the institution of *Zaddikism* and Cabbala which he regarded as 'the spiritual essence of Judaism, its inner kernel which supplied it with the spirit of life'. In his foreword to Horodezky's book *Leaders of Chasidism*, Gaster stated that 'Chasidism brought hope and joy to the downtrodden, to the weak, to the ignorant. It opened up a new outlook upon the world, a new feeling of satisfaction and happiness.' He once again reiterates the assertion that 'a careful study of Chasidic practices and theories reveals a curious similarity to the practices and beliefs among the Buddhists and their doctrine of the reincarnation of Buddha, notably the Mongolian Buddhists and those from Tibet'.[32]

It is incredible that Gaster, a native of Romania, the heartland of the Chasidim of Sadagora, Bohush and Ruzhin, should describe the *Besht* as

an 'unknown, half-learned beadle and teacher of *Miedzyboz'*. Nevertheless, Gaster concedes Chasidism's doctrine that

> the world is not a vale of tears and all the energy of man is not to be
> devoted to self-annihilation, in order thereby to purge himself from all
> sin of the present life, or of the lives gone by. On the contrary, this world
> is full of God. Everything is divine. Nature is there to be enjoyed. The
> world is there to be happy in.[33] God is not to be served in a self-sacrificing
> manner but one must be animated by the highest exercise of love and
> lifted up by an inner enthusiasm, longing to be conscious of and to feel
> His presence.[34]

Like Israel Solomon, Elkan Adler and David Solomon Sassoon, Gaster
was a dedicated bibliophile. His 20,000 printed books and 2,000
manuscripts included many noteworthy works relating to the Bible, to
the Midrash and the Cabbala. In 1924 the British Museum (now the
British Library) acquired for the sum of £10,000 over 1,300 of Gaster's
manuscripts, including many works relating to the Cabbala.

With the help of the Pilgrim Trust, the John Rylands Library,
Manchester, also acquired 350 manuscripts in Hebrew, over 300
Samaritan manuscripts and 12,000 Geniza fragments. Mysticism is well
represented. An outstanding item is a remarkable compendium of
homilies, discourses, commentaries, *kitvei kodesh* (sacred writings) in
18 volumes, compiled at the behest of Chayim Jacob of Velitz, Riga.
This is, in fact, almost an encyclopaedia of Chasidism. Its 5,000 pages
comprise every branch of Chasidism.[35]

'These eighteen volumes,' writes Dr Gaster in his catalogue

> all of the beginning of the nineteenth century and copies of autographs
> made from the writings, speeches, sermons – all, as far as I know,
> hitherto unpublished and quite unknown – are of one or more of the
> most prominent representatives of the Chasidic movement. Chief among
> them is Rabbi Schneersohn, I believe better known as the Lubavitcher
> Rebbe. One of the small manuscripts is signed by his son, Dov Baer.
> They were all made by order of a certain very great Chasid who lived
> somewhere near Riga. He died in poverty and so the manuscripts came
> over to England and Mr Lutski bought them for me.

Lutski was a London bookdealer who specialised in Orientalia, and
Gaster bought these books from him on 13 April 1931. One volume[36] is
by Rabbi Dov Baer, known as the 'Mittler Rebbe', the 'Middle' Rabbi,

since he was the second of the three men who laid the foundations of the Chabad dynasty.

Chasidism now received the imprimatur of Chief Rabbi Dr Joseph Hermann Hertz (1872–1946), a graduate of the Jewish Theological Seminary of New York, who was probably influenced by Dr Solomon Schechter who had 'a loving sympathy for everything Jewish'.[37]

In his essay on 'The Rise and Development of the Cabbala', Hertz stated:

> The last country from which a new doctrine of mysticism was to issue is Poland. Chasidism is a new and original mystic movement from the people, and is among the most remarkable in the history of religion. Its founder, Israel Baal Shem Tov, around whose life there soon arose a whole mythology, preaches humility, joyful trust in God, and enthusiasm in religious life as the whole duty of man . . . Baal Shem's most famous successors were Nachman Bratzlav and Shneur Zalman Ladier. Nachman Bratzlav, a grandson of the Baal Shem, emphasized the Pantheistic leanings of the founder. He was a poetical soul, an original fabulist, and a true Chasidic superman (*Zaddik*).[38]
>
> And the other was Ladier (1747–1812), the Azriel of Chasidism, who places it on a metaphysical basis. He is a profound Talmudist and a deep student of Luria.[39] In him the *Zaddik* ceases to be a miracle-worker and becomes a Teacher. We may well conclude our survey of Jewish mysticism with these heroes of Chasidism, who nobly reflected some of the highest traits of the Jewish mystic – strength of personality, saintliness, coupled with independent thought.

And the Chief Rabbi concludes: 'that to ignore Cabbala is to leave unexplored large portions of the map of Jewish life and thought; and that to remain ignorant of Jewish mysticism is to fail to grasp a distinctive side of the Jewish genius and one of the great driving forces in Jewish history.'[40]

Hertz's successor, Rabbi Israel Brodie, in a message dated 27 December 1951, on the occasion of the twelfth anniversary of the existence of the United Lubavitch *Yeshivot* in the USA and Canada, paid tribute to Lubavitch activities: 'The Jewish world knows with pride of the great achievements of this organisation in spreading Torah and the fear of Heaven during the short years of its existence. In particular we have been impressed by the high moral and intellectual level achieved by the students of the Lubavitch *Yeshivot*.'[41]

Emeritus Chief Rabbi Lord Jakobovits, in an address in Jerusalem on

3 July 1990, stated: 'This messianic streak became ever more pronounced after the establishment of the Jewish State among secular leaders . . . or at a different level altogether the messianic fervour generated by Lubavitch in the Chasidic world.'[42]

He defended his views by pointing out that he had spoken in support of Lubavitch institutions in five continents over some 30 years: 'I believe I have promoted the Lubavitch movement no less than any of my critics. The personal associaton of my wife and myself with the Rebbe over the past forty years has been warm and enduring.'[43]

Dr Isidore Epstein (1894–1962), the Principal of Jews' College, in his book *Judaism*, gives a sensitive and authoritative analysis of Chasidism. 'The important contribution of Chasidism lay rather in the strong emphasis it gave to certain ideals, whilst relegating others to the background. By these means Chasidism injected a new and vital part into Jewish religious life with transforming effect upon those men and women who came under its spell and influence.'[44]

4 • Early Chasidim in England

In 1734 the Jewish population of England was estimated to be 6,000.[1] By 1850 the Jewish community numbered between 20,000 and 30,000.[2] Chief Rabbi N M Adler remarked that owing to the Crimean war 'there is a great influx of fugitives of Russian Jews'.[3] Adler even complained to Rabbi Solomon Eger of Posen that he 'had virtually no free time in London due to the many cases of divorce, *agunot* and *chalitzah* which came to me mostly from Poland and Russia'.[4]

The new immigrants were not particularly welcomed by their co-religionists. The *Jewish Chronicle* in an editorial entitled 'A hint to Russia',[5] suggested that 'Russian authorities should allow their Jews to be settled in the newly acquired provinces of Central Asia [where] they would bring an element of commercial prosperity'.[6] Similarly, Samuel Montagu (1832–1911), the first Lord Swaythling, stated: 'I have striven for years to keep away from our shores poor Jewish refugees.'[7]

The London Board of Guardians not only repatriated Russian Jews to Russia, but sent the following letter to the Jewish Press on the continent and to all places where the emigrants might pass through on their way to England:

> In order to avoid trouble in the coming days, we beseech every right-thinking person among our own brethren in Germany, Russia and Austria to place a barrier to the flow of foreigners, to persuade such voyagers not to venture to come to a land they do not know. It is better that they live a life of sorrow in their own native place than bear the shame of famine and disgrace of missionaries and perish in destitution in a strange land.[8]

These sentiments of the lay-leaders were fully endorsed by the German-born spiritual head of Anglo-Jewry, Chief Rabbi N M Adler who was then 85 years old. 'It is proper for you to remain in your land,' he wrote, 'and walk in the ways of the Lord.'[9] He urged his East

European colleagues 'to preach in the synagogues and houses of study to publicise the evil which is befalling our brethren who have come here, and to warn them not to come to the land of Britain, for such an ascent is descent.'[10]

Such sentiments were even voiced in the House of Commons by the Jewish Conservative Member of Parliament, Sir Benjamin Cohen (1844–1909), the President of the London Jewish Board of Guardians, who said: 'The Board of Guardians has always set its face against those who did not leave their country on account of persecution, but who came over here to better themselves.'[11]

We have no concrete evidence that any Chasidim came to England in the first half of the nineteenth century. In Eastern Europe Chasidim and *Mithnaggedim* suffered equally from the oppressive Czarist regimes. The Chasidim, however, were not encouraged to uproot themselves from their familiar environment, hence the number of those who emigrated was small. They were reluctant to leave their familiar environment, their rebbes and their fellow-Chasidim. They feared to expose their children to the spiritual dangers of the godless countries even more than they feared the violent and murderous mobs at home. America, popularly known as the *goldene medina* (golden country), was also regarded as the *frei land* (godless country), free in too many ways.

There were, however, in London at the end of the nineteenth century quite a number of small congregations. The Polish Synagogue in Cutler Street, Houndsditch, was established in 1790.[12] The Little Scarborough Street Synagogue was established in Goodmans Fields in 1873 and eventually merged with the Kalisher Shul or the Great Alie Street Synagogue.[13]

The first Polish Chasid of note to settle in London was Abraham Sussman (1802–81).[14] He was a native of Siedlice in Little Poland, and the grandson of Rabbi Eliezer, the Cabbalist of Siedlice and Sanok. Sussman's stepfather, Jacob ben Ezekiel, was a Chasid who observed the ritual of *tikkun chatzot* (getting up at midnight to recite Psalms and dirges on the destruction of the Temple). Abraham Sussman received *cabbala* (authorisation to serve as a ritual slaughterer of animals) from the Chasidic Rebbe, Rabbi Jacob Simeon Ashkenazi (Deutsch), the Rabbi of Barnov and Zelichov.

In 1820 Sussman was appointment *shochet* in Shenitsa, near Kalushin.[15] In 1840 he left Poland and after living in Leeds for a short time, moved to London. At that time London does not appear to have had a *minyan* which followed the Chasidic ritual. Sussman, therefore, patronised the

Bevis Marks Sephardi Synagogue whose ritual has affinities with the Chasidic mode of prayer, in that *Hallel* (Psalms CXIII to CXVIII) is recited on the eve of Passover as part of the festival service. He never joined the Sephardi community but availed himself of its facilities. Eventually he became chief *shochet* of the London community and was the author of a number of learned books written in Hebrew.[16]

His sixth and last book, *Millel Avraham*, published in 1882, was the first Hebrew book to be printed in England, and gives an account of Chasidic rebbes.

His works are full of stories of Chasidic life in Poland. He gives a graphic description of the Chasidic wedding in Zelichov of the grandson of Rabbi Jacob Isaac of Lublin.[17] One of the wedding guests was the famous Rabbi Israel, the *Maggid* of Kozienice, one of the most powerful pillars of Polish Chasidism. Sussman describes the *Maggid* as a 'short man and much older than our holy rabbi of Lublin';[18] and also portrays the Rabbi of Zelichov.[19]

In another work, Sussman recalls the cholera epidemic in Oswiecze near Lublin, which, two days before the New Year in 1848, killed 230 people, including eight Chasidim, journeying to visit their Rebbe.[20] He frequently refers to the saintly Rabbi Levi Yitzchak of Berdichev and recounts an incident when the Rebbe, after the service, greeted his congregants with 'Shalom Aleichem, Shalom Aleichem' (Peace upon you). When he was asked to explain this greeting – normally extended to those returning from a journey – the Rabbi stated: 'While they were reciting the silent *Amidah*, their thoughts were on the fairs and market places, and they were far away from real *Kavanah* (devotion). Hence I welcomed them home.'[21]

One story Rabbi Sussman relates is about Rabbi Israel Baal Shem Tov who visited a house where his host offered him some meat. The Baal Shem said to him: 'Do not eat it, it is *trefa*.' His host afterwards found that the ritual slaughterer had made a mistake and that the Baal Shem Tov was right.[22] He quotes comments by Rabbi Shmelke Horowitz (1726–78) of Nikolsburg, then Rabbi in Ryczwol, and by Rabbi Jacob Simeon of Zelichov.[23] Sussman's son, Baruch Juda Leib, became a *dayan* of the Sephardim, dying young in 1863 at the age of 32, and his grandson, Israel Abrahams, was a scholar and Hebraist who was a teacher in Jews' College and later became Reader in Hebrew at Cambridge University.

By 1914, London's Jewish population had grown to some 150,000.[24] They settled in Spitalfields, Whitechapel, Goodmans Fields, and Mile

End New Town in the East End of London. This influx resulted in a proliferation of small *chevrot*. They were set up in backyards of private houses, in rooms in tenement blocks, in converted workshops, in disused chapels and churches, abandoned by the departing Christian population.

The Federation of Minor Synagogues (*Chevrot Bnei Yisrael*) was formed by Mr Samuel Montagu, MP, at the Spital Square Synagogue in the East End on 6 November 1887. This Federation included the following *chevrot*: 'Konin', Hanbury Street; Marshall Street; the 'Kalisher'; the 'Peace and Truth', Old Castle Street; the 'Voice of Jacob', Pelham Street; and *shtieblech* in Dunk Street, Windsor Street and Hope Street.[25]

Whether these *chevrot* included any Chasidim is impossible to ascertain today. There must have been one Chasidic *shtiebl* among them, for Zangwill, in the *Children of the Ghetto* describes such a place of worship. 'In England their [Chasidim] idiosyncrasies are limited to noisy jubilant services in their Chevrot, the worshippers dancing or leaning, or standing, or writhing, or beating their heads against the wall, as they will, and playing like happy children in the presence of their Father.'[26]

Several prominent Chasidim participated in the formation of the *Machzikei Shomrei Hadath* in 1890. They included families who later founded the North London Beth Hamidrash. It became known as the *Machzikei Hadath*, the Spitalfield Great Synagogue, one of the spiritual fortresses of Anglo-Jewry.[27] Among its founders were the Chasidim Hanoch Heinoch Bloomstein, Mendel Chaikin and, particularly, David Frost who was a trustee and a leading member for over 40 years. 'To him alone,' testified Dr Bernard Homa, 'the existence of the building owes its thanks.'[28]

Mendel Chaikin arrived in England in 1905 and established the house of Chaikin and Company, the first importers into England of wine produced in Palestine in the cellars of Petach Tikva and bearing the name of Bozwin, the acronym of the words *Beauty of Zion Wine*.[29]

Other Chasidim prominent in *Machzikei Hadath* were Asher Zeigermacher (the father of Simon Weingarten) and the Alexander Chasid Baruch Mordechai Wolkowitch (d. 1953).[30] From 1891 to 1912 the spiritual leader of the Congregation was Rabbi Abraham Abba Werner, formerly the Chief Rabbi of Finland.[31] He was an ardent follower of the Vilna Gaon and was a convinced *Mithnagged*.[32] In an interview with the *Jewish Chronicle* on 9 June 1911, dealing 'with the Chasidic movement on the one side and the Haskalah or Mendelssohn period on the other side', he remarked: 'These two movements have, in my opinion, greatly weakened Judaism. From different points of view both made light of Jewish learning, the one being swept by emotionalism, the other by rationalism; they diverted attention from the study of Judaism.'[33]

Rabbi Werner was not the only *Mithnagged* in London. On 6 March 1912 the Federation of Synagogues on the recommendation of Rabbi Dr Moritz Guderman of Vienna appointed Rabbi Maier Zevi Jung (1858–1921) as the Chief Minister. Born in Tirsza Eszlar he studied under Maharam Schick of Huszt. He also studied in the universities of Marburg, Heidelberg and Leipzig. After serving as rabbi in Mannheim Germany from 1886 to 1891, he became rabbi in Ungarisch Brod in Moravia, Austria.

He was a great educationalist and he opened up the very first Jewish day school in 1901. 'The aim of my school,' he said, 'was merely to train business and professional men who would be true to their people and the Torah.'[34] When he opened a school in Cracow, he was violently opposed by Rabbi Issachar Dov Rokeach of Belz.[35] From contrary sides pressure was brought against the school, by the assimilationist Edler von Horowitz as well as by the Chasidim, with the result that the government closed the school in 1906. Rabbi Jung then published a *kol koreh* (a proclamation) in which he stated that the 'Rebbes of Belz and Sanz thought that the school would steal Jewish boys from the *Beth Hamidrash*.'[36] He subsequently appealed to Jewish parents that they should 'offer their children a general education in the spirit of purity and you will understand how right our Sages were when they said: "How good it is to combine our Torah with secular education!"' He was opposed by 36 rabbis, and the Chasidim placarded the streets of Cracow with the Hebrew words: *haMashchit bo el haIr* (the destroyer has come to town).[37]

In London Rabbi Jung did not show any trace of ill-will against the Chasidim. On the contrary, in 1914, he established a branch of the *Aguda* which encompassed a number of prominent Chasidic leaders in England.[38] He also founded the *Sinai* League 'to preserve and promote traditional Judaism amongst Jewish young men and women',[39] a movement which lasted for several years.

5 • East End Chasidic Shtieblech

The new Chasidic immigrants had little in common with the English Jews whose order of service in the synagogue was strange to them, and whose standard of living was far above their own, and they gravitated to the *shtiebl*. The *shtiebl* was very primitively furnished but the worshippers came regularly, morning and evening, and prayed with fervour. These people had been nurtured in Jewish learning and practice. Although ceremonial was not lacking, no one stood on ceremony. Here, harassed and poverty-stricken Jews who struggled hard to eke out a meagre living, often working more than 13 hours a day in sweatshops and other unhygienic surroundings, could forget for a short while that they were strangers in a strange land and escape momentarily into spiritual ecstasy. Joy was the keynote. The Chasidim emerged from the material hardships of their lives and worshipped with what the late Dr Gaster called 'a fiery enthusiasm which seemed to break all the bonds of traditional ceremonial. They danced when they prayed and prayed dancing.'

It is a comparatively easy task to establish a *shtiebl*, the Yiddish word for a little room which will serve as a place of worship and a house of study. Some may need cathedrals, massive choirs, great tenors to move their hearts. Not so a Chasid. For him, any room can easily be converted: just an Ark, some tables and benches or chairs, and a *shtiebl* is born. A Chasidic *minyan* is a gathering of a select number of faithful Guardians of the Law. They meet together in a friendly and informal atmosphere. They feel at home in their place of worship. Everyone knows and is known by his neighbour. Here familiarity breeds content, for each individual matters.

A problem of paramount importance is who is to have the honour to act as a *Baal Tefillah* (officiant). The voiceless are often vociferous while the mellifluous retire from the proffered privileges and must be wooed. True, there are traditional melodies, but these melodies are mainly for the guidance of officiants who may insert some of their own cantorial accents. Melody is regarded as an aid to contemplation and prayer. The Chasidim believe with the Psalmist that, 'Though he goeth on his way weeping, he beareth the measures of the seed, but if he goeth with joy he shall bear his sheaves.'[1] Chasidism brought about a veritable renaissance of Jewish music. For the masters of mysticism, melody was rich with mystical meaning. None the less, it was very rare for a *shtiebl* to engage a *chazan*, a professional cantor.

Chasidim today no longer turn somersaults, as they did in the past, nor do they engage in loud shouting during prayers, but they still maintain gestures which they find aid concentration. 'All my bones shall say: Lord, who is like You?'[2]

Chasidic liturgy contains elements of the old Sephardi prayer book, elements of Ashkenazi rites and of the Lurianic prayer book by the Safed Cabbalist, Rabbi Isaac Luria. The Chasidim of Lubavitch use the *Rebbe's Siddur* by Rabbi Shneur Zalman of Liady, which contains meditations and was published in 1800. The practice of *shnoddering* (offering a donation for the privilege of being called to the Reading of the Law) and auctions of *aliyot* and certain honours, such as the opening of the Ark before *Neilah* or reciting *Maftir Yona* on the Day of Atonement, are a primary source of income and do not, in any way, affect the decorum of the *shtiebl*. Some Chasidim don two pairs of *tefillin* each morning. Rabbi Jacob ben Meir disagreed with his grandfather Rashi as to the order of the texts on the four parchments of the *tefillin*, which led to two versions of *tefillin* becoming available. To satisfy both authorities, devout Chasidim use both sets. On intermediate days of a festival, Chasidim, like the Sephardim, refrain from wearing *tefillin*.

On Passover, Chasidim eat only *matza shemurah*, unleavened bread made from flour that has been supervised from the moment the wheat was harvested, for these are 'cared for' matzot. In June or July, a trusted representative goes out to the farm and selects the wheat. Then it is stowed away in air-conditioned strongrooms in the bakery basement. In December, the wheat is ground by hand in a special mill. When the baking season opens, the water is drawn at sundown from a nearby well. The Chasidim work and chant *leShem matzot mitzvah* (we are making these matzos in fulfilment of the precept). *Shemura matzot* are made by hand; they are also made by heart.

The Chasidim recite *Hallel* (hymns consisting of six Psalms) with the benediction after the evening service in the Synagogue on both nights of Passover. They blow the *shofar* during the silent Additional Service on the New Year. They have *hakafot* (processional circuits around the *bimah* with Scrolls of the Law) on the eighth day of the festival of Tabernacles, as well as on the day of the Rejoicing of the Law (the festival immediately following *Sukkot*). Though they say 'Shikkur is a *goy'* (only a Gentile gets drunk), a Chasid in his *shtiebl* enjoys his liquor.

'Permissible pleasures are not scorned.' At a *siyum* (completion of the study of a tractate of the Talmud), on the anniversary of a Zaddik's death, or even on the *yahrzeit* of any Chasid, on *Purim* and *Simchat Torah*, at a circumcision and at a Redemption of a first-born male, at weddings and engagements, Chasidim would drink spirit in careful measure and wish each other *l'chayim* (to life) and thus banish grief from their hearts.

In the *shtiebl*, *shalosh seudot* or *seuda shlishit*, the third meal, is the highlight of the Sabbath. In Cabbalistic literature it is referred to as a 'time of favours', when God is kindly disposed towards Israel. At a *seuda shlishit* the menu generally consists of herring and *challa* (the Sabbath loaf), but the sparse meal is uplifted by the spiritual fare. In the gathering dusk, the rebbe speaks and all listen devoutly, and the Chasidim sing mystical melodies by Rabbi Yitzchak Luria, based on the Zohar, such as *Askinu Seudasa* ('Prepare the meal') and *Bnei Hechala* ('Members of the Sanctuary'). Together they dance in an ecstasy that transcends the barriers of time and place. They are reluctant to let the honoured guest, the Sabbath, depart, and prolong the day as much as they can. On Saturday evening, after the conclusion of the Sabbath, a time between holy and profane, they celebrate the *Melave Malka* ('accompanying the Queen'), chanting hymns and relating Chasidic tales.

THE DZIKOVER SHTIEBL

The most prominent and influential *shtiebl* in London in the first half of the twentieth century was the *Dzikover shtiebl*, also known as the *Austrian Dzikover shtiebl* at 35 Fieldgate Street. Dzikov in Galicia was famous for its joyous prayer and song, which these Chasidim brought with them to London. Even on the Days of Awe when the Lord sits in judgement, the service was one long song of praise. As the *Baal Tefillah* began the *Kaddish* on the Holy Days, a deep sense of awe descended on the congregation. When the Reader sang 'He nourishes the world with kindness', Naftali Gerstler, one of the prominent worshippers, in his black jacket and striped trousers, his ginger beard aloft like a banner, would jump in front of the Ark, singing and dancing and clapping his hands in joy. At the conclusion of the service which lasted some seven hours on the New Year, the Reader Reb Ezriel would rest exhausted, his shirt collar undone, completely bathed in perspiration, but his face aglow with holiness. The whole service was conducted exactly according to the traditions of Dzikov. Woe betide anyone who attempted to change a note or an inflection. All were equals in the *shtiebl*, the milkman and the grocer, the shopkeeper and the garment worker, the bookseller Cailingold and the textile manufacturer Gerstler.

Standing in prayer before the Almighty, there were no rich or poor. For when Chasidim pray, they pray with ecstasy and with a passion that overcomes the barriers of time and space. The Reading of the Law was a period of concentration. Everyone followed the reader, repeating every word quietly to himself, but bursting out from time to time whenever he made the slightest mistake in a great correcting chorus. To err is human, to amend is divine.

Three decades before any Chasidic rebbes settled in London the *Dzikover shtiebl* was a cynosure for all who had been brought up in a Chasidic milieu. The voice of prayer and study was heard from early in the morning until late at night. A number of worshippers would even spend an hour or two in study first thing in the morning before starting their daily work. Within two decades this *shtiebl* became one of the richest in the East End of London. On the Sabbath men would come to the *shtiebl* wearing silk top hats (before the advent of the *shtreimel*) as a sign of their increasing affluence.

The *shtiebl* which was originally occupied by the Cracow Synagogue and known as *Chevrah Tiferet Jacob* consisted of a ground floor with seats for 60 men, and a gallery for 40 women.

On 14 March 1903, the members instituted their own bye-laws (*takkanot*) which consisted of 17 articles. According to these, a general meeting of members was to be held annually during the month of *Tishri*. The executive committee comprised the President (first *gabbai*), the Vice President (second *gabbai*), six members of the Committee, a Treasurer, two Trustees, a Secretary and a Collector. Each member was to pay a contribution of three pennies per week; an additional penny was charged if his wife was to be included. In the event of six weeks' non-payment, membership was to be withdrawn. The President had the right to spend up to ten shillings without consulting the Committee. A balance sheet was to be presented annually. A minimum membership of 12 months was required before one became eligible for membership of the executive. No one was allowed to officiate at the Reader's desk or to read the Law without the express permission of the Wardens. A committee meeting had to be held once a month, and a quorum of four members was required.

High moral and religious conduct was expected of each member. He was urged not to criticise the *shtiebl* in public, as such action would be detrimental to its interests. These rules were strictly followed, and at one time a member was suspended for a period of six months for insulting behaviour to a Warden.

Each worshipper, when offered an *aliyah*, had to make a *misheberach* in honour of Rabbi Joshua Horowitz of Dzikov (1848–1913) and later on, in honour of his son Rabbi Alter Yechezkel Eliyahu (1884–1943). The *yahrzeits* of their rebbes were to be commemorated annually by a festive meal, that of Rabbi Naftali Zevi of Ropczyce (1760–1827) on 11 *Iyyar*, that of Rabbi Eliezer (d. 1861) on 3 *Cheshvan*, Rabbi Joshua's on 11 *Tevet* and Rabbi Alter's on 15 *Adar*.

On 13 May 1914, the *shtiebl* acquired a 90-year lease of 30–32 Dunk Street at a cost of £1,250 with a loan of £400 from a bank. The premises were in one of the narrow streets of East London's Whitechapel. But at that time it was distinguished from all others in accommodating no fewer than three *shtieblech*. Dzikov no longer had to make do with a converted house, but for the first time it could boast of a purpose-built place of worship, with a women's gallery, and a total seating capacity for some 150 men and women.

The *shtiebl* was later known as the Dzikover Klaus. It was fortunate in its lay-leaders. One of its founder members was the hosiery merchant, a Chasid of Ropczyce, Zevi Hirsh Israel (d. 1945), known as 'Hershel President' or 'Uncle Fetter' to distinguish him from his namesake, another Hershel Israel from Mile End who, with his two sons, Lippa and Chayim, and his brother Moshe, was a regular at the *shtiebl*. 'Hershel President' who came to London in 1899, remaining President until 1939, was a witty and jovial man, who was instrumental in the acquistion of the freehold at Dunk Street. 'The *shtiebl*', he proudly proclaimed, 'will now survive.'

It was Hershel Israel who, together with Mr B Bernstein of Bedford Street Synagogue, Mr P Larholt of Sidney Street Synagogue and Mr M Rosenoff of Grove Lane Synagogue, urged the Federation of Synagogues to appoint a competent rabbi 'in the neighbourhood of Commercial

Road to replace the late Dr Jung and Rabbi Maccoby, for the sake of young Jewry in the East End of London'.

In 1925, Israel was unanimously elected Honorary Life President, and two years later he helped to purchase the freehold of the synagogue. He was loyally supported by the first *Gabbai*, Naftali Gerstler (1876–1942), known as 'Roiter Naftali'.[3] Born in Oleszyce, near Lvov, at the turn of the century he and his three sons came to London, where he established a leading textile business. For nearly a quarter of a century, until 1930, he acted as *gabbai* and represented the *shtiebl* at the Federation of Synagogues and the Board of Shechitah. He was never happier than when he could do someone a good turn. His home and his place of business were always open to the poor and needy. He was also vice-chairman of the Board of Jewish Education, and prominent in the *Yeshivot Shaar Torah* and *Etz Chayim*.

Another *gabbai* was the manufacturing furrier and wholesaler, Hershel Steinhart (1886–1975).[4] Born in Ostrowiec, he was steeped in Chasidic teachings. He came to London in 1908 and immersed himself in communal affairs while remaining in constant touch with the Rebbe of Dzikov. He represented the Federation on the London Board of Shechitah, the Board of Deputies, the London Board of Jewish Religious Education and the Initiation Society. Following the retirement of the Sexton of the Federation of Synagogues, Steinhart undertook the administration of the Burial Society. He was instrumental in establishing a *mikveh* in Dunk Street. His self-opinionatedness, his inability to listen to the views of others, made it virtually impossible to get him to change his mind once it was made up.

The *shtiebl* was well organised. Nothing was left to chance. The officiants for the High Holy Days were carefully chosen and their duties recorded. The distribution of *aliyot* (Torah honours) was no easy matter – not when you deal with claimants whose genealogies would confound the compilers of Debrett! No regular paid officiant was employed but occasionally paid help was sought. Rabbi Zevi David Frankfurt was paid 'every Monday £4 10s a week'.[5] In the 1930s, Rabbi Moshe Eichenstein, known as the 'Schwartzer Rebbe', gave regular *shiurim*.[6]

Among the notable worshippers was the wine merchant Elisha Horowitz (1880–1932), a cousin of the Rebbe of Dzikov and a native of Tarnov where he studied. When he came to London in 1912 he lived next door to the *shtiebl*, and when prominent rabbis visited London, such as Rabbi Meir Shapiro of Lublin and the Rebbe of Dzikov, they stayed in his home. Hershel Neiman (d. 1937), who for a quarter of a century taught Talmud at the *Yeshiva Etz Chayim*, was another erudite congregant.

The *shtiebl* had many interesting congregants: Yitzchak Strauss (1902–88), known as 'Reb Itchele Krakower', named after his grandfather, was orginally a *baal tefillah* at the Court of the Rebbe of Belz. Born in Krakowice, Galicia he came to London in 1930 and became a *shochet* for the *Machzikei Hadath*. His home in Spellman House and later in Montagu Street, was a veritable shelter for refugees who stayed there sometimes days and sometimes weeks before continuing their journeys to different parts of the world. His nephew is the Circuit Judge Henry Lazarus Lachs of Liverpool.

Another scholarly congregant was the dairyman Mordechai Frankfurt (d. 1972), a native of Przemysl. He was a renowned *baal koreh*. Together with Aaron Feigenbaum (1898–1926) he would get up before dawn and study diligently until the morning service. Azriel Katz, the son of the Rebbe of Yanov, was not only an outstanding *baal tefillah*, but also a linguist of distinction. He acted as honorary legal adviser to the new arrivals. Anyone in need of a visa extension, advice on a lease, help with the filling out of forms for naturalisation, the sending of affidavits to relatives abroad or dealing with problems with the Inland Revenue, would find in Katz competent assistance freely given.

Naftali Chayim Gastwirth (1895–1956) of Tarnov, the father of the former principal of the Judith Lady Montefiore College, Rabbi Ephraim Levy Gastwirth, was popularly known as the 'quiet gentleman', the 'gentle Chasid' or 'Reb Naftali from Dzikov' and was one of the stalwarts of the *shtiebl*. His Chasidism was internal rather than demonstrative, profound rather than obtrusive and above all, tolerant. Every Dzikover custom was sacred to him. He was a tuneful *baal tefillah* and frequently led the services. Two things governed his religious life: the love of learning Torah and the love of song in prayer, and hardly a day passed without indulging his passion for both of them. Of medium height, he was a giant in humility, although totally unaware of it. Jacob Joseph Rubin (1893–1978), the son of the Rebbe of Glogov and a descendant of Rabbi Naftali of Ropczyce, was another pillar of Dzikov. He came to London in 1928 and, being a gifted calligraphist, he soon qualified as a *sofer*.

The high point of the *shtiebl's* history was the visit of Rabbi Alter Yechezkiel Eliyahu Horowitz, the Rebbe of Dzikov (1884–1943). He arrived in Dover on 23 January 1936 and was welcomed there by Mr N Gerstler and Mr H Israel. Chasidim from the then fashionable districts of Cricklewood, Willesden and Brondesbury spent the Sabbath in the East End in order to be with the Rebbe, who stayed at the home of Elisha Horowitz, where his food was prepared by Mrs Getzel Berger. On Friday night the Rebbe conducted *tisch* (festive meal) and, as a mark of respect for the late King George V who had died on 20 January, the Rebbe discouraged his Chasidim from dancing.[7] This was a very sensitive act, and on that Sabbath, too, special memorial prayers were recited in all synagogues.[8] The Rebbe sent a message of condolence to King Edward VIII which the Palace duly acknowledged. The textile merchant, Mordechai Birnhak, a native of Tarnov, who, with his three sons, Shalom, Yitzchak and Izzie, had been a regular worshipper in the *shtiebl* since the beginning of the century, held a reception for the Rebbe in his home in Warwick Grove, Clapton.

The Rebbe was disappointed at the meagre donations offered by the *Dzikover* worshippers at the Reading of the Law. 'I note here,' he said, 'that congregants devoutly kiss the Scroll of the Law with their "hands" and offer small donations with their "mouths". Would,' he continued humorously, 'that they reversed the process. They should offer donations with their "hands" [in other words, generously] and kiss the Torah with their "mouths".' The Rebbe left London on 12 February 1936.[9]

Writing about the religious state of the East End of London in 1937, Rabbi Louis Rabinowitz, at that time Minister of the Cricklewood Synagogue, stated that he found a surprising number of young people patronising the *shtiebl*.[10] The annual balance sheet submitted on 8 April 1938 records that the sum of £42 12s. was sent to the Rabbi of Dzikov. The Shofar blower received a remuneration of two pounds and the payment to the cantor amounted to £67 10s. for that year.

Before the Second World War Mr Getzel Berger began to take an increasingly active interest in the *shtiebl* and together with Moshe Landau and Anshel Kesselman maintained it throughout the war. In March 1946 a memorial service was held for Rabbi Horowitz, who had been a victim of the Nazis. Three years later, in 1949, a new *mikveh* was opened there by Chief Rabbi Israel Brodie, the first to be built by the London Board of Mikvaot.[11]

The bombing of the East End of London brought about a marked diminution of its Jewish population. In 1954, the possibility of the Dzikover *shtiebl*'s amalgamation with that of Black Lion Yard (see next section) was discussed.[12] Further abortive attempts to amalgamate the *shtieblech* of Black Lion Yard, Dzikov and Rosener were made by Mr Steinhart.[13] A committee was set up to negotiate, but nothing came of it. A compulsory purchase order was served on the Dzikover *shtiebl* in 1956 and implemented in 1967. By that time, 90 per cent of its members were no longer residing in the area. The last honorary secretary, A Kesselman, transferred the remaining members to different East London synagogues. Some of the funds were utilized by Messrs. Steinhart and Berger to establish a *mikveh* in Ilford. The *sifrei torah* were given to Wembley Synagogue (where Steinhart's son-in-law Rabbi Meyer Berman was the rabbi) and to the Marble Arch and Cricklewood Synagogues where Leon and Hyman Gerstler were active congregants.

THE AUSTRIAN SHTIEBL

Not far from the Dzikover *shtiebl* was the Austrian *shtiebl*, also known as *Beth Hamidrash Kehal Chasidim Estreich Polin*. Originally it was called *Anshei Oestreich* and located at 156 Whitechapel Road, but in 1909 it moved to 85/87 Fieldgate Street. In 1927 it was the first Chasidic *shtiebl* to join the *Adath Yisrael* Burial Society, whose cemetery at Enfield was opened in 1925. This affiliation was arranged by Chanina Blusenstein with Rabbi Dr Avigdor Schonfeld, the spiritual head of the *Adath*. In the 1930s his son and successor at the *Adath*, Rabbi Dr Solomon Schonfeld, would regularly walk from his home in Highgate to preach at the *shtiebl* during the High Holy Days. The *shtiebl* observed the *yahrzeit* of Rabbi Ezekiel Halberstam (1813–99) of Sianawa on 6 *Tevet* and Rabbi Chayim Halberstam of Sanz on 25 *Nisan* by a festive meal which was preceded by the annual elections.

A regular worshipper, until he moved from the East End in 1936, was the colourful Moshe Leib Cailingold (1895–1967), a son-in-law of Jacob Elijah Fenechele (d. 1960), the president of the *shtiebl*. For three generations the Cailingolds had been booksellers and publishers in Warsaw and the Holy Land. Born in Warsaw, of Lithuanian origin, into a family of Chasidim of Karlin, he studied for a time at the *Yeshiva* in Vilna. When his father Naftali emigrated to the Holy Land, Moshe Leib came to London in 1920 for the sole purpose of obtaining certificates to enable his relatives in Eastern Europe to settle in the Holy Land, but he soon engaged in bookselling, first in Church Road, and then at 6 Old Montague Street, and for four decades until his death in 1967 was not only a prominent bookseller but a publisher of many liturgical works and Anglo-Judaica.

For a time he also had a branch at 21 Bury Street near the British

Museum. His shop became the Mecca for all book-lovers and a rendez-vous for Jewish scholars. His uncle Aaron who had a flourishing book-shop in Nalewka, Warsaw, would regularly supply him with the latest Hebraica published in Poland. His customers turned to him with their literary problems, and he gave unstintingly of his knowledge. A *maskil*, a bibliophile, he would willingly look up their *yahrzeits* and the dates of their *bar mitzvot*. A great lover of Zion, he was shattered when his daughter Esther was killed in the Old City in 1948 during the War of Independence. His other daughter, Mimi, married Yehuda Avner, who later became the Israeli Ambassador to the Court of St James's. Active in the administration of the *shtiebl* until 1930 was Chayim Rechtand (Wulkan), the grandfather of Cyril Domb. Chayim, who was named after Chayim Halberstam of Sanz, was born in Auschwitz and settled in Mulberry Street in the East End of London.

Another prominent worshipper was Abraham Maslo (1899–1985), a native of Struszov, who, after spending some time in Danzig, came to London in 1938, and was a *gabbai* of the *shtiebl* from 1944 to 1955. In the twilight of the *shtiebl's* existence Rabbi Abraham Muschel (d. 1965) was its spiritual leader. Born in Bragel, Galicia, he was ordained by Rabbi Meir Arik (1855–1926) of Jaslowice. Muschel is reputed to have known by heart the complicated commentary on the *Shulchan Aruch Pri Meggadim* by Rabbi Joseph Teomim (1727–92). Muschel came to London in the 1930s and was authorised by the London *Beth Din* to resolve ritual problems with regard to the *kashrut* of fowls. Apart from the rabbinate he was the proprietor of an antiquarian book shop in Old Montague Street. Like the proverbial Jewish bookseller of Sholem Aleichem's tales, he was more interested in studying the book than selling it. Part of his library was given to the *Beth Hamidrash* of Bobow. The *shtiebl* closed in December 1957.

BLACK LION YARD

In 1896, a *Shtiebl Kehal Chasidim*, with a membership of 70, was estab-lished at 36 Old Montague Street under a Mr S Goldstein. On 6 November 1896 it became affiliated to the Federation of Synagogues and in 1904 it moved to a one-storey building at 14 Black Lion Yard, a narrow turning off Whitechapel Road. This tiny alleyway became the centre of the Jewish jewellery trade with practically every shop selling silver and precious stones. The Nazi bombing during the Second World War destroyed the street, and Black Lion Yard totally disappeared in the post-war rebuilding of the area.[14]

The mainstay of the *shtiebl* was the herring merchant David Frost (1861–1938).[15] David Frost's father Nathan, who died at the age of 57 in 1900, was a member of the Great Synagogue, where he and Lord Swaythling were jointly given the honour of being 'Bridegrooms of the Law' one *Simchat Torah*. In 1877, Nathan established a delicatessen business in Brune Street – a business that is still trading. He was so devout that he had his own private *shtiebl* adjoining his premises, and he and his wife, Dora Rebecca, fed and cared for his fellow worshippers, to whom he gave regular subventions. Nevertheless, he would advise his seven children, saying: 'If you want to be a *Mensch* (human being), join the United Synagogue.'

David, an infant when he arrived in London from Poland, received a very thorough Jewish and secular education. He continued his father's business, and travelled regularly to Scotland on business. Unlike his siblings who became members of the Establishment, David somehow became attached to the Chasidic way of life. He married Jane Fredman of Plymouth, who came from an Anglicised but Orthodox family. Though supportive of her husband's way of life, she never consented to a *sheitel* (wig), which remained unworn in her wardrobe. His contemporary, Dr B Homa, describes him

> as a man with a full flowing beard who spoke the Queen's English with perfect pronunciation in a deep rich voice . . . He was a man of vigour and determination, vehement and forthright in the opinions he held. There was no nonsense about Mr Frost and his temper would quickly rise, particularly against any opposition based on misunderstanding or insincerity. Rigid and unyielding in his Orthodoxy, he would fight any attempted infraction of Jewish law or custom, for, as a *Cohen*, he took his religious duties and responsibilities most seriously.[16]

Frost was instrumental in freeing the *Machzikei Hadath* of its debts. He acted as a trustee and was a leading member for 40 years. He even travelled to Lithuania in search of a suitable rabbi for the *Machzikei Hadath* congregation.[17]

He did not allow any mugger to get the better of him. On one occasion on his way to *shul* in the Whitechapel Road on a Sabbath morning, he was attacked by a ruffian. Frost retaliated in such a way that the assailant had to be taken to hospital by ambulance.

His participation in the administration of *Machzikei Hadath* did not affect his involvement with the Black Lion Yard *shtiebl* where he was a regular worshipper. He had a high standard of ethics, and he expected the same standard from others. He who deviated, in any way, had no place in the *shtiebl*, and was literally thrown out. 'I will break every bone in his body,' Frost would say, 'should he ever reappear here.' He would not allow outsiders to come and recite Kaddish. 'We are not a place of refuge,' he asserted. Nor did he welcome the newly arrived Chasidic rebbes. Though not scholarly, few would or could dispute his knowledge of the rubric or liturgy. When Dayan Abramsky left the *Machzikei Hadath* and joined the *Beth Din*, Frost seriously considered instituting legal proceedings against the United Synagogue 'for the enticement of an employee'.[18]

Harmony and accord did not always prevail in the *shtiebl*. David Frost rarely arrived on time for the Sabbath morning service scheduled to commence at 10 a.m. 'Could you not have waited a few minutes longer before commencing,' he would say to the *baal tefillah*, no matter how late he was. There were also constant clashes between him and another congregant, the grocer Isaac (Isser) Assistant. Isser was a lovable person. He would stop children in the street and reward with a coin anyone who wore *arba kanfot* (ritual fringes). Yet there were continuous arguments between him and Frost. On Saturday afternoons after *Mincha* the *shtiebl* divided into two hostile factions, Frost and Isser each conducting their own *Seudah Shlishit*, each intoning different melodies. Annually, prior to the *Kol Nidrei* Service, the two adversaries reconciled and, with tears in their eyes, asked each other's forgiveness. This truce lasted only until the termination of the Day of Atonement when they reverted to their normal behaviour. Though David's four sons, Lionel, Bertie, Cyril and Nat, regularly attended their father's *shtiebl*, none of them maintained his Chasidic way of life.

On one bitterly cold winter night, Isser used a reading stand for firewood. When reprimanded the following morning, he justified his actions by saying: 'Don't I pay my weekly contribution of six pence? Surely, this entitles me to sleep, to pray, to study and to get some warmth here.'

Only those with flowing beards and whose wives wore *sheitels* (wigs) were allowed to officiate at the reader's desk. There were no facilities for women worshippers, who were allowed only a glimpse of the *shtiebl* at *Simchat Torah*.

Henry Bloomstein, born in Polutsk in 1871, came to England in 1881, and eventually became a manufacturer of rabbit fur goods. His wife, Catherine, was a cousin of the Rebbe of Ger. Henry was a treasurer of the *Machzikei Hadath*, but like David Frost, he and his four sons were regular worshippers at the *shtiebl*.[19]

Another controversy over the appointment of a *shammash* split the *shtiebl* and resulted in a splinter group meeting in nearby Union Street. After only a short time, the group returned to the fold.

The First World War brought a large influx of continental refugees. *Simchat Torah Hakafot* at Black Lion Yard became renowned. The inter-war years saw many distinguished visitors from Eastern Europe, such as Rabbi Meir Shapiro of Lublin and Rabbi Meir Dan Plotzki. In the course of its existence the *shtiebl* was patronised by a number of interesting personalities: one of them was a certain 'Rabbi Shaul' who was considered a walking encyclopaedia, had no fixed abode, dressed like a tramp and slept on the benches of the *shtiebl*. Prominent, too, were Yisrael Yitzchak Mintz and his son Louis (1909–87) who celebrated his *Bar Mitzvah* in the *shtiebl* and later became a Maecenas in Anglo-Jewry. He was a business man of remarkable breadth of outlook. His involvement with the fashion firm Selincourt was paralleled by his interest in property development. He financed the Jewish Soup Kitchen for the Poor and shared the presidency of the East London Jewish Boys Club with Viscount Bearsted. He was a great benefactor to Israel and a governor of two Israeli universities. At one time he stood as a Labour candidate for Marylebone.

Chayim Nata Katz, Baruch Mordechai Wolkowitch (1833–1953) and Abraham Pinchas Landau (d. 1948) were the guiding lights of the *shtiebl* in the inter-war years. Regular *shiurim* were given by Rabbi Bromberg of Commercial Road and Rabbi Meir Berger (d. 1930). Congregants of the calibre of Menasheh Adler would not allow any halachic point to go unchallenged. The last decade of the *shtiebl*'s existence, before its destruction by enemy action, saw an influx of pious and learned congregants: the jeweller Simon Winegarten, Moshe Yitzchak Turner (1873–1938), Reuben Oberman and the restaurateur Velvel Silverstein. Though his restaurant at 27 Whitechapel Road was not supervised by any *kashrut* authority, its standard of *kashrut* was deemed sufficiently high even for the highly meticulous Dayan Abramsky to eat there.

Abraham Sugarwhite (d. 1945), known as Avrom Warshaver, was a colourful character. A hardworking and poor 'boot-clicker', he had to struggle to maintain his family of eight children. He was an exceptionally gifted *baal tefillah* and was a *gabbai* at the *shtiebl* for many years, who acquired a block of 50 burial places for the members at the Federation Cemetery at Edmonton. His son, Yitzchok Meir (1909–91), worshipped there until he moved to Clapton in 1935. By 1933 the membership had dwindled to 25, ten of whom were living in North London.

The *shtiebl* had a *bikkur cholim* fund (aid for the sick) and provided wheelchairs, stretchers, crutches and other medical equipment at a time when there was no other voluntary organisation doing so.

The *shtiebl* was totally destroyed by Nazi bombs in 1940 and the diminished membership prayed at *Chevra Shass*, 42 Old Montague Street. They negotiated with the *Yesodey Hatorah* School, Stamford Hill, for a room to be used as a *Beth Midrash*. Nothing came of this scheme. The trustees of the *shtiebl*, Noah Landau, Wolf Silberstein and J Turner, donated some of the assets received from the War Damage Commission to the school.[20] The remaining 17 surviving members were transferred in June 1971 to Federation congregations in the districts in which they lived.

13 BUXTON STREET

In 1899, the *Bnei Ruzhin and Sadagora Shtiebl* was established at 13 Buxton Street. One of the founders was the milliner Jacob Meir Binstock (1870–1939), a descendant of Rabbi Moshe Chayim of Sudlykow (1748–1800), a grandson of the Besht. Binstock, accompanied by his five brothers and three sons, almost made up a *minyan* (quorum). Another of the founders was the police helmet-maker, the Odessa born Israel Spivak (d. 1966) who later founded his own *minyan* in Hendon. The *shtiebl* enacted its own 19 regulations in Yiddish and in Hebrew which were ratified in 1913 and published in 1920 under 38 signatories.[21]

Their liturgy was to conform to the custom of the Rebbes of Ruzhin and Sadagora from which there should be no deviation.

The affairs of the *shtiebl* should be controlled by two *gabbaim* and an elected committee. The principal *gabbai* was to be a Chasid of Ruzhin and Sadagora and could be elected only by the followers of these sects. No such restrictions were applied to the election of the second *gabbai*, who need not necessarily be a Chasid, but had to conform to the Orthodox way of life.

If a member suffered a bereavement, four of the community were required to accompany the cortège to the cemetery in a carriage at the

Synagogue's expense. Half a *minyan* of members should attend prayers – expenses to be defrayed by the *shtiebl* – during the *Shivah* period to enable the recitation of *kaddish* by the bereaved.

Should a member commit an unseemly act, cause dissension in *shul*, behave in an impertinent manner, or transgress Jewish Law, it was the solemn duty of the Wardens and the Committee to warn him three times. Should he persist in his ways, a General Meeting of members should be convened to consider expelling the offender by a majority vote.

New members were to be vetted by a full committee before being accepted, so as to make sure that the conduct of the prospective member conformed to the Jewish way of life. New members had no voting rights for the first six months, and could not stand for Committee in their first year. The dismissal of a collector or *shammash* could only take place with the approval of the Committee.

Enactment 13 expressed the pious wish of the founders that 'A spirit of harmony, brotherhood and friendship should permeate all members, so that they should at all times be worthy of the title "Chasid".'

The *shtiebl* observed the *yahrzeit* of Rabbi Israel of Ruzhin on 11 *Elul*. When the Rebbe of Boyan visited London in 1925, he stayed at Binstock's home at 41 Quaker Street.[22]

Among its spiritual leaders were Rabbi I Grynhouse and Rabbi Taub of Modzitz who officiated during the High Holy Days. In 1955 the *shtiebl* amalgamated with *Old Castle Street* which was then renamed *Agudat Achim Nussach Ari Ubet Haknesset Chasidei Ruzhin.*[23]

THE OLD CASTLE STREET SHTIEBL

Originally there was a synagogue at 113 Old Castle Street, but in 1895 another was established at number 42, calling itself *Agudat Achim Kehal Chabad.* In 1896 its membership numbered 130.[24] but by 1904 it had declined to 70.[25] Four years later Rabbi Moses Tellier, its spiritual leader, was authorised by the Chief Rabbi to answer halachic queries.[26] It kept a *yahrzeit* Record Book which included the anniversaries of Rabbi Israel Baal Shem Tov, all the Rebbes of Lubavitch and that of the Cabbalist Rabbi Chayim ben Moses Ibn Atar (1696–1743), the author of *Or HaChayim.* Every six months they held a committee meeting and any member who failed to attend, was fined a half-crown. Honorary officers who desecrated the Sabbath were forced to resign.[27]

A number of its Chasidim were making a name for themselves in the community. One of them was Rabbi Moses Avigdor Chaikin (1852–1928), the author of many works in French, English and Hebrew, including *Sefer Kelalei HaPoskim* (rules of the codifiers).[28] This fervent Chasid of Chabad was born in Shklov, Russia, on 22 *Iyyar* 1852 and was educated at St Petersburg (Leningrad). He received *semicha* from Rabbi Yitzchak Elchanan Spector of Kovno and from Rabbi Abraham Shmuel Diskin. From 1884 to 1887 he was the spiritual head of the Russian and Polish Jews in Paris. He then returned to Russia and was Rabbi in Rostov-on-the-Don until his appointment as Minister and Chief *Shochet* in Sheffield in 1892. Chief Rabbi Adler would not at first permit him to call himself 'Rabbi' but described him as 'Darshan' (preacher). On 15 December 1901 he was appointed Chief Minister of the Federation of Synagogues until he became *dayan* of the Beth Din at a salary of £100 per annum in 1911.[29] He served Anglo-Jewry until 1926. His home at 47 White Lion Street, Aldgate, was open wide to anyone in need. He was president of the *Rabbi Meir Baal Haness* Charity and the *Chaye Olam Yeshiva* in Jerusalem, and the president of the London Branch in support of *Mir Yeshiva* in Russia.

After the death of his wife in 1926, Rabbi Chaikin, at the age of 74, resigned his post and settled in Jerusalem where he died two years later on 29 *Sivan* 1928. At the memorial service in Bevis Marks Synagogue on 28 June 1928 Chief Rabbi Hertz said:

> He was in truth a never-failing fountain of Jewish lore; a river flowing on with ever sustaining vigour . . . of Moses Avigdor Chaikin the Saint, it is only necessary to say that he was a born Chasid, a Chasid by nature even more than by upbringing. His character was marked by the selflessness, transparency and simplicity which are the very flowering of culture, intellectual, aesthetic and spiritual.
>
> His was the joyfulness of the true Chasid, the optimism, the clarity in judgment, the obstinate refusal to despair of his fellow mortals and their destiny, which made him the friend to all, beloved by all, loving God and loving all of God's children. And his was the self-effacement which the Founder of Chasidism declared to be of fundamental importance in the spiritual life – modest, long-suffering and forgiving of insults.[30]

The mainstay of the *shtiebl* was Chayim Mordechai Zevi Rapoport (d. 1956) whose son Rabbi S Rapoport is the Minister of the Higher Crumpsall *Beth Hamidrash*, Manchester. Chayim Mordechai, a native of Dvinsk, was the soul of the *shtiebl* and would allow no deviations from

Nusach Ari. He was, moreover, a great *baal zeddakah* (man of charity). To avoid embarrassing the recipients, the *Maot Chitin* (Passover charity for the poor) was put into sealed envelopes and anonymously inserted into the letter-boxes of the needy in time for Passover.

Officiants included Israel Dov Olivestone (d. 1928) whose father had been the *baal musaf* at the Court of Ger,[31] Simon Leib Greenberg, a Chasid of Lubavitch, the Reverend Joseph Kacenelenbogen,[32] Rabbi Mordechai Zeev Gutnik (1897–1932), who received a salary of £388 per annum in 1930, Rabbi Asher Abramson and Rabbi Abraham Rapoport (1907–73), who during the Second World War served as rabbi in Bedford and was subsequently appointed Rabbinical *kashrut* supervisor and later *dayan* of the London *Beth Din*. He was born in Pereyaslav, Ukraine. He purposely absented himself from the representative service at Bevis Marks to celebrate the Tercentenary of Jewish Settlement in Britain in 1956, because of the presence there of the representatives of the Reform and Liberal congregations.[33] The *shtiebl* had a *Chevra Tehillim* under the guidance of the shoe manufacturer P Blackman.

After extensive redecoration the *shtiebl* was re-opened on 12 December 1933 with the participation of Dayan Asher Feldman and Mr Barnet Janner MP (later Lord Janner) presiding. The synagogue was damaged during the war and repairs amounting to £477 were carried out subsequently. At that time its membership stood at 30. As late as 24 June 1951 a consecration of seven Scrolls of the Law, donated by members, took place. The synagogue was independent, the Federation having no proprietory interest in its assets. Its trustees, A Kramer and H Brown, hoped to perpetuate the name of the synagogue elsewhere, but none of the various schemes materialised.

There were a number of other *shtieblech* who used *Nusach Ari*.[34]

6 • Controversial Rebbes

Rabbi Alter Noach HaKohen Michalenski (1852–1920), the first Chasidic Rebbe to settle in England, was a colourful, fighting, enigmatic and erratic personality. He had lived a most unsettled life, wandering from place to place, persecuted by *Mithnaggedim* and Chasidim alike, imprisoned, libelled, mistrusted and maligned. No one has yet been able to fathom why he aroused such hostility – maybe he suffered from a psychosis which took control of his personality. Yet none could deny either his mastery of the Cabbala or his great erudition. Despite his great learning, he was the 'suffering servant' of Chasidism in the twentieth century.

Rabbi Michalenski was born in Neschitz, near Kovel in Volhynia. His father, Rabbi Aryeh Meir, was a descendant of the scholarly Rabbi Naftali ben Isaac HaKohen Katz (1645–1719). When Rabbi Aryeh died in the prime of his life, the boy's mother, Tame Simah, brought him to Rabbi Yitzchak of Neschitz (1788–1868), a disciple of Rabbi Jacob Isaac Horowitz, the 'Seer of Lublin', and of Rabbi Levi Yitzchak of Berdichev.[1] Rabbi Yitzchak had no children and he welcomed the young Alter Noach to his home, where he stayed until he was 15. This enabled him to visit the many Chasidic courts that were flourishing at that time in the Ukraine.

In 1870 he made his way to the Holy Land where he spent five years studying Cabbala in Safed, Jerusalem, Hebron and Meron, under the guidance of the great Cabbalist, Rabbi Mordechai Abadi (d. 1923). In 1877, he became the rabbi at Remet, near Sighet. Here he styled himself a Rebbe and thus antagonised both Rabbi Yekutiel Yehuda Teitelbaum of Sighet and Rabbi Moses Schick. In 1879, in collaboration with Mordechai Abadi, he published a Cabbalistic book entitled *Chen Mordechai – Darchei Chen*.[2] He then spent some time in Bulgaria and in Trieste.

During the Russo-Turkish war in 1877 Rabbi Michalenski was arrested by the authorities on the charge of espionage. Nevertheless, in 1888 he became the rabbi in Jassy, Romania, and had to plead eloquently before King Carol I and Queen Elizabeth of Romania on behalf of his fellow Jews.[3] In 1890 he settled in Yardanov, near Cracow where he acted as a Chasidic rebbe and for many years he was popularly known as the 'Yardanover Rebbe'. One day, as he was donning his prayer-shawl and phylacteries, he was arrested and languished, without trial, in prison for two-and-a-half years. His house was burnt down, his family miraculously escaping with their lives.

Through the intervention of Nethaniel Berger he was released from prison and, in January 1895, came to London where he lived first at 27 Sidney Square and later at 37 Tredegar Square, Bow. The *Jewish Chronicle* gives a vivid and graphic description of the very first Chasidic Rebbe in London:

> He was a great Talmudist, and still greater Cabbalist; he prayed much, wore two sets of phylacteries at the same time, was consulted upon questions not only of ritual but of practical affairs of the business of life, and answered his consultants with an almost infallible wisdom, had been known quite recently in Paris to prescribe for a sick child with an accuracy which astonished the ordinary medical attendant, and was waited on by a Meshores – a man servant – as remarkable as his master . . . The Rav – or to give him his full style Rabbi Alter Noach Michalenski Kohen-Zedek – is somewhat under 40, has a fine powerful face – good features – clear grey eyes, long Peot and flowing black beard of patriarchal dimensions and a tendency to curl. He wore a gown of thick black corded silk reaching to his feet, confined about the waist by a handsome girdle. On his head he wore a high sable hat with velvet crown, a sable such as any lady might have envied.
>
> Reb Noach rose slightly from his arm chair, bowed his visitors to seats and the grey eyes sparkled with the utmost keenness of observation . . . He was, he said, Russian by birth, had studied from his earliest youth, had visited Jerusalem, and studied there, and had finally settled down as Rav in Jardonow in Galicia where he possessed fields and farms of his own and enjoyed credit as a Rav and a Cabbalist. His success had aroused the bitter jealousy of a family of Rabbis who were of a type of Chasidim more stringent than his own. They and their clients had plotted against him and succeeded in procuring his imprisonment for six months as a Russian spy. Not content with this, they set fire to his house and accused him of arson. He was totally ruined by these accusations, and in the end he had been compelled to leave. He had been some little time in Paris and was now in London, his intention being to study his

case, perfect his pleas and then return to clear his name and reassert his position.

A few respectful interrogatives elicited the information that his work as a Rav was mostly done at home. He did not preach in synagogues, though he gave expositions to the privileged few on occasions. He studied and prayed continuously and answered questions which were asked him day by day in such quantities as to keep him always occupied. He 'Paskened' when required, but his speciality was advice to those in difficulties. . .[4]

In the same year, he published in London a 76-page Cabbalistic work, entitled *Netivot Chen*.[5] He stayed in London for seven years. He became a British citizen and changed his name of Michalenski to Kaizer[6] – the Hebrew for Kaizer being *Keter*, numerically equivalent to 620 (combining the *Taryag Mitzvot* – the 613 commandments contained in the Pentateuch – with the seven laws traditionally given to Noach and therefore binding upon Jews and Gentiles alike).[7] Noach Alter studied ancient Jewish manuscripts of Cabbalistic interest at Oxford and Cambridge.[8] He then visited Poland and the Holy Land where he was anxious to acquire land for the settling of religious people. Rabbi Abraham Isaac Kook gave him every encouragement, and addressed him as the 'righteous rabbi', the 'source of wisdom' and the 'master of secrets'.[9]

At the outbreak of the First World War, he and his brother took refuge in Cairo and Alexandria, where he became ill after drinking unboiled milk. He returned to the Holy Land after its capture by the British in 1917 and lived in Tel Aviv in great poverty, his home having been ransacked and despoiled by the Turks. He then became involved in complex litigation with a hotel proprietor, Warshavski. A leaflet, the title of which referred to him as 'the Bandit of London', was published. In vain did Rabbi Kook try to reconcile the irreconcilable.

Rabbi Michalenski died in Jerusalem on 8 *Elul* 1920 and was buried on the Mount of Olives.[10] He left an unpublished manuscript, *Chen Tefillin*, on the phylacteries of Rabbenu Tam (Jacob ben Meir, 1100–71) the grandson of Rashi, who disagreed with his grandfather over the correct order of the verses inserted in the phylacteries. (As a result of Rabbenu Tam's ruling, many pious people wear two pairs of phylacteries.) Kaizer was survived by two sons. One, Arnold Meir (1896–1967), later became the general secretary of the Federation of Jewish Relief Organisations in London and was the author of a book *This Whitechapel of Ours*, humorous sketches of Jewish life in East London, which was published in 1944. His other son, Shlomo, was associated with the Old Castle Street Synagogue and wrote an uncritical biography of his father. It is a sad fact that the Rebbe suffered more than any other contemporary Chasidic figure from unfair and malicious criticism and hostility.

RABBI MORGENSTERN

Another controversial rebbe who received unfavourable publicity was Rabbi Shlomo David Morgenstern (1904–62) the son of Rabbi Jacob Mendel of Wengrow, a descendant of the famous Chasidic rabbi, Rabbi Menachem Mendel Morgenstern of Kotzk (1787–1859). He married Chavah, the daughter of Rabbi Joshua Siroka. He came to London in 1932 and established the *Shtiebl Beth David* first at 179 Hanbury Street, and later at 37 Buxton Street in the East End of London.[11] He was a stormy petrel who sued the London Yiddish daily *The Jewish Daily Post*, and the Yiddish journalist, Leon Creditor (the father of Dora Gaitskell) for libel because they questioned the authenticity of his rabbinic qualifications. To avoid unsavoury publicity the parties agreed to arbitration under the chairmanship of Neville Laski KC, who was then the president of the Board of Deputies of British Jews. He found in favour of the Rebbe, and the paper went into voluntary liquidation. Rabbi Morgenstern's *shtiebl* was damaged in enemy action in October 1940, and his claim for war damage compensation involved him in litigation.[12] Following that, he opened a *Shtiebl Beth David* at Brentmead Place, Hendon, and later emigrated to Chicago in the USA.[13]

RABBI JOSEPH SHAPOTSHNICK

In the inter-war years the East End of London was the home of the remarkable 'religious anarchist', Rabbi Joseph Shapotshnick, one of the best known and most controversial Jewish clerics of his generation.[14] Throughout Rabbi Shapotshnick's life he fought the Establishment as composed of the Chief Rabbinate, the London *Beth Din* and the Shechita Board. He made a virtual career of non-conformity, rarely avoiding controversy. People either loved or hated Rabbi Shapotshnick, there was no middle path, and his personality was so complex and his ideas so conflicting that there can be no definitive assessment of him.

He was outspoken, saying exactly what he thought. He enjoyed giving discourses on unpopular topics, and he liked to attach himself to lost causes along completely independent lines. He allowed his heart to rule his mind, taking a one-sided view on many issues. He wrote prodigiously – a monument to his tireless genius – but his words did not enhance his reputation or his integrity. His last years in particular were beset by controversy. He explored the most diverse of areas, dreamed up extravagant schemes, and went into prodigious disputes or fantasies. He rarely finished any work that he began.

Always dressed in a *kaftan* of black satin and an imposing fur hat, he cut a stately figure for a period of over 26 years, as he sallied forth from his various homes in East London.[15] Ideas flowed from him but he could control neither himself nor his pen. He habitually took up a cause, convinced himself of its justice and championed it with unflagging zeal. He started many projects, but carried few of them to fruition. He remained an enigma even to his friends. He was often simplistic and unpredictable, often bashful and humble. It is not surprising that his talents and enthusiasm were exploited by unscrupulous people to further their own ends. He was a tragic figure, a genius whose brilliance misfired.

He was born on 19 February 1882 in Kishinev, Bessarabia, the son of a Chasidic rebbe, Rabbi Yehuda (Arye), known as the Belziszer Rebbe, a follower of Rabbi Yacov David Kalish (1814–78) of Amshinov and his son, Rabbi Menachem (d. 1918). When Joseph was barely 14 years old, his father died. By then he was already known as an *illui* (child prodigy). Joseph studied under Rabbi Abraham Joel Abelson. In 1903 Joseph published in Odessa his first book *Birchat Yosef*, and was ordained by Rabbi Shalom Mordechai ben Moses Schwadron (1835–1911) of Brezany who stated that 'all doors of Halachah are open to him . . . He is fit to be a rabbi of a large community'. 'Fortunate indeed is the community that will avail itself of his services,' wrote the Rebbe of Sadagora in 1908. Joseph continued his rabbinic studies in Odessa where his widowed mother Chavah (d. 1914) had a shop. He also studied Greek and general modern philosophy, specialising in psychology, which he utilised to throw light on many difficult passages in the Talmud. He had a great admiration for the founder of psychoanalysis, Sigmund Freud, and also acquired some knowledge of folk medicine.[16] In 1909, he married Chayah Gitel (d. 9 June 1963).

During a short stay in Berlin he printed his *Midrasch Joseph – Randglossen und Indices zum Talmud*.[17] He then moved to London where he soon published the first of his broadsheets and periodicals *Roshei Alphei*

Yisrael,[18] the only one of his many periodicals to even have as many as 17 issues. Among his notable contributors were Rabbi Abraham Yitzchak Kook, then rabbi of the *Machzikei Hadath*; Rabbi Zevi Hirsch Levine of Manchester; Rabbi Yehuda Leib Levine, Rabbi of Philpot Street; Rabbi Levi Yitzchak Brill (1841–1917) who lived in London for the last seven years of his life; and the Chief Preacher of the Federation of Synagogues, the *Kamenitzer Maggid*, Rabbi Chayim Zundel Zalman Maccoby, who often castigated the sweatshop employers and slum landlords.

Joseph became known as a 'miracle worker'. He endeavoured to cure people suffering from rheumatism, neuritis, certain forms of paralysis, asthma, bronchitis and kidney trouble. In this connection he published a news sheet entitled *The World Doctor* in which he printed letters, and photographs, names and addresses of people who had been cured by him of all kinds of maladies.[19] He maintained that treatment of mental disorders and cognate ailments could be cured through the rhythmic sounds of music. He let it be known that he was prepared to give 'Free advice to the ailing on all matters relating to General Health. Jew and Gentile are welcome to avail themselves of this unique opportunity. Consulting hours 12 noon to 10 pm.'[20]

One year after his arrival in London, in January 1914, he convened a meeting of representatives of 13 East End synagogues including the *Machzikei Hadath*, Philpot Street and Black Lion Yard, at which it was decided to publish a new Yiddish weekly called *Der Emes* (The Truth).[21] He also wrote a letter to the *Zeit* (The Jewish Times), expressing his concern that in the West End of London there are 'fifty Jewish butchers' shops which publicly desecrate the Sabbath'.[22]

In January 1915, he addressed meetings in the *shul* at 44 Philpot Street and at Cannon Street Synagogue with the aim of strengthening and revitalising Judaism.[23] He made an impassioned appeal for the setting up of a hostel for refugees and vehemently denied the suggestion that he had given Kashrut licences to bakers.[24] He issued a statement refuting the allegation that he had declared all oils to be *kosher*.[25] He authorised the wine produced by Harry Ratsker of 48 Vallance Road, declaring that 'he himself would drink the wine on Passover'.[26] Ratsker advertised that he was willing to sell 500 bottles of wine below cost price, at one shilling per bottle, provided the would-be purchaser produced a letter from a rabbi or president of a synagogue certifying that he was a needy person.

Shapotshnick appealed to the London *Beth Din* to ban the use of mincing machines in butcher shops, for, once the butchers were given a free hand, no one would know what sort of meat was put through the machines. He also alleged that some manufacturers of *matzot* used *chametz* (leaven) meal. He approved the use of a motor invented by the electrical engineer A Barnett for the controlled cooking of all kinds of beef.

Shapotshnick was a prolific author. The British Library lists only 21 items from his pen, but there were more.[27] He wrote commentaries on, and translations of, the Talmud in Yiddish and published a *Siddur* and many tracts on a variety of subjects.

He originated from a Chasidic background and his synagogue was originally named *Chevra Beth Yoseph Chasidei Amshinov*.[28] But it is noteworthy that, in a very rare eight-page booklet, printed in London in 1920,[29] he criticises Chasidism as if he were a *Mithnagged* or a *Maskil*. 'Chasidism today,' he writes, 'consists only of (people) drinking whisky and taking of snuff.'[30] 'The rebbes today bless and take money. Their families live a life of luxury. They adorn themselves from head to foot with diamonds and do nothing for the good of Judaism.'[31] He castigated the Chasidim for allowing their young children to carry on the Sabbath, for not observing the right times for the recitation of the *Shema* (the name given to the three biblical passages which must be read morning and evening), and above all for talking during the reading of the Law. He strongly condemned the hereditary principle of Chasidism, whereby a son or grandson succeeds as rebbe. He refers critically to the Rebbe of Talno.[32] He calls him facetiously the 'precious' Rebbe of Talno. 'The profanation of God's name that the Rebbe of Talno caused in Russia is not to be estimated.'[33] He propagates a new type of Chasidism to which the masses would be attracted not merely by snatching *shirayim* (left-overs) of the rebbe, but by providing the people with good books, that is, tractates of the Talmud, and encouraging them to study the Talmud daily.[34]

On the death of Kamenitzer Maggid, who had collaborated with him in his periodical, Shapotshnick delivered a eulogy at 44 Dunk Street,[35] but he never occupied a salaried rabbinical position at any of the innumerable East End *shtieblech*, although for a short time he officiated at the *Beth Hamidrash Haggadol* at Dunk Street, where he delivered a talmudical discourse on *Shabbat Haggadol*. He also gave discourses on the Sabbath at the *Chevra Torah Ubnei Melave* at 93 Wilkes Street.[36]

To enlist financial support for his vast literary works, he addressed meetings at Cannon Street Synagogue[37] and *Chevra Doresh Zion*,[38] and at Montague Road *Beth Hamidrash* where he was supported by Rabbi

Jacob Rabinowitz of Edinburgh.[39] He widely publicised his projected commentary on the Talmud, *Kenos Lachachamim* (based on 100 commentaries) and asked for subscriptions of one shilling per week.[40] Insertion of a subscriber's name was to cost £3 and to commemorate a loved one, £5.[41] In May 1920 it was announced in the Yiddish press that Shapotshnick had been elected chief Rabbi of America and that he would visit the United States in *Elul*.[42] However, no American visit followed.

He persevered in his activities. His *Beth Midrash* was renamed *Chevra Beth Yosef* and he outlined a new plan for the establishment of a *yeshiva* named *Gehender Yeshiva*.[43] He also announced the publication of his commentary to the Pentateuch at one shilling a copy.[44] At a meeting presided over by Mr H Lass, he pleaded for financial support for his envisaged educational projects.[45]

He claimed that he was the 'Presiding Rabbi' of the *Chevra Mefitze Torah* whose members were 48 rabbis from Poland, Lithuania, Norway, Romania, Czechoslovakia and the Holy Land. He published a brochure containing letters from world famous rabbinical authorities recognising 'Chief Rabbi Joseph Shapotshnick as one of the greatest talmudical scholars and authority on rabbinical law'. Among these authorities were Rabbi Meir Yechiel Halevi Halstock of Ostrowiec, Rabbi Samuel Deutsch of Bucharest, Rabbi Mordechai Deutsch of Velatin, Czechoslovakia and Rabbi Aron Kagan of Nowo-Swieciany.

His home was described as a *Beth Din* 'with offices at 60 Myrdle Street, open every day from 10 am to 10 pm'. He made it known that he had a special school for male and female proselytes, whom he undertook to prepare 'within a three week period'.[46] In 1930 he established the Amhurst Road *Talmud Torah* at 36 Amhurst Park. The classes met on Sunday, Monday and Thursday.[47] On 7 January 1934 he dedicated his new *Beth Din* at 7 Frostic Place. He gave a *hechsher* (permit) to *matzot* and *matza* meal baked by Peek Frean whose manager was Rakusen of Leeds. He was ahead of his time in seeking to establish an *eruv* (to make it possible to carry objects on the Sabbath) for London and he urged Jewish landlords not to harass their Jewish tenants but to maintain a high ethical standard.

THE GREAT CONTROVERSY

Rabbi Shapotshnick's literary activities did not fully absorb his energies. He turned his attention to the task of resolving the problem of the *agunah*. Few are so tragic as the *agunah*, the married woman who cannot remarry either because her husband will not give her a divorce, or because there is no conclusive evidence that the missing husband is dead. This also applies to a *yevamah* (a 'levirate widow') if she cannot obtain *chalitzah* (the rite by which the widow is free to remarry).

For a long time there have been attempts to introduce some kind of measure to deal effectively with these problems. At the close of the First World War there were 10,000 women in Europe who, with their husbands declared missing, could not receive a divorce. Many rabbis have made heroic efforts on behalf of the *agunah* but no solution to satisfy all Orthodox rabbis has ever been found. Some twentieth-century *Halachic* authorities, such as Rabbi Solomon Eliezer Alfandari of Jerusalem, the Conservative Rabbi Louis M Epstein of Brookline, Mass., and Rabbi Joel Zusman Hodes, Rabbi of the Birmingham *Beth Hamidrash*, have maintained, having regard to a clause in the *ketuba* (marriage contract), that all Jewish marriages are conditional, as the husband at the time of the wedding declares that the bride is married to him 'according to the law of Moses and of Israel'.[48] This obliges him to live with his wife and perform his conjugal duties. If he does not do so, according to this argument, the marriage becomes *ipso facto* invalid.

Shapotshnick felt that there was no legal reason why this problem should not be resolved and took it upon himself to extricate the *agunah* from a life sentence. His work *Cherut Olam (Everlasting Freedom)* and *Likro L'Asirim Dror (To Proclaim Freedom for the Prisoners)* was aimed at mitigating their plight. He even published the draft text of a new *ketuba*. East End Jews watched in amazement as Shapotshnick released live doves as a symbol of freedom for the chained wives. He scattered his thoughts unsystematically. His decisions were not the result of prolonged meditation or consideration. It is difficult to give his writings *Halachic* plausibility. His views were, therefore, not admissible from an *Halachic* standpoint, as the weight of rabbinical authority felt that he was legalising possibly adulterous unions.

He was strongly opposed by the great contemporary *Halachic* scholars: by Rabbi Chayim Ozer Grodzinsky of Vilna who stated that 'his (Shapotshnick's) views are contrary to the Talmud and those of the rabbis';[49] by Rabbi Israel Meir HaKohen Kagan, the author of the six-volume *Mishnah Berurah*, an authoritative updated commentary on Jewish Law; by Rabbi Elijah ben Naftali Hertz Klatzkin (1852–1932) of the Holy Land, known as the '*Shklover Illui*';[50] by Rabbi Abraham Mordechai Alter of Ger who wrote, 'Far be it to rely on him',[51] and by the Talmudical genius Rabbi Joseph Rozin of Dvinsk, known as the 'Ragochover Gaon'.[52]

The Polish rabbinate reacted with unaccustomed speed. They even published a special supplement attacking him.[53] Letters were published by the Chasidic rebbe, Rabbi Meir Yechiel Halevi Halstock of Ostroviec, and his son, Rabbi Yechezkel Halevi Halstock of Nashelsk and Rabbi Chayim Yosef of Opatov, who categorically denied that they ever associated with Shapotshnick.[54] 'He must not be relied upon,' wrote Rabbi Yechezkel Halevi.[55] 'He is confused and not rational,' stated Rabbi David Zevi Auerbach. Similar sentiments were expressed by Rabbi Menachem Halevi Steinberg of Brody.[56]

In all, 600 rabbis in Poland signed a protest denouncing him. He was also attacked by the rabbis in the Holy Land, such as Rabbi Zevi Pesach Frank, the Chief Rabbi of Jerusalem and an expert on the problem of *agunot*; Rabbi Pinchas Epstein of Jerusalem; Chief Rabbi Abraham Yitzchak Kook who wrote, 'I have known him in London when I was at the *Machzikei Hadath* during the war, and he is a man who is not rational.' Rabbi Moses Mordechai Epstein, known as the '*illui* of Bakst' and the head of the *Yeshiva Knesset Yisrael* of Hebron even accused Shapotshnick of having forged the signatures of rabbis to support his distorted *Halachic* views.[57] Rabbi Shalom Yitzchak Levitan of Oslo vehemently denied that he had ever supported Shapotshnick's rabbinical organisation.[58] The London scholar Menasheh Adler called him 'a heretic'.[59]

This avalanche of abuse did not affect Shapotshnick. He continued to call himself 'Chief Rabbi of the Rabbinical Association' and alleged that he had the support of many rabbis. He challenged Dayan H M Lazarus and Chief Rabbi Hertz to appoint a Committee of learned men with 'profound knowledge of the Talmud to pit his erudition against theirs for in Judaism it is the paramount knowledge that could entitle someone to assume the position he occupies'.

He desired to establish his *Yeshivat Beth Yoseph* at 36 Amhurst Park. In his prospectus he stated that, starting with the *Aleph Beth* (Hebrew alphabet), he undertook to teach beginners the Pentateuch within a period of six months. Teaching would be based on scientific pedagogic methods and would cover Bible, Talmud, logic and general knowledge. The College welcomed boys and girls from the age of seven, and the hours of instruction would be from 5 p.m. to 9 p.m.

In the course of carrying out his routine rabbinical duties Shapotshnick announced that the unemployed would not be charged any fee for 'selling their *chametz*' (leaven).[60] When he celebrated his fiftieth birthday on 6 March 1932 at the Shoreditch Town Hall, he received a congratulatory message from Rabbi M Sinson of Leeds. One of his favourite ideas was the plan to erect a large synagogue in Jerusalem to serve as a 'supreme religious world centre'.[61]

He addressed members of the World Congress of Faiths, held at University College on Wednesday 8 July 1936, where he pointed out that the Talmud itself was a mine of scientific information. In it were to be found references to botany, algebra, geometry, anatomy, physiology, astronomy and other sciences. His fertile mind constantly gave birth to new ideas. He maintained that working in unity with the League of Nations would inspire worldwide support and could more readily solve the intricate and complex problems confronting the world. He advocated that the representatives of every religion in the world (there being over 300) should form a 'League of Religion' or a 'Parliament of Religion'. He felt that if the representatives of every religion were to form a Parliament and work in harmony with self-assumed power to arbitrate in international disputes, no single nation would dare resist it. He wrote on this matter to Sir Arthur Wauchope, the Governor of Jerusalem, the Pope, Sigmund Freud and the Archbishop Canterbury. In 1928 he made national headlines when he sent a herbal remedy to King George V and was thanked by Lord Dawson of Penn, the King's physician.

He was very charitable. He distributed two-thirds of his meagre income to charity and regularly supported widows, poor rabbis and authors in Eastern Europe. He would send registered letters containing money to needy scholars. He was a life-long vegetarian, and apart from his charitable deeds, the bulk of his income was spent on innumerable literary publications.

Apart from his non-conventional *agunah* intervention, Shapotshnick established a rival *Board of Shechitah*. By 1928 there were five butcher shops under his personal supervision, presenting the biggest challenge to the Establishment since the *Machzikei Hadath* controversy of 1892. On 18 October 1934 Chief Rabbi Hertz and the *Beth Din* issued a directive that 'All hindquarter meat sold at any shop under the control of the *Beth Din* and the *Shechitah Board* must be porged and one of the conditions of the licence must be that no customer shall be served with hindquarter meat unporged.'[62] This directive caused much discontent among many butchers.

By 1937, there were 11 butcher shops under his supervision, some of the butchers paying him 30 shillings per week for his services.[63] He visited each shop once or twice a week. He offered to take – at his own expense – any would-be patron of the shops under his supervision to view the slaughterhouse 'where the method of Jewish Ritual Slaughter is carried out in accordance with Jewish law, to satisfy themselves of the *kashrut* of the Meat.'

The rabbi became a tool in the hands of unscrupulous butchers. The Board for the Affairs of *Shechitah*, on the advice tendered by its then solicitors, Messrs. Teff & Teff, and the joint opinion of Mr Norman Birkett KC, and Mr F M Landau, published in the *Jewish Chronicle* and the *North West Jewish Mirror* the information that quantities of *trefah* (non-kosher) meat were found in eight of the butchers' shops. The London Board of *Shechitah* was concerned that 'there are in London a considerable number of unscrupulous men who were deliberately foisting upon the Jewish public *trefah* meat and selling it as kosher'. They had no difficulty in proving in the civil courts that *trefah* meat which had been sold was obtained from Spitalfields Market and sold as kosher in Shapotshnick-supervised shops.[64]

To counteract his *shechitah* activities, a crowded public meeting was held at the Whitechapel Art Gallery with Reuben Lincoln in the chair. The speakers, Chief Rabbi Hertz, Councillor M H Davis LCC, Dayan A Feldman, Isaac Landau, President of the London Board of *Shechitah*, Dayan Abramsky, Rabbi Rabinowitz of Vine Court Synagogue, Rabbi A Singer and his father-in-law, Rabbi Pekarowitch of Bethnal Green Synagogue all stressed that only the *Beth Din* and the *Kashrut* Commission could provide *kashrut* in London.[65]

For the best part of his life he carried on a bitter vendetta against Chief Rabbi Joseph Hermann Hertz. It could accurately be said that 'Joseph' Shapotshnick 'knew not Joseph', for he refused to accept the authority of Chief Rabbi Hertz.

Eight months before Shapotshnick's death, Chief Rabbi Hertz encouraged Rabbi Isser Yehuda Unterman of Liverpool (later Chief Rabbi of Israel) and Rabbi Zevi (Hirsch) Hurwitz (1863–1946), senior rabbi of the Leeds community, to make peace with this rabbinic revolutionary. At a meeting held in the Cumberland Hotel, Marble Arch, Shapotshnick, accompanied by his son and the warden of his *shul*, was offered an annual stipend to enable him to pursue his literary work in return for dissolving his rabbinical organisation.

Another meeting took place at the home of Dr Hertz on 15 March 1937. The Chief Rabbi assured him in the presence of Rabbi Unterman that 'he would treat him like a brother'. A signature was obtained from Shapotshnick in exchange for a verbal promise of an annual subsidy. Despite four reminders addressed to Dr Hertz and Rabbis Unterman and Hurwitz, nothing came of this 'gentleman's agreement'. The President of the Union of Orthodox Hebrew Congregations, Dr Bernard Homa, wrote to the *Beth Din* as follows:

> Gentlemen, Public statements have been made that you are effecting a compromise with 'Rabbi' Shapotshnick, who has given his sanction to a number of shops which to your knowledge have made purchases of *trefah* meat, and who has been involved in other grievous wrongs.
>
> My executive feel it to be their duty to state that if this agreement matures they would consider it a severe blow to Kashrut in general such as would jeopardise any future possibility of cooperation between the Orthodox forces in the Community.[66]

In letters dated 8 May and 8 June Shapotshnick addresses Dr Hertz as 'my friend and dear one' and said that he was anxious to see him once again, as he felt that they have common interests. 'I studied psychology,' Shapotshnick wrote, 'and I immediately took to you', and he felt that one of the *Dayanim* was an obstacle to their agreement. 'I am not,' he writes, 'an extremist, nor am I a fanatic. I am, indeed, a progressive, and I always try to be a helpful rabbi.'[67]

On 11 June 1937, Shapotshnick, in a letter written in English by another hand and signed by him, writes:

> The Very Rev Dr J H Hertz, Relating to our recent meeting, with a view of reaching an amicable settlement in our communal differences, I regret to learn that the conditions verbally agreed upon at that time, have up to now not been fulfilled.
>
> If you do not propose to abide by the promises made both by your good self and your intermediary Rabbi Unterman, I must demand an immediate return of the conditional signature obtained from me; failing which I will be compelled to seek advice as appertains to this matter. Writing to you as one Rabbi to another I fully trust it will not be necessary for me to seek recourse to a court of law, and that you will see fit to respect your unfailing promise made not once but several times at our interview, and previously substantiated by your learned emissaries, Rabbis Unterman and Hurwitz. Before acting on further advice I hope to hear from you by Wednesday next. I hope and trust that you will avoid any inconvenience and *Chillul Hashem* [profanation of the Divine Name].[68]

The disappointment of the abortive 'peace moves' caused the final breakdown of his health. Too poor to pay for medical care, he was finally admitted to the London Jewish Hospital in Stepney Green where he died after surgery on Thursday, 16 *Cheshvan* 1937.

His sudden death did not appease his opponents. The Federation of Synagogues under the leadership of Councillor Morris Harold Davis, LCC (d. 1985), refused to bury him. The *Adath Yisroel* agreed to inter him on condition that his son would not continue his father's various controversial activities and that he would pay a fee of £15.

The funeral took place on 22 October 1937. For several hours weeping men and women waited in the rain. The traffic was held up for a considerable time as the cortège passed along Whitechapel Road. Police had to link arms to hold back the 5,000 people who attended the funeral. 'He had a sway,' records the *Jewish Chronicle*, 'over the minds, at any rate the emotions, of many members of the community as the scenes at the funeral amply demonstrated.'[69] He was buried at the *Adath Yisroel* Cemetery at Enfield.[70] The poet Aaron Rumyanek (1876–1946), principal of the Modern Hebrew School, Leeds, delivered the memorial address.[71] No rabbi was present, however. Dr Bernard Homa was the only communal personality who attended. The Reverend Hoffman officiated.[72] The coroner gave the cause of his death as 'misadventure'. Many people would regard this an apt description of Rabbi Joseph Shapotshnick's turbulent life.

His only son Louis Levi (1909–82) was promptly summoned to an informal meeting at the Committee Room of the Board of Deputies of British Jews. Its President, Neville Laski KC, and Dr Homa, the President of the Union of Orthodox Hebrew Congregations, urged him to affirm in writing that 'he agreed that the activities of the Synagogue which had been held in his late father's house, should be confined strictly to religious matters.'[73] He was later appointed minister of the Great Garden Street Synagogue where he served for 43 years. He maintained that he had in his possession a number of his father's unpublished manuscripts.[74] He was warned that he would lose his employment should he ever publish them. The *Beth Hamidrash Maharish*, established by the son in a disused chapel at 62 Fieldgate Street in his father's memory, housed a Young Social Circle, Hebrew Classes, an Institute where lectures in Hebrew, Yiddish and English were delivered, and a Talmudical study circle. It was not successful and closed after a short period.[75]

7 • *The Inter-war Years*

The East End of London in the first decade of the twentieth century was crowded with *Yidden fun der heim* (Jews from 'home' countries), from Russia, Lithuania, Poland and Romania, who came to try their luck in London. By 1912, some 142,000 Jews were living in Whitechapel, Mile End, Poplar, Stepney and Hackney.[1] Among them were a number of *meshullachim* (emissaries) from various *yeshivot* who had decided to settle here.

The East End became a centre of Chasidism, the headquarters of Chasidic rebbes, before they branched out northwards and westwards. Dramatic scenes took place in those small squalid streets. On the first day of *Rosh Hashanah* (New Year) hundreds of Jews would wend their way to the City of London, to Tower Bridge, to recite *Tashlich*, the symbolic ceremony (of drowning one's sins), on the banks of the Thames. On occasions when new Scrolls of the Law were consecrated, the Scrolls would be borne under a canopy through the streets of the East End from the house of the donor to the synagogue amid public rejoicing. Before Passover the rebbes and their followers would actually bake their own hand-made *matzot*, performing this task with scrupulous care and energy that transformed it into a labour of love. Many of the *shtieblech* regularly held a *melaveh malka* (a gathering held after the termination of the Sabbath) which became popular for the accompanying songs and melodies.

The East End of London blossomed with *batei midrashim* which not only used *Nusach Sephard*, but, in Great Garden Street, also observed the *yahrzeit* of the Chasidic Rebbe, Rabbi Yechiel Meir Lipshitz (d. 21 *Shevat* 1888 in Gostonyn).[2]

In Dunk Street there were three *shtieblech*: Dunk Street *Beth Hamidrash* at 44a, Dzikov at Number 30 and Mile End New Town (founded in 1886) at Number 39. In Philpot Street there were two synagogues: Philpot Street Great at Number 44 (founded in 1901) and Philpot Street *Sephardishe*. In Princelet Street there were also two and there were several more in Fieldgate Street.

The Chasidic rebbe's task in London was not an easy one. He had to perform the miracle of interpreting eighteenth-century East European Chasidism in the light of twentieth-century West European culture. He had to demonstrate its peculiar relevance to an age of moral disintegration, social upheaval and economic depression. His efforts to do so brought colour and richness to the drab impoverished lives of London's Jews.

The climate was favourable for Chasidism. The Romanian-born Morris Myer (1878–1944), the founder and editor of the Yiddish daily paper, *Die Zeit (Jewish Times)*, exerted a strong influence on East End Jewry for 31 years.[3] He was active on the Board of Deputies, Zionist Federation, Federation of Jewish Relief Organisations and the World Jewish Congress. Every Friday a double number of his paper was issued and for 20 years (ending in 1939) he also published a Yiddish evening paper, *Ovent Zeitung*. His premises at 325 Whitechapel Road were the meeting place for London literati. He enlisted the services of Ben A Sochachewsky (1889–1958), a Yiddish poet, satirist, lyricist and teller of Chasidic stories, as well as Leo Koenig (1889–1970) who, during his 35 years in London, wrote innumerable articles on a variety of subjects.[4]

Myer's paper had many other distinguished contributors, including Sholem Aleichem, Sholem Asch and Abraham Reisen. He commissioned Meir Eidelbaum, a native of Mezerich and a religious Labour Zionist, to write a series of biographical articles on the London rebbes.[5] Myer himself, under the pseudonym Yechiel Meyer, wrote a series of popular articles on Rabbi Israel Baal Shem Tov, which he later published in book-form.[6] He dealt with the ten main principles of Chasidism: love of the deity, *Devekut* (cleaving to God), prayer, *Kavanah* (devotion), *Hitlahavut* (enthusiasm), *Hisbodedut* (seclusion), humility, charity, Torah study, and serving the Almighty. Myer stressed that the Besht revitalized the Jewish community not by revolutionary methods but by reviving ancient Jewish precepts. Myer's relations with all the rebbes was cordial, and he faithfully recorded their activities, their marriages and, above all, he published regular annual reports on the High Holy Day services.

In his first year of publication he printed a Chasidic story about a rebbe's Chanukah lamp.[7] He gave a detailed account of the activities of the Rebbe of Boyan,[8] and a sensitive appreciation of Rabbi Nachman of Bratslav[9] in eleven articles. He encouraged a contributor who wrote under the pseudonym 'Historicus' on Rabbi Arye Leib of Shpola,[10] Rabbi Levi Yitzchak of Berdichev,[11] Rabbi Shneur Zalman of Liady,[12]

Rabbi Isaac Meir Alter of Ger,[13] Rabbi Uri of Strelisk,[14] and a series of articles on Rabbi Nachman of Bratslav,[15] Rabbi Mordechai of Czernobiel,[16] and Rabbi Samuel Eli Taub.[17] He also serialised the Chasidic novel *The Kaiser and the Rebbe*[18] by the Hebrew and Yiddish writer Zalman Shneour (1887–1959). It is, therefore, not surprising that the Trisker Rebbe sent Morris Myer cordial greetings on the Silver Jubilee of the paper.[19]

A regular contributor to the paper was Rabbi Joshua Szpetman (d. 1964), the rabbi for 30 years of the Nelson Street *Sephardishe* Synagogue. He was a native of Lublin, of Chasidic background and a disciple of the author and thinker Hillel Zeitlin (1871–1942), who translated the *Zohar* into Yiddish and wrote extensively on Chasidism and Mysticism. Rabbi Szpetman was a prolific writer of articles and High Holy Day booklets.[20] In his Yiddish book *Bigilufin* he depicts Chasidic observance of happy and social occasions. His aim was to describe the Chasidic way of life, especially in his native town Lublin, the cradle of Polish Chasidism. He was not afraid to criticise spiritual or lay leaders. He hated untruths, dishonesty and hypocrisy. He frowned on displays of pretentiousness and was unique in tolerance and sympathy. He spoke more like a prophet than a preacher. He enlivened any gathering with his wit, his eccentricity and his healthy irreverence. He befriended the Chasidic rebbes in London and graced most of their functions.[21] He was popularly called the 'Red Rabbi', the Jewish counterpart of his contemporary the Dean of Canterbury, Dr Hewlett Johnson.

In a letter to the *Jewish Chronicle* in 1947, Rabbi Szpetman wrote:

> In view of the recent grievous occurrence (when the Chief Rabbi of Italy converted to Catholicism) which deeply shocked the Jewish Communities of the world, I suggest now that Anglo-Jewry is about to elect its spiritual head, would it not be appropriate earnestly to consider dispensing with the so-called title 'Chief Rabbi', particularly where European Jewry is concerned and in its place substitute a dignified title.[22]

The favourable climate for Chasidism created by the press was expressed by the rabbis of the Federation of Synagogues, many of whom came from Chasidic backgrounds and were very sympathetic towards the new arrivals. In his paper, *Die Zeit*, Morris Myer had a regular column entitled *Menora* by Rabbi Israel Joseph Lew – a column devoted to discussion of religious topics and brief homiletical notes.[23] Rabbi Lew (1884–1951), a devotee of Ger, was born in Vengroff, Poland and studied in Warsaw where he received *semicha*. On his marriage he lived in his father-in-law's home in Siedlice for a time. Later he held a rabbinic position in Warsaw and became involved in the *Agudas Yisroel* in Poland. In 1922, together with Rabbi Asher Spitzer, Rabbi Dr Meir Hildesheimer, Dr Nathan Birnbaum and Rabbi Meir Dan Plotzki, he went to the United States to enlist help for Eastern European Orthodox Jewry.

On the return journey, the rabbinic delegation visited England, and Rabbi Lew addressed a large gathering at the Embassy Hall, Mile End, on the financial plight of Polish Jewry. He was offered, and accepted, the position of rabbi of the independent Lincoln Street congregation in Bow. Some time later, this synagogue amalgamated with a neighbouring *shul*, and they acquired a disused chapel in Harley Grove, Bow, for their combined use. By 1929 the congregation was known as the Mile End and Bow District Synagogue and had become part of the United Synagogue. Rabbi Lew was the first 'foreign rabbi' to join the Establishment. He preached in Yiddish and in English on alternate Sabbaths. However, he never conformed to the United Synagogue requirement of wearing 'canonicals' and continued wearing a *kapote*.

Rabbi Lew served the community for 26 years until his retirement in 1950. Broadminded and tolerant, he was so alienated by the anti-Zionist policies pursued with such vigour by the British *Aguda* under H A Goodman, that he became a Mizrachi sympathizer. His weekly column 'Menora' in *Die Zeit* grew into a book. His two-volume Yiddish work, *Yalkut Yosef* was an anthology of selected passages from the Talmud and Midrash on the Pentateuch and Prophets, with brief explanations of homiletical comments.[24] Of his nine children, two sons followed his footsteps: one son, Meyer Lew (1907–87) was the minister of the Stoke Newington and Hampstead Garden Suburb Synagogues. He was also a *dayan* of the London *Beth Din*, and the author of a doctoral thesis *The Jews of Poland*.[25] The younger son, Rabbi Maurice Lew (1909–89) was the minister in Highgate, London, Parkview, Johannesburg and the West End Great Synagogue.

Rabbi Yerachmiel Mett was the District Rabbi of Stamford Hill and author of *Even Yechezkel*, novellae on the Talmud, which had *haskamot* from Rabbi Meir Yechiel Halevi Halstock, Rabbi Moses Friedman of Boyan and Rabbi Menachem Zemba of Warsaw.[26] It also has a five-page preface by Rabbi Yechezkel Halevi Halstock of Nashelsk. Rabbi Mett was an extraordinary, modest and rather private person.

Rabbi Abraham Israel Kon (1892–1968), a Chasid of Radomsk, was loved for his humane and understanding nature. He was born in Lodz, the son of a Chasid of Alexander. Abraham was educated in the *yeshiva* of Lomza under Rabbi Meir Dan Plotzki of Ostrova. He was subsequently 'converted' to Radomsker Chasidut. After living with his in-laws at Izbice, and intending to settle in the Argentine, in 1924 he accepted a position as teacher and *shochet* in the *Adath Yisroel* community in Stettin, Germany.[27] When deported to the Polish frontier town Zbanszyn by the Nazis in October 1938, he, together with some 5,000 to 8,000 Jews, lived in cramped conditions in military barracks and former horse stables, and life was only made tolerable through the efforts of the Warsaw Jewish Relief Committee and the Joint. He came to this country just before the Second World War, and was put in charge of a refugee children's hostel in Ely, Cambridgeshire, whence the Jews' Free School was evacuated.[28]

After the war, Rabbi Kon returned to London, where he was in charge of another refugee hostel in Amhurst Road, Stoke Newington. He combined this position with the job of ritual slaughterer for the London Board of *Shechita*, and in 1954 became the rabbi of the nearby *Rutzon Tov* Synagogue. He was the author of *Siach Tefilla*, a collection of selected definitions on matters relating to prayer and synagogue, to enable the layman to get a basic understanding of Judaism.[29]

The Rabbi of Philpot Street Sephardish and Romanian Synagogue was Rabbi Abraham Twersky. Born in Trisk in 1903, he was the son of Rabbi Moshe Mordechai Twersky, popularly known as 'Rabbi Moishele Trisker', who settled in Lublin in 1918. Rabbi Abraham married Shifra, a daughter of Rabbi Alter Yisrael Shimon Perlow of Novominsk, in 1924. He became deeply attached to the charismatic personality of Rabbi Meir Shapiro, the founder of the *Yeshivat Chachmei Lublin*. When the *yeshiva* was in great financial difficulties and almost facing closure, Rabbi Shapiro persuaded Twersky to undertake a fund-raising rescue mission in France and England. It was while on this visit to London that he was appointed rabbi of the Sephardishe Synagogue at a salary of £3 per week. An excellent orator and a melodious singer, he soon made an impact on the Jewish East End. His soul-stirring rendition, at the termination of the Sabbath, of the Yiddish prayer attributed to Rabbi Levi Yitzchok of Berdichev

> *Gott fun Avrohom, Yitzchok un Yakov,*
> *Der heilige Shabbos koidesh geht shoin aweg . . .*

(God of Abraham, Isaac and Jacob, the Holy Sabbath is passing away. May the coming week bring us health, life and all good. May it bring us sustenance, good tidings, deliverance and consolation) attracted large crowds of women and there was not a dry eye in the audience. His ability to dramatize whatever he did, made him a memorable figure.

Apart from pursuing his rabbinic duties, he immersed himself in communal affairs. He was active in the *Keren HaTorah* (Torah Fund of the *Aguda*) and the Federation of Jewish Relief Organisations of Great Britain under Dr D Jochelman, whose object it was 'to assist the suffering Jews in Poland, Russia, Bessarabia and other countries'. It helped Polish refugees with monthly grants. The Federation rescued 150 children who had been kept with their parents as virtual prisoners in a camp at Zbanszyn. Rabbi Twersky was also the editor of the *Jewish Weekly* (*Die Wochenzeitung*) and was deeply involved in the work of the *Aguda* and the Union of Orthodox Hebrew Congregations.

After the war, he ran the Grosvenor Court Hotel in Bournemouth for a time, eventually settling in the USA where he was joined by his brother Baruch Meir (1913–81) who had spent the war years in London and later became the public relations officer of the Rabbinical Council of America.

There were also a number of learned Chasidic laymen in London during that period. They combined 'the study of the Torah with worldly occupations' and were authors of halachic works. Moses Aaron Kutchinsky (1874–1960) was born in Grobova, Poland. He studied under Rabbi Yehuda Leib Kowalski, a disciple of Rabbi Abraham of Sochaszew. With his parents and his only sister Frimet he came to London in 1892. In 1908 he married Miriam Chanah, the daughter of Ezekiel Wetzer, a diamond merchant in Bamberg. He later became the owner of a very prosperous jewellery shop, at first in Cannon Street Road, and from 1914 at 171 Commercial Road. He never ceased learning and even conducted a daily *shiur* at Cannon Street Road Synagogue. He was the author of a 213-page rabbinic commentary with the title *Gevurot Moshe V'Aharon*.[30] He was survived by three sons: Benjamin Zevi, Yekutiel and Joseph. His only daughter, Gitel, married the Reverend Wolf Morein, later Minister of the North London Synagogue.

Yechiel Nathan Swimer (d. 1952), who lived in Church Street, Whitechapel Road, was a trimmings merchant as well as the author of a 206-page learned work of 39 responsa *Chikrei Halachot*.[31] This work had a *haskamah* from Rabbi Abraham Yaakov Helevi Horowitz of Probiszna. Swimer corresponded with Rabbi David Menachem Munish Babad of Tarnopol, Rabbi N Greenspan, Rabbi S Moskowitz, Rabbi S J Rabinow, Rabbi Issachar Dov Finkelstein and Rabbi Yerucham Leiner.

Rabbi Meir Yechiel Halevi Halstock of Ostrowiec describes him as 'a Gaon, renowned for his works'. His 39 responsa reflect his wide range of erudition. He was exceptionally well-versed in the *Hassagot* (criticisms) on Maimonides' *Mishneh Torah* by Rabbi Abraham ben David of Posqueres (1123–98), and he supported the views of Maimonides against his critics. His considerable business interests did not diminish his devotion to learning.

London was no longer devoid of facilities for Talmudic studies. The *Yeshiva Etz Chayim*, originally established in Dunk Street in 1904, later moved to Landau House, Hutchinson Street, Aldgate, and in 1924 to Thrawl Street. The Yeshiva building was consecrated by Chief Rabbi Hertz in June 1926.[32] By 1930, the Yeshiva had over 80 full-time students and a further 90 evening students. On the staff were many well-known teachers.[33] Its destiny was guided by the great *Musar* teachers Rabbi Elia Lopian and Rabbi N D Greenspan.[34]

The Yiddish Theatre in London provided the public with Chasidic plays. A great attraction was the *Dybbuk*, a play by Solomon Zainvel Rapoport (under the pseudonym of S Anski, 1863–1920), based on folklore and the belief that the spirit of a dead person may enter the body of a living one and has to be exorcised by a *Zaddik*. Crowds packed Her Majesty's Theatre, London, in 1935, when Maurice Schwartz staged the play *Yoshe Kalb* – by Israel Joshua Singer (1893–1934) – a fictitious account of a sinner/saint protagonist of nineteenth-century Galician Chasidism.[35] *The Brothers Ashkenazi*, staged at the Phoenix Theatre in July 1938, was set in Lodz, the textile centre of Poland, and is the saga of a Chasidic textile baron.[36]

The dream to provide a secular education in a Jewish environment was soon to become a reality. Rabbi Dr Avigdor Schonfeld (1880–1930) was a native of Sutto on the Danube.[37] In 1911, he accepted the post of rabbi of the North London *Beth Hamidrash*, the forerunner of the *Adath Yisrael*. In 1927 he founded the Union of Orthodox Hebrew Congregations which he described as an amalgamation of synagogues which not only profess but practise traditional Judaism.[38] One of his principal aims was the establishment of a Jewish Secondary School. He opened one in the Finsbury Park area in September 1929. He died a year later. His son, Rabbi Dr Solomon Schonfeld, expanded the Jewish Secondary School Movement after the Second World War.[39] Unlike the old-established Jews' Free School which did not generally permit the wearing of a *kipah* except for Hebrew Studies, the new movement enforced its wear.

A number of Chasidic personalities visited England on fund-raising missions. One of the earliest visitors was Rabbi Menachem Chayim Landau (1862–1938) of Zarwitz, a descendant of Rabbi Abraham of Ciechanow. He visited the *Chevra Bnei Avrohom V'Zichron Yaakov* at 26 Heneage Street which observed the *yahrzeit* of Rabbi Abraham.[40] Others were Rabbi Meir Shapiro, the founder of the famed *Yeshivat Chachmei Lublin;*[41] Rabbi Eliezer Hager; Rabbi Leibel of Hornistopol;[42] Rabbi Jacob Friedman of Boyan; Rabbi Aaron Yechiel Hofstein of Otwock; Rabbi Jacob Safrin; Rabbi Chayim Baruch Hager of Vishnitz and Rabbi Moses of Kozienice.[43]

The sympathy with Chasidism spread to many sections of Anglo-Jewry. Nachum Sokolow, the author and Zionist leader, one of the most colourful and many-faceted personalities in Jewish life, was born in Wyshograd, Poland, in 1859. He traced his ancestry to Rabbi Nathan Shapira, the author of *Megalleh Amukot*. A child prodigy in Talmudic studies, he was in the words of Sholem Asch 'a legend among the synagogues in the Polish towns'. He came of a Chasidic family and his grandfather was a follower of Rabbi Elimelech of Lejask.

In 1874 Sokolow wrote: 'Let not the Maskilim be hasty to despise the Chasidim: let not the Chasidim be eager to curb the Maskilim.' In 1901 in a series of articles under the title *L'Moranan V'Rabbanan* (to our Masters and Teachers), he endeavoured to refute the contention of the holders of extreme religious views that Zionism was flouting God's will. On the contrary, he asserted, it was fulfilling the words of God as revealed in the Torah and the sacred literature.[44] Sokolow visited the court of Rabbi Yehuda Arye Alter of Ger, to elicit Chasidic support for Zionism, but, as Herzl before him, was unable to evoke any positive response. The Rebbe of Ger could not be persuaded that political Zionism would not weaken Orthodoxy.[45]

In an address on Chasidism, delivered at the Whitechapel Art Gallery under the auspices of Ben Uri, on Sunday, 5 February 1928, Sokolow expressed his admiration for the Chasidic movement.[46] Chasidism was like a melody which cannot be translated and cannot be interpreted. He was critical of the historian Graetz who classified Chasidism as reform. In his view a better term would have been revolutionary. The *Mithnaggedic* war against Chasidism was not a 'seven-year war' nor a '30-year war' when so much innocent blood was shed. It was a 'Jewish war', fought with 'Jewish weapons', and the *casus belli* was when or when not to recite certain passages of the liturgy. Sokolow also attacked Yitzchak Erter who maintained that Chasidism had encouraged superstition and invented the concepts of *gilgul* (transmigration of souls), *dybbuk* and *tashlich*. His response was that it was common knowledge that these beliefs were part of Judaism for many centuries before the advent of Chasidism.

He similarly refuted the views of Lilienblum and Smolenskin who held that Chasidism 'invented miracles'. This, too, had no foundation, for even Manasseh Ben Israel believed in miracles, and the *Mithnaggedim* attributed miracles to Solomon Ibn Gabirol and to Rashi. He stated that class divisions in Eastern Europe were clear cut. The scholars had little in common with the unlettered masses. They lived in a rarefied world of their own. Chasidism cut down class distinctions with the rich helping the poor, and at the court of the rebbe all were equal. Sokolow was encouraged by the Chalutzic activities of a number of Chasidim in *Nachlat Yaakov* who had turned farmers. Towards the end of his life, Sokolow started a series of articles on the leaders of Chasidism, but he only managed to complete an essay on Rabbi Nachman of Bratslav.[47]

At the beginning of the twentieth century there was a small Chasidic *shtiebl* at 85 Sandringham Road, Dalston, the home of Naftali Oster, a Chasid of Dzikov. Moses Samuel Schiff (1860–1936), a dealer in pots and pans in Commercial Road, a native of Tarnov and a brother-in-law of Oster, came to London in the 1880s and was then a regular worshipper at the Austrian *shtiebl* in the East End. On his moving to Dalston, he, together with a number of the First World War Belgian Jewish refugees, founded a *shtiebl* at Number 1 Sandringham Road, Dalston, which became known as *Schiff's shul*. The synagogue was a converted dance hall with a section for women worshippers. Among the scholarly worshippers were Abba Richman (father of Joe Richman) and Moses Weinstein. Though Jacob Morris Witzon (who had a clothing shop in Wentworth Street) was officially the warden, President Schiff, in spite of his move to Amhurst Park, retained full control of the synagogue's administration.

In 1946 the *shtiebl* premises were sold to a manufacturer of walking sticks, Mr Pinner, on condition that one room should remain a place of worship, but this closed down within a short space of time.

Schiff's autocratic rule alienated some of the worshippers, especially Leibish Rickel (1860–1928) who formed a breakaway *shtiebl* at his own home at 70 Colvestone Crescent.[48] He had 18 children of whom 11 survived. His three sons-in-law, Israel Orlinsky (1901–51), Berl Kleinman (1891–1968) and Willy Keller (1893–1946), a native of Cracow and the son of a well-known restaurateur, formed the nucleus of the

minyan. Berl, or Bernard, was a native of Warsaw, where he studied in
a *yeshiva*. After a short stay in Antwerp, he came to London in 1916 and
made his home in a three-storey house in Cazenove Road. His brother
Isaac (1886–1963) joined him in 1924. Berl and his brother-in-law
established a large ladies' clothing manufacturing business opposite
Gardiner's Corner, Whitechapel, under the name of Orlinsky and
Kleinman, which flourished until 1932. The firm then went into
liquidation and the partnership was dissolved, each one establishing
his own showroom within a few yards of the other.

Though there was now fierce competition and dissension within the
family, all of them felt at home in the *shtiebl*. Berl and his son Emanuel,
Isaac and his four sons, Jack, Joseph, Maurice and Mark, worshipped
there regularly until they moved to Willesden in 1941.

Among its congregants were the scholarly Chayim David Orlinsky
(1854–1937) and Juda Waller (1871–1953), popularly known as Reb
Yiddele, a devoted Chasid of Bobow. He had a little shop in Hessel
Street, Commercial Road, and until the outbreak of the Second World
War made annual pilgrimages to the Rebbe of Bobow in Galicia.

Harmony at Rickel's *shtiebl* was of short duration. A fiery liturgical
controversy soon erupted over the recitation of a Sabbath table-hymn,
Baruch HaShem Yom Yom (Blessed is the Lord day by day), which was
composed in the tenth century by the poet Shimon Bar Yitzchak. Rickel
adhered to the Galician custom which began the hymn at the sixth
stanza, commencing with the words *Bvo'o M'Edom* ('Who came from
Edom'); others felt that the melody should be recited in its entirety at
the midday meal. The *shtiebl* was soon split. Another place of worship
was opened on the corner of Colvestone Crescent and St Marks Rise
and became known as Zelig Semion's *Shtiebl*.

Hirsch Zelig Semion was born in Warsaw in 1860 into a family of
Grodzisk Chasidim. He left Warsaw in 1904 and lived in Antwerp for
ten years. At the outbreak of the First World War he came to London
where he established himself as a ritual slaughterer, later joining the
Board of Shechita. His home at 20 Sandringham Road, Dalston, was
a veritable shelter for homeless refugees. No one was ever refused
hospitality. Rabbi Joseph Lew stayed with him for more than a year
before his appointment as rabbi in Bow. Semion was a violent opponent
of Rabbi Shapotshnick, whom he regarded as a charlatan. He published,
at his own expense, a news-sheet entitled the *Londoner Yiddish Vort* (*The
London Jewish Word*), in which he drew the attention of the general
public to Rabbi Shapotshnick's activities.

Among the regular worshippers at his *shtiebl* were Berl (Barnet) Weisfogel (1881–1953) whose son Alec became a rabbi in Springfield, Mass., and whose sons-in-law were also rabbis: Dr Isaac Cohen the Chief Rabbi of the Jewish Communities in Ireland (1958–79) and Jona Indech the rabbi in Bournemouth.

During the height of the London blitz, Semion and his family spent the nights in the air-raid shelter at the Kingsland Road Cinema, Dalston. On the night of 21 *Elul* 1940 he deviated from his regular practice, and, unaccountably, spent the night at nearby Downs Park Road air raid shelter, which tragically received a direct hit, killing him, his wife Sara Lea, his daughter Esther, his son-in-law, the Shochet Moshe Brown, and his granddaughter.

The proliferation of *minyanim* within the confines of two streets created problems. *Es fehlt a Yid zu minyan* (a tenth man wanted) became a common cry. This was a *mitzva* (good deed) that could not wait. Jews would leave their meals uneaten, they would leave their armchairs, some of them men of learning, and all of them earning an honest living the hard way, often working far into the evening for it, but none of them would refuse the call.

Occasionally one *minyan* would borrow a man from another *minyan*. At other times the *shamash* (beadle) of the *shtiebl* was quite capable of 'press-ganging' any co-religionist who happened to be passing. No excuse availed. 'I am not *frum* (religious)' the passer-by would say hopefully. 'I have an urgent appointment,' another would say despairingly. '*Es fehlt a Yid zu minyan*,' the *Shamash* would reply inexorably. Providence never deserted the *shtiebl*. At the last moment, the tenth man always turned up, often in the guise of a breathless workaday Jew. The prophet Elijah could hardly have had a warmer reception. *Yidden lommir davenen* (Jews let us pray).

8 • The Sassover Rebbe

In the inter-war years a number of Chasidic rebbes made their homes in London. The first of them was Rabbi Chanoch Heinoch Dov Rubin, the Rebbe of Sassov.

It was said of Rabbi Israel Baal Shem Tov that he could not sleep at night unless all the money in his house had been distributed among the poor. Rabbi Rubin was a man cast in the same mould, a *baal zeddakah* (man of charity) who never refused an appeal for help. Many were the worthy causes he supported generously and anonymously. He was compulsively attracted by any cause needing help. He cultivated a large and unusually heterogeneous number of friends.

The Rebbe was born in Sassov, a town near Lvov, in 1889. His father, Rabbi Eleazar Rubin, was renowned as a miracle-worker. The Rebbe's mother was a descendant of Chanoch Heinoch Dov of Olesk (d. 1888) who married Devora, daughter of Rabbi Menashe Eichenstein, the author of important Halachic works.[1]

Rabbi Rubin studied first under his father and later under Rabbi Menashe of Rzeszov. During the First World War the family lived for a time in Lvov. In September 1922 Rabbi Chanoch Heinoch Dov visited London where he worshipped in the Broder Shul at 32 Fieldgate Street. In 1925 the 34-year-old Rebbe, his wife and three young children (Simcha, Shlomo and Meir) came to London and established a *beth midrash* at 14 Fordham Street in the East End.

He radiated such genuine warmth and kindliness that he attracted followers from all over London and the provinces. To those who poured out their hearts to him he offered not only counsel but also practical help. No task that might spell relief for the afflicted was too difficult for him. He supported unstintingly every cause that came to his attention. He was overjoyed when he was able to arrange the marriages of orphans.[2] His genuine piety, his readiness to take on any task which came his way, his affection for his fellow-Jews, his innate simplicity and lack of pride, and, indeed, his true humility as a servant of God, all combined to make him the object of veneration and love.

At the age of 40 in 1929 he became very ill and an appeal for funds was publicly launched in *Die Zeit*.³ He died in Westcliff, Essex, on Sabbath, 13 *Tammuz* 1929. News of his demise cast a gloom over London's East End. His body was taken from his Fordham Street home to the Dzikover *shtiebl* at 30 Dunk Street where eulogies were delivered by Rabbi Shulman, the rabbi of the King Edward Street Synagogue, and by the rebbes of Premishlan and Biala, as well as by other rabbis. Even Chief Rabbi J H Hertz attended the funeral. The interment took place at the Edmonton Federation Cemetery where additional eulogies were made by Rabbi Dr Avigdor Schonfeld.

An *ohel* (sepulchre), one of only two in the whole cemetery, was erected and consecrated on 26 September 1929 and is still visited by many Chasidim who pray at the graveside of this compassionate rebbe who passed away at such an early age. In accordance with the Rebbe's express wishes, his eldest son, Simcha, who was born in 1911, succeeded him as the Rebbe of Sassov.

On 26 June 1930 Simcha married Chava, the daughter of Rabbi Dov Heschel of Lvov, a descendent of Rabbi Abraham Joshua Heschel of Opatov. The wedding took place at the Portman Rooms, Baker Street. The bridegroom was married from the home of Chaim Parnes (d. 1933) at 20 Brondesbury Park, and the bride from the home of Yechiel Zalman Parnes at 76 Christchurch Avenue, both addresses in Willesden. The *unterfirers* (those who lead the bride and bridegroom to the wedding canopy) were Mr and Mrs N Gerstler.⁴ One thousand people attended the wedding festivities, including the distinguished Flora Sassoon, the mother of the bibliophile David Solomon Sassoon. She was a diligent student of Hebrew and rabbinics and, in the words of the late Chief Rabbi Isaac Herzog, 'a living well of Torah and piety'.⁵

In 1938 the Sassover *shtiebl* amalgamated with the one at 34 Settles Street, where the Rebbe later established a Talmud Torah.⁶ After his wife's death, he married Minna, the widow of Yehuda Frankel. After the war, the Rebbe moved to 843 Finchley Road, Golders Green,⁷ and then to nearby Helenslea Avenue, but maintained the *shtiebl* at 34 Settle Street, East London.⁸ He became involved in business activities, and it was said of him that he was 'a *socher* (merchant) on weekdays, and a rebbe on the Sabbath'. For the last 20 years he has devoted himself exclusively to the rabbinate. It was he who, in 1957, encouraged Rabbi Eleazar Wahrhaftig (d. 1961) to establish the *Yeshiva Chaye Olam* with only two students in his *shtiebl* in Finchley Road, Golders Green. Later he found them accommodation at the *beth hamidrash* of Rabbi Chune Halpern and eventually the *yeshiva* found a permanent home at 961 Finchley Road, under the leadership of Rabbi B Z Rakov and Rabbi J Lieberman. In 1973, the Rebbe encouraged the publication of the periodical *Yad Eleazer*, containing Halachic novellae written by the students.

Rabbi Simcha Rubin has been described as one who has a sympathetic heart, an open hand and closed mouth.[9] He dispenses charity amounting to almost £250,000 annually, for which he appeals regularly to the general public. 'There are in our midst,' he writes, 'many poor families who are in desperate need of help. They are unable to cope with their financial burdens and are too shy to disclose their plight.'[10] 'The poor and the needy gravitate naturally to our Rabbi, knowing that they can confide their problems to him,' remarked his wardens, Naftali N Rokach and Moshe Feld.[11] The Rebbe maintains: 'Our entire existence depends on *zeddaka* . . . This *mitzva* of *zeddaka* must be practised constantly and diligently . . . since we engage ourselves in the practice of charity, we, in turn, can hope to expect the benevolence of Heavenly kindness.'[12]

Before Passover, the Rebbe together with five colleagues visits 18 Jewish Homes for the Elderly to explain the importance and requirements of *kashrut* to the non-Jewish staff there. He has been instrumental in arranging full *kashrut* supervision in some of the homes. At the North London Jewish Home and Hospital at Tottenham he told staff: 'You are not just earning a wage, but enriching the lives of the unfortunate people in your care by alleviating pain and creating their inner happiness.'[13] He is particularly saddened by the apparent neglect of some of the elderly residents whose children rarely visit them. He is frequently asked by residents to contact their children and encourage them to visit.[14]

He regularly offers advice on moral issues, not only to his Chasidim but to Anglo-Jewry as a whole. 'To me,' he says, 'all Jews are the same and I hope they will take notice.'[15] He stresses that women and girls must remember that it is wrong to contravene the laws of *zeniut* (modesty in the matter of clothing) at all times. He urged women to remember that 'the current fashion of slit dresses and skirts is contrary to the laws of modesty'. He does not forget the children: 'All these modern fashion books and magazines are not meant for the daughters of Sarah, Rebeccah, Rachel and Leah.' He regards the effects of television as poisoning the minds not only of adults but especially those of children.

He urges people taking holidays 'to join groups of families who are Torah-observant, so that a daily *minyan* will be available.'[16] He further stresses: 'I think it is most important to mention the case of TV because whereas in very many religious homes there are no sets, most holiday homes and flats are already equipped with TV sets. They must be put away and not made use of at all . . . One must observe the same degree of strictness on holiday as at home. This includes the use of supervised milk.'[17] He has furthermore emphasised the prohibition of mixed bathing which applies not only to adults but also to children from the age of three.[18]

The problem of *au pair* girls did not escape his attention. 'When she takes your child to the park, do you know whom she meets and what she does there? Do you know what reading material she brings into your home? *Au pair* girls should not be allowed to wear dresses without sleeves or of insufficient length, or jeans and slacks.' He gives parents advice on how not to spoil their children. 'Over-generosity with spending money or lavish presents is very unwise.'[19] The importance of ethical behaviour is continuously stressed. 'We have an overwhelming obligation to ensure that not only do we behave legally and correctly in all our dealings, but also that it should be manifestly obvious that this is our invariable practice, whatever the temptation and inducements to the contrary.'[20]

The Rebbe is rigid, demanding and severe. Although he has a great capacity for affection, he has much difficulty in expressing it. He demands a high standard of decorum during the service at his *shtiebl*, and he often chides congregants for speaking during the services, saying:

> The Beth Hamidrash is for *davening* (prayer), not for talking . . . Some of us are in special need of health, some for a happy family life, some for easier and better *parnossa* (living), some for *nachas* (joy) from our children. Therefore, let us *daven* properly and remember, the less we talk in *Shul*, the more chance our *Tefillot* (prayers) will be answered[21] . . . A person who talks during prayer without restraint, displays either total ignorance of the basic laws of prayer and *Derech Eretz* (respect), or he has completely surrendered to the *Yetzer Hora* (evil inclination).

Rabbi Rubin also criticizes those congregants who browse through *Sefarim* (sacred books) during prayers. He interprets the verse 'I have forgiven according to your words' to mean 'Our Father in Heaven tells us that He will forgive and fulfil your prayers according to the way in which you pray.'[22]

It grieves him to witness the distribution, and the distraction caused by the frequent selling, of raffle tickets in synagogues during prayers. Inevitably such activities divert the attention and concentration of the worshippers. He regards such activities as disrespectful in a place of worship.[23] He has also warned the community of the danger of missionary activity.[24]

He expressed his full support for a letter dated February 1990 and headed 'Regarding *Kedushat Am Yisroel*', by an anonymous writer who urged the prohibition of illicit sexual behaviour and advocated self-discipline, 'especially in our day and age when all bounds of modesty have been disregarded.'

In a special message on the occasion of the 15th *Shevat* (the New Year for Trees) the Rebbe stressed the importance of gratitude not only to the Almighty for his manifold blessings, but to our parents 'for the infinite amount they provide for us: food, clothing, shelter and education.'[25] He criticises those who waste time and urges the young, 'those who are at school, seminary or *Yeshiva*', who are free from family worries and responsibilities, to make good use of time. 'Some people say that time is money, but we Jews maintain that money is time. It is a precious gift from God.'[26]

Together with Rabbi C Halpern the Rebbe is the spiritual guide of the Beth Yaakov Primary and Grammar Schools. His *shtiebl* in Helenslea Avenue, Golders Green, is one of the wealthiest Chasidic *shtieblech*. Seventy to eighty people pray there every Sabbath, and there are *minyanim* and *shiurim* throughout the week.

In the *shtiebl* of Sassov, *aliyot* on the High Holy Days are auctioned for very large sums of money, as much as £5,000 being paid for each of these honours, especially for *Maftir Yona* (recitation of the Book of Jonah on the Day of Atonement) and *Pesichat Neilah* (the opening of the Ark at *Neilah*). More than £25,000 has been raised in this way. The Rebbe receives no salary, but a rent for the *shtiebl* is paid to him.

The Rebbe is a renowned *baal tekiah* (blowing of the *shofar*). On the Sabbath he delivers a discourse at the *seudah shlishit* (the third meal on the Sabbath). The *shtiebl* has its own *mikveh*.

When the Bank of England opened an enquiry into possible illegal deposit-taking by his son, David Menashe, the Hendon South Conservative Member of Parliament wrote a personal letter to the Rebbe, offering him moral support 'as one father to another'.[27]

There is hardly a rabbinic function or Chasidic *simcha* which the Rebbe does not grace with his attendance. When called upon to speak, he does so very briefly, in accordance with the maxim 'say little and do much'. He is faithful to, and even enhances, the great Sassov traditions of *zeddaka* and *gemilut Chasadim* (practice of charity).

9 • The Trisker Rebbe

Few social virtues rank higher than the practice of hospitality which is regarded as one of 'those things of which man enjoys the fruit in this world while the stock remains with him in the world to come.'[1] 'Let your house be open wide and let the poor be members of your household.'[2] This rabbinic adage was the motto of Rabbi Jacob Arye Twersky of London. His hospitality was renowned and anyone in need of food or shelter was sure of finding a warm welcome in the Rabbi's home. No questions were asked and help was immediately forthcoming. Many poor rabbis or *meshullachim* (emissaries) from Poland, Romania and the Holy Land would spend days, weeks and even months in the Rebbe's house. The Rebbe was quick to offer sympathy and practical help to anyone in real difficulty. Whatever the pressures, his kindliness and gracious demeanour never deserted him. He was a man poised and dignified yet shy, reserved and undemonstrative. Frail in body and often unwell, he nevertheless lived productively into great old age. He was blessed with a fine voice, sound common sense and great strength of character.

He was possessed of great charm. Everyone who came into contact with him was captivated. He could meet many situations with a smile or a jest. The influence which he exercised on his followers was based on trust – trust in his sense of justice, his honesty and his tolerance, the advice which he was always ready to give and his compassion for the underprivileged. His common sense was blended with kindliness. His ability to understand people and to gain their confidence was very helpful in his dealings with the many who came to consult him. His ability to understand a situation quickly, to get to the heart of the matter, were gifts which he used to great advantage. A homeless man once asked him whether he and his family could stay in the Rebbe's house for the festival of Passover. 'You cannot stay in *my* house,' was the Rebbe's reply. The petitioner felt very perplexed at this response by the Rebbe. However, he was soon put at ease. 'Certainly, you and your family will be most welcome to stay with us for the Festival . . . But take note that it is not really my house. We are all mere custodians for the Almighty. Nothing really belongs to us.'

Rabbi Jacob Arye's father was Rabbi Mordechai Zusya (d. 1937), a well-known Cabbalist, and his great-great-grandfather was Rabbi Abraham Twersky (1804–87) of Trisk, known as the Trisker *Maggid*. The *Maggid* was famous for his knowledge of numerology and was one of the most important rebbes in the latter part of the nineteenth century. Chasidim came to him from Russia, the Ukraine, Hungary and Lithuania. His court was regal. He even had a throne of gold made. At one time during the reign of Czar Nicholas, he was imprisoned for five weeks. When his book was published, the Rabbi of Ger, said: 'Young men may even pawn their *tallit* and *tefillin* in order to acquire such a precious diamond.' He was one of the first of the Chasidic rebbes of the house of Chernobyl to give public discourses on the Sabbath.

'Why don't you give charity?' he once asked a Chasid. 'I am looking for a poor man who is really in genuine need and I have not as yet found one,' replied the Chasid. 'The Almighty bestowed wealth upon you,' the *Maggid* replied 'He did not discriminate. So why do you discriminate?'

Jacob Arye was born in Trisk in 1883 on the eve of *Tisha B'Av* (ninth of Av). He was educated by private tutors and married Blima Reizel (d. 1948), a descendant of Rabbi Abraham Joshua Heschel of Opatov. Jacob Arye spent a number of years in the courts of Sadagora and Bohush, and was, for a time, the rabbi in Zinkov, his father's home town.

For six years from 1917 to 1923, Rabbi Jacob Arye lived under Soviet rule in Odessa, Zinkov and Kamenetz–Podolski.[3] He experienced the vicious new anti-religious campaigns, designed to decimate the clergy and to reduce the number of houses of prayer to a bare minimum. Hundreds of rabbis, ritual slaughterers and religious teachers were arrested or deported to far-distant provinces. In Odessa, the largest and one of the most beautiful synagogues in the country, the 'Broder Synagogue', was closed down. Teaching Hebrew was forbidden and religious instruction for children under 18 was made a punishable offence. All central Jewish organisations were suspended. Restrictions were imposed on the production of Jewish religious articles necessary for the observance of the Jewish rituals – prayer shawls, phylacteries, Torah scrolls, prayer books and Jewish calendars.

The Rebbe was in Russia when the civil war broke out. Former Czarist generals mobilised considerable armies to fight the Bolsheviks, but they also attacked the Jews. As a result, hundreds of Jewish communities in the Ukraine and White Russia were destroyed. Nearly a quarter of a million Jews were killed or maimed in pogroms reminiscent of the worst days of Czarist rule. Almost all of them had been organised by the anti-communist military group under the command of Petlura, Denikin and Machno.[4]

The Rebbe left Russia and lived for some time in Warsaw and in Vienna. On the advice of Rabbi Israel Friedman of Czortkov he made his home in Berlin. 'My heart, however, told me not to stay there,' related the Rebbe. When the Nazi Party became more noisy and menacing, the Rebbe left for Belgium. In August 1922, the Rebbe came on an exploratory visit to London and stayed at the Osborn Hotel, 25 Osborn Street.[5] He officiated as the *baal musaf* (reader for the additional service) during the High Holy Days at the *Sephardishe shul* in Philpot Street in East London. His melodious rendering of the services, his spontaneous Yiddish addresses and his infectious enthusiasm made a tremendous impression, and a number of people persuaded him to settle in London. At first he stayed with Chayim Shapiro, but soon a house was acquired at 22 Sidney Square, which enabled his wife and five children (three sons and two daughters) to join him in August 1923.[6] The *shtiebl* joined the Adath Yisroel Burial Society on 19 December 1924, and soon the Rebbe began baking *matza shemura* (*matzot* produced from specially supervised wheat).[7]

Together with Dayan Hillman he was responsible for the founding of a synagogue called *Or Chayim Bnei Berdichev Nusach Sephard.*[8] He tried to transplant the warmth of Trisk into the foggy atmosphere of London. An excellent *baal tefillah*, he attracted followers with song and melody which resounded in Sidney Square, and his *tisch* on Friday night was very popular.

At that time there was no Orthodox Jewish day school in London. As he would not allow his children to attend the Jews' Free School in Bell Lane, Spitalfields, he obtained permission from the London County Council to have his children privately tutored.

The Rebbe enjoyed travelling. He visited the United States in 1929, Belgium, Karlsbad and Jassy a year later.[9] He was no writer of books, but in 1929 he gave a *haskamah* (approbation) to Israel Brod's work *Tal Hashamayim.*[10] In 1933 he was host to Rabbi Shlomo Yoskovitch, the son-in-law of the Rebbe of Ger.[11]

After the First World War, Jews began to leave the East End for the more salubrious areas of Clapton, Dalston and Stamford Hill, the East End remaining the home mainly of the ageing. In common with his congregation the Rebbe moved to 51 Upper Clapton Road in 1931, and in 1940 to 111 Cazenove Road where he established a *mikveh*, a *matza* bakery and a *beth midrash*.[12] During the High Holy Days it was impossible to accommodate all those who wished to worship in the regular *beth hamidrash*. A special marquee was therefore erected in the garden for the period. The Rebbe had a beautiful voice, and he was ably supported by his three sons.

In the 1930s many 'grandchildren' of Chasidic rebbes came to England in the hope of securing visas for the United States, and they usually lodged with the Rebbe who kept an open house. Among his 'guests' were the Gorlitz grandchildren, Rabbi Mendel, Rabbi Arale and Rabbi Cheiskel. The Rebbe employed a private tutor for his children who was nicknamed 'Einstein', because he showed great interest in astronomy and prepared special pictures of the sun, the moon, and the stars in their orbits.

In 1934 he visited Glasgow.[13] He was frequently ailing and at one time spent 14 weeks in hospital.[14] Even during the heavy bombing of London the Rebbe remained in his *beth midrash* and maintained the services, though he spent a short time at 30 Chiltern Lane Parade, Harrogate.[15]

One of his most constant and faithful followers was Chayim Eliezer Lass (1883–1947), a native of Mlava near Warsaw, who came to London in the early 1900s. He made a meagre living making ladies' clothes. He then progressed to working as a sub-contractor for manufacturers, and soon became a manufacturer himself. By dint of hard work he was successful in his endeavours, and in 1936 his firm became a public company.

Chayim Lass was a supporter of many worthy causes, and was particularly fond of the Trisker Rebbe, living opposite him in Sidney Square. Whenever the Trisker was in financial difficulties, Lass would help him. He even took him to Harrogate and Watford for medical treatment. It is told that on Friday afternoons, when Lass paid his workers their weekly wage, both Jews and non-Jews had to put some money into a charity box allocated for the benefit of the Rebbe.

Lass's interest was not confined to the London rebbes. He made regular financial contributions to Chasidic rebbes in Poland, as is evidenced in the autographed letters from Rabbi Abraham Mordechai Alter of Ger; Rabbi Israel Meir HaKohen Kagan of Radun; Rabbi Alter Horowitz, the Rebbe of Dzikov. He was a particular adherent of Rabbi Aaron Menachem Mendel Guterman of Radzymin. In 1933 the Rebbe sent Lass an *etrog* (citron) Box containing a *kameya* (amulet) to be worn 'near his heart', an unusual and special gesture from the Rebbe to a faithful friend.

Yeshivot and scholars in Eastern Europe found him a real Maecenas. He even contributed £150 for the repairs to the *mikveh* in his native town of Mlava. Lass helped many refugees to settle in London, and was guarantor to the Home Office for 12 Jews released from German concentration camps. The signatures of the Chasidic Rebbes on the acknowledgements of his contributions – to charitable, educational and religious bodies – read like a 'Debrett' of Eastern European luminaries.[16] On the advice of the Rebbe of Ostrowiec he brought over Rabbi Y Mett, a *mohel* (person authorised to perform circumcision) and *shochet* from Mielec, Poland.

Lass financed the publication by Rabbi Yechiel Meir Morgenstern of London of the work *Bikkure Aviv*, written by Rabbi Yaakov Arye of Radzymin, and he helped Rabbi Dov Straus (who had established a *shtiebl* in 34 Sandringham Road in 1934) to procure private treatment for his only son Pessach who was seriously ill. He was also a Trustee of the North East London *Beth Hamidrash*, Ainsworth Road, Hackney.

On Friday afternoons, poor Jews went to his office in Ford Square and received small sums of money for the celebration of the Sabbath. A number of poor rabbis received a regular pension from him. He became a Life-President of the Sidney Street Synagogue, and was given the honour of opening many other synagogues. He was also a Governor of the London Hospital and the Jewish Hospital.

Other supporters of Trisk were Yechiel Kossoff who established a Jewish bakery in north-east London, Philip Larholt (1901–73), the President of the *Chevra Tehillim* (whose son Louis Larholt later became the President of the St Albans Hebrew Congregation) and Abraham Yitzchak Krieger who presented the Rebbe with a *Sefer Torah* (Scroll of the Law).[17] In 1950, the Rabbi became unwell once again and had to spend some time in Switzerland to recuperate.[18] In 1964, the Rebbe emigrated to Israel and made his home at 4 Rechov Rabbi Tarfon, Bnei Brak, where he established a small *beth hamidrash*. He lived there in comparative retirement, saying, 'Everyone is a rebbe here. We are not short of rebbes, but we could do with more Chasidim.' He visited London on a number of occasions to participate in family celebrations.[19] He last visited London in June 1979, and died on *Hoshanah Rabba* (the seventh day of the Festival of Tabernacles) of that year and was buried on the Mount of Olives in Jerusalem.

The Rebbe of Trisk truly deserves the epithet of a *guter Yid* (a good Jew). He was survived by his son Rabbi Yitzchak David (born 1920) who succeeded him as Rebbe in Bnei Brak and by two other sons who live in London: Rabbi Chayim Menachem Avrohom (Chamunyu) who maintains a *shtiebl* in Stamford Hill, and Rabbi Pinchas who was a Cantor at Bethnal Green Synagogue. His elder daughter, Chavah Esther Gitel (1922–94), married Rabbi Mordechai Roberboy (Rabin), a native of Cracow and the son of a Chasid of Sanz.[20] Mordechai studied in the Gerer *shtiebl* in Cracow. In April 1939 he came to Manchester to study under Rabbi Moses Yitzchak Segal and from 1940 to 1945 studied under Rabbi Yitzchak Dubow. He was ordained by Rabbi Yehuda Potock, of Manchester and by Rabbi Ehrenberg, the head of the Tel Aviv *Beth Din*. Subsequently he studied at the *Mesivta* in London. From 1949 to 1955 he gave discourses at Montague Road *Beth Hamidrash*, and from 1955 to 1957 he was rabbi at Teesdale Street Synagogue in the East End of London. He had his own *shtiebl* from 1957 to 1976 at 310 Watford Way, Hendon. He now gives regular *shiurim* at the Ohel Yisrael *Skoler Beth Hamidrash* at the *Adath Yisroel* Synagogue in Hendon.

The Rebbe's younger daughter Rachel married Rabbi Elimelech Spira in 1951. Elimelech (Marks) Spira (1903–83) was born in Tarnov, Galicia. He studied in Vienna and then at the *Yeshiva Etz Chayim* in London from 1923 to 1931. In 1924, as a young man of 21, he officiated at Teesdale Street Synagogue, on the High Holy Days,[21] and in 1929 he received his rabbinical diploma from Rabbi E Lopian and Rabbi Steinberg of Brody, as well as from the Cracow *Beth Din*. He received his secular education at University College, London, where he graduated with BA Honours in philosophy and psychology.

His *semicha* was endorsed by Chief Rabbi Israel Brodie in 1948. In 1933 he was appointed Minister, Secretary and Headmaster of the West Willesden Hebrew Congregation which later became part of the United Synagogue, and which he served until his retirement in September 1968. Spira was the first son of a Chasidic rebbe to join the United Synagogue. He was a melodious reader and a very thoughtful preacher who introduced a number of Chasidic innovations into the liturgy of the synagogue. On *Shabbat Haggadol* (the Sabbath before the Passover) and on *Shabbat Shuvah* (the Sabbath before the Day of Atonement) he delivered traditional discourses in Yiddish.

His discourses were replete with *Gematriot* (a method of Biblical exegesis based on the numerical value of the Hebrew letters). He was an able lecturer and did much to popularise talmudical studies among the youth and adults in synagogue circles of north-west London and beyond. He often gave lectures on Chasidism and wrote on Chasidic and literary topics for the *Jewish Chronicle*.[22] For many years he was engaged in research on the Italian scholar, Samuel David Luzzatto (1800–65) one of the pioneer students of mediaeval Hebrew literature.

He was a lifelong member of the Mizrachi movement and was the vice-chairman of the Education Committee of the Zionist Federation and vice-president of the World Union for Hebrew Education. As a man, he was shy, reserved and undemonstrative, but he possessed a decisive and penetrating mind, wide cultural interests and meticulous scholarship. He combined general culture with deep talmudic learning. On his retirement to Jerusalem, he reverted to the lifestyle of his illustrious Chasidic forebears. Wearing a *streimel*, a long *kaftan* and a flowing beard, he devoted his days to scholarship and religious contemplation. He is survived by his wife and five children.

The Trisker Rebbe's *mechutan* (in-law) Rabbi Jacob Joseph Spira (d. 20 Av 1946), a descendant of Rabbi Zevi Elimelech Spira of Dynov (1783–1841), came to London in 1926 and lived at 33 Greenfield Street, Commercial Road.[23] In 1927 he established the *Shtiebl Kehillat Yaakov* at 81 Cazenove Road, Stamford Hill, and was rabbinical District Supervisor of *Kashrut*.[24] He was of retiring disposition and encouraged his learned congregants, Yechiel Swimer and M A Kutchinsky, to give discourses in the *shtiebl*. Rabbi Jacob Spira was the author of *Mili D'Hespedah*,[25] a 15-page eulogy on Rabbi Issachar Dov Rokeach of Belz (d. 1927); *Rishmei Sheela*, a 22-page learned treatise on the construction of a ritual bath, addressed to Rabbi David Menachem Munish Babad of Tarnopol; and homilies entitled *Maamar Hayashar V'Hatov*,[26] and *Sefer Hayashar V'Hatov*. Rabbi Spira's wife Gitel (d. 1958), the daughter of Rabbi Chayim Ungar, was a forceful and dominant personality, and ran a bookshop at 92 Wentworth Street, East London.

10 • The Biala Rebbe

Prominent among the early Chasidic rabbis in England was Rabbi Nathan David Rabinowicz of Biala. The founder of the Biala dynasty was Rabbi Yaakov Yitzchak (1847–1905), a direct descendant of Rabbi Yaakov Yitzchak, the Holy Jew of Przysucha.

Barely 26 years old when he succeeded his father-in-law, Rabbi Yaakov Yitzchak moved to Biala–Podolsk, a town in the province of Lublin. Following the teachings of Przysucha, the Rebbe of Biala discouraged protestations of piety. He maintained that sincerity is measured by service, charity and loving kindness, and not by words. He was known far and wide for his open heart and his open house. A special kitchen at his court provided meals for visiting Chasidim and for poor townsfolk. As a practical demonstration of his wish that the poor be treated as members of his household, the Rebbe himself regularly sampled the dishes to make sure they were up to standard. He would spend a long time preparing for the statutory service by reciting devotional prayers.

Rabbi Yaakov Yitzchak left an Ethical Will which bears eloquent witness to the writer's humility and kindliness. He advised his four sons to settle in different localities should they decide to take up the rabbinate, thereby lessening the likelihood of fraternal friction. In the Will he requested that notification of his death be conveyed by his Chasidim to his father (whose grave was in Szydlowiec), to his father-in-law (whose grave was in Warsaw) and to the Holy Jew (whose grave was in Przysucha), so that his ancestors might intercede for him in the Heavenly Court. 'I would urge you to announce by means of posters and through the newspapers that I ask forgiveness of those who pressed gifts into my reluctant hands. They regarded me as a *zaddik*, but verily, I am unworthy.' He died in 1905. One of his sons, Rabbi Abraham Joshua Heschel, made it his life's task to publish his father's writings.[1]

In obedience to their father's Will, the four sons established their own courts at Parszev, Siedlice, Miedzyrzec–Podolski and Lublin respectively. The youngest son, Rabbi Yerachmiel Zevi, was famed in Chasidic circles, not only for his learning and piety, but as an artist and musician. He excelled as reader for the congregation. Once when he was ill, his anxious mother urged her husband to dissuade their son from officiating at the reader's desk, but to no avail. 'The entire heavenly court waits to hear the prayers of my son. How dare I stop him?' He died in 1906, barely six months after being appointed Rebbe at the age of 26. His wife Chava, daughter of Rabbi Arye Leib Epstein of Ozarov and mother of six small children, survived him. She subsequently married Rabbi Emanuel Weltfreid of Lodz.

Heir to centuries of rabbinic culture and tradition, the eldest and most illustrious of the sons of Rabbi Yerachmiel Zevi, Nathan David, was born in Ozarov on the 11th *Iyar* 1900. They said of him as a young boy that he would set the world on fire. From his earliest youth he spent his days and nights in study, and his teachers predicted that he would one day be a *gadol B'Yisrael*, a great one in Israel. He learned from his earliest youth to scorn delights and to live laborious days. After studying for some time at the *yeshiva* at Ozarov, he spent several years at Radzymin (a town in Warsaw Province), at the home of his uncle, Rabbi Aaron Menachem Mendel Guterman (1860–1934), the Rebbe of Radzymin who was married to Matele, the daughter of Rabbi Yaakov Yitzchak of Biala. Nathan David was welcomed there, as his aunt Matele had no children, and his uncle became his surrogate father who looked after his education, progress and material welfare. Despite many communal preoccupations, the Rebbe of Radzymin never missed delivering a daily discourse at his *yeshiva*, which was one of the earliest Chasidic *yeshivot* in Poland, established in 1912. The Rebbe had a mercurial temperament, and he was anxious to have an heir. 'I can see my children, as I can see my fingers,' he would say. In 1922, after 46 years of childless marriage, at the age of 62, he coerced his wife into granting him a divorce. This became a *cause célèbre* in Poland. He remarried in 1924, but died without issue 12 years later.

In 1918, Nathan David received *semicha* from Rabbi Meir Yechiel Halevi Halstock of Ostrowiec, and Rabbi Ezekiel Zevi Michaelson, a rabbi on the Warsaw *Beth Din*, known as the 'Rabbi of Plonsk'. On 15 *Kislev* of the same year he married Sheindel Bracha, the eldest daughter of Rabbi Alter Yisrael Shimon Perlow of Novominsk (1875–1933), who was one of the most prominent rebbes in Poland in the inter-war years and a scion of the Chasidic dynasties of Ustillo, Koidanov, Chernobyl, Karlin and Berdichev.[2]

The home of the Novominsker at 10 Franciskanska Street, Warsaw, quickly became one of the thriving centres of Chasidism. Chasidim of all kinds flocked to him. He knew the whole *Mishna* by heart, and towards the end of his life he rehearsed 21 chapters daily. On Shabbat he spoke only in *Lashon Hakodesh* (Hebrew); crowds thronged to his famous Shabbat discourses which were remarkable for their length as for their profundity. A typical *seudah shlishit* discourse would last for nearly two hours. His eloquent addresses, his stirring prayers, his melodious voice and his mature wisdom spread his fame far and wide. Once heard, the melodies of the Rebbe of Novominsk were never forgotten, as they elevated his listeners. His prayers on the High Holy Days, particularly at *Neilah*, were high points in the lives of the Chasidim. On *Kol Nidrei* night he recited aloud the entire book of Psalms.

Rabbi Nathan David, having lost his father at six years of age, was greatly influenced and affected by his father-in-law from whom he received *kest* (board and lodging) for nine years. He could not but admire the manner in which the Rebbe of Novominsk ministered to his people. Twice every day there were long lines of men and women who flocked to him for help, guidance, comfort and inspiration. With infinite patience, the ailing rabbi would listen and dispense practical counsel. At night he would say to his family: 'I cannot eat. I am sated with the sufferings and tribulations of the children of Israel.'

The Novominsker Rebbe had 12 children (four sons and eight daughters). Economic conditions in Poland were bad. The resurrection of Poland after more than 100 years of political non-existence brought neither equality nor economic security to Polish Jewry. The ink on the Treaty of Versailles was hardly dry when Jewish blood began to flow. Pogroms became an everyday occurrence and Jewish life was the cheapest commodity in the market-place. The much vaunted tolerance which had existed in mediaeval Poland vanished beyond recall, as every section of Polish society embraced the convenient old-new creed of anti-Semitism. The Polish government adopted anti-Jewish administrative measures. Unemployment affected the Jews more than the non-Jews, for various forms of state welfare were barred to them. Thirty per cent of Polish Jewry were reduced to dire financial straits.

In vain did the British Government send Sir Stuart Samuel (1856–1926), President of the Board of Deputies of British Jews, and Captain Peter Wright on a mission to Poland in 1919. The first Prime Minister of Poland and famous pianist, Ignacy Jan Padarewski (1860–1941), arranged a Kosher dinner in honour of the two Englishmen. Dr Samuel Poznanski (1864–1921), the spiritual head of the Tlomacki 'Choir'

Synagogue in Warsaw and the uncle of Nathan David, the Rabbi of Radzymin, also attended the dinner.[3] The situation was reviewed with clarity and compassion by Sir Stuart. He refuted the allegation that the Jews were Bolsheviks and declared: 'It is for the Poles to choose whether they will follow the example of Great Britain, the United States of America, France, Holland, Italy and the other liberal-minded states which have treated the Jew equitably, or link their fate with ancient Egypt, mediaeval Spain and modern Russia.'[4] Sir Stuart further made 12 practical recommendations, one of which was, 'that a secretary who understands and speaks Yiddish be added to the staff of His Majesty's legation in Warsaw.'[5] Sir Stuart's colleague, Captain Wright, estimated that the Chasidim constituted half of Poland's Jewish population.[6]

The strained conditions in the large household of the Rebbe of Novominsk, consisting of sons, daughters, daughters-in-law, sons-in-law and grandchildren, led to a desire and necessity for some of the family to find new pastures. The Rebbe's eldest son, Rabbi Nachum Perlow, settled in New York, where he was known as the Novominsker Rebbe; this title is now held by his son, Rabbi Yaakov. A younger son, Rabbi Aaron, at first settled in Antwerp, as did the Rebbe's son-in-law, Rabbi Eleazar Eichenstein, but they eventually made their home in New York.

Rabbi Nathan David arrived in London on 18 December 1927. He spent the first two days in the home of his *landsman* (fellow-countryman) Jacob Weisman (d. 1944) (his grandson is the Reverend Malcolm Wiseman, the Minister to the Small Communities and Chaplain to the Forces) and his wife Chana Golda (d. 1951), who lived at 52 Pyrland Road, Highbury. Jacob or 'Reb Yankel', as he was popularly known, was a native of Siedlice where he knew the Rebbe's father, Rabbi Yerachmiel Zevi. Yankel married the daughter of the Shochet Moses Flasterstein of Mezerich. While living there, he became friendly with the Rebbe's uncle, Rabbi Meir Solomon Juda.

Reb Yankel left Poland in 1910 and lived in Antwerp for four years where he worked for the *Shechita* Board. At the outbreak of the First World War he came to London and found refuge in the Jewish Shelter which had an additional hostel in Poland Street in West London. He prayed in the *Beth Hasefer* in Soho Square. Reb Yankel subsequently taught Talmud under Rabbi Schwartz at the *Yeshiva Shaarei Torah* in Ford Square, East London. He then became a leather merchant and moved to Highbury where he regularly conducted *shiurim* in Talmud and encouraged the young Solomon Schonfeld in his Talmudic studies, prior to the latter's departure for the Hungarian *yeshivot*.

Reb Yankel then patronised the *Nusach Ari Shtiebl* at 139 Highbury New Park, established in 1925 by the metal merchant and property dealer Zevi (Henry) Goldblum (1880–1930). A native of Rovno, Ukraine, Goldblum founded the *Adath Yisroel* Synagogue, under the paternalistic spiritual leadership of Dr Avigdor Schonfeld, too *Yekkish* (too Germanic and dogmatic) for his taste, and his *shtiebl*, which flourished for many years, was patronised by scholars and rabbis, especially Rabbi Leiner.

Goldblum helped many recently arrived rabbinic scholars to remain in this country by appointing them as 'honorary rabbis' of his *shtiebl*. 'You are creating too many rabbis,' Chief Rabbi Hertz grumbled, 'you are causing me great embarrassment with the Home Office.'

Reb Yankel organised a *melave malka* in his home on a Saturday night during Chanukah in honour of the youthful Biala Rebbe, whose address made such an impact on the gathering that a fellow-*landsman*, the journalist and writer Meir Eidelbaum anounced in *Die Zeit* that 'a *Zaddik* and *Gaon* has arrived here.'

'I will pay your passage to New York,' a London rebbe advised the newly arrived Nathan David. The 27-year-old declined the offer and remained to compete against the rabbinic establishment. For this was a new-style rebbe, a modern miracle worker. The miracle he wrought was to transplant the traditions of his ancestors into London's inhospitable and unreceptive soil.

The Rebbe established a small *shtiebl* at 6 Osborn Place, Chicksand Street, off Brick Lane in London's East End. Later, in 1931, he acquired a house at 10 St Marks Road (later St Marks Rise), Dalston, then a middle-class suburb with large Victorian houses. He established another *shtiebl* there and was made welcome by the Rabbi of the nearby Montague Road *Beth Midrash*, Jacob Rabinowitz (1867–1932).[7]

The new Dalston *shtiebl* attracted people from all walks of life and of all ages. They came, they saw, and they were conquered by his humanity, his personality and his genuine friendship and approachability. The Rebbe brought with him a fiery enthusiasm that was foreign to the Jews of north-east London. There were some who had known his grandfather Rabbi Yaakov Yitzchak of Biala, others had been adherents of his maternal grandfather, Rabbi Leibish Epstein of Ozarov. There were still others for whom this was the first introduction to Chasidism.

The *shtiebl* originally formed by Leibish Rickel now joined with the Biala *Beth Hamidrash*. They came to see him *prave tisch* (conduct the table) and to hear him expound Torah at *seudah shlishit* and *melave malka*. His preaching and his teaching were marked by passionate intensity. When he officiated at *Neilah* (closing service on the Day of Atonement) his voice shook with tears of anguish as he wrestled in prayer for his people. His life was Torah, and wandering through its fathomless profundities, he found challenge and fulfilment. But at the same time he was keenly interested in day-to-day issues and students enjoyed debating with him and sharpening their young wits against the whetstone of his fiery intellect. He was approachable, emphatic and perceptive, able to communicate equally with the old-time Chasidim as with their semi-alienated children.

Londoners who had never heard of Chasidism found a friend in the Rebbe, for he genuinely loved his fellow-men, and his approach was positive. Like Rabbi Levi Yitzchak of Berdichev, he looked for man's good points rather than his failings. Often he would quote the verse: 'For the House of Israel is the vineyard of the Lord of Hosts',[8] adding 'Who am I that I should disparage or condemn that which belongs to the Almighty himself?' No one was denied or neglected. Not with 'fire and brimstone' but with love were people brought back to their Father in Heaven. For he was both a mystic and a man of the world, paradoxically blending asceticism with worldliness, rigid uncompromising piety with tolerance and humanity.

We have heard of the mystics of ancient times, those learned rabbis who sought to free their souls from earthly bonds in order to achieve a yet closer and more intimate communion with the Creator. They lost touch with reality and lived in a world of their own, hovering between heaven and earth. We have seen, too, how sometimes our spiritual leaders in this, the twentieth century, after spending their time on contemporary scholarship, have little left for sacred study. The Biala Rebbe combined the two.

There were no visiting hours, the Rebbe divided his time between his Dalston home and the *shtiebl* in the East End of London which he maintained and regularly visited. The Rebbe's door was open wide; all were free to consult him and most left his presence comforted. He was always ready to minister to the spiritual and even material needs of his followers. No forms of recreation, no personal ambition, no desire for temporal honour, no social distinction, ever distracted him from his own austere and devout life. He was always happy and when life was a struggle and at times tempestuous, he remained serene and optimistic, maintaining even in the darkest days of the war, when the Nazi invasion seemed imminent and the bombs were destroying London, that all would be well, and that justice would triumph.

There was no barrier between the *zaddik* and the Chasid. To his Chasidim he was a father and a friend who never failed them. He sought to instil the same spirit of joyous animation, the very essence of Chasidic ideology, into all who came into contact with him. Carried out cheerfully, energetically, conscientiously, the ordinary tasks of day-to-day existence, could, according to the Rebbe, become ennobled and imbued with spiritual significance. The Chasid should rejoice in the glory of the universe because he sees in every manifestation of nature the loving handiwork of the Creator. The Chasid rejoices in his life and he rejoices even at his death, because everything comes from the Almighty.

His brother-in-law, Rabbi Abraham Twersky, came to London in 1932, and he and his family stayed at the Rebbe's house until Rabbi Twersky was appointed Rabbi of the Philpot Street *Sephardishe Shul*.

In 1935, the Rebbe visited Paris in response to a request by Chasidim there who wanted to renew their links with Biala.[9] The Rebbe, at his own expense, arranged the marriage of a Polish girl, Lea Butt, who had found refuge in his home, to Phil Levkovitch, on 14 June 1936. A year later he was host to his brother-in-law Rabbi Shalom Alter Perlow, the Koidanover Rebbe of Baranowicze who spent a month in London.[10]

One of the prominent members of the Dalston *shtiebl* was the Rebbe's neighbour, Elkanan Hillel (d. 1973). A furrier by profession, he loved to officiate as Reader on the Sabbath. Another was the scholarly Abraham Samuel Beresticky (1889–1981), a handbag manufacturer, a native of Lodz and a Chasid of Alexander, who lived in Berlin from 1920 to 1939 and prayed in the Radomsker *shtiebl* there. When he came to London in March 1939 with his wife and four children, he made his first home in a damp cellar in Colvestone Crescent and later in nearby Amhurst Road, North London, and became a devoted adherent of the Rebbe. He read the Law, officiated at *Kol Nidrei*, blew the *shofar* and was *kolbo* (general helper) at the *shtiebl*. He spent his last years in Israel where he was buried on the Mount of Olives.

Zevi Elimelech Uri (d. 1973), the scion of Chasidic families and a diamond merchant in Hatton Garden, acted as *gabbai* for many years. Though small in stature, he became transformed when he intoned the melodies of Ropczyce and Sanz at *seudah shlishit*. He was nicknamed 'bushy-brows', as he had very large black eyebrows.

A native of Glagov, Poland, he arrived in London from Belgium on the eve of the Second World War. In May 1940 he was interned on the

Isle of Man. His six-year old son Max died of leukaemia. Despite his tribulations he always appeared jovial, as if he had no care in the world. His surviving son, Dr Norbert Uri (1920–74), also prayed at the *shtiebl* A graduate in Chemistry of the Hebrew University and a Research Fellow of Leeds and Manchester Universities, his work for the Ministry of Defence was top secret. Despite his repeated vociferous disclaimers he was regarded as a top nuclear scientist and was known as the 'Tizard' (Sir Henry Tizard, the scientist) of the *shtiebl.*

Wolf Oster (1892–1956), an egg wholesaler, who ran his business from a small garage attached to his house, professed dual loyalty: he was active at the Stoke Newington United Synagogue under Dayan Myer Lew where he was chairman of the Education Committee and also at the *shtiebl* where he regularly officiated during the High Holy Days. He had a fine ear for music.

Another unique character was Mr Morris Lewis, the son of Mr Leibish Rickel. He looked like an Al Capone character with his huge trilby hat, very expensive suits and silk shirts. Though rumoured to be the proprietor of many amusement arcades in the West End of London, he felt very much at home at the *shtiebl* his late father had founded.

Harry Binstock (d. 1986), the son of Israel, acted as honorary collector for the *beth hamidrash* for many years. Despite his many business commitments, he devoted some of his time each day to this purpose. An interesting worshipper was Harris Louis Cohen (1880–1964). Born in Brest–Litovsk, he came to London at the age of nine. During the First World War he was minister-reader at the Ostwind's Synagogue in 75–79 Wentworth Street at a salary of £56 per annum. He devoted half his day to study and corresponded with the *Chafetz Chayim* and Rabbi Chayim Ozer Grodzinsky. Cohen's shoe shop in Wentworth Street was a meeting place for *meshullachim* (emissaries). He and his five sons, one of whom is Mr Joseph Conway, the ophthalmic surgeon, were of tremendous help in making up the daily morning *Minyan.*

A noteworthy character was Chayim Stark (d. 1953), the vice-president of the *shtiebl* from 1936. Originally he earned his living as a milkman. Every morning, on his round, he would leave his horse and cart outside the *shtiebl* while he prayed with great devotion. He later opened a grocery shop in Amhurst Road. So devoted was he to the Rebbe that he left instructions in his will that he wished to be buried next to him.

Mr and Mrs Michael Caplin were devoted and dedicated followers of the Rebbe. Michael (1882–1962) came to London in 1902, and from

1928 onwards was a vice-president of the *shtiebl*. Mrs Jane Caplin (1884–1974) was a remarkable woman even among the older generation of Jewish matriarchs. She was generous, full of zest, vitality, courage and enthusiasm. Her lack of pomposity, her simple and ardent faith were a shining example to her family. No task was too menial for her. She would regularly scrub the floor of the *shtiebl* in Chicksand Street on a Friday morning. 'An hour at the Rebbe's *shtiebl*,' she used to say, 'does me more good than an outing to Westcliff.'

Even when the Caplins moved to 23 Northfield Road, Stamford Hill, they kept up their association with the Rebbe, and the *bar mitzvah* of their youngest son Charles took place at the *shtiebl*. All their six sons served in the British forces during the Second World War, stationed in different parts of the world, while their mother would light six candles on Friday nights, praying fervently for their safe return. When they returned, her determination and powerful personality spurred her children to pursue academic studies: two became doctors, one a solicitor, one an architect, one a stockbroker, one a brilliant advertising executive, one daughter in charge of Rimmel, the cosmetic conglomerate, and another, Judith, in the antique business. The eldest son, Maurice, was the Treasurer of the Federation of Synagogues and President of the Sinai Synagogue in Golders Green until 1988.[11]

Chayim Lyons (1898–1944), a native of Parszcv (the home town of the Rebbe's uncle), came to London in 1911. He was a noted *baal tefillah* and a *baal tekiah* and regularly officiated at the Pavilion Theatre in the East End of London at High Holy Day services. The Sabbath found him at the Rebbe's *shtiebl*. He was a tall, lean man, a presser by trade, whose love of *Yiddishkeit* was contagious. In 1924, he was approached to raise money for the London Jewish Hospital in Stepney Green, and was inscribed in their Book of Life Governors in recognition of his services.

The President of the *shtiebl* from 1928 to 1939 was Leibish (Lewis) Yehuda Freedman (1877–1951).[12] A native of Zychlin, near Lodz, he came to this country at the beginning of the century. Originally trained as an 'upper machinist' in the shoe trade, on his arrival in England he became a ladies' tailor. He found his *métier* when he eventually joined his son Maurice as an artistic embroiderer. He was a perfectionist and this was exemplified in his fine Yiddish style and calligraphic writings. He and his wife, Alta Toba (d. 1961) and their eight children, carried out gladly and thoroughly all they were asked to do.

When the Rebbe's son became *bar mitzvah*, Leibish organised the celebrations with almost military precision. There were no funds to engage a caterer. With the aid of 15 hard-working Chasidim, Leibish planned the function. Tailors, pressers, cabinet-makers were transformed into 'professional caterers', whose wives spent an entire week cooking and baking. Early on the morning of Sunday, 4 June 1932, equipped with wheelbarrows, the men carried out the arduous task of collecting the dishes, cutlery and crockery from the various 'authorised' Kosher homes under the overall command of Leibish Freedman. Ostwinds the caterers supplied, gratis, cakes and biscuits, the butchers Samuel Greenspan, meat and chickens. All were taken to the Old Kings Hall, 85 Commercial Road.

In the afternoon the women took over, laying the tables and setting out the food. After that the wheelbarrow men transformed themselves into waiters and served the assembled 300 guests a sumptuous meal of six courses. Leibish's task was not yet over. As President of the congregation he acted as toastmaster and chairman. He took for his text the passage from the book of Genesis: 'And Jacob went near and rolled the stone from the well's mouth and watered the flock of Laban, his mother's brother.'[13] He appealed to the community to remove the burden of debt from the Rabbi to enable him to concentrate on his sacred work to be a true shepherd to his community.

The blowing of the *shofar* at the *shtiebl* in the East End on New Year's Day, always an unforgettable experience, was the highlight of the service. The Rebbe walked for one hour from Dalston to the East End of London. Before the service, at around 7 a.m., he went to the *mikveh* (ritual bath) in nearby Dunk Street. The *shacharit* (morning) service began at about 8.30 a.m., and after the Torah and *Haftorah* readings at about 10.30 a.m., the Rebbe, accompanied by his *shammash* (beadle), once again visited the *mikveh* in Dunk Street. The Rebbe returned to the *shtiebl* his hair still wet, wearing a heavy Turkish *tallit* over his *kittel*, the *tallit* fully covering his face. He carried two old *shofrot*, family heirlooms, on either side of his *gartel* (belt). By this time the small *shtiebl* was filled to overflowing with many worshippers from the nearby *shtieblech* of Black Lion Yard, Dunk Street, Dzikov, Lodz, 80/81 Davis Mansions and from the Romanian Synagogue in Chicksand Street. Though not regular worshippers, they came to witness the blowing of the *shofar*. No seats were available, there was standing room only. There was an air of expectancy, and suppressed sobbing and heavy sighs were faintly audible from behind the thick partition wall that divided the women from the men.

The Rebbe in a tearful voice began to read the pre-*shofar* prayers. Psalm 47 was recited with its call to the nations to hail the awesome God. The Divine Name occurs seven times in this Psalm, and is repeated seven times by the worshippers, in order that their prayers may soar through the seven heavens. The Rebbe then recited a number of appropriate passages from the *Zohar* and from the Prayer Book of Rabbi Isaac Luria. He then gave a stirring discourse on the signficance of repentance. Seven biblical verses were then chanted by the *baal tekiah* and responded to by the congregation. These preliminaries lasted for over 40 minutes. The Rebbe then recited the two blessings, praising God 'Who has commanded us to hear the sound of the *shofar*' and 'Who has kept us alive and sustained us and brought us to this season'. To enable the *baal tekiah* to concentrate single-mindedly on his task, the sounds are called out note by note by another person, known as the *baal makrei*.

On one occasion, the Rebbe took the *shofar*, and placed it in the right position, but no sound emerged. *'Tekiyah'*, cried Reb Osher Zelig Rubinstein, the *baal makrei*. The Rebbe tried again to blow, but try as he might, no sound emerged. Once again, the *baal makrei* called out *'tekiyah'*, but despite frantic and almost superhuman efforts not one sound issued. In the overcrowded, stifling hot little *shtiebl*, the worshippers were terribly anxious. This was an unprecedented event. Never had such an incident occurred. The Rebbe had been a master of the art of *shofar*-blowing since his youth, had done so at Siedlice, at Radzymin and in the Novominsker *shtiebl*, continuing this practice in England. Satan had a field day. The Rebbe soon realised that he was fighting a losing battle, and now completely exhausted and perspiring profusely, handed over the *shofar* without saying a word (as speaking is prohibited) to Osher Zelig Rubinstein who, with trembling hands and a fearful heart, took the *shofar*, so that they reversed roles, with the Rebbe now calling out the notes and Osher Zelig almost effortlessly blowing the *shofar*.

Osher Zelig Rubenstein was a Hebrew teacher in Stepney Green who died in 1941. His grandson is Lord Max Rayne, Life Peer, Chairman of London Merchant Securities, Officer of the Légion D'Honneur, and a patron of the Arts, who served as chairman of the National Theatre for 16 years.

11 • The Biala Traditions

During the Second World War most of the relatives of the Biala Rebbe perished in the Holocaust. His aged mother Chava died in Lodz. His sister, Perele, the wife of Rabbi Alter Shlomo Chayim Perlow, the Koidonover Rebbe of Baranowicze, was murdered in Vilna in 1941. Perele had become famous in the Vilna Ghetto during the Nazi occupation as the founder of a religious institute for women. She was a valiant woman of great courage who gave comfort and strength to the other women throughout their terrible agony.

The Rebbe's *shtiebl* in the East End of London closed down during the war, and the Rebbe's followers now came to his Dalston home from many parts of London: wealthy Chasidim such as Abba Myers of Riverside Drive, Golders Green; the jeweller Simon Winegarten (d. 1949) of Stamford Hill; Harry Binstock of Bridge Lane; the restaurateur Harry Ostwind of Wentworth Street; Avidgor Shaikowitz (1883–1975) (father of Cyril Shack) of West Hampstead, an Elder of the Federation of Synagogues and an honorary member of the *Chevra Kadisha*. His solicitude for and kindness to others were a byword in the community. Solomon and Golda Bloomstein (parents of Alfred and Bertie) supported him generously and the Rebbe was now free from all financial worries. A number of survivors of the Holocaust found a welcome refuge in his Dalston home. These included his nephew Herschel (later the Przysucha Rebbe in Jerusalem), one of the many who were rescued by Dr Solomon Schonfeld and brought to England. Many of these had to sleep on the benches of the *shtiebl* and stayed there until they established their roots in London.

All day and well into the night, men and women tramped through the house. They were invited: 'Come when you please, go when you want, eat in the kitchen and make yourself at home.' They hung their coats in the hall and deposited their burdens at the Rebbe's feet. Should Mrs Greenberg have an operation? Dr Schwartz says yes, Dr Weiss says no. So what does the Rebbe say? Should Mr Cohen's elder son grant a divorce? Could Mr Bamlison be persuaded to bring his old mother back from the Jewish old people's home where she was so unhappy? Could

101

Mr Popperman, who shamefully overcharges, be prevailed upon to go to the rent tribunal or submit to private arbitration? And where could Mrs Shindler get a suitable match for her marriageable daugther, and how can she help her husband Jonah who is suffering from consumption and is working in a sweatshop until 10 o'clock at night? These were the types of problem his followers brought to the Rebbe, believing his wisdom would provide the solutions.

The Rebbe steadily protested that he had no special *protektsia* (influence) with the Ultimate Arbiter. His followers were not convinced, however. They wanted and needed to believe, especially when times were bad, that '*Nur der Rebbe ken helfen*' (only the Rabbi can help). It was the very essence of their faith, reflecting the intimate and unique relationship between the Rebbe and his followers, for whom he was mentor, father confessor, oracle and mediator.

The Rebbe also befriended the local rabbinic scholars who enjoyed talking to him and conducting Talmudic discussions with him. Among them were Rabbi Abraham Zevi Weinstein (1900–75). A native of Azhore, near Grodno, he studied in the *yeshivot* of Grodno and Slabodka, and was rabbi of Liskova, Lithuania, until he came to England in 1928, to become the rabbi of the Princelet Street Synagogue.[1] In 1940 he became *Rosh Hashochtim* (chief adviser in religious matters to the London Board of *Shechita*) where he worked until his retirement in 1966. He also acted as the rabbi of the Montague Road *Beth Hamidrash*, Dalston. He was the author of *Shaarei HaMitzvot*,[2] a concise Hebrew compendium on the 613 Commandments as listed by Maimonides. He was renowned and loved for his Yiddish discourses which demonstrated his profound learning and humour and contained a wealth of rabbinic maxims. Though a *Litvak* (of Lithuanian origin) and the son of a *Litvak*, Rabbi Weinstein walked all the way from Meynell Gardens, Hackney, to engage in Talmudical duels with the Rebbe.

Another regular visitor was the scholar and leader of the Lithuanian *Musar* Movement, Rabbi Eliezer Desler (1891–1954), a scholar and a thinker of the first rank, who settled in Dalston in 1925 and was the rabbi of the Montague Road *Beth Hamidrash* until 1941.[3] He was brought up in Kelm, Lithuania, and encountered Chasidism at Homel, the hometown of his father-in-law, Reuben Baer. The great *Musar* teachers, Moshe Chayim Luzzato, Jonah ben Abraham Gerondi and Rabbi Israel Salanter were continually quoted in their discussions. Rabbi Desler was amazed to learn from the Rebbe that the Novaredok system, by which a man trained himself to subdue his animal nature by an inner psychological self-examination (a system developed by Rabbi Joseph Jossel of Novaredok) was part of Chasidism and to be found in the teachings of the Yehudi of Przysucha.

Also in close touch with the Rebbe was Rabbi Samuel Joseph Rabinow (1889–1963). He was born in Chaimiak, suburb of Kovno and could trace his ancestry to the Gaon of Vilna. He studied under Rabbi Israel Meir HaKohen Kagan, the *Chafetz Chayim*, at his *yeshiva* in Radun. His first post was as *dayan* in Vilna. He then accepted a position in Lubeck, Germany, and, encouraged by Rabbi Joseph Carlebach, established a *yeshiva* in Hamburg where he remained for 16 years before accepting a call as *dayan* to the *Machzikei Hadath* Community in Antwerp. When the Nazis invaded Belgium, he escaped to England on one of the last boats to leave Dunkirk, and became the rabbi of the Stamford Hill *Beth Hamidrash* in Grove Lane. He was one of the most lovable personalities in London, a profound scholar, overflowing with Torah, a fiery preacher, whose discourses often lasted several hours and kept his audiences spellbound.

From his home at 57 Cazenove Road, Stamford Hill, he regularly visited the Rebbe. '*Es is a mechayei zi reden in lernen mit dem rebben*' (it is a joy to learn Torah with the Rebbe), he would say. After decades of a childless marriage, his wife died, and he consulted the Rebbe about his impending remarriage. In spite of the Rebbe's advice not to be too hasty, Rabbi Rabinow, in his longing for children, remarried. This second marriage to Miriam, the daughter of Rab Shalom Frishman, also proved to be childless. In 1955 he suffered a stroke which greatly curtailed his activities. Four years later he settled in Bnei Berak where he died on *Chol Hamoed Pesach* 1963.[4]

A regular youthful visitor was Rabbi Mordechai Rabin (son-in-law of the Trisker Rebbe). With him the Rebbe discussed the complex problems of tractate *Yevamot* (dealing with Levirate marriages). 'A visit to the Rebbe', said Rabbi Mordechai 'transplants one to another world, the world of Abaya and Rava (teachers of the Talmud).' The Rebbe reciprocated the compliment: 'He is a real *tachshit*. He is *mole v'gadish*.' (He is a really precious person. He is full of knowledge.)

The Rebbe was in correspondence with the rabbi and scholar Arthur Marmorstein who, from 1912, until his death, taught at Jews' College. The Rebbe admired his painstaking research and his vast knowledge of Midrashic sources. Dr Marmorstein, replying to the Rebbe's query on a Midrashic problem, wrote: 'A wise man's question is already half an answer.'

The Rebbe always enjoyed good health and never suffered a day's illness in his life. He walked there and back from Dalston to his *shtiebl* in the East End (one hour's walk each way) without much effort. After Passover, 1947, he suddenly felt ill. His doctor and lifelong friend, Dr Michael Oster (d. 1976) soon diagnosed a malignant growth on the colon. He underwent surgery at University College Hospital under Mr Simon Isaac Levy, FRCS, and subsequently, by Mr Gabriel at St Marks Hospital. The doctors could not disguise the seriousness of the situation and the Rebbe realised that his days were numbered. On his return home, after a short convalescence in Westcliff, where he was taken by car by one of his Chasidim, I Joseph, he was confined to bed, but never betrayed any sign of distress.

He enjoyed brief remissions which were enough to keep alive the unspoken hope of a recovery. This was not to be, and he summoned his last strength to pray in the *shtiebl*. To see before him so many familiar faces, many of whom had walked long distances, gave him a new lease of life. The worshippers sensed the seriousness of the situation. 'Rebbenu' (our beloved Rabbi), wept Zevi Elimelech Uri, one of the wardens, 'I freely make you a gift of the remaining years of my life.' Although several Chasidim made similar offers, alas! this was not a negotiable transaction. In any case, the Rebbe asked his Chasidim to live rather than to die for him.

Even when ill health drained his physical resources, his enthusiasm spurred him on. Nineteen days before his death he delivered his last discourse before *Neilah*, the closing service on the Day of Atonement. He based it on the Talmudic passage that 'the Almighty sits on the throne of justice with the books of life and death before him'.[5] On the Day of Judgment it is understandable that the Almighty should scrutinise the 'Book of Life', to judge the living, and to place their past actions on the heavenly scales before judgment can be pronounced, whether they should live or die. But why open the 'Book of the Dead?' Surely, those who have gone the way of all flesh have already received their verdict when they presented themselves before the Heavenly Tribunal. Why reopen their case? They have already received their merited reward or punishment.

The Rebbe explained this Talmudic anomaly with a simple simile. The function of an advocate or barrister is to do his utmost to defend his client, for which he is fully trained. If, however, the advocate himself is on trial, despite his legal knowledge, it is usually very difficult for him to defend himself and to marshal his facts. He, therefore, employs another advocate to plead on his behalf. Similarly, on the New Year and on the Day of Atonement, we stand on trial before our Father in Heaven. How can we, who are full of transgressions, full of sins of commission and omission, defend ourselves and plead for Heavenly mercy and forgiveness. We, therefore, call upon the 'Book of the Dead', on our fathers and ancestors – our *zechut avot* (ancestral merit) – to take up our case and to act as our advocates before the Heavenly Throne.

For one who always hated to show any signs of physical weakness, his decline must have been particularly hard to bear. Yet he retained his consideration for others to the last and he frequently apologised to Dr Oster for being such a 'troublesome' patient. With his last strength he officiated, as was his custom since his youth, at the *Neilah* service, and despite doctors' orders, he fasted on the Day of Atonement. He ate in the *sukkah*, but could no longer sleep there, and he could not even participate in the *Simchat Torah* celebrations, but listened attentively to the melodies and watched the dancing in the *shtiebl*. He was very appreciative of the frequent visits by Rabbi Szpetman and the Kielcer Rebbe. He loved the Kielcer Rebbe for his sincerity, and Rabbi Szpetman for his keen sense of sardonic humour. On the eve of *Rosh Chodesh Cheshvan* (29 *Tishri* 1947) he died at the age of 47.

In the *beth hamidrash*, the customary *hakafot* (circuits) around the coffin took place. Moving tributes were paid by Rabbi Dr S Schonfeld, Rabbi S Rabinow and the Kielcer Rebbe. The coffin was then taken to Monague Road *Beth Hamidrash*, where Rabbi Szpetman read in full the 'Ethical Will' which the Rebbe had written four weeks before his death. Another tribute was paid by his relative, Rabbi J Heshel. At the cemetery of the *Adath Yisroel* at Carterhatch Lane, Enfield, the only tribute was paid by his son, then minister of the St Albans Hebrew Congregation, who concluded his oration with the words from the Book of Psalms: 'Cast us not away from Thine Presence and take not Thy holy spirit from us.'[6]

He was interred at Enfield according to his instructions: 'A space of four cubits (as prescribed by the Law) should be left around my grave, in which no one should be buried nor any tent (*ohel*) erected thereon.' He further desired that

the tombstone should be as plain as possible, inscribed with only my name and the name of my saintly father. I should be designated merely as 'Rabbi Nathan David' without any further complimentary epithets. I should prefer to dispense even with the title 'Rabbi', but since my revered father-in-law (the Rabbi Novominsk) addressed me by this title several times, and also in deference to the wishes of my family and relatives. I will leave just this.[7]

In this respect he faithfully followed the traditions of his grand-father, the Rabbi of Biala. When the latter died in Warsaw on 23 *Av* 1905, no *ohel* was erected over his grave, but according to his wishes, a space of four cubits was marked off around it, and the site purchased in perpetuity. However, a Warsaw *Beth Din* later ruled that this prohibition did not apply to his children, and that they could be buried near him.[8] Even today, in the vandalised and derelict Warsaw cemetery, a tablet stands on his grave, indicating that 'by the permission of the rabbinate his son was buried there'.

The Rebbe's Ethical Will was not written with a view to publication. As mentioned at its end, it was written during the Rabbi's illness. But it contains matters of high spriritual value which appeal to a circle much wider than those for whom it was primarily intended. On the advice of Rabbi Rabinow it was decided to publish it, and Rabbi Szpetman trans-lated it into Yiddish. A special publication committee, consisting of Abba Myers, Harry Binstock and Henry Oliver, published the Will in 1948, and within four weeks the 1,000 printed copies became collector's items. It had a preface by Dayan H M Lazarus (the Chief Rabbi's deputy) in which he said:

> On reading through the Will of the saintly Rabbi of Biala, I was moved to tears and remained a while deep in thought. They were not tears of sorrow, but of an overwhelming sense of veneration for the meek, saintly friend who, on his impending departure, wrote a fatherly message of sweet counsel and directions to all those he loved. And who knows how wide was the beloved circle of this great-hearted man![9]

There were other tributes. 'The [Biala Rebbe's] Ethical Will breathes the air of traditional Jewish saintliness,' wrote Rabbi Kopul Rosen (d. 1962), the Principal Rabbi of the Federation of Synagogues. 'We see the soul of one whose daily life was overflowing with the holiness of the Torah', said Rabbi Dr S Schonfeld.

This slim volume, the Ethical Will, written on the brink of death and in the darkening shadow of illness, revealed his true greatness. It is a remarkable document, a loving and enlightening message to his children, his wife and closely-knit Chasidim. There is nothing in contemporary ethical writings to compare with this unique document.

The Rebbe's unpublished output was considerable: he wrote incisive commentaries based on his weekly discourses on the Torah, the *Pirkei Avot* (Ethics of the Fathers) and on the *Zohar*. In his Ethical Will he clearly stated: 'My manuscripts on the Torah have so far not been revised. Therefore, if I am able, I shall burn them while I yet live, and if I do not burn them myself, I request my dear son to burn them immediately after my burial and on no account to disregard my instruction on this matter.'[10] However, on the advice of Rabbi Rabinow, Rabbi Szpetman and Rabbi Dr Solomon Schonfeld, it was decided that the manuscripts should not be burned but should remain unpublished. The Rabbi, being a perfectionist, did not want anything published without his thorough revision.

A Memorial Service was held at the Stamford Hill *Beth Hamidrash* on Sunday, 16 November 1947, and eulogies were delivered by Rabbi S Rabinow, Dr S Schonfeld, Rabbi J Szpetman and Rabbi A Weinstein.

In his Ethical Will the Rabbi requested:

> I beg of those who attend the *Beth Hamidrash* to keep up the *Beth Hamidrash* and pray there regularly. Even if they find it necessary to pay some men for the evening service, they should do so. They should also arrange *Seudah Shlishit* every Sabbath as they did during my lifetime without any change whatsoever. They will then perform a kindness to my soul which needs the mercies of the Holy One, blessed be He.[11]

The Rebbe further stated that,

> I beseech the members of the *Beth Hamidrash* always to live in harmony and not to secede from the congregation, for great is the blessing of peace, and if God grants I will plead on their behalf in the world of eternity.
>
> I would also beg of them to make no offerings throughout the year, for such has been my own custom while alive, only on Festivals and at joyful celebrations of their fellow congregants.[12]

The *Beth Hamidrash* was maintained for 14 years despite the shift of population when most of the congregants either moved to other parts of London or died. During the decade following the Rebbe's death an annual *melave malka* was held either at the Rebbe's *shtiebl* or at the Kielcer Rebbe's *beth hamidrash* where eulogies were delivered.[13] Normally celebration is hardly the word one would use for the commemoration of a *yahrzeit*, but among Chasidim this is so. Tradition tells us that on every *yahrzeit* the soul ascends yet higher in the celestial heavens.

The Rabbi's widow, Sheindel Bracha, died in New York in 1963. The Rebbe in his Will had entreated her:

> I further beg of you, my beloved wife, knowing how your soul has been bound up with my soul, how tender-hearted you are, and liable to break down – therefore, I implore you earnestly with all my heart and all my soul, I pray you, my dear one, not to give way too much to grief. You are indeed the daughter of a king [in rabbinic literature scholars are likened to kings] – you come of a highly noted family, tracing your descent to Rabbi Israel Baal Shem Tov. By doing so, you will set to all your descendants an example of submission to the will of God, all the more so as it is now incumbent on you to fill my place as well as your own. You must now watch over our dear children and I beg of you to see that the house is conducted as it was when I was alive. I desire that you should make *Kiddush* every Sabbath, and provide all the requirements of Sabbath just as in my lifetime.

He paid her a glowing tribute:

> My dearly beloved wife, know that the small part of saintly sentiment to which I have been privileged to attain through the study of the Torah came to me through the influence of the home of your saintly revered father, of whose pious deeds I never tired of observing, and who was particularly fond of me, as you know, in nearly all his letters he addressed me as 'my son-in-law whom I regard as my own son'. Therefore, I leave you the following small gift. In all the Torah which I have learned and in all the precepts – however few – which I have performed from the time when I became responsible for my actions until my decease, you shall have an equal share.[14]

She was survived by her son in London and by two daughters, Miriam Rose, an artist, and Rachel Anne, who died in 1987 in New York. The latter was born in London and was a graduate of London University. She was a frequent contributor to the *Jewish Chronicle*, the *Manchester Guardian* and *The Times*,[15] and a prize-winning copywriter for several companies. She wrote Jewish cookery books under the pseudonym of Miriam Field and also wrote *Junior Classic Comics*. She was the author of *The Land and the People of Israel*,[16] and in 1982 was the editor of *The Feast of Freedom*, the Passover *Haggadah* of the American Rabbinical Assembly – the only *Haggadah* ever edited by a woman.[17] She also wrote a manual for the High Holy Days, and just before her premature death, wrote a poem, *The Princess Sabbath*. Her radiant personality, her profound commitment to Jewish tradition and learning, her skill in transmitting the abiding values of Judaism, her unassuming piety and extraordinary gift for friendship were well known. In a commentary to Psalm 79 she wrote: 'Jewish existence is a tapestry woven of silk on a loom of steel, woven with tears and blood, mystery and martyrdom, exultation, anguish, ecstasy, peril and paradox.'[18]

The Biala tradition was maintained by the Rebbe's elder brother, Rabbi Yechiel Yehoshua who survived the Holocaust and made his home in Israel in 1947, where he was known as a 'miracle worker' and a great servant of the Lord. He died in 1982 and is survived by a daughter in Tel Aviv and four sons who all became rebbes: Benzion in Lugano, Switzerland, Herschel in Jerusalem, David Mattisyahu in Bnei Berak and Yaakov Yitzchak in Ramat Aaron, Bnei Berak.

12 · The Premishlaner Rebbe

Przemishlany, a town near Lvov, was, in the nineteenth century, the home of Rabbi Oron Leib (d. 1803) and of his son Rabbi Meir (d. 1850) who was renowned as a 'miracle worker'.[1] He was also known for his hospitality and maintained that 'the Gates of Heaven are open to those who keep an open house.'

It was through Rabbi Meir's daughter, Esther Zinah (who married Rabbi Herschel Frankel), that the Premishlaner Rebbe of London, Rabbi Israel Arye, traced his descent. Rabbi Israel Arye was also a direct descendant of Rabbi Chayim Mordechai Margaliot (d. 1823). Rabbi Chayim Mordechai's brother, Rabbi Ephraim Zalman, rabbi and author, lived in Brody. He owned flourishing commercial establishments in Vienna. It was said of him that from the time of the financier Saul Wahl, a court agent to Polish King Sigismund III in 1589, 'there has not been Torah and wealth' such as that of Rabbi Ephraim Zalman whose writings became classics and were reprinted many times.[2]

Rabbi Israel Arye was born in Przemishlany on 7 *Tishri* 1893 and was named after his grandfather, Rabbi Israel Leib (Arye) Frankel. The Premishlaner's father, Rabbi Ephraim Zalman (d. 1922), was at first Rabbi in Lanko and later in Drohobycz. He was a descendant of Rabbi Meir ben Yehuda Leib (Hakohen) Poppers (d. 1662),[3] and a devoted Chasid of Rabbi Joshua Rokeach, and later, of the son, Rabbi Issachar Dov Rokeach of Belz. The Premishlaner's mother, Udel, was a daughter of Rabbi Israel Leib Frankel, a descendant of Rabbi Moses Chayim Ephraim of Sudylkov,[4] a grandson of the *Besht*.

The Premishlaner Rebbe was ordained by Rabbi David Menachem Munish Babad – the Rabbi of Tarnopol – and Rabbi Abraham Menachem Halevi Steinberg of Brody. In 1913, Rabbi Israel Arye married Peshah (d. 1970), the eldest daughter of Rabbi Isaac Babad (d. 1929), a descendant of Rabbi Heschel (d. 1664), the head of the *Yeshiva* of Cracow.[5]

Rabbi Arye Leib lived for a time in Tartikov where he acted as *rav zair* (junior rabbi), then in Budapest (1914–19) where he officiated as rabbi in several synagogues. When Chasidim complained to the Rebbe of Belz that Rabbi Arye Leib was taking *qvitlech* (petitions), he was told, 'Let him. He is ready for it.' In August 1920, Rabbi Arye Leib visited Mannheim, Germany, where he officiated at the marriage of Perl to her cousin Benzion Margulies (1890–1955). Benzion was one of the nine children of Mordechai of Skalat, Western Galicia (part of Austro-Hungary), a devoted Chasid of the Rebbe of Husyatin (Rabbi Jacob Friedmann, 1878–1953, a scion of Ruzhin). The family sprang from a long line of rabbis, tracing their descent back to Rabbi Isaiah Horowitz (1565–1630). The Margulies family had moved to Mannheim, Germany before the outbreak of the First World War.

In 1931 one of the sons, Alexander (1902–91), generally known as Alex, settled in London, and established a thriving business, assembling imported clock movements into British-made cases. He was joined two years later by his brother, Benzion.

Benzion was a man of wide-ranging knowledge, a true autodidact, who acquired a mastery of Hebrew and had a profound natural curiosity about people. After serving as a corporal in the Austro-Hungarian army, he settled in Essen in 1922 where he became involved in helping the large contingent of poor Polish Jews. On his arrival in England, with the encouragement of Abba Bornstein, he interested himself in the *Mizrachi* and *Bachad*, and the Board of Deputies. During the Second World War, while living in Waddesdon, he supervised the religious needs of the refugee hostel, 'The Cedars', set up by James and Dorothy de Rothschild. He organised religious services at which he himself officiated. He was unstintingly generous with his time and money in his work for the Polish Jewish servicemen, and he worked with S M Zygelbojm, the Polish Bundist leader, and the Zionist leader, Isaac Schwartzbart, who represented Polish Jewry in London in the Polish Government in Exile. He helped Joel Cang to publish the *Polish Jewish Observer*, and Chaim Lewis with the Mizrachi *Jewish Review*. He worked tirelessly with the British author, Joseph Leftwich (the director of the Federation of Jewish Relief Organizations of Great Britain) and Louis Questle, to alleviate the suffering of the Jews in Poland.

Benzion, in the words of his brother was 'a *maskil* in the traditional mould'.[6] Just as scripture links Zebulun, the merchant and the man of action, with Issachar, the student and the man of spirit,[7] so Alexander regarded his brother as playing the role of Issachar and he that of Zebulun.

He befriended the Yiddish writers H Leivick, Itzik Manger, Leo Koenig and A I Lisky. His visit to Poland to commemorate the first anniversary of the Warsaw Ghetto Uprising completely shattered him. During the last years of his life he regularly visited the Premishlaner Rebbe, who became his soulmate.

Alexander was an astute businessman, whose firm Elco Clocks and Watches was, by 1939, one of the largest importers in the field of horology, importing two million watches per year, its slogan being 'value, quality and service'. He also established a wartime aircraft component factory in Aylesbury, and employed many refugee workers. In 1962 his enterprise 'Time Products' was floated on the London Stock Exchange. Today it has factories in France and Hong Kong, and distributes many leading Swiss watch brands. Its Sekonda range is the biggest selling brand of watches in Britain.

During the Second World War the brothers founded, with the help of Oscar Philip, a non-profit-making publication society, 'Ararat', in order to foster Hebrew literature and encourage Jewish learning. Between 1942 and 1948, with the scholarly help of Dr Simon Rawidowicz (1897–1957), a lecturer at Leeds University and later Professor of Jewish Philosophy at Brandeis University, it published seven volumes of the Hebrew annual *Metzudah*, a worthy successor to *Yalkut* (a Hebrew supplement published in this country before the war by the Zionist Federation). *Metzudah* provided a forum for Hebrew scholars in the free world. 'Ararat', so named because it was conceived as a haven of Jewish culture at the height of the Nazi annihilation of European Jewry, also published *Sefer Shimon Dubnow*,[8] essays and letters of the historian Simon Dubnow, and two volumes of philosophical essays *Bavel V'Yerushalayim* (Babel and Jerusalem) by Simon Rawidowicz.[9] Benzion and Alexander contributed towards the publication of the two volumes of *Letters of Jews Throughout the Ages*, collected and edited by Dr Franz Kobler; a volume of poems by the Yiddish poets Nachum Stencl and Itzig Manger; and two historical works by Josef Fraenkel.[10]

In 1942 the Margulies brothers established a club, the *Ohel*, in Central London (Gower Street) which catered for Polish Jews in war-time London and served as a meeting-place for Polish Jewish servicemen, Jewish writers and artists of Polish origin.

Alexander Margulies became an outstanding communal figure, a renowned philanthropist and a great patron of the Arts. It is difficult to think of a cause which did not draw on his munificence. He was the mainstay of the Ben Uri, the Jewish Art Society and Gallery. Together with his wife Stella, whom he married in 1935, he amassed a large and valuable collection of paintings and sculptures of the *École de Paris*, many artists such as Jacob Epstein, Mané Katz, Joseph Herman and Yankel Adler becoming his personal friends. He presented a number of his paintings to the Tate Gallery in London and to the New Art Museum in Tel Aviv. In 1983 a centre for *Bnei Akiba* youth in Golders Green was named after him, as was an Old Age Home in Beer Sheva.

He particularly befriended Rabbi Samuel Sperber and the Chasidic research scholar Joseph Weiss. He was a member of the Actions Committee of the Twenty-second Zionist Congress, held in 1946, the first post-war Congress and the last to be held in the Diaspora. He helped to acquire a farm in Thaxted, Essex, for the Bachad Fellowship, and was active in the *Mizrachi*; the Anti-Tuberculosis League of Israel; the first Hillel House for Jewish students; the Institute of Jewish Studies; Carmel College, the only Jewish public school; the Joint Israel Appeal; the *Jewish Quarterly*,[11] and the Ruzhin *yeshiva* in Jerusalem. He maintained his links with the Rebbe of Husyatin in Tel Aviv, whom he never failed to consult when visiting Israel.

In 1927, the Premishlaner Rebbe came to London with his wife and young children. At first he lived in the home of Moses Zeev Linder at 86 Chicksand Street, East London. Through the generosity of Hyman Spector of Willesden, £100 was collected for the acquisition of a home at 45 Umberston Street, where he established the *Shtiebl Kehillat Yisrael*.[12] The dedication took place on 18 November 1927.[13] Three more childen were born to him there. The Rebbe attracted many followers, who were drawn by his melodious voice and warm personality. In 1932, he felt the need to move to more spacious accommodation at 14–16 Vallance Road, East London, a converted public house.

On 21 March 1930 the Rebbe addressed a public meeting at the Princess Academy in the East End of London, held in protest against the persecution of religious Jews in Russia. In December 1938 he moved again, to 6 Minster Road, Cricklewood, North West London. The *beth hamidrash* (which had a private *mikveh*) was consecrated by Dayan M H Lazarus and Revd A Schechter.[14] Among the worshippers were Rabbi Dr Hirsch Jacob Zimmels, later Principal of Jews' College; Professor Cyril Domb (of Imperial College and now at Bar Ilan University); Meyer Barsam (1892–1961) and his brother-in-law Eliezer Bornstein together with his son Abba and son-in-law, the bibliophile Moshe Sanders (1905–86) (son of a Chabad Chasid). R Moshe Schwartz (1912–93), a native of Nemirov and a Chasid of Belz, came to London in 1935, and soon became a prominent figure in the *beth hamidrash*. He subsequently moved to Hendon where he became the Treasurer of the Hendon Adath Congregation, a position he held for 24 years. He was also active in the Hendon *Chevra Kadisha*, and was chairman of the North West London Communal *Mikveh*. He settled in Israel in 1972.

Rabbi Kopul Rosen, who had by then been appointed Principal Rabbi of the Federation of Synagogues and lived in the area, often worshipped there and occasionally addressed the congregation in faultless Yiddish. The Rebbe's *shammash* (beadle), Mordechai Leib Ansell, who had previously been associated with the Shatzer Rebbe, was a man of many talents, a superb organiser, administrator and general factotum. Having no immediate family, he dedicated himself completely to the *shtiebl*. He possessed a keen sense of humour and a brilliant memory for names and faces which he put to effective use. He played many roles, culinary, secretarial and advisory; he was marriage broker and counsellor, and made every visitor feel welcome.

On *Simchat Torah* all roads in the north-west London area led to Minster Road. Congregants of all 'denominations', from the United Synagogue *shuls* of Cricklewood, Brondesbury, Dollis Hill and Willesden, from the Federation Synagogues Ohel Shem, and Ahavat Shalom of Neasden, and from the other *shtieblech* (Yudeleib and Freedman), made a point of celebrating *Simchat Torah* with the Rebbe and joining in the Chasidic joy and fervour. The major *aliyot* of the evening were sold by auction, and everyone was thrilled when high figures were achieved. Ephraim Zalman, the Rabbi's son, actively participated in the auctions.

The Premishlaner Rebbe was a man of most equable temperament, worldly-wise, a good listener with a great capacity for absorbing valuable information, and renowned for his hospitality. Along with his ten children, he fed and sheltered the needy and the homeless, refugees and *meshullachim* from Poland and the Holy Land. The refugee boys from the hostel at No. 1 Minster Road found a second home in the Rebbe's house. A generous and tolerant person, he was happiest when ministering to others and attending to their needs. Anger was foreign to him. Strangers responded instantly to his warmth. His particular claim to a place in the hall of fame is not for his scholarship or his discourses, but for his warmth and the friendship he extended to all who came to him.

Although personally associated with the *Aguda*, the Rebbe strove to avoid politics in the *Beth Hamidrash*, and to ensure that everyone felt at home. For example, when Rabbi J L Maimon, the Mizrachi leader, visited the *shtiebl* as a guest of Abba Bornstein, he was asked to address the congregation. After the Sabbath service there was always a *kiddush* at which the Rebbetzin's *kugel* (a dish made on Friday, cooked overnight for serving hot on Saturday) would be served, and where the Rabbi or any honoured guest would deliver a short discourse. But the Rabbi was very pragmatic, and if the *kugel* arrived during the discourse, he would abruptly interrupt the speaker with the maxim, 'the Torah will not get cold, but the *kugel* will'.

The Rebbe was deeply interested in education. Before the Second World War he was active on the religious education committee, the *Vaad HaChinuch*. In 1942, he helped his son-in-law, Rabbi S Pinter, establish the *Yesodey Hatorah* school. Three years later, after intensive preparation in tandem with his son Meir (d. 1981), he was instrumental in opening the North West London Jewish Day School at 28 Minster Road on 1 May 1945. A kosher kitchen, under the chairmanship of the industrialist, Mechel Rabinowitz, provided midday meals.

The school's founders included Rabbi Aaron Godal Klepfish (d. 1969), a student of the *Slabodka Yeshiva* and Rabbi of the *Ein Yaakov Shul*, Artillery Lane in the East End from 1936 to 1940 in succession to Rabbi Desler.[15] The Rebbe insisted on setting and maintaining high standards in both secular and religious studies. He applied himself diligently to collecting the funds that enabled the school to expand and move to new premises at 180 Willesden Lane, and he had the satisfaction of seeing it achieve state recognition and become a voluntary-aided (mixed) infant and primary school. He had the ability to see what could be accomplished and the courage to translate plans into practice in situations which others might have deemed hopeless.

He was deeply involved in the work of the Union of Orthodox Hebrew Congregations under Rabbi Dr Avidgor Schonfeld and his son, Rabbi Dr Solomon Shonfeld. As a member of the *Moetzet Gedolei HaTorah* (Council of Jewish Sages) he was given the privilege of opening with a recitation of Psalms the *Fourth Knessiya Gedola* in Jerusalem on 10 February 1954.[16] He was a passionate supporter of the development of the Holy Land and visited Israel many times. He sensed that the centre of gravity of Yiddishkeit was moving from Cricklewood: he moved in 1954 to 30 Linden Lea, Hampstead Garden Suburb, where he re-established his *shtiebl*.

He died of a heart attack on 24 *Tevet* 1955 and was buried at the Enfield *Adath Yisrael* cemetery. Eulogies were delivered by Rabbi A M Badad, Rabbi Rabinow, Rabbi Dr S Schonfeld, Rabbi Chune Halpern, Rabbi Simcha Rubin of Sassov, and Rabbi Zeidel Semiatizsky. The children of the North West London Jewish Day School lined the streets in a sorrowful farewell to their beloved patron as the cortège passed the school.[17] Among the mourners was Chief Rabbi Sir Israel Brodie.[18]

The *shtiebl* was maintained for a short time by his son-in-law, Rabbi Uziel Herbst. None of his sons or sons-in-law felt able to take on his mantle and the *beth hamidrash* lapsed. The Rebbe was survived by three sons and six daughters. His second son, Ephraim Zalman, born in 1924 and educated at the Davenant Foundation School, married Martha (Rivkah Sarah) Stern. After a chequered career, including a spell in the British Navy, he became a very successful entrepreneur and was, until 1990, group chairman of S & W Berisford, a multinational company which acquired British Sugar in 1982. He restructured the group into four core divisions: food, financial services, property and commodities.

In 1990, he not only resigned as chairman, but sold his remaining stake in the company, ending a 20-year association. In 1982 he initiated an ambitious building project, 'Emanuel' in Israel, a housing project for Orthodox settlers in the hills of Samaria, on the West Bank. By the end of 1987, over 400 flats had been built in the new town, which acted as an overspill for families from areas such as Bnei Brak and the strictly Orthodox parts of Jerusalem. His son Joseph, one of his 11 children, was in charge of this project.[19]

In 1984 he founded the S & W Berisford Charity Trust for general charitable purposes. All his sons and grandsons study in *yeshivot* and *kollelim*, and are educated in the Chasidic way of life.

The well-known communal worker, the late Fritz Nussbaum of Gateshead, summed up the character of the Rebbe of Premishlan: 'If anyone could convert me to Chasidism, it would be the warm-hearted Rebbe of Premishlan.'

None of the Rebbe's sons succeeded him as Rebbe, but the work of two of his Chasidic sons-in-law made a notable impact on Anglo-Jewry.

13 • The Progeny of the Premishlaner

The first of the Premishlaner's sons-in-law, Rabbi Abraham Moses Babad (1909–66), was born on 22 *Kislev* in Mikulince. The name Babad is an acronym of *Ben Av Beth Din* (son of the head of the court). It was a family that produced many learned rabbis. There were 41 rabbis of that name active in pre-war Poland, all belonging to the same family.[1] Abraham Moses studied under his uncle, Rabbi Menachem Munish Babad, an outstanding halachic authority, and was his companion on a trip to Switzerland for medical treatment. After a year and a half his uncle returned to Tarnopol, and Babad came to London in 1936 and married his cousin Chaya, the eldest daughter of the Premishlaner Rebbe. The wedding took place at *La Bohème* rooms, Mile End.[2] Babad's first rabbinical post in London was at *Ahavat Emet*, a small synagogue in the East End of London.

In 1937, he was appointed by Dr S Schonfeld as Principal together with Rabbi (later Dayan) Michael Fisher of the *Yeshiva Or Yisroel* at 109–111 Stamford Hill and later at 65 Lordship Road. The *yeshiva* catered for 20 refugee boys whom Dr Schonfeld had rescued from Nazi-dominated Europe.[3]

In 1943, he was appointed the rabbi of the Edgware *Adath Yisroel* Synagogue and also acted as the official spokesman of Orthodox Jewry in the Polish government-in-exile in London. In 1947 Rabbi Babad was elected Rabbi of the Sunderland *Beth Hamidrash*, and was inducted into office by Dayan I Grunfeld on 30 March 1947.[4] He soon felt at home in this *Mithnagged* community, largely of Lithuanian origin.

In his *Beth Hamidrash* every *yeshiva* emissary was invited to occupy the pulpit on a Sabbath morning. Each of the numerous emissaries was found a well-respected congregant to accompany him on his 'tour' of the town.

Babad's mastery of the English language, his genuine concern with the needs of every individual and, above all, his robust common sense, soon endeared him to all sections of the community, despite his prolonged and frequent absences in London or abroad on communal affairs. At one time, after the departure to Israel of Dayan Y Ambramsky, he was invited by the then president of the United Synagogue, Sir Robert Waley-Cohen, to join the London *Beth Din*, an invitation which he declined on the advice of the Rebbe of Belz.

In a lecture to the *Bnei B'rith First Lodge of England* on Chasidism, he stated that Chasidism safeguarded Judaism from the fate which had befallen Jewry in Western Europe and from the philosophical theories of materialism.[5]

At the Fourth *Aguda* World Conference (*Knessiya Gedola*) in 1954 he declared that 'the *Agudat Yisrael* was not and never will be Zionism in a *Shtreimel*'.[6] He believed that the establishment of Zionist schools in England was fraught with danger for the future.[7] He was strongly opposed to the Reform and Liberal Movements. He publicly declared that 'a marriage in a Reform Temple is tantamount to a marriage in a Catholic Church'.[8] He was against the establishment of a new Sanhedrin as advocated by the Mizrachi leader, Rabbi Maimon: 'The new project,' he stated, 'springs from a scarcely hidden desire for Reform.'[9]

He was communally minded and headed the praesidium of the British *Aguda* from 1944 and chaired the *Vaad Hapoel* (executive) from 1957. He was also a member of the *Moetzet Gedolei HaTorah* (Torah Sages) and chairman of the *Vaad Harabbanim* of the British *Aguda* from 1964. He worked tirelessly with Rabbi N Shakowitsky and Rabbi Leib Gurwitz, collecting funds for *Chinuch Atzmai* (*Aguda* Schools in Israel) in Gateshead, Newcastle and Sunderland. He regularly wrote editorials for the *Jewish Tribune* and for the fortnightly *Aguda Bulletin*. He was a born leader, tolerant and broad-minded, gentle in manner and conciliatory in character, possessed of a formidable intellect, sharp wit and a photographic memory.

His discourses and responsa, one addressed to Chief Rabbi Israel Brodie, dealing with electrical stunning before *shechita*, were published posthumously by his son, under the title *Imre Tava*,[10] together with letters of approval by Rabbi Issachar Dov Rokeach of Belz and Rabbi Eliezer Menachem Shach.

Although he was friendly with the Rebbes of Satmar and Ger, he was a devoted Chasid of Belz. He often recalled with pride that the Rebbe of Belz had said of him, 'He is one of us.' He supported Belz institutions in Israel, London and Antwerp. Before his death, he expressed the wish that his cortège pass by the *Beth Hamidrash* of Belz, 'for there my ancestors worshipped.' In a letter dated 1 March 1966 he urged the

Sunderland Community to appoint his son-in-law as his successor, for the period of the minority of his son. On 30 December 1966 the London *Beth Din* ruled: 'That according to Jewish Law and traditional practice, a son or a son-in-law, adequately qualified, of a deceased incumbent of a rabbinical office, has an entitlement to succeed to such office and is to be accorded precedence in the appointment.' The Community was deeply divided on this issue, and no appointment was made.

'His home was wide open like the Patriarch Abraham's', are the words inscribed on his tombstone and are a fitting epithet to the Rabbi. His son, Joseph Dov, born in 1949, studied in Gateshead and in Israel, and is the *dayan* of the London 'New' Belz community.

The Premishlaner's third son-in-law was Rabbi Samuel (Shmelke) Pinter who in 1943 married Gitel (Gertude), a younger daughter of the Rebbe. Rabbi Pinter was a man of natural friendliness, a tireless administrator with a tremendous eye for detail. He had a charismatic, gregarious and extrovert personality. The pioneer and founder of the *Yesodey Hatorah* Schools, Stamford Hill, which now have a roll of over 1,000 pupils, he has been described as a 'leading entrepreneur' in the Jewish educational world.[11]

Rabbi Shmelke's father, Rabbi Chayim (1881–1941) was the rabbi of Bukovsk, western Galicia, a direct descendent of Rabbi Shmelke Horowitz of Nikolsburg (1726–78) who was noted for his singular religious devotion. To guard against oversleeping, he would endeavour to choose the most uncomfortable sleeping positions. He often sat upright with his head resting on his arms, a lighted candle in his hands. When the candle burnt low, the heat of the flame would wake him, and he would instantly resume his duties. His prayers were often impassioned improvisations. 'Alas, Lord of the Universe,' he exclaimed on New Year's Day, 'all the people cry out to You, but what of their clamour? They think only of their own needs and do not lament the exile of Your glory.' In 1778, when on his deathbed, he confided to his disciples: 'Today is the day of my death. You should know that the soul of the prophet Samuel is within me. For this there are three outward signs: my name is Samuel, just as his was; I am a Levite, as he was; and my life has lasted 52 years as did his.'

During the First World War, like many other rebbes from Galicia, Pinter's father, Rabbi Chayim, made his home in Vienna, where Shmelke was born in 1919. In 1923 Rabbi Chayim spent six months in England for medical treatment.[12] Shmelke studied under his ailing and disabled father, at the same time attending a Jewish secular school in

Vienna. To deepen his rabbinical studies he returned to Poland in 1930, where, for three years, he studied under his elder brother. He then returned home to Vienna, where he was ordained by Rabbi Zevi Schmerler. In February 1938, with the help of Dr S Schonfeld, he and his father came to London.

Though classified as an 'enemy alien', Rabbi Shmelke was not interned as he had to look after his invalid father, and they remained in London throughout the Nazi bombing. 'One minute under Hitler was worse than all the London bombing,' he said. At the age of 20 he became the head of the *yeshiva Merkaz HaTorah*, established by Rabbi J H Cymerman. The *yeshiva* soon had 35 students between the ages of 13 and 14. His father, who had a *shtiebl* in Jane Street, off Commercial Road, died in 1941. Some time thereafter Rabbi Shmelke established his own *shtiebl*, *Yeshuot Chayim*, at 39 Bethune Road, which was bombed, and in 1951 the *shtiebl* reopened at 43–45 Heathland Road, North London.

It was Rabbi Abraham Issacher Halevi Pardes (1894–1950), a former member of the *Beth Din* of Ostrowiec, a man of great erudition, deep piety and sincerity, who encouraged and inspired Rabbi Shmelke to launch his educational activities.[13] It was Rabbi Pardes's goal and ambition to establish in England in institution parallel to the *Torah V'Daat Yeshiva* of New York.

One *Yom Kippur* during the war, Rabbi Pardes, clad in *tallit* and *kittel* (white shroud) before the *Kol Nidrei* service, extracted a solemn pledge from Rabbi Shmelke to establish a Jewish day-school. 'We are in serious danger', he said. He was not referring to the dangers of war or to the air raids; he was speaking of the serious void that existed in this country in the field of Jewish religious education, aggravated by war conditions and evacuation. He pointed out that valuable as the old type of *Talmud Torah* had proved in the past, something different was now needed to save Jewish religious education in this country.

A meeting was held in 1942, attended by Saul Bodner, Pinchas Landau, Getzel Berger, Wolf Schiff, Avrohom and Mendel Getter. As a result the *Yesodey Hatorah* School was established. Its beginnings were very humble. It started with six children in a classroom attached to the Stamford Hill *Beth Hamidrash*, Lampard Grove, where Rabbi Rabinow was the Rabbi.[14] The first headmaster was Meir Domnitz, later the Secretary and Education Officer to the Central Jewish Lecture Committee of the Board of Deputies. Heavy bombing forced the school to evacuate to Manchester for a few months.

In 1948, Rabbi Pinter, for the sum of £9,000, acquired a disused nursing home at 2/4 Amhurst Park, Stamford Hill, to house the school. Various fund-raising events were held, including a boxing match at the Seymour Hall. It was Rabbi Pinter's avowed purpose 'to establish a learned laity, able to acquire the knowledge to study a *blatt* (page) of *Gemara* without any difficulty, which till now, has been the privilege of rabbi and minister. We want the children to grow up as practising Jews who understand our Torah and Codes.'[15]

The boys' school and kindergarten are now centred at 2/4 Amhurst Park. The senior and junior girls' school are located at 153 Stamford Hill. The principal was Rabbi Shmelke Pinter, and the vice-principal is his son, Rabbi Abraham Pinter. Out of a total staff of over 100, fourteen are rabbis. Pupils in the girls' schools have the opportunity to choose from ten GCSE subjects.

A new wing, consisting of 14 classrooms, was opened in 1969. Rabbi Pinter's educational empire now consists of the *Yesodey Hatorah* Mixed Nursery School where ten hours per week are given to Jewish studies; the *Yesodey Hatorah* Infants' and Primary Boys' School with nearly 200 pupils, and the Senior Boys' School with 100 boys where 23 hours per week are devoted to Jewish studies (the curriculum of secular subjects includes English, mathematics, geography, history, French, science, British constitution and physical education); *Yesodey Hatorah* Infants' and Primary Girls' School with nearly 400 pupils and 15 hours each week devoted to Jewish studies, and the Senior Girls' School at 51 Amhurst Park with 160 pupils on the roll and 16 hours per week devoted to Jewish studies (secular subjects are English, mathematics, geography, history, nature study, physical education, needlework, current affairs, art, French and British constitution). Generally the school day is divided into a morning session from 8.45 a.m. to 1 p.m. devoted to Jewish studies, and an afternoon session from 1.25 p.m. to 4.30 p.m. when secular subjects are taught.

The schools now have a combined staff of 125 and a budget of nearly £800,000 per annum. GCSE examinations are normally taken at the age of 15, a year in advance of the national average, and the subjects favoured are mathematics, English, French, science and Classical Hebrew. There are no facilities for Advanced level work, as the boys are expected to continue their Jewish studies at a *yeshiva*, and the girls at seminaries, either in England or abroad. Girls are expected to dress modestly, and school rules forbid the wearing of short sleeves and socks. Thick navy or white tights must be worn. A high percentage of former pupils are now teachers at the schools. Rabbi Pinter saw three generations of families passing through them.

Some have become white-collar workers, accountants, teachers, business men and others, manual workers. As many pupils come from large families, nearly 80 per cent do not pay full tuition fees. However, no children are turned away because of their parents' inability to pay the fees, and none of the pupils has ever appeared in a juvenile court. Apart from the nursery, which receives a grant from the local authority, the schools are not state-aided and have to survive on fees, fund-raising activities and donations. Despite the proliferation of other religious dynastic Jewish day schools in the area, *Yesodey Hatorah* Schools still have a waiting list, as they cater for all shades of the Chasidic and even the non-Chasidic community.

Beth Hamidrash Yeshuot Chaim also has as *kollel, Imre Chaim*, at 43–45 Heathland Road. It is one of the largest *kollelim* in Europe, offering two courses in advanced rabbinics. The first, a general course, is open to all graduates of Talmudical colleges and mature students who wish to take up teaching or rabbinical studies as a profession. The second is a rabbinical diploma course and is only open to those students who have graduated from Talmudical college with distinction. Time is set aside in both courses for the study of *Musar* and ethics. Study is full-time over 40 weeks a year. The running costs of the *kollel* are £250,000 per annum.

When Rabbi Pinter's wife died in 1983 after many years of ill heath,[16] he married his *machutaneste* (his son's mother-in-law), Babche, whose husband had been Rabbi Avrohom Eichenstein (d. 1967), the Zhydaszower Rebbe in Chicago.

Rabbi Pinter was active in the *Aguda* and enjoyed cordial relations with all the Chasidic groups in Stamford Hill, from Satmar to Lubavitch. Few Chasidic gatherings took place without his participation. He was interviewed – and very successfully, too – on television. Rabbi Pinter's phenomenal success as a pioneer of Orthodox education was due not only to his firm determination, but also to his affable character, equally at home with the non-observant Jew as with the ultra-Orthodox. All admired his zeal. All respected his sincerity and dedication. He was an army in himself and all are agreed that the miraculous survival and constant expansion of the schools in the face of overwhelming financial problems was the result of his self-sacrificing zeal. True, the schools are overcrowded and under-resourced, the buildings in need of repair, with many classes being held in temporary premises. There is a lack of audio-visual equipment, laboratory and gymnasium facilities, but the schools nevertheless survive and have a future. It is hoped that the local Hackney Council will grant the schools long overdue state aid.

Rabbi Pinter not only faithfully followed his forebears' traditions, but was also the founder of an ever-increasing dynasty of rabbis and teachers. Of his sons, Rabbi Issachar is the head of the *kollel*, another, Rabbi Abraham, is the vice-principal of the schools and a past Labour Councillor of Hackney – 'my Communist' his father jokingly used to call him; a third son, Yitzchok, commutes between Bnei Brak and London, and is in charge of *Yeshiva Hamasmidim* – a youth study group – and Rabbi Chayim is the executive director of the *Yesodey Hatorah* Schools.

One of his daughters married the erudite *Dayan* Yitzchok Dov Berger, formerly of the London *Beth Din*, and the other married Rabbi Azriel Weinberg, who works for the *Baalei Teshuvah* (Return to Judaism) movement in the Holy Land.

Rabbi Shmelke Pinter died on 11 *Tammuz* 1994.

14 • Rabbi Schulim Moskowitz – The Rebbe of Shatz

At the Enfield *Adath Yisrael* cemetery, London, can be found the *ohel* (sepulchre) of Rabbi Schulim Moskowitz, Rebbe of Shatz. Inside the *ohel* is an extract from his Ethical Will and Testament.

> It is well-known that I have always tried to help people to repent of their evil ways, and thanks to the Almighty I have succeeded many times. Therefore, whosoever is in need of any kind of *Yeshuah* (help) or a *Refuah* (speedy recovery from illness) for himself or for someone else, should go to my tomb – preferably on a Friday before noon, and light a candle for my *Neshamah* (soul) and make his request. Let him state his name and his mother's name. Then I shall certainly intercede with my saintly forefathers that they should awaken God's mercy for a *Yeshuah* or a *Refuah*.

The Rebbe of Shatz, however, made one condition for his efforts.

> But there is a definite condition attached: the person concerned must promise to improve his standard of *Yiddishkeit* (Jewishness). For example, he whose business is open on Sabbath must promise to keep it closed. He who shaved his beard with a razor blade, should now remove it in a way that is permissible. A woman who does not cover her hair must promise from now on to wear a *Sheitel* (wig). All this must be clearly known to those who come to my tomb. They must keep their promise and should not try to deceive me, God forbid, for I shall be very angry. Unfortunately, there is already too much deceit in this world.

Rabbi Schulim was born on 17 *Kislev* 1878 in Verbreparove, near Lvov, one of 17 children and was a descendant of Rabbi Yechiel Michael of Zloczszow.[1] Rabbi Schulim's grandfather, Rabbi Joel (d. 1886), was the son-in-law of Rabbi Meir of Przemyshlany. Only on Friday nights did Rabbi Joel use his bed, and on his tombstone are engraved the words: 'He devoted to charity one-fifth of his wealth.' All the members of the family were staunch Chasidim of Belz. Rabbi Schulim's mother Feige used to say: 'True, we are living in Romania, but in my home the spirit of Belz permeates.'

Rabbi Schulim studied under his relative Rabbi Elijah Samuel Schmerling, the *dayan* of Bobruisk, and under Rabbi Shalom Mordechai Schwadron, the Rabbi of Brzezny, and the author of four volumes of responsa which analysed *Halachic* problems with painstaking clarity. Schulim also studied Cabbala with his uncle, Rabbi Leibish Halperin. Rabbi Schulim maintained that he received his 'rabbinical ordination' from the Rebbe of Belz, Rabbi Issachar Dov Rokeach (d. 1927). On one occasion in Belz when the discussion centred on an unresolved *Halachic* problem, the Rabbi of Belz remarked: 'As Rabbi Schulim Shatzer is here, let him decide.'

The Rabbi of Shatz had a very imposing appearance. He was tall and handsome, and he found it difficult to stoop, metaphorically or physically, to those who could not rise to his heights. He had a long white beard and wore silken garments even on weekdays. He was stern, sometimes quick-tempered, but was deeply concerned about the welfare of his followers, and always found time for the younger generation. For 16 years he was the rabbi in Shatz (Suczawa), Bukovina, near Czernowitz. He left the community after a disagreement with the local *shochet*, giving up his post without thought as to how he would earn a living elsewhere, for he was unable to compromise where religious problems were concerned.

Among his early disciples was Rabbi Meir Shapiro, who was brought up in his home. The idea of the *daf yomi* (the study of the daily page of the Talmud) which later became universally accepted, was actually the brainchild of Rabbi Chayim Joel, the Rabbi of Sambor and Rabbi Schulim's brother.

Rabbi Schulim married his cousin Shlomtze in 1897. They lived in Tarnow during the First World War, and from 1920 to 1927 in Cologne, Germany, where he established a *shtiebl* on one floor of an apartment building in Thebedgasse. He enjoyed cordial relations with Rabbi Emanuel Carlebach, the Rabbi of the *Adass Yeshurun*. Rabbi Schulim was keenly interested in astronomy and botany, and frequently visited the *Sternwarte* Planetarium in Munich, on one occasion drawing the attention of the curator to two errors in the description of the exhibits.

He visited London in November 1922, and stayed in the home of Shlomo Bardiger at 180 Brick Lane. In 1929 he settled in London and opened the *Beth Hamidrash Brit Shalom* at 67 Chicksand Street in the East End where he remained until the outbreak of the Second World War. He actively participated in the *Shemirat Shabbat* (Sabbath observance) conference which took place at the Stern Hotel, London, in June 1937.[2]

During the war he lived for a time in Leeds and later in Gateshead. After the war he moved to Stamford Hill where, from 1945 to 1947, he lived at 47 West Bank, from 1948 to 1957 at 119 Lordship Road, and finally at 51 Queen Elizabeth Walk. His home was always open to vistors.

Rabbi Schulim was a *masmid* (diligent student) *par excellence*. He spent 18 hours a day in prayer, study and meditation. He had lived in this way since he was a young man, retiring to his study in order to pore over the Torah. The Talmud chant could be heard throughout the house. He lived a spartan existence, in the same way as his father and grandfather had done before him. He continued studying the entire Talmud – a taxing task – taking four years to complete it. Absorbed as he was in the ivory tower of the Torah, the Rebbe had little understanding of mundane materialistic matters. Money meant absolutely nothing to him. Such money as his followers cared to give him was handed over immediately to his children who managed the day-to-day details of his household. Only when a follower called upon him for advice, to invoke a blessing or intercession in the Heavenly Courts, did the Rebbe lay aside his book, and attend to his caller.

He took a long time over his prayers. On weekdays, after listening to *Borechu* (Blessed) and the *Kedushah* (Sanctification), which are part of the Morning Service and can only be recited in the presence of a *minyan* (quorum), he retired to his study where he completed his prayers in private. He did not wish to burden his fellow-worshippers with his lengthy and prolonged prayers. Many Chasidim would stand outside his door to listen to him praying, and only when he had finished would he undertake any work. 'I do not want to confuse my mind before I recite the prayers,' he said. He would not trouble anyone, not even his children or grandchildren, to do any errands for him. This was against his nature. 'It is forbidden,' he would say, 'to utilise an Israelite to perform any menial task.' He was a true ascetic and ate only once a day.

He was renowned for his erudition and Rabbi S J Rabinow testified that 'there was not a paragraph in the Codes which he did not know by heart'. When he visited Rabbi Yeshayahu Karelitz, the latter remarked: 'The Rebbe of London *kenn lerenen'* (the London rabbi is a scholar). After the establishment of the State of Israel, the Rebbe published a 20-page open letter to its leaders, urging them to establish the State on the basis of the Torah. 'Know,' he wrote, 'that this is no orphaned generation. We still have great scholars like Rabbi Zalman Meltzer, Rabbi Karelitz, the rebbes of Belz and Ger.' He strongly opposed the conscription of women. He was against television, which he called an 'abomination'. He endorsed, in this respect, the views of Rabbi Joseph Hirsch Dunner, the rabbi of the *Adath Yisrael* Synagogue of the Union of Orthodox Hebrew Congregations and Rabbi Chanoch Dov Padwa, the principal rabbinical authority of the Union. Though he was not a member of the *Aguda,* he was one of the signatories of a *kol kore* (proclamation) to enlist support for that movement.

The Shatzer Rebbe was zealous for the Law. He would dismiss with contempt any argument which was not entirely based on *daat haTorah* (Torah point of view). The ardour and haste of his temperament gave a false impression of his true character. He had the courage to denounce anything that he felt was detrimental to the community, and he never moved one iota from the grand Chasidic heritage which he had brought from Galicia. He often quoted Maimonides, who, basing himself on the verse in Deuteronomy 'Ye shall not be afraid of the face of man',[3] stated that this verse applied to religious leaders, who must never show partiality to any person. A spiritual leader must have the courage to express his views without fear or favour. He was apt to be forceful in expounding any views he felt deeply. His hot temper stemmed from a genuine passion to improve religious conditions.

He worried about a market that flourished along the Whitechapel Road on Saturday, causing Jews publicly to desecrate the Sabbath. It pained him to notice, as he walked to the *mikveh,* that Jewish children were queuing for the Saturday morning show at the local East End cinema. He was concerned about the involvement of Jewish youth in left-wing politics, which even attracted the son of a learned *dayan* of the London *Beth Din.*

The state of Jewish education, too, appeared to him to be unsatisfactory. He felt that the Hebrew Classes held after school were proving inadequate as an attempt to provide a proper Jewish education for the sons of the immigrants. Nor could he find any common ground with spiritual leaders such as the Reverend J F Stern, of the East London United Synagogue, with his 'dog collar' and 'canonicals', which appeared to him as *chukkat hagoy* (customs imitating the Gentiles). He found it intolerable that the Establishment accepted mixed choirs in the synagogues at Hampstead, East London and New West End, and that the Revd Stern carried an umbrella on the Sabbath.[4]

The Rebbe urged Chief Rabbi Israel Brodie and the London *Beth Din* to close down Jews' College which he regarded as 'an unclean house which defiles'. In his Ethical Will he wrote:

> When a physician visits someone who is ill, he tries hard to diagnose the roots of the disease so that he can proceed to a cure. One of the root causes of the disease from which the Anglo-Jewish community suffers is the existence of Jews' College, where are trained rabbis, reverends, ministers – that is to say, ignoramuses, whose false ideas, foreign to the tradition of our holy sages, of blessed memory, by whose mouth we, the people who are old Israel's children, live. They should not say, 'after all, a minister is not a rabbi'. This is not so, for such a person has a great influence on the laymen, who look to him as if he were a rabbi. When he preaches, what does he preach? Not the fear of Heaven and the whole-hearted observance of the Torah. All his preaching is not from his heart, for he is not God-fearing in private as he tries to appear in public.
>
> They (the Anglo-Jewish ministers) should be judged in the scale of merit. For after all, a minister has never seen the light, never spent years in a Yeshiva for his soul to be sated with Talmud, Tosafists and the fear of Heaven. It is at Jews' College that he receives the final tap of the hammer that makes him one of the most indifferent to piety. For who are the teachers there, for our many sins, and what further subjects for a goy and an assembly of goyim . . . I know for certain that the Chief Rabbi himself, long may he live, spoke adversely of Jews' College to someone, declaring that the College was no good. 'Woe to the dough against which its baker testifies.' This house has leprosy in it. It is absolutely unclean. 'The house shall be torn down – its stones and timber and all the coating on the house – and taken to an unclean place.'[5] But if other stones are taken and other earth, the plague will revert to the house for it is accursed leprosy, it is unclean. No reforms are possible by bringing in new teachers.[6]

Rabbi Kopel Kahana, a pupil of the *Chafetz Chayim* who had a long-established reputation as a *illui* and a *gaon*, was a lecturer in Talmud and Codes at Jews' College in the years 1946–68 and attracted back to the College some of its former students for the Rabbinical Diploma

Course. He did not escape this censure. He was criticised for giving the College an air of respectability.[7] The Shatzer Rebbe was a fierce opponent of the establishment of day schools by the Zionist Federation. He wrote many letters to leading personalities on this subject. He drafted proclamations which were displayed in the *shtieblech*, drawing the attention of the community to the dangers inherent in a Zionist-controlled education project.[8] However, he highly esteemed Rabbi Yechezkel Abramsky, a profound thinker, forceful preacher and staunch fighter for *Halachic* supremacy.[9] In a letter to his grandchildren, the Shatzer Rebbe urged them not to use perfume: 'It is better to have the odour of good deeds.'[10] He also opposed the idea of female emancipation and urged his granddaughters to encourage their husbands to study and not to burden them with domestic chores. He strongly urged the retention of Yiddish as an everyday language.

So far the following of the Shatzer Rebbe's works have been published: *Shulchan Aruch Orach Chayim* under the title *Daat Shalom*, edited by his son-in-law, Rabbi Yissachar Baer Halevi Rothenberg, New York; *Hagaot* on Rabbenu Bahya on the Torah under the title *Heorot V'Hagaot*, printed by his grandson, Rabbi Moses Halberstam, in Jerusalem in 1958; *Vayomer Shalom* on Responsa *Nodah B'Yehuda* in two parts published in New York in 1966. Work is in hand to publish his commentary on *Pirke Shirah*, glosses on the Babylonian and Palestinian Talmud and on the Zohar. 'I am not a Cabbalist,' the Rabbi asserted, 'but without mysticism we are without understanding.'

He left clear instructions that the term *zaddik* should not appear on his tombstone. 'My son Jacob,' he wrote, 'deserves the epitaph of *zaddik*.' Rabbi Schulim died while on holiday in Westcliff on Tuesday, 22 *Tevet* 1958. The funeral took place at 9 p.m. on the same day and more than 1,000 people attended. Eulogies were given by Rabbi Padwa and Rabbi C Halpern.[11]

The Shatzer's life had been beset by personal tragedy. Except for one daughter, Miriam Chaya, all his children had died in his lifetime. His son Yitzchak died at the age of 42 in 1931, his second son Yisrael Yaakov in 1953, and his third son Yechiel Michel in 1956. His daughter, Adel Halberstam, died in Jerusalem in 1956, and another daughter, Malkah, died in New York in 1958. His son-in-law, Rabbi Issachar Baer Rothenberg (d. 1986) of Wodzislaw, an outstanding orator, was, at one time, the rabbi in Dunk Street, later settling in New York where he was a close associate of Rabbi Yoel Teitelbaum of Satmar.[12] His daughter,

129

Miriam Chaya, had married Rabbi Yoel Moskowitz (1907–79), who at first settled in Montreal, but later moved to Bnei Brak.[13]

The Rebbe's *yahrzeit* is commemorated annually at *Beth Shalom* in Stamford Hill which is under the guidance of Rabbi Moses Deutsch. Rabbi Moses Deutsch's father, Joshua (1910–90), was a native of Makova and studied under Rabbi David Dov Meisels of Ohel and Rabbi Joseph Zevi Duschinsky of Huszt. In 1948, Rabbi Joshua Deutsch settled in Katamon, Jerusalem, near the Rebbe of Belz, who appointed him Principal of the Belz *yeshiva* in Jerusalem. He established a publishing firm *Mein Hachochma* which published a number of rabbinical works.

His son, Rabbi Moses, was born in Braszow, Romania, in 1934 and emigrated to Israel with his parents, where he studied at the *yeshiva* of Belz and under Rabbi Berish Weidenfeld. For four years he lived with the Shatzer Rebbe and had two daily *shiurim* with him. After the Rebbe's death he moved to Hendon where he established the *Shtiebl Shaare Avrohom* at 19 Green Lane.[14] When Mr Freddy Greenwood established a *kollel*, Rabbi Deutsch joined him, and when the *kollel* closed down he established a *Shtiebl Bet Shalom* at 27 St Kilda's Road, Stamford Hill, where four to five *minyanim* worship regularly. He and his 11 children, together with other descendants of the Shatzer Rebbe who live in Israel and the United States, maintain the scholarly traditions of Shatz. Rabbi Moses recently published the Shatzer's commentary on the Passover *Haggadah, Or Ganuz*.

Rabbi Deutsch has criticised individuals who consult psychologists and marriage counsellors, believing that 'all psychologists give advice which originates from impure thoughts and ideas foreign to true Jewish traditions'.

1 Mr Alexander Margulies

2 Rabbi Joseph Shapotshnick

3   Rabbi Joshua Szpetman   4   Rabbi C H D Rubin of Sassov

5   Rabbi S Rubin of Sassov   6   Rabbi J A Twersky of Trisk

7 Rabbi N D Rabinowicz of Biala

8   Rabbi I A Margulies of   9   Rabbi A M Babad
    Przemyshlan

10   Rabbi S Pinter and Rabbi S Halberstam of Bobov (centre)

11   The Rabbi of Vishnitz visiting the Yesodey Hatorah School

12   A Talmud Class at Yesodey Hatorah School

13   Rabbi Shulim Moskovitz of Shatz

14 Rabbi Yehuda Chaim
    Schonfeld of Kielce

15 Rabbi Issachar Dov Hager of
    Vishnitz

16 The Vishnitzer Rebbe visiting Hager's Beth HaMidrash

17   Rabbi Mendel Hager   18   Rabbi Yerucham Leiner

19   Rabbi E Halpern   20   Rabbi Jacob Heshel

21   Rabbi B Finkelstein   22   Reverend J Kacenellenbogen

23   Rabbi Joel Teitelbaum of Satmar   24   Mr Getzel Berger

25 Rabbi Menachem M Schneerson 26 Reverend A D Suffrin

27 Students at the Lubavitch Yeshivah, London

28   Lubavitch Mitzvah Tank, London

29   Lubavitch School Outing

30   Lubavitch Function

31   The Lighting of the Chanukah Menorah by Lubavitch

32   The Rebbe of Belz   33   Rabbi Y H Cymerman

34   The new Yeshivah of Ger in Stamford Hill

35   Rabbi P M Alter of Ger in London (far right)

36   Rabbi Meshullam Ashkenazi   37   Dayan Y Weiss

38   Rabbi C B Padwa

39   Chasidic Rebbes at a Melaveh Malkah

40   A Mizvah Dance at a Wedding

41   Dedication of a Sefer Torah in Stamford Hill

42   Chasidim on a bus in Stamford Hill

43   A Street Scene in Stamford Hill

44   A Rebbe gives a Discourse

45   A Beth Yaakov Girls' Group

46   Siyum HaShas

47   Dressing-up at Purim, Lubavitch in Glasgow

48   A Satmar Junior Class

15 • Chasidic Personalities

RABBI YEHUDA CHAIM SCHONFELD – THE KIELCER REBBE

Rabbi Joseph ben Rabba, a Talmudical sage, said of his illustrious father, that 'he was most particularly concerned with the law relating to ritual fringes'.[1] This dedication to a particular religious precept calls to mind the special concern of the late Rabbi Yehuda Chaim, the Kielcer Rebbe of London: his leitmotiv was *Taharat Hamishpacha*, the law relating to family purity. His commitment to it in his later years almost verged on obsession.

The statistical returns collected by Chief Rabbi N M Adler in 1845 show that only half the congregations of England had access to a *mikveh* (ritual bath).[2] This situation did not change much in the century that followed. In the years between the wars and in the immediate post-Second World War years this was a taboo subject, hardly ever raised in public. In 1936 only six public *mikvaot* were listed for the whole of London, all of them in the East End.[3] By 1945 there were only five.

The Rebbe of Kielce was a most lovable, easy-going and approachable man. But he was implacable on the subject of *Taharat Hamispacha*. On this matter his zeal knew no bounds. Publicly and privately, he never ceased directing appeals to the Chief Rabbi J H Hertz and all the *dayanim*, Rabbi Yechezkel Abramsky, Dr Isidor Grunfeld, Dr Julius Jakobovits and Rabbi Morris Swift.

He addressed meetings in London, Leeds and Westcliff, arguing that the building of a *mikveh* took precedence over the building of a synagogue or a religious school. He frequently pointed out the beneficial effects of the laws of *niddah* (the ritual ablutions a woman undergoes after her period of menstruation) and *tahara* (ritual purity), but his main emphasis, citing Maimonides, was that these laws were of Divine origin and do not belong to those matters which can be explained rationally. His pronouncements on family purity appeared regularly in *Die Zeit*.[4]

His generous and amiable personality won him many friends. He had a special gift of friendship, which arose from limitless compassion.

131

He was willing to help in any difficulty, however trivial. Added to these qualities was his jovial personality which endeared him to all those who came into contact with him.

Rabbi Yehuda Chayim (Yiddel) Halevi Schonfeld was born in 1892 in Wloclawek, Poland. He was a grandson of Yechiel Meyer, a brother-in-law of Rabbi Yehuda Arye Leib Alter of Ger. Yehuda Chayim studied under his great-grandfather Rabbi Elchanan Ungier at Piontke. When he was 13 years old, he was taken to Ger to see Rabbi Yehuda Leib Alter. Later, he moved with his parents to Kielce which then had a Jewish population of 15,430 which was 13.6 per cent of the total population.

In 1917, Yehuda Leib married Malka Chana, the daughter of Rabbi Elimelech Jacob Isaac Rabinowicz, (d. 1937) a direct descendant of the Holy Jew of Przysucha. For the first ten years of his marriage Yehuda Leib lived in Kielce, then in the homes of a number of Chasidic rebbes.

In 1929, after a short stay in Belgium and in France, he arrived in London and took up residence at 17 Fenton Street, East London. Two years later when he was joined by his family, he moved to 45 Umberston Street, to the former home of the Rebbe of Premishlan. He visited Poland in 1934 and 1936 to participate in family weddings. In 1938 he moved to 120 Manor Road, Stamford Hill, where he remained throughout the war. He finally moved to 39 West Heath Drive, Golders Green, in January 1947, and the dedication of his *Shtiebl Kol Yaakov* took place on 20 April 1947, with the participation of Rabbi J Szpetman.[5] His wife died on 18 *Av* 1963, and three years later the Rebbe settled in Israel where he remained until his death in 1967, aged 75, and was buried on *Har Hamenuchot*, Jerusalem.

He is survived by his son, Mordechai Chanoch, a diamond merchant, and a regular worshipper at the Sassov *shtiebl*.

RABBI YERUCHAM LEINER

Rabbi Yerucham Leiner of Radzyn was an outstanding scholarly rebbe who lived in London for twelve years (1935–47). He was born in Radzyn in 1888. His great-uncle was Rabbi Gershon Chanoch Heinoch Leiner who was an original thinker in *Halachic* studies. The last-named was the author of a monumental anthology called *Sidrei Tohorot*, a compendium of the commentaries and interpretations of the sages found in rabbinic literature. He designed his book in the form of a pseudo-*Gemara* with a commentary set out as Rashi's, bordering the text on the left side of the page, with *Tosafot* on the right, flanked by the commentaries of *Messorat HaShass, Ein Mishpat* and *Ner Mitzvah*. This work received enthusiastic and glowing praises from many rabbis, but was also censured by those who objected to the publication of a book in the format of a *Gemara*.

He was also the discoverer of *petil techelet* (the cord of blue). Jews are required to wear ritual fringes, each of which should have seven white threads and one blue (*petil techelet*) in accordance with the verse: 'And bid them put on the fringe on each corner a thread of blue.'[6] The dye was derived from a native mollusc called chillazon. However, the dye became increasingly difficult to obtain and eventually disappeared from the ritual fringes. Reference to it is made by Natronai, the Gaon of Pumbedita, in the early eighth century. Maimonides, too, in his commentary on the Mishna, maintains that it had been lost. Rabbi Gershon was determined to rediscover the source of the dye, and to restore the thread to its rightful place. He fervently believed that this restoration would hasten the redemption.

Rabbi Gershon travelled to Naples in 1887 and again in 1888 to study marine life, on which he became an expert. He claimed to have rediscovered chillazon (*Sepia officinalis*), a member of the cephalopod family, a relative of the octopus and squid families. A factory was established in Radzyn for the manufacture of ritual fringes containing a blue thread, and soon 12,000 Chasidim were wearing the thread of blue.

During the Second World War, with the extermination of Polish Jewry, the secret of making the dye was lost once again. A Russian Jewish immigrant to Israel then carried out lengthy experiments and eventually succeeded in finding a satisfactory method of obtaining the blue dye of the chillazon.

Yerucham Leiner, a descendant of Rabbi Gershon, was known as a child prodigy, and as a youngster was already in correspondence with Rabbi S M Schwardron of Breziny. When his father died in 1920, he succeeded him as Rebbe of Chelm. He was ordained by Rabbi Moshe Hakohen Adamashik of Kelm who declared 'that he is fit to be a Rabbi and a leader of the largest community.'[7] He married Rebecca, a descendant of Rabbi Abish of Frankfurt-am-Main.

In 1934, Rabbi Leiner left Poland and settled in North London. With characteristic modesty he never looked for publicity and only a small number of perceptive people were aware of his great knowledge and erudition. He was at home 'in all corridors of learning'. He regularly visited Antwerp where he addressed the Chasidic community at Feiner's *Beth Hamidrash*. He greatly impressed Rabbi Samuel Halevi Brodt who said: 'He is not one of those Chelmer *naronim* (fools) but an outstanding scholar.' Apart from his rabbinic erudition he was well-read and fully conversant with current political and economic affairs.

In 1935, with the financial help of Abba Bornstein, who gave £50 towards the deposit, he dedicated his *Shtiebl Beth Hamidrash Kehal Yisrael* at 185 Willesden Lane. The official opening took place on 7 April 1935 in the presence of Dayan Y Abramsky, Dayan H M Lazarus (then Minister of the Brondesbury Synagogue), Rabbi Louis Rabinowitz of the Cricklewood Synagogue, and the orientalist and bibliophile Abraham Shalom Yahuda, later Professor at the New School for Social Research of New York. Greetings were received from Chief Rabbi J H Hertz.[8]

He was befriended by Mechel Rabinowitz, the brother of the Skoler Rebbe. Mechel had arrived in England from Vienna in 1939 and settled in Birmingham where he produced aircraft components for the Ministry of Supply. In 1942, he moved to London and married a niece of the Trisker Rebbe. In his home in Teignmouth Road, Cricklewood, he had his own *mikveh*. After the war he expanded into the manufacture of radios (Emor Radios), but, when this venture proved unsuccessful, he emigrated to the United States, and finally settled in Israel.

In a letter to the *Jewish Chronicle* in 1943, Rabbi Leiner strongly criticised Chief Rabbi Hertz for his controversial comments on sacrifices in his commentary to the Authorised Daily Prayer Book.[9] He disliked the quotation from Dr M Friedlander who comments that 'References to the Sacrificial Prayer, especially prayers for its restoration, are disliked by some.' 'This opinion,' wrote Rabbi Leiner, 'was favoured by the founders of Reform in Judaism.'[9]

In 1947, he wrote again to the *Jewish Chronicle* when the election of a new Chief Rabbi was being considered: 'The most pressing need for the moment is to change the whole system of election of the Chief Rabbi, and to bring it in line with traditional Jewish law and ethics. The Chief Rabbi must be a *Talmid chacham* in the highest sense of the term, but may I point out that according to Jewish law, he must be selected by *Talmidei chachamim*.'[10]

In response to calls from many of his Chasidim he settled in New York in 1947, where he died in 1964. He was a prolific and profound writer on *Halachah*, *Aggadah*, and *Cabbala*, and 81 of his articles appeared in the rabbinic periodicals *Sinai*, *Hapardes*, *Hadarom*, *Talpiyot*, and *Kol*

Torah. He published a commentary on the Passover *Haggadah*,[11] and reprinted the works of his grandfather and uncle to which he added long introductions. His son, Rabbi Joseph (1918–91), and three daughters survived him.

RABBI FINKELSTEIN

'The sun also rises and the sun goeth down,' says Ecclesiastes.[12] This verse can be applied to the Cricklewood area. When Rabbi Leiner emigrated to the United States, the void was soon filled by the establishment of a *shtiebl* by Rabbi Finkelstein. Though not a blood-relation of the Radzyn–Isbice dynasties, as was Rabbi Leiner, he was, nevertheless, heir to the Radzyn tradition.

Rabbi Issachar Dov (Beresh) Finkelstein was born in Radom, Poland, the son of Alexander Ziskind, a Chasid of Radzyn. He eventually became the Rabbi in Novozivkov, Russia, and for nine years he was on the city council of Chelm, later holding the presidency of the Jewish community for 25 years, as well as being the head of the *yeshiva*. Through his wife Sarah he was related by marriage to the dynasties of Crimilov, Sochaczev and Radomsk. He was thus, through family links and study, totally immersed in Chasidism which he loved with fervour and joy. He was a devoted disciple of Rabbi Samuel Solomon Leiner (d. 1942), a protagonist of the Radzyn–Isbice Chasidic school, and he was one of the very few men in England to wear *techelet* (the cord of blue) in the ritual fringes.

Rabbi Leiner arranged for him to come to England in 1935 and, at first, he lived for over a year in Gateshead, then in Newcastle from whence he travelled to supervise the baking of Bonn's *matzot* in Carlisle. Later he moved to Leeds where he worshipped in the *Chasidische* Synagogue where he conducted *shiurim*.[13] He left Leeds for London in September 1947 and opened a *Shtiebl Keser Torah* at 62 St Gabriel's Road, Cricklewood.[14]

Cricklewood was then a still-growing Jewish community, receptive to *shtieblech*. It was the location not only of the Premishlaner Rebbe, but also of the *shtiebl* of Rabbi Zevi Hirsch Friedman (1886–1960), formerly minister in Tredegar, South Wales, and in Manchester,[15] who came to England as a young man and lived in Leeds. He was sent to study at a *yeshiva* in Hungary where he obtained *semicha*. His *shtiebl* in Dollis Hill existed until he was knocked down by a car while crossing the road near his home.

The Dollis Hill *Beth Hamidrash*, at 152 Fleetwood Road, was originally established by a Mr A Eisenberg, and was later guided by Rabbi Gershon Henoch Yudeleib (1901–81), the son of a Radzyner Chasid. Furthermore, Rabbi Melech Spira was the rabbi of the Willesden Synagogue, and the Reverend Abraham Schechter (d. 1958) was the reader of the Cricklewood Synagogue. Reverend Schechter was a native of Warsaw who studied at the Lomza *yeshiva*. He was a Chasid who had learned his *chazanut* at the Court of the Rebbe of Ger, to which he remained loyal.[16] He came to England after the First World War and served as a Cantor at Commercial Road Great Synagogue, Newcastle-upon-Tyne, Southend and Westcliff, before he became the Reader of the Cricklewood Synagogue in 1930.

In addition, the Reverend Joseph Kacenelenbogen (1917–73) was inducted as Cantor of the *Ohel Shem* Federation Synagogue by Rabbi Kopul Rosen on 7 September 1947. The son of a Chasidic Rebbe, Rabbi Aaron of Serotzk (d. 1927), he was a descendant of Rabbi Yitzchak of Neshchitz. When his father died, he and his brother Baruch (who later became a judge in Tel Aviv) were very young, yet the two of them became 'boy' rebbes in Warsaw. Crowds would gather around them to watch how they conducted themselves. Joseph was one of the survivors of the Warsaw Ghetto from where he escaped together with his brother and sister Zipporah and reached the Holy Land in 1941. For a time, he was the cantor of the Hurvah Synagogue in Jerusalem. After joining the Polish Army, he came to London and married Connie Greenstock in November 1947. He occupied positions as cantor in the New Road Synagogue, East London, and Croydon, South London. In 1961 he settled in Israel where, for a time, he was cantor in Jerusalem, later at the *Beth Haknesset Yehoshua ben Nun* in Tel Aviv, and finally at Holon. In 1973 he was killed in a motor accident.[17]

Moreover, the warden of the *Ohel Shem* Synagogue was the Chasid Elchanan Chanan (d. 1975), a former vice-president of the Federation of Synagogues. Among the notable Chasidic residents was Rabbi Simon Baumberg (1872–1940), the District Supervisor of the Board of Shechita. He was a native of Lodz and studied under Rabbi Moses Baruch Cohen of Isbice. He was authorised by the Chief Rabbi to decide on ritual matters regarding *schechita*.[18]

It did not take Rabbi Finkelstein long to make an impact on the area. His encyclopaedic knowledge of Chasidism, of Radzyn in particular, soon manifested itself. His followers were impressed by his fascinating discourses, his humanity and immense learning. He was visited by

Mrs Rivkah Schatz-Uffenheimer, the author of *HaChasidut KeMistika* (Chasidim as Mysticism). 'She is a truly remarkable woman,' was the Rebbe's verdict.[19] He was often consulted by Shalom Zalman Shragai, the religious Zionist leader, later mayor of Jerusalem, a member of the Jewish Agency Executive, a devout Chasid of Radzyn and the author of a number of works on this subject.

In October 1954, the Rebbe was instrumental in the setting up of the *Yeshiva Keser Torah*.[20] At first, it was in temporary premises at the *Ohel Shem* Synagogue, later it moved to a permanent home on the premises of the North West London Jewish Day School, at 180 Willesden Lane.[21] Students aged nine and upwards received advanced tuition in Bible and Talmud on weekday evenings and on Sundays. The principal was Rabbi Simcha Lapian, the rabbi of a congregation in Mile End. Advanced students attended a *shiur* every Friday evening at the home of Rabbi Finkelstein.[22]

Chief Rabbi I Brodie was the guest of honour at a festive *melave malka* held at the Cricklewood Synagogue to mark the conclusion of the Tractate *Baba Kama*, when a number of boys delivered *Halachic* discourses.[23]

In 1957, Rabbi Finkelstein was appointed by the *Machzikei Hadath* for the purposes of supervising *kashrut* and *shechita*.[24]

Though he shunned publicity, he none the less protested vehemently that Liberal and Reform rabbis had been allowed to take part in the Tercentenary Service held at the Bevis Marks Synagogue on 22 March 1956. In a letter to the *Jewish Chronicle* he wrote:

> There could have been no objection to inviting the leaders of any sect to be present at such a service; but to have asked the spiritual heads of the Liberal and Reform communities as such, to participate in the service by carrying Scrolls of the very Law against which, in the main, they militate, is repugnant to traditional Judaism. Such participation by Liberal and Reform ministers who incidentally wore their canonicals for the occasion, implies recognition of their ecclesiastical status within the Jewish religious community and must give rise to much perplexity in the mind of the average layman, particularly as they were given the same rabbinical title as their Orthodox colleagues.[25]

In another letter he quoted Rabbi Joseph B Soloveitchik of Boston:

> From the Torah standpoint, the gap between Reform and Orthodoxy is much greater than the distance that separated the Pharisees from the Sadducees in the time of the Second Temple, and the Karaites from

traditional Jews in the days of the Geonim. The doctrines of the Liberal and Reform sects cannot be regarded as a form of Judaism . . . Any act of fraternisation in religious matters with the liberal and reform communities is an implicit recognition of their status within the Jewish religious community.[26]

Apart from the *yeshiva* he established a Talmud circle which met every Thursday. Despite the fact that he belonged to the old world, he made a great impact on a number of young people who changed their way of life due to his influence and guidance.

The Rebbe's most striking characteristics were his gentleness, his willingness to listen to all opinions, his profound understanding of the motives of men and, above all, his total immersion in and love for Jewish learning. He was always delving into the commentaries of the great thinkers. While everyone in his house was sleeping, he would sit reading and evaluating the great works into the early hours of the morning. He loved repeating Chasidic sayings and experiences to groups of his friends and followers. He was at his best and most inspired when giving discourses sitting around the table with members of his congregation. Quotations from the Bible, the Talmud and the Zohar, and tales of Chasidic dynasties, would flow from him in a wonderful and apparently never-ending flood. He spoke in a gentle, melodious voice, with a glow of holiness on his face, which appeared to be filled with unearthly inspiration. He had a special gift of fascinating young people with the romance of mysticism, and he won their affectionate regard. His influence had a far-reaching impact and won him outstanding acclaim as the 'Torah-Jewel of Cricklewood'.

The Rebbe contributed many articles to Torah journals. He died during *Sukkot* 1977, and was buried in Enfield.[27] He was survived by his second wife, Ela, two sons, one of whom is Joseph Finklestone, formerly Foreign and Diplomatic Editor of the *Jewish Chronicle*, and by two daughters. One of his sons-in-law is Rabbi Nathan Vengroff, at one time the rabbi of the Brondesbury Synagogue.

Despite the death of the Rebbe, the *shtiebl* survived under the dual guidance of Rabbi Chune Unterman (son of the late Chief Rabbi of Israel) and Rabbi Myer Frydman. The Rabbi's Chasidic library was handed over to Rabbi Schneebalg of Edgware.

At a *siyum mishnayot* held on the tenth anniversary of the Rebbe's death at the *Beth Hamidrash* of Rabbi David Halpern in Hendon on 25 October 1987, Rabbi Chune Halpern strongly urged the publication of the Rebbe's unpublished works.[28] He had written on Nachmanides, on *Mai Hashiloach* and on other Cabbalistic works.

RABBI JACOB HESHEL

Heir to a long line of Chasidic rebbes, Rabbi Jacob Heshel, who spent 32 years of his life in London, never became a rebbe, but exerted a beneficial influence on a wide circle of friends. A modest and tolerant man, completely devoid of ambition, he was, as the rabbi of the *Adath Yisrael* Synagogue in Edgware, a true shepherd to his community.

Rabbi Heshel was the son of Rabbi Moses Mordechai (1873–1917) of Pelcovizna, near Warsaw, a direct, fifth-generation descendant of Rabbi Abraham Joshua Heschel of Opatov, known as the *Ohev Yisrael*. Heshel's grandmother, Rachel Leah, after the death of her first husband, Rabbi Abraham Joshua Heschel of Miedzyboz, married Rabbi David Moses Friedman of Czortkov, and it was there that Jacob's father, Moses Mordechai, was brought up. He married Rifka Reizel, the daughter of Rabbi Jacob Perlow of Novominsk, a twin sister of Rabbi Alter Yisroel Shimon Perlow of Novominsk, a scion of the dynasties of Berdichev, Koretz, Karlin and Chernobyl.

Jacob was born on 18 March 1903 in Minsk–Mazowiesk, Poland. He was only 14 when his father died, and he and his widowed mother, brother and four sisters moved to Warsaw, to 40 Muranowska Street. The Rebbe of Novominsk greatly influenced the orphans. 'His life,' observed A J Heschel, the brother of Jacob Heshel

> was consistent with his thought . . . He was a complete person. Not one minute of the day was allowed to pass without attempting to serve God with all of his strength. He gave himself over to a tremendous task: the service of the Almighty at every moment with every act. An ordinary Afternoon prayer by him was like the Day of Atonement prayer elsewhere, and on the Sabbath, as he put each morsel of food into his mouth, he would say, *Lekoved Shabbos Kodesh* (to honour the holy Sabbath). The Novominsker was truly an extraordinary man.[29]

'The picture I have in my mind is of a perfect Zaddik,' wrote Rabbi Yedidya Frankel, the former Chief Rabbi of Tel Aviv. 'His profound wisdom, his constant learning, the depth of his Cabbalistic mastery, his majestic face, the smile which never left his face, his love of all Israel, his refusal to utter a critical word about another, were unforgettable.'[30]

Jacob Heshel studied at the *Mesivta Yeshiva* in Warsaw. The *yeshiva* was established in 1919 by Rabbi Meir Dan Plotsky, the Rabbi of Ostrowiec. No one was accepted there unless he was able to master unaided a page of Talmud and commentaries. Unlike other *yeshivot*, the *Mesivta* devoted two hours each day to the study of the Polish language, mathematics and history. Jacob Heshel obtained *semicha* from Rabbi Horowitz of Stanislaw and Rabbi J Rosen of Romania.[31]

Heshel's sister married Rabbi Abraham Joshua Heschel, the Rebbe of Kopyczynica who later made his home in Boro Park, New York. When his brother left Warsaw to study in Vilna and subsequently in Berlin, Jacob went to Vienna to stay with his sister. In 1931, he married his distant relative Sarah, the daughter of Rabbi Nachum Mordechai Friedman of Czortkov, who then lived in the ninth district of Vienna, but settled in Israel in 1939.

In 1939, Rabbi Jacob Heshel came to London. He first served as an education officer of the Board of Orthodox Jewish Education and for the *Ben Zakkai* Youth Organisation, established by Rabbi Dr Victor Schonfeld. In 1949 he succeeded Rabbi A Babad as rabbi of the Edgware *Adath Yisrael* Congregation which was then at 21 St Margaret Road, Edgware, and later moved to enlarged premises at 261 Hale Lane. In addition to these duties he was rabbinical district supervisor for the London Board of *Shechita*. He helped to edit the homiletical book *Doresh Tov* by Rabbi Nachum Mordechai of Czortkov.[32] He also contributed an essay on the 'History of Chasidism in Austria'[33] and wrote a number of other articles for the Federation of Synagogues' periodical *Hamaor*.[34]

He died on 3 *Tevet* 1971 and was buried in Enfield.[35] A new hall in Edgware was dedicated to his memory in May 1983. He is survived by an only daughter, Thena (Kendal), who is a producer for the BBC. His brother, Abraham Joshua Heshel, who during his short stay in London established an Institute of Jewish Learning,[36] was later professor of Mysticism at the Jewish Theological Seminary in New York, and one of the most distinguished Judaic scholars of the twentieth century. He exerted a great influence on both Jewish and non-Jewish thought throughout the world. He contributed major works on the Bible, Rabbinics, Chasidism, theology and ethics.

ABBA BORNSTEIN

Abba (Abraham) Bornstein (1900–79) was a patriarchal figure with a long, flowing beard and an imposing countenance. He was not a rebbe himself, but he was a lifelong and dedicated Chasid of Rabbi Shlomo Chanoch HaKohen Rabinowitz of Radomsk.

Born in Frankfurt-am-Main, he was the eldest of seven children. His family originated from Cracow and settled in Germany after the First World War. Abba came to England in 1931. He became a very successful businessman. At a time when so many people were complacent and indifferent he helped numerous Jewish refugees to come and settle in this country. Many people alive today owe their lives to his foresight and willingness to help. During the war he found accommodation for many evacuees from the London bombings in Letchworth where he owned property. He supported the establishment of prayer houses and study circles there. He was a man who had the means and above all the willingness to help. On his return to London after the termination of the war he worshipped at the Cricklewood *Hashkamah* service where he was the officiant for the morning service, covering the entire service in the record time of 29 minutes.

He identified himself with almost every cultural and Zionist activity. His presence graced every Zionist congress and conference. He was a lifelong supporter of the *Hapoel Hamizrachi* and the *Mizrachi*, and served for decades as chairman, governor, treasurer and trustee of many organisations. He saw in *Mizrachi-Hapoel Hamizrachi* the only framework for religious Jews. He identified himself with Weizmann's Zionism which advocated a policy of 'dunam after dunam'. He associated himself with the group of religious Zionists *Oz VeShalom* and he was worried lest the activities of the *Gush Emunim* might falsify the basic ideas of Jewish ethics. In 1944 he wrote in the Mizrachi journal *Chayenu*: 'What mental aberration to think that Zion can be built on a foundation desecrated by the spilling of human blood.'[37]

Abba justified his attachment to religious Zionism in these words:

> History has proved that the policy of the Mizrachi in joining and being an integral part of the World Zionist Organisation from the beginning, was the right one. We were there from the start and we made our voice heard. While the land was being bought dunam by dunam from the Turks, we safeguarded Jewish values among the people who did not care for them. So when the State was established we had a right to be heard and be listened to.[38]

In 1971 he opposed the decision of the Board of Deputies to amend Clause 43 of its Constitution to establish the right of Progressive religious leaders to be consulted on all religious issues concerning them. He resigned from the Board where he was vice-chairman of the *Eretz Yisrael* Committee, having been a deputy since 1938.

Abba was one of the founders of Judith Lady Montefiore College at the Brodie Institute in Golders Green, established in 1952, a joint activity of the Torah Department of the Jewish Agency and the Spanish and Portuguese Jews' Congregation in London. It was a matter of great satisfaction to him that over 200 former students of the college became active as rabbis, headmasters and teachers in several countries.

He was also active in the Bachad Fellowship, the Yeshiva *Etz Chayim*, *Mifal HaTorah*, *Machzikei Hadath*, World Jewish Congress, World Zionist Organisation, and the North West London Jewish Day School. When he died, his valuable library was divided between *Mosad Harav Kook* in Jerusalem and the Sephardi Community in Lauderdale Road, London.

RABBI SAMUEL SPERBER

'Even a Scroll of the Torah in the Ark', says the Zohar, 'needs *Mazal*.'[39] This aphorism applies to Rabbi Samuel Sperber (1904–84). Learned and erudite, he was not taken up by the Anglo-Jewish establishment and never obtained an academic post either at Jews' College or at a university. His father, Rabbi David of Brasov, the author of *Michtam L'David*,[40] was a Chasid of Rabbi Moses Hager of Kossov. Brought up in such a Chasidic and learned milieu, it is not surprising that Samuel wanted to be a rebbe.[41]

He came to London in 1934 and stayed for some time at the home of the Trisker Rebbe, addressing his congregation on the High Holy Days.[42] For three years he was the rabbi of the Brondesbury *Chevra Torah* at 9 Brondesbury Road, London at a salary of £1 per week. Among his learned congregants were Dr Adolph Buchler, the principal of Jews' College, and Dr Simon Rawidowicz. During the war he acted as spiritual director of the Mizrachi *Hachshara* Centre at Crwych Castle, Wales, and then lived for some time in Manchester where he studied at the Department of Semitic Studies, at the same time being the head of the Manchester *Merkaz Limmud Torah* (Jewish Study Centre).

With the financial help of his brother-in-law, Mechel Rabinowitz, Sperber moved to London in 1945, and became the spiritual guide to Abba Bornstein and Alexander Margulies. He maintained that we live in order to serve God, our fellow-men and poor people who are in dire need of unselfish service.[43] His literary output in Hebrew, English,

Yiddish and German was very considerable and included a volume of *maamarot*.[44]

In 1948, Sperber became the director of the Department for Torah Education and Culture of the Jewish Agency and was involved with the Judith Lady Montefiore College. 'A Chasid,' he maintained, 'was not, as some might suppose, a person isolated from Jewish society, or from the affairs of the common people. He might seem, in his extremism, to be an isolated human being, but he exerted a conscious influence and was a tremendous force for the moral future of a society.'[45] On his retirement in 1971 he settled in Jerusalem. Chief Rabbi Lord Jakobovits described him as a 'scholar and saint, a leader and a thinker. I cannot think of anyone who, in his unique way, has contributed more to the richness of our religious heritage than he.'[46]

RABBI MOSHE ROKEACH

Rabbi Moshe Rokeach was born in 1891 in Vanovitch, a descendant of Rabbi Shalom of Belz. In 1930, he came to London where he established a *Shtiebl Kehillat Moshe Anshei Belz*. His wife, two sons and two daughters joined him in 1936, and they lived at 8 Fairclough Street.[47] During the war they moved to 69 Sidney Street. He was closely associated with the Belzer *shtiebl* at 90 Commercial Road,[48] which, in 1936, amalgamated with Nelson Street Synagogue.[49] Very few of the congregation thus formed were Chasidim of Belz. In 1938 he moved to nearby 63 Cavell Street.

It was the custom of Rabbi Rokeach to send wine to his congregants for *arba kossot* (four cups) on Passover. He eventually became a wine merchant and began dealing in property. He moved to 46 Menelik Road, West Hampstead, and prayed at the Premishlaner *shtiebl*. He subsequently moved to 34 Ridgeway, Golders Green, and joined the Sassover *shtiebl*. In 1971, he went to Israel to attend a family celebration and spent the *Seder* nights with the Rebbe of Vishnitz. He died on 18 *Nisan* 1971 in Bnei Brak. His son Norman was for many years the *gabbai* of the Sassover *shtiebl*.

16 • The North-west Passage

After the end of the Second World War, the Jewish population of London moved in great numbers to Golders Green and Hendon. The extension of transport facilities, the high-quality, moderately-priced housing and the possibility of Jewish day schools in the area brought an influx of religious Jews. Of the 1,500 ultra-Orthodox Jewish families, nearly 400 are Chasidic, and the wearing of *shtreimlech* in Golders Green Road on a Sabbath is no longer a rare sight.

North-west London now has several boys' and girls' schools. There is a Lubavitch Senior Boys' Grammar School at Kingsley Way, Hampstead Garden suburb. Originally a small, privately owned school, it was so popular with Jewish parents that the headmaster, a non-Jew, felt compelled to sell out to Lubavitch. An extension was built in 1972, comprising extra classrooms, an assembly hall, a *beth midrash*, physics and chemistry laboratories and a gymnasium. The school provides a high standard of secular education integrated with Jewish studies. It has 50 pupils on the roll, and they are prepared to A-level standard. Most of the students are British-born, and in their free time devote their energies to activities within the community.

Tuition for boys is also provided by the Pardes House Junior and Grammar Schools. From 1979 both schools were housed in an Edwardian listed school building at 246–250 East End Road, Finchley. In 1991 the schools acquired for £2.5 million the former Christ College building, a Grade II listed building on a 2.2 acre site, a short distance from Golders Green.[1] The Pardes House Junior School was originally founded in 1953 with four pupils at premises in Sneath Avenue, and later moved to 181 West Heath Road. Over 500 children aged from three to 16 now attend the kindergarten, Primary School and Grammar School (established in 1974). In January 1991 the Grammar School returned to its original site at West Heath Road vacated by the girls' *Beis Yaakov* Junior School.[2] Eighty-five per cent of the boys come from north-west London, 40

144

coming from North London. The majority of children are taken to and from school by special buses, and many children are taught in temporary classrooms in the playground.

The spiritual leaders and founders are the Rebbe of Sassov and Reb Chune Halpern, who visit the School regularly and examine the pupils on their work. Only children of ultra-Orthodox families are admitted. A *Shacharit Minyan* takes place daily at 7.30 a.m.

Yiddish is the language of instruction for Jewish Studies, and half the school day is devoted to it. English language, French, history, geography, mathematics and physics are compulsory subjects in the grammar school, and are taught up to the GCSE-level examinations of the London University. The boys are highly motivated, and there is an examination pass rate of 80–90 per cent. Many complete the GCSE in at least five subjects by the age of 15. Recently 21 out of 26 pupils obtained five or more passes at grades A to C in this examination. An A-level syllabus of one year's duration is offered to the small number of interested pupils. Sporting activities are of low priority. The school day for the first three years finishes at 5 p.m., and for the GCSE and A-level classes not until 6 p.m. Occasionally extra classes are held on Sunday afternoons.

Hebrew studies are so designed that pupils will reach *yeshiva* standard. Intensive Talmud study from the age of nine develops the logical faculties of pupils, preparing them to feel at home in their subsequent further studies. Pupils are encouraged to continue their studies in Gateshead or Manchester for at least another four years.

The school has a well-equipped IBM computer laboratory, as well as a woodwork and design workshop where boys can acquire carpentry skills. There is also a commercial department that teaches accounts and business studies at GCSE and A-level. Certain subjects such as church history and geological structure are avoided and the National Curriculum is carefully scrutinised so that there is no clash with Jewish traditional teachings.

No school lunch is provided. The headmaster administers corporal punishment if pupils seriously misbehave. While half the secular subject teachers are non-Jewish graduates, the Jewish studies teachers are all graduates of *yeshivot* in England and in Israel, and are mostly from Chasidic backgrounds. The school is supervised by an Education Committee headed by Rabbi S Rubin, Rabbi C Halpern and his son, Rabbi David Halpern. They are responsible for appointing teachers and lay down the syllabus.

No child is refused entry to the school for lack of means. As a large number of parents are unable to pay the fees, the school has a large annual deficit, which is covered by donations from private donors, who include the Freshwater family and Mr William Stern, the Chairman of the Governors.

Though the spiritual leaders and a large number of teachers are Chasidic, the school also caters for the ultra-Orthodox and non-Chasidic element. Forty children come from the Munk community. The teachers maintain a neutral attitude, and in no way try to convert the children to Chasidism.

GIRLS' SCHOOLS

Two *Beis Yaakov* schools were established for the girls of the Chasidic and ultra-Orthodox community. The Junior School was founded with three children in 1972 in an attic of a house at 835 Finchley Road, next door to a hostel founded by the late Mr O Freshwater, and subsequently moved to West Heath Road, the premises vacated by the Pardes House Boys' School. It now caters for girls aged four to eleven plus, and has a roll of 320. In March 1991 it moved to the former Kilburn Polytechnic Annexe at 373 Edgware Road, Colindale, which was acquired for £3 million.[3]

The school was the brainchild of Mr Benzion Freshwater, who felt that a school to cater for 'lovers of the Torah' was urgently needed. It was the first single-sex primary school in north-west London, and admits only daughters of religious and observant parents. Though not labelled Chasidic or Agudist, the school attracts many Chasidic girls. The language of instruction is English and half the time is devoted to secular studies.

A girls' grammar school was founded in 1980 and is now established in two adjoining houses in Finchley Road, the property of the Freshwater family. The 220 girls on the roll, aged between 11 and 17, are divided into six classes. Nearly half of the school day is devoted to Jewish studies, and the girls take GCSE and A-level examinations in a variety of subjects. They are very highly motivated and their examination results are well above the national average. Modern Hebrew to GCSE-level is taught after school hours and Yiddish classes are held on Sunday mornings. Forty girls come daily by special buses from Stamford Hill. The girls are encouraged to go to a teachers' seminary, and to postpone taking a university course (if they so wish) until after marriage. Sacred studies cover Bible, Rashi, grammar and liturgy. Jewish history is taught up to the destruction of the Second Temple, and a special course of Jewish literature, which has been approved by the University of London, is available in place of the normal English literature paper.

The school prefers to have part-time staff, fully committed to Judaism, rather than employ non-committed Jewish full-time teachers, and has 30 part-timers on its pay-roll. In addition to its regular teaching staff, five visiting rabbis give special instruction. The girls continue their studies at seminaries in Gateshead, Manchester, Switzerland or Israel, and some return as teachers. A site in Bell Lane, Hendon, has been acquired for £1 million for the erection of a new purpose-built school.

The schools are not state-aided, and as some parents cannot afford to pay the full fees, there are large deficits each year in the junior and grammar schools. Their survival is in no small measure due to Mr Benzion Freshwater and his family, who take a tremendous interest in the affairs of the schools.

In September 1938, a few families started the Hendon *Adath Yisroel* Synagogue, and in 1940 Rabbi Mordechai Knoblewicz (1900–1982) became their spiritual leader. A native of Dobri, Kalish, Poland, he was a disciple of the Chasidic scholar, Rabbi Meir Dan Plotzki, and though he lived for many years in Germany, he remained a Chasid of Ger. In the synagogue, however, he conformed to Ashkenazi ritual. However, no *tachanun* was recited on the seventh day of *Adar*, the *yahrzeit* of Moses. 'For Moses, our teacher', he said, 'is surely greater than any Chasidic rebbe.' He had expert knowledge of Chasidic folklore, and he resented very much a view expressed by secular historians that Israel Baal Shem Tov was a pious *am haaretz* (unlearned). 'It is inconceivable', he said, 'that the *Maggid* of Mezeritch, an outstanding talmudical scholar of his generation, could have sat at the feet of an *am haaretz*.'

The first *mikveh* in Hendon was established at 10 Shirehall Lane by the Biala Chasid Abba Myers.[4]

The *Adath* community accommodates the Skoler *Beth Hamidrash*. In 1942, Rabbi Israel Rabinowicz (d. 29 *Elul* 1971) established the *Ohel Israel Skoler Beth Hamidrash* at 29 Green Lane, Hendon. It had a membership of 60 and later moved to Shirehall Lane. The Rabbi was a son of Rabbi Baruch Pinchas Rabinowitz of Skole, a prolific writer and a descendant of Rabbi Yechiel Michael of Zloczow. Rabbi Israel married the daughter of Rabbi Mordechai Zusya Twersky. He reprinted his father's works.[5]

Rabbi Israel came to London from Vienna before the outbreak of the Second World War where his family had lived since 1914. Afterwards, in July 1948, he left for Miami Beach, Florida where he became known as the 'Kishinever Rebbe'. The *shtiebl* ultimately affiliated with the Hendon *Adath Yisroel* Synagogue, Brent Street, where it is housed on the first floor of its building, and maintained as an independent, self-financing *minyan* using Chasidic liturgy. Rabbi Knoblewicz even permitted the *minyan* to have *hakafot* on the night of *Shemini Atzeret*. *Shiurim* were originally given by the late Rabbi Leib Rakov and his son Rabbi Lippa, and this tradition is continued by Rabbi Mordechai Rabin.

Another *shtiebl*, *Beth Avraham* at 46 The Ridgeway, was formed by the late Abraham Goschalk (1884–1961). A native of Warsaw and a Chasid of Grodzisk, he was trained as a *menaker* (porger) in Poland. On his arrival in London he worshipped in Black Lion Yard, and when he opened a butcher's shop in Mare Street, he prayed at the *Yavneh* Synagogue, 25 Ainsworth Road, Hackney, under Rabbi (later Dayan) M Fisher. Owing to a controversy, he later joined a splinter group in King Edward's Road, Hackney, and when he moved to north-west London in 1945, he worshipped at the Kielcer and Sassover *shtieblech*. When he lost the use of his legs, he started a *shtiebl* in his house. This *shtiebl* now has 50 members, and is carried on by Rabbi S Schmahl, a teacher at the Hasmonean Grammar School.

The establishment of the *Beth Shmuel* Synagogue at 171 Golders Green Road was a landmark in the evolution of Chasidism in north-west London. The story is told that when Rabbi Ezekiel Halberstam of Sianawa, the author of *Divrei Yechezkel*, was in Marienbad, he heard a man calling his name: 'Rab Ezekiel'. The Chasidim were disturbed and felt that the right appellation should be 'Rabbi of Sianawa' or '*Divrei Yechezkel*', but the Rebbe, to their surprise, was not perturbed. 'At least,' he countered, 'someone still knows that I have a personal name.'

Similarly, Rabbi Chune Halpern is not known as the Rebbe of Radomysl, but simply by the name 'Reb Chune'. The verse in Proverbs, 'Find favour and good understanding in the eyes of God and man',[6] surely applies to Rabbi Chune. He was born in Kosice on 25 *Kislev* 1922, and was a grandson of Rabbi Shmuel Engel of Radomysl, one of the greatest Chasidic scholars of the inter-war years. Rabbi Shmuel was renowned for his immense scholarship and masterly ability to argue coherently. He generally adopted a lenient approach, and consequently hundreds of women who were left without definite evidence of their husbands' deaths were spared lives of loneliness and grief. His rulings were invariably upheld by his contemporaries. In fact, according to Rabbi Yosef of Rymanov, the rulings of the *Maharash*, as Rabbi Shmuel Engel was known, were accepted by the Heavenly Court. He was a prolific writer, and his work covers many volumes.

Rabbi Chune's mother, Mindel, perished in Auschwitz in 1944, and his father, who survived, died of typhus in 1945. Rabbi Chune studied under his grandfather, Rabbi Shmuel, until 1935, and then under Rabbi Saul Broch of Kosice. In 1939 Reb Chune came to London and stayed with Rabbi Joel Moskowiz, the son of the Shatzer Rebbe then in Leeds. In 1942 he married Hena Chayah Lidzbersky, originally from Frankfurt, whose grandfather was Rabbi Dov Yehuda Wallach. Rabbi Chune moved to 5 Oakfield Road, then to 18 Alba Gardens, Golders Green. Two years later he moved to 171 Golders Green Road, where eventually two adjoining houses were converted into a purpose-built synagogue.

The synagogue, with its 200 members, is open all day for prayer and study. There are four daily *shiurim*. It was Rabbi Chune who founded Pardes House School and is the Honorary President of the Union of Orthodox Hebrew Congregations. He follows the traditions of Sanz and Ropczyce, and has made it his life-work to reprint the works of his grandfather. He himself has written extensively for the rabbinic annual *Yagdil Torah* and is the author of a weekly Torah bulletin on homiletics and law. He is known for his great common sense and believes in fair play. Though held in high respect by all sections of the community, he is approachable and makes everyone feel at ease. He has five sons and four daughters. Two of the sons have established their own *batei midrash* within walking distance of his *beth hamidrash*: Rabbi David has his Hendon *Beth Medrash* in Brent Street, and Rabbi Chayim has a *Beth Hamidrash Divrei Chayim* in Bridge Lane.

One of the busiest of the Torah centres in Golders Green is the *Beth Hamidrash Yissochor Dov*, popularly known as Hager's *Beth Hamidrash*, at 2–4 Highfield Avenue.[7] On 14 November 1988, the Centre celebrated its jubilee at the Brent Town Hall. Hager's Centre is a beehive of activity, reminiscent of the old *Machzikei Hadath* in the pre-war East End of London. Four services take place consecutively every morning and evening. A three-and-a-half hour *kollel* for *Baalei Batim* (*Kollel Boker*) takes place between 8.30 a.m. to 12 noon. There is also a *Kollel Erev* from 6.30 p.m. until midnight, which is attended by past and present *yeshiva* students.

There is a *Chayim Meirim* Youth Group and a library for young people. Twice a day, at 6 a.m. and in the early evening, there is a *Daf Hayomi Shiur*. In 1975 a *kollel* was established on the premises of the *beth hamidrash*. There are now 12 regular students and another 12 attend frequently. It has a large annual budget, and has at its disposal two houses for student accommodation. In 1976 the first completion of Tractate *Pesachim* was made. Since then the *kollel* has completed another six tractates, and many leading scholars have delivered discourses. Among them have been the heads of the *yeshivot* of Gateshead, Ponevezh and Hebron. Many of its graduates now occupy positions in education and in the rabbinate.

The first one of the Hager family to come to England was Rabbi Shalom Hager of Storzhinetz. During the First World War, Rabbi Shalom had a *minyan* in Staudingergasse, Vienna. On his arrival in England just before the Second World War, he formed a *shtiebl*, first in Blenheim Gardens, Willesden, then in Belsize Road, Swiss Cottage. He died on 14 *Sivan* 1950, at the age of 75 and was buried in *Nachlat Yitzchak* in Israel.[8] He was survived by three sons, Eleazar (d. 1968), Mechel and Moshe who did not continue in the rabbinate. He was thus the last representative in the male line of a famous family of Chasidic rebbes who played a great part in Eastern European life and in Yiddish folk legend.

The rabbi who put Hager's on the map of Chasidic life in London was Rabbi Issachar Dov Berish Hager (1877–1967), the son of Rabbi Yitzchak Yaacov David of Storzhinetz, Bukovina, a scion of Kossov and Vishnitz. He married his cousin, Sheine Rachel, of Pecenezin, Galicia, the daughter of the wealthy merchant Avish Kaner. He served the community in an honorary capacity and during the First World War, in common with so many other rebbes, he found refuge in Vienna, where he established a *Beth Hamidrash Beth Yitzchak*. In 1932 he succeeded his father as Rabbi of Storzhinetz.

Through the initiative of a Chasid, Meshullem Scharfstein (d. 1944), and Rabbi Yehuda Hirsch Hager of Stamford Hill, the North-West *Sephardishe* Synagogue was opened in 1938, and its first task was to bring Rabbi Issachar Dov Berish, his wife and his mother, to London. He was soon followed by his two sons.

The *shtiebl* started in rented premises on the second floor above a shop on the corner of Alba Gardens and Golders Green Road. A Talmudical study group was soon formed. In 1940, he moved to 4 Highfield Avenue, and in 1960 the *shul* was extended to accommodate the growing number of worshippers. He refused to take Restitution money from Austria, calling it 'blood money'. He constantly avoided the limelight and spent his years in London in prayer and study.

The Rebbe died on 20 *Kislev* 1967. He had been Rebbe for 36 years, the first seven in Vienna, the others in London. He was succeeded by his eldest son, Rabbi Herschel (Zevi). Rabbi Herschel, who combined his diamond business with the rabbinate, died in 1972 at the age of 64. His younger brother, Rabbi Mendel, is the titular head of the community.

Rabbi Herschel was survived by two sons, Gershon and Yankel. Gershon, who became the Rebbe – one of the few native-born English rebbes – was educated at the Hasmonean Grammar School. He continued his studies at the Gateshead and Hebron *yeshivot*. He has 11 children and is a member of the *Beth Din* of the Union of Orthodox Hebrew Congregations.

His younger brother, Rabbi Yankel, gives three *daf hayomi shiurim* daily.

In the mid-1970s, the *Beth Hamidrash* acquired the adjoining house and while extensive rebuilding took place, the Sobel Centre in Beverley Gardens served as temporary premises. The new *Beth Hamidrash* opened in 1980.

In the history of Chasidic *Shtieblech* it has not been uncommon for *ahavat Yisrael* (love of one's fellow-Jew) to give way to *sinat chinom* (hatred without cause). This does not apply to Hager's where Rabbi Mendel and his nephews, Rabbi Gershon and Rabbi Yankel, work in harmony and in close proximity – *kinat sopherim tarbeh chochmah* (rivalry between scholars increases wisdom).[9] Rabbi Gershon is prominent in creating a Hager Chasidic empire, while Rabbi Yankel concentrates on maintaining a high standard of learning, and Rabbi Mendel efficiently supervises the administration. In the words of Rabbi Gershon:

> From the Jewish point of view, Golders Green is a really vibrant, alive area, and it is becoming stronger all the time with an ever-increasing resurgence of orthodoxy . . . There was a great need for a place somewhere in Golders Green where local people, many of whom are former *Yeshiva* students, could come and continue their studies for a few hours when they have the time.

17 • The Jerusalem of England

Rabbi Abraham Yeshayahu Karelitz once described Kiryat Vishnitz as the spiritual guardian (the *mezuzah*) of Bnei Brak. He predicted that its Torah institutions would warm and illuminate the Holy Land. Whilst the Hager family in north-west London, the real descendants of Vishnitz, primarily concentrate on adult education, the Chasidim of Vishnitz in Stamford Hill are making tremendous progress in the education of the young.

In 1986, the Vishnitz Community acquired the Stamford Hill *Beth Hamidrash*, Lampard Grove (formerly Grove Lane), originally established in 1916, whose spiritual leaders in the past had been Rabbi Bloch, Rabbi Dr E W Kirzner and Rabbi S Rabinow. With the help of the local authority, central government and Inner London Education Authority Youth Service, more than one million pounds was spent in adapting the premises for their present use, and the centre was opened by the Vishnitzer Rebbe, Rabbi Moshe Hager, on 25 January 1987.[1]

The Vishnitz Talmud Torah *Chayim Meirim*, founded in 1980 with five pupils, now has over 200 pupils between the ages of three and 14, and is divided into nine classes. Half the school day is devoted to sacred studies which are conducted in Yiddish, the rest of the time is spent on secular subjects: English, mathematics, geography and history, which are taught in English. A number of young children know over 400 *mishnayot* by heart. Pupils in the top four classes arrive at 7.30 a.m. for morning service and breakfast. School starts at 9 a.m. and ends at 6 p.m. On Sunday, classes are held from 9.30 a.m. to 5.30 p.m. Vishnitz plans to build a kindergarten for the under-fives on land belonging to the school, part of a disused engineering works.[2]

Vishnitz also has an expanding Junior *yeshiva*, headed by Rabbi Pinchas Schneebalg, a son of Rabbi Menachem Mendel Schneebalg, the Rabbi of the Manchester *Machzikei Hadath*. So far, there has been no provision for the higher education of girls.

Vishnitz, like Belz, is not a unified community. Those who follow Rabbi

Mordechai Hager, the second son of Rabbi Chayim Meir, now living in Monsey, New York (a Chasidic settlement 30 miles from Manhattan) have their own *Beth Hamidrash* at 21 Upper Clapton, consecrated by the Rebbe in May 1972. (This had previously been the *shtiebl* of Zydaszew under Rabbi Naftali Labin who emigrated to the United States.) In 1991 Rabbi David Hager, the son of the Monsey Rebbe, was appointed its spiritual leader and its adherents follow the ideology of Satmar.

Today, among the prominent supporters of both branches of Vishnitz is Chayim Moshe Feldman, born in Satmar in 1934. During the Second World War, Chayim Moshe found refuge in the Holy Land, where he stayed until 1956. He married Devora, a daughter of Getzel Berger, and afterwards settled in London. Both Rebbes of Vishnitz are welcome in his house.

Vishnitz in London goes back to the immediate post-war years. In 1947, Rabbi Baruch and Rabbi Chayim Meir Hager of Vishnitz participated in the *Aguda* Conference held in London.[3]

The first Vishnitz *minyan* was established at 97 Stamford Hill (now the home of the *Aguda*) and subsequently at 2 Colberg Place, N16. Later, in 1978, it moved to the more spacious premises at Numbers 87 and 89 Stamford Hill. The present spiritual head of the *minyan*, which is attended by more than 70 congregants on the Sabbath and on weekdays, is Rabbi Shraga Feivish Schneebalg. His father, Rabbi David Zevi, was formerly the head of the *Beth Din* and principal of the *yeshiva* of Vishnitz. He can trace his descent back to one of the first pioneers to introduce Chasidism to Moldavia and Bukovina, Rabbi Chayim Tyrer, or, as he was popularly known, Rabbi Chayim of Czernowitz. He well deserved the name of 'the man of the Sabbath', as legend has it that when Rabbi Chayim emerged from the ritual bath on Friday afternoon and donned his Sabbath garments, his height increased, and he was said to have become a head taller.

The Schneebalg family lived through the Russian invasion of Poland in 1939 and the subsequent German occupation of 1941, when the entire family was taken to Transnistria. Rabbi David Zevi came to Manchester and became the rabbi of the *Machzikei Hadath* in 1947. Sixteen years later, he settled in Bnei Brak where he died in 1968. His son, Rabbi Menachem Mendel, succeeded him in Manchester.

Rabbi Shraga Feivish studied under his father and under Rabbi Weingarten in Staines. He also spent one year in the Chebiner *yeshiva* and received *semicha* from Rabbi S Rabinow, Rabbi Selig Reuben Bengis and Rabbi D Sperber of Braszov. In 1954, Shraga Feivish married

Freidel, the ony daughter of Rabbi Moses Munt (1895–1958). A native of Russia, Rabbi Munt had succeeded his father Rabbi Eliezer as rabbi of Mikolayev. In 1935, he settled in Paris and found refuge in Switzerland during the Second World War. In 1952, he came to London, where he established a *Beth Hamidrash Damesek Eliezer* in north London. He was the editor of a rabbinical periodical *Olat Chadash* (Paris, 1949) and worked on *Toldoth HaRabbanim*, a biographical dictionary of rabbis and authors throughout the world.

Rabbi Schneebalg is a prolific writer. It has been said that one needs a whole bookcase to accommodate his printed works. No other rabbi in England, apart from Rabbi H Ferber, has produced so much. In all he has published 22 books, ranging from responsa to *Halachic* works. He is known for the remarkable breadth of his knowledge.

In 1988, Rabbi Schneebalg's son, Rabbi Eliezer Lieber, opened a Chasidic *Shtiebl Machzikei Hadath* in Edgware. Between 40 and 70 people attend services and his religion school has 90 children in seven classes.

In June 1988, 120 people attended a *seudah shlishit* at his *shtiebl* to mark the visit of the Ratzforter Rebbe, Rabbi Yoel Beer from Sao Paulo, Brazil, a descendant of the Besht. On 21 July 1988, 300 people attended the Edgware United Synagogue to watch Rabbi Israel Chayim Weisz of Spinka conduct a *tisch*. 'The establishment of a *mikveh*', said the Rabbi, 'can hasten the coming of the Messiah.'

In January 1967, the *Mesivta* Talmudical College – one of the foremost *yeshivot* in England – moved into its new purpose-built palatial home in Cazenove Road, North London. It was established in the early 1940s by Rabbi Pardes, Rabbi Yankl Hornstein and Rabbi Melech Rumpler in a few rooms in Manor Road. It soon moved to Cazenove Road under the leadership of Rabbi Abraham Rand, ably supported by Messrs G Oestreicher, Z Matyas, H Diamond and P Herzka. It receives an annual grant from the Central British Fund in London.

Despite the growth of Chasidism in London, the prominent Chasidic rebbes did not establish courts here. Chasidic rebbes regularly visited London, but none settled here permanently. In this respect London cannot compare with Bnei Brak or Boro Park. The nearest rebbe whom post-war Chasidim would consult was Rabbi Moses Isaac Gevirtzman (1882–1977) of Antwerp, popularly known as 'Reb Itzikel'. He was a descendant of Rabbi Elimelech of Lejask and was known as a miracle worker. He was the most venerated *zaddik* of post-war Europe and many Chasidim from London would frequently make their way to Antwerp to consult him.

RABBI YIDELE HOROWITZ

Rabbi Yidele Horowitz of Dzikov, who spent his last years in London, had been reluctant to become a rebbe. 'There are so many rebbes,' commented the late Rabbi Joel Teitelbaum of Satmar, 'who do not merit to be rebbes, and yet one who is so worthy to be a rebbe refuses to act as one.' 'Reb Yidele', as he was popularly known, was born on 18 *Elul* 1905 in Dzikov. His mother was Chava, the daughter of Rabbi Israel Hager of Vishnitz, and his father was Rabbi Alter Yecheskel Eliyahu, who perished in 1943 in Plaszow near Cracow. Rabbi Yidele was his only surviving son. 'Thousands of souls waited for him to be born,' said his proud grandfather. He studied for five years under Rabbi Meir Arik of Tarnow who greatly admired him: 'No one can compare with him in Galicia,' he said. Yidele was brought up in the house of his grandfather, Rabbi Israel ben Baruch of Vishnitz, and in 1928 he married his cousin, Channa Miriam Sima, the daughter of Rabbi Chayim Meir Hager. After ten childless years he divorced her, but they then remarried and once again divorced. She subsequently married Rabbi Weisz of Jerusalem.

Rabbi Yidele was a great admirer of Rabbi Moses Sofer (1762–1839), known as the *Chatam Sofer*, whose seven-volume responsa of that name he knew almost by heart, as well as his sermons and novellae on the Talmud. His works never left his desk, and he used to say, 'the *Chatam Sofer* speaks to my heart'. He encouraged Rabbi Joseph Naftali Stern of Hungary to publish these works, giving up his own dowry for this purpose. Rabbi Yidele was ordained by Rabbi M. Arik and by his uncle, Rabbi Chayim, and by Rabbi Chayim Eleazar Spiro of Munkacz. At the age of 30, Rabbi Yidele was appointed *dayan* at Klausenburg. In 1939, at the outbreak of war, he was in the spa town of Krenice. He returned to the Dzikov Ghetto and then to Cracow. He subsequently lived in Arad, Bucharest and Klausenburg, and miraculously survived the Holocaust.

In 1947, he settled in Israel, first in Tel Aviv where he was befriended by Rabbi A Y Karelitz, then in Jerusalem in *Rechov* Hosea. Here he was highly respected by Rabbi Joseph Zevi Duschinsky, the rabbi of the separatist Orthodox community of Jerusalem. 'I have never found a person with whom I could converse in both Halachah and Mysticism as I can with Rabbi Yidele,' said Rabbi Duschinsky.

His uncle, Rabbi Eliezer Hager, urged him to become a rebbe and to continue the great traditions of Dzikov. He himself gave him a *qvittel*. Rabbi Yidele, however, was adamant. He categorically refused to allow people to treat him as a rebbe, though he acted for a time as principal of the *Kollel Tarbitza* in Jerusalem.[4] His discourses lasted three to four hours. He would concentrate on just two or three pages of the Talmudic tractate *Chullin*, studying it in great depth.

From 1985, he lived in London at 10 Jessam Avenue, Stamford Hill, as the honoured guest of Eliasz Englander, the son-in-law of the late Getzel Berger. He hardly ever spoke, nor did he deliver any discourses, but spent his days in study and prayer. However, he regularly officiated even in London as a *sandek* (the one who holds the baby at a circumcision) and would himself put *tefillin* on *bar mitzvah* boys. He used the liturgical ritual with a Cabbalistic commentary edited by Rabbi Shneur Zalman of Liady.

Rabbi Yidele was an ascetic who lived a very frugal life. He would eat meat only on the Sabbath, and during the week he never ate bread. In honour of the Sabbath he himself would wash some of his clothes. The moneys showered upon him by his admirers and Chasidim were immediately distributed to orphans and widows. 'I am terrified', he would say, 'of the sighs of a broken-hearted widow.' He was greatly concerned about the material well-being of the underprivileged.

He died at the age of 84 on the 11th *Sivan* 1989. He left no will or final instructions. After much heart-searching and telephone communications with relatives in Israel and in the United States, he was, on the advice of Rabbi C Padwa, interred at Enfield *Adath Yisroel* Cemetery, and not in Jerusalem or at Vishnitz, Bnei Brak. The elaborate *ohel* erected over his grave at the back of the Prayer Hall is frequently visited by all sections of the Chasidic community.

The Rebbe left many unpublished writings, glosses on the works of Moses Sofer,[5] on *Toldot Yaakov Yosef* by Rabbi Jacob Joseph of Polonnoye, on the responsa of Rabbi S M Schwadron and on the works of Rabbi Chayim Joseph David Azulai.[6] His nephews, of Boro Park and Bnei Brak, took over his printed Hebrew books, and original autograph manuscripts. His *shtiebl* at Jessam Avenue was closed down one year after his death.

RABBI MESHULLAM ISSACHAR ASHKENAZI

The doyen of post-war Chasidic rebbes in London was Rabbi Meshullam Issachar Ashkenazi, the Rabbi of Stanislav. Though he lived in Vienna and in London for the best part of his life, his ways remained unchanged.

His entire day was devoted to prayer and study. He was a true full-time servant of the Lord, conveying his message through gentle persuasion. Though a great friend and blood relation of the late Rabbi Yoel Teitelbaum of Satmar, who stayed in his house when he visited London, Rabbi Ashkenazi was not heir to his temperament. He was a disciple of Aaron, 'a lover of peace and a pursuer of peace'. No Chasidic gathering in London was complete without his benevolent presence. No manifesto was ever issued without his signature. Despite physical handicaps and much discomfort, he endeavoured not to vary his way of life. He was greatly helped by the warmth and love of his wife, children and grandchildren. His grandson supported him when he held the *Kiddush* cup and prayer book. With patience and resignation he served the Almighty. He followed the traditions of Belz.

He was born in Stanislav (now Ivanov Frankovsk), a city in the Ukraine, which, until 1918, was under Austrian rule. In May 1919, units of the pogromist Joseph Heller entered the city and went on the rampage. The family took refuge in Kolomyja, in Satmar and in Budapest, eventually settling in Vienna, where Meshullam studied under Rabbi Steinberg of Brody and Rabbi Benjamin Katz of Braszov. In 1937, Meshullam married Esther, a descendant of Rabbi Uri Hakohen Yolles of Sambor.[7] After the Nazi occupation of Vienna, his parents returned to Stanislav, which came under German administration after the start of the Soviet–German war in 1941. In a ruthless 'action' on 12 October 1941, over 100,000 Jews were put to death in that region. His parents, too, perished in the Holocaust.

Rabbi Meshullam lived in Vienna under the Nazis until, through the intervention of the late Mr Getzel Berger, he was given permission to settle in Manchester in 1939 where he established a *minyan*.

In 1943, he moved to London, living first in Allerton Road, then for 20 years at 55 Lordship Park, eventually settling at 93 Lordship Park. In 1976, he won an appeal against the refusal of the Hackney Borough Council to grant him planning permission for the continued use of his premises as a synagogue. Both Rabbi Yoel Teitelbaum and Rabbi R Z Portugal had stayed in his home on their visits to London. He had two sons and three daughters. In 1977, he suffered a stroke and in 1989, at *Neilah*, a heart attack. He reprinted the *Siddur Lev Sameach*.

He died on 3 *Kislev* 1994 and was succeeded by his son Uri.

18 • The Power of Satmar

When the Rabbi of Ger came to town, it was in the nature of a state visit, surrounded by pomp and ceremony. Mr (later Judge) Neville Laski, the President of the Board of Deputies of British Jews (1933–40), gives an eye-witness account:

> An extreme instance of the power of the Rabbis is afforded by the 'wonder-working' Rabbis, who are almost worshipped by a section of the population. I heard much talk of the wonder-working Rabbi of Ger, and I managed to obtain ocular demonstration of his popularity. I went to see his arrival from his cure at Carlsbad, and was presented with a spectacle such as I had never imagined. Hundreds and hundreds of, to me, Mediaeval-looking Jews wearing strange hats and kaftans crowded on to the platform, alongside which steamed a train of the latest type, composed of *wagons-lits*. Excitement reigned supreme. I stood on a railway truck against a fence to obtain a better view, but soon repented, as a surging crowd, marching step by step with the Rabbi, nearly turned me and my truck into the roadway. Four policemen in front, four behind, and two on either side pushed a way through a seething and excited mob for a very small, bent old man who took not the slightest notice of the crowd of admirers who had come specially to see him, and went to a motor car, in which he was whisked away preparatory to his going to his *Nachkur* (convalescence).[1]

Laski's description came to my mind when I observed a similar scene, not in Warsaw, Poland, but in Hendon, north-west London, on Sunday, 16 July 1989, when Rabbi Moses Teitelbaum, the Rabbi of Satmar, arrived on a three-day visit to London. His host was Mr Maurice Markovits, a financial Management Consultant of Allied Dunbar, then living at 8 Holmfield Avenue.[2] The police cordoned off the street for three days and local residents could not use their cars. A marquee to accommodate 1,000 people was erected over an area of three gardens. Bus-loads of adults and children arrived from Stamford Hill and the crowds had to be controlled by security guards. It took nearly three hours of queueing before one could file past the Rebbe who sat at a table flanked by his entourage. Class by class, Satmar pupils under their respective teachers paraded in front of him. Each one was presented with a copy of a book by the late Rebbe of Satmar, *VaYoel Moshe*.

The following day the Rebbe participated in the completion of a Scroll of the Law donated by Mr Shalom Berger in memory of his father, Getzel Berger. A festive dinner for over 1,000 guests was held at the Stoke Newington Town Hall. Several million pounds were collected, at a dinner held at Mr Markovits's home, in support of a new Satmar *Talmud Torah* now being built in Williamsburg, New York, large enough to contain 60 classrooms. Notable rabbis from Lucerne, Antwerp, Zurich, Strasbourg and Manchester, came to pay court to him. Chief Rabbi Lord Jakobovits paid the Rabbi a one-hour visit.

This imposing spectacle was an indication of the growing might of Satmar in London and elsewhere. Satmar adherents form the most visually colourful and distinctive Chasidic group, the most vigorous of all Orthodox Jewish sects in the world today. The name Satmar has become an expression of strong partisanship, and is frequently synonymous with anti-Israel and anti-Zionist activities, aggressively defying general public opinion.

Within three decades, Satmar has surpassed numerically all other Chasidic groups. It is probably the fastest growing Chasidic sect of Stamford Hill. It has extensive backing which enables it to maintain and expand its educational institutions. Its supporters have the confidence and the self-assurance to counter opposition not only from their vociferous opponents but also from their fellow Chasidim. Unlike the Lubavitch movement, Satmar does not reach out and build bridges to the wider Jewish community. Though not hostile to outsiders, as often alleged, Satmar concentrates on the strengthening and expansion of its own community from within its own ranks.

Today in Stamford Hill, there are three Satmar *Batei Midrash*. A new *Beth Hamidrash* at 26 Upper Clapton, formerly the British Home for Deaf and Dumb Women, was acquired for £550,000 in 1985 after intense competition with the Belz community and a housing association.[3] It was opened by the Rebbe of Satmar in November 1988. This is in addition to the Synagogue *Yitev Lev* at 86 Cazenove Road. The nearest synagogue at 14 Heathland Road on the premises of the Squarer *Talmud Torah* also attracts a large congregation. Satmar also has a *Cheder Yitev lev* at 111 Cazenove Road attended by 350 boys from the age of three to 13, the language of instruction being Yiddish. Only two hours daily are devoted to secular study. There is a girls' school (*Beth Rochel*), a Junior *yeshiva* and a girls' seminary. Rabbi Chayim Meir Wosner, the son of the *Rosh Yeshiva* of Bnei Brak, is the spiritual leader of the London Satmar Community.[4]

Satmar arrived comparatively late on the London scene. Number 86 Cazenove Road was the *shtiebl* of Rabbi Parnes who was brought from Leeds by Yechiel Swimer and Saul Bodner. After Bodner's death the house was bequeathed to the *Yesosdey Hatorah* school, and in 1954 was acquired by Getzel Berger. It originally accommodated the Chasidim of Bobow, and it was not until 1962 that it became the first exclusive Satmar *shtiebl* in London.

ELIKUM GETZEL BERGER

The life and soul of Satmar was Elikum Getzel Berger. He was born in Toparoff, Galicia, in 1895, into a family who were devoted Chasidim of Alesk. Getzel studied under Rabbi Juda Greenwald who was the Rabbi of Satmar since 1898, and it was there that he first met Rabbi Yoel Teitelbaum. He also studied under Rabbi Yekutiel Aryeh Kamelhar.

Getzel lived for a time in Simleni, Romania, where in 1920 he married Bracha (1897–1993), the daughter of Issachar Berish Laufer, a Chasid and *dayan* of Dzikov. His first business endeavour was to export oil to Galicia. In 1923, Getzel, after a short stay in Berlin and Antwerp, arrived penniless in London. His wife joined him three years later, leaving behind their son Shalom, then five years old. Getzel, whose first home in London was at 28 Dunk Street, regularly worshipped at the adjoining Dzikover *Shtiebl*, where he felt at home and soon became the mainstay of the *shtiebl*. His other two sons, Mendel and Berish, were sent to study rabbinics in Hungary, and in 1930 Getzel moved to 22 Sidney Square, the former home of the Trisker Rebbe.

After many endeavours to eke out a meagre livelihood, he, together with a fellow-countryman who had come with him to London, Leibish Lempel, opened a garment factory trading under the name of 'Lempel and Berger' first in Arbour Square, later in Brick Lane, and then in Great Alie Street, where they employed outdoor workers.

In 1940, realising that torches were indispensable in a blackout, Berger, with the financial support of fellow Dzikover Chasid, Hershel Steinhart, set up a factory in Johnson Street, Stepney, and with the help of many religious workers produced 100,000 torch batteries each week. His son Berish, who was at that time in the Budapest Ghetto, was killed there in a bombing raid at the age of 16. Another son, Mendel, who had lived with his aunt in Hungary, reached Britain after the war.

At the age of 50, Getzel became a property tycoon by sheer accident. Due to the bombing of his home, he moved to Number 9 Myrdle Court in the East End of London, and at Succot was anxious to erect a Succah. The Jewish landlord would not give him permission to do so at first, so Getzel enlisted the good offices of his Gentile bank manager, Mr Smith, of the Stepney Branch of Barclays Bank in Commercial Road, and he persuaded the landlord to grant this request. It was at the manager's advice that Getzel later acquired Myrdle Court, his very first property acquisition. He was a shrewd judge of character. Estate agents, surveyors and bank managers respected him for his common sense, his formidable mastery of detail and natural flair for business. He was determined always to accomplish what he planned.

The Bergers kept an open house, always crowded with visitors and *meshullachim*. His wife, during the London air raids, would distribute food to those who took shelter with the family in Tilbury, Commercial Road, giving each their dietary requirements. When Rabbi Yoel Teitelbaum escaped the Nazi inferno, Getzel regularly corresponded with him and became not only one of his most generous supporters but also his devoted Chasid. He wholeheartedly supported the Rebbe's institutions in New York and in the Holy Land.

Getzel was a man of immense compassion, and he never forgot his humble beginnings. He was responsible for countless unobtrusive good deeds, and he enabled many newly arrived refugees to set up in business by recommending them to his banks, and guaranteeing loans and mortgages. There was scarcely a Torah charity with which he was not connected. He was one of the founders and constant supporters of the *Mesivta Yeshiva*, *Yesodey Hatorah* Schools and the Jewish Secondary Schools Movement. From 1943 to 1947 he was the President of the Union of Orthodox Hebrew Congregations.

In 1952, he accompanied the Rebbe of Satmar to the Holy Land and stayed with him there for 11 days. On his return to London, Berger uncharacteristically wrote to the *Jewish Chronicle*, stating:

> Reports have been published in the press to the effect that the Satmar Rebbe, in the course of his call to religious Jewry not to take part in the voting at recent elections in Israel had offered $15 to every individual

who would obey his line of thought . . . I wish to state that to my knowledge these reports are completely without foundation.[5]

For the last 20 years of his life, Berger lived at 1–2 Warwick Court in Stamford Hill. By nature shy and retiring, he shunned publicity. He was a solitary and diffident man, whose hesitant manner belied a lively mind, and great strength of character. He lived an austere and disciplined life, as if unconscious of the great wealth he was daily amassing.

He died on the eve of *Yom Kippur* in 1977,[6] and is survived by his two sons, Shalom Zevi (Sigismund) and Menachem Mendel. Sigismund is one of the largest landlords in Britain with 100,000 rented units. His son Berish, born in 1957, continued, until recently, the family tradition of dispensing charity, which he did on Wednesday evenings from his home in Craven Walk. No one was turned away empty-handed.

The family has endowed charity trusts: *Trudene*; the Gershon Berger Association; and the Keren Association. These trusts distribute over £500,000 per annum to Torah institutions in Israel, England and the USA.

After the death of Getzel Berger the validity of the will was disputed by the family, and five rabbis tried unsuccessfully to settle the matter. It was brought before the British Court of Appeal, Civil Division, on 28–29 March and 21 July 1988.[7] The question was whether the estate should be distributed in accordance with his English will, dated 15 July 1975, or the Hebrew will of 6 August 1977. Lord Justice Mustill ruled that the Hebrew will should be admitted to Probate.

The four surviving children, two sons and two daughters with their husbands, give their allegiance to different Chasidic groups: Shalom and his sons belong to Satmar, and Mendel is a Chasid of Rabbi Yankele Leizer of Antwerp. He and his five children worship at Rabbi Padwa's *shtiebl*. Getzel's son-in-law, Eliyahu (Eliasz) Englander, a native of Crenice, at the age of eight, found refuge during the Second World War in Siberia. After the war he lived and worked as a diamond merchant in Antwerp. In 1952, he married Sarah, Getzel's elder daughter. He is an adherent of the *Old Belz Beth Hamidrash* in Bethune Road and was a staunch supporter of Rabbi Yidele Horowitz.

The descendants of Getzel Berger are brought up in the Chasidic way of life, and marry into well-known Chasidic families in Israel and the United States. Wealth has not robbed them of their natural humility. They are modest, unostentatious, approachable and utterly without pomposity.

RABBI YOEL TEITELBAUM

No Chasidic rebbe of the twentieth century has inspired both antagonism and veneration as has Rabbi Yoel Teitelbaum of Satmar (Satu Mare in north-western Romania). Brilliant and controversial, he was widely loved and is remembered as a saintly figure. Rabbi Yoel was a direct descendant of Rabbi Moshe Teitelbaum (1759–1841), to whom Chasidim attribute the soul of the prophet Jeremiah who lamented the destruction of the First Temple. Yoel was born in Sighet, Hungary, on 18 *Tevet* 1887. He studied under his father, Rabbi Chananiah Yom Tov Lipa and under a private tutor, Jacob Hirsch Turner. He accepted a rabbinical post in Yenice and moved to Orshove in 1911. Thirteen years later he became the Rabbi of Korolle Carei (Nagy Kallo) in Transylvania.

Though elected Rabbi of Satmar in 1929, he did not take up this position until 1934 owing to controversy, which he always seemed to generate. Until the outbreak of the Second World War, he devoted himself single-mindedly to transforming Satmar into a stronghold of Orthodoxy. There he served both as the local rabbinical authority and as a rebbe, and attracted a rapidly spreading following of Chasidim by virtue of his extraordinary piety, scholarship and religious, social and political leadership. His *yeshiva* had 350 students. His personal life, though, was beset with tragedy. Of his three daughters, two died before the Second World War, while the third, Chayah Rachel, died in New York after the war. His wife died in Satmar in 1936. Two years later he married Alta Feige Rachel, the daughter of Rabbi Avigdor Shapira, the Rebbe of Czenstochowa.

Within three months of Eichmann's arrival in Budapest, a total of 437,402 Hungarian Jews were deported to Auschwitz. Rabbi Yoel, together with his wife and beadle, Yosef Ashkenazi, escaped to Klausenburg in a Red Cross ambulance. On 3 May 1944, they were arrested and taken to the Ghetto of Klausenburg and then to Bergen-Belsen where they remained until December 1944. Dr Rudolf Kasztner, the vice-president of the Zionist Organisation in Budapest, and Joel Brand, a leading member of the Jewish Aid and Rescue committee in Hungary, were approached by Adolf Eichmann with an offer of 'Ware für Blut' (merchandise for blood). The Nazis offered to spare the lives of the 350,000 Hungarian Jews and even let them leave the country, if Brand were to obtain for Germany 10,000 army lorries, to be used on the Eastern Front, 80 tons of coffee, 20 tons of tea, 20 tons of cocoa, and two million bars of soap. Brand conveyed what he had been told but neither the Allies nor the Jewish leaders believed in the reality of the offer.

Kasztner negotiated for a special 'convoy' of 1,684 Jews, including the Rebbe of Satmar, to leave Hungary for a neutral country. The train, known as 'Noah's Ark', reached the Swiss border on 7 December 1944 (21 *Kislev*), now commemorated by Satmar Chasidim as a festive day. Through the efforts of the Chief Rabbi Y Herzog, the Rebbe was allowed to enter the Holy Land, where he arrived in 1945. He decided, however, to emigrate to Williamsburg, New York. Here he made his home at 554 Bedford Avenue, in which street many Hungarian, Czech and Romanian Chasidim had settled. He personally initiated and dominated every one of the numerous educational, social and economic activities of Satmar. No major decision was made without consulting the Rebbe.

The Rebbe established *Kehal Yitev Lev DeSatmar* which became a self-sufficient and cohesive entity. It has its own welfare network, including a holiday fund for orphaned children, employment agency, hospital clinic with female gynaecologists, an oxygen service, a special nursing service, a publishing enterprise which prints a weekly newspaper, insurance and pension schemes, an emergency rescue service and a burial society. It operates its own butcher shops and supervises the production of a variety of processed foods. The building, acquired by Getzel Berger, houses one of the largest *yeshivot* in the world. After completing the *Talmud Torah*, the children of Satmar continue their education in the *yeshiva*, and eventually in the *kollel*. The girls can choose between commercial and teaching diploma courses. With the exception of *Yeshiva* University, Satmar has the largest Jewish educational organisation in the western world.

Rabbi Yoel was the author of *VaYoel Moshe*,[8] *Kuntres Al HaGeula VeAl HaTemura*, and *Divrei Yoel*, a seven-volume commentary on the Torah and responsa, published posthumously. Rabbi Yoel was one of the most outstanding Chasidic leaders of his generation. Rabbis and rebbes gathered around his Sabbath table. It was not unusual for over 100 people to seek his counsel in the course of a single day.

He had a complex personality, uncompromising in religious issues, yet kindly, considerate and generous, with a keen sense of humour. Many Satmar Chasidim owed their financial success to a monetary gift from the Rebbe, whose acts of kindness were always imaginative and discreet. He was sought after by politicians. In 1968, Vice-President Hubert Humphrey called upon the Rebbe at his home in Brooklyn to discuss tensions between some black militants and the Jewish community. In March 1979, the Rebbe appeared at a rally in Madison Square Gardens to protest against a road project in Jerusalem which he considered would interfere with the observance of the Sabbath.

He believed that the Holocaust was a punishment for the Jews because they sought the path to redemption through political means – the implementation of the Zionist dream in the State of Israel. 'Only God can put an end to Israel's exile,' he asserted. Those who want 'to hasten the end' were rebels in his eyes. He referred to the Talmudical tractate *Kethubot* which states that the people of Israel were bound by an oath neither to revolt against the nations where they were held captive nor to try to hasten the end of the Exile.[9] As a result, he was a consistent opponent of the State of Israel.[10] He regarded Zionism as an evil creed and recommended that religious Jews should not vote in *Knesset* elections. He believed that the Promised Land for the Jews could only be established after the arrival of the Messiah. The years did not diminish this implacable belief, which he made public again and again. According to him, the establishment of the State was a dangerous interference with God's wishes. He objected to the secular character of the State and its use of Hebrew as an everyday language, but as Israel was no worse than any other country, he did not oppose individual Chasidim settling there.

He attacked the Israeli government's policy of enlisting women into the army. He instructed his followers not to visit the Western Wall in Jerusalem as long as it remained under Zionist domination.[11] Nationalism to him was an imitation of Gentile behaviour. At the time of the Hungarian uprising he advised a number of his followers against settling in Israel.

After the death of Rabbi Zelig Reuben Bengis (1864–1953), the Rabbi of Satmar became the spiritual head of *Eda Haredit* of Jerusalem. This includes the *Neturei Karta*, a group of about 300 Jews, who were led by the late Amram Blau. Blau, too, regarded Zionism as the product of false messianism founded on assimilationist ideologies.

The *Neturei Karta* view the secular State of Israel as a scandal, an abomination, and the Government of Israel as a government by Gentiles. They are convinced that Zionism is in direct opposition to all that constitutes Judaism, and they refuse to pay Israeli taxes.[12] Hebrew to them is a sacred language, used only for prayer. They do not vote and their young men do not serve in the army. They refuse to be registered as citizens or to accept identity cards. Amram Blau issued certificates to his followers which bore as a slogan a verse from the Scroll of Esther: 'And Mordechai did not bow nor did he prostrate himself before Haman.'[13] Their anthem is a poem 'The Lord is our King, and we are his servants. We do not recognise the state of heretics.'[14]

The walls of the houses of *Mea Shearim* (the ultra-religious quarter) in Jerusalem are covered with posters. 'The decrepit walls of *Mea Shearim*', the Rebbe once said humorously, 'would have collapsed long ago, were it not for the posters that hold together the crumbling stones.'

Satmar organised protest meetings in Washington and London against the alleged desecration of graves during archaeological excavations in Jerusalem.[15] Banners saying 'Zionism is the enemy of Judaism' and 'Zionism does not care for the dead or the living' and 'Let our people rest in peace not pieces' were displayed by demonstrators in London's Kensington High Street close to the Israeli Embassy.

Rabbi Yoel visited London in August 1952. Nearly 200 Chasidim from Belgium, France and Austria joined him. At Dover he was greeted by 200 youths from the *Aguda* Camp at Bexhill-on-Sea.[16] Among the notables who welcomed the Rabbi were Rabbi Rabinow, Rabbi Dr Krausz of Leeds, Rabbi Babad and Rabbi Dr S Schonfeld. The five-day visit was one of the most impressive demonstrations of Jewish religious fervour seen in London for a long time.[17] Rabbi Yoel revisited London in June 1955, in June 1959 and in August 1965. 'There must be,' he stated, 'a strong body of Orthodoxy in the *Galut* (Diaspora) to reinforce the efforts of those who are waging the War of the Lord in the Holy Land.'[18]

The Rebbe condemned television as one of those things which brought an unholy atmosphere into the home, enabling a person to see profane things without even having to go outside the home. Rabbi Yoel died on 26 *Av* 1979 and was interred in *Kiryat Yoel*, in Monroe, New York State, a Chasidic colony which Getzel Berger helped to establish.[19] He was succeeded by Rabbi Moshe, the son of Rabbi Chayim Zevi Teitelbaum (1880–1926) (Rabbi of Sighet and the author of *Atzei Chayim*, a treatise on the festivals[20] and other works).[21] Rabbi Moshe was born in Sighet in 1915 and brought up by his uncle, Rabbi Yoel. He was in Auschwitz and Theresienstadt concentration camps during the war. He eventually settled in New York and became known as the Rebbe of Sighet.

He is opposed by a very small minority of Chasidim and by Mrs Feige Teitelbaum, the widow of Rabbi Yoel.[22]

19 • Lubavitch – A Global Challenge

Lubavitch is one of British and world Jewry's most dynamic movements. In 40 years it has become a household word. No other section of Chasidism receives so much publicity in the Jewish and non-Jewish press. No one can deny the selfless dedication of its emissaries who are to be seen everywhere.

The name Lubavitch is derived from the town of that name in Russia where the movement originated. Unlike other Chasidic groups such as Satmar who are completely withdrawn from the mainstream of Jewish life, Lubavitch Chasidim use every means to communicate with their fellow Jews. They argue, they persuade, but they do not denounce. Their zeal is truly evangelical. Though scrupulously Orthodox, the Lubavitch movement never slights other less committed Jews. Every Jew is potentially a prospective Lubavitch Chasid. The love of every Jew is its basic tenet. Its aim is not to snatch souls from other types of worship, but to ignite the spark of Jewishness in those whose Jewish belief is not completely extinct.

In London there are 1,500 children, cared for by 80 teachers, in Lubavitch schools. The Lubavitch House Junior Boys' School is located at 135 Clapton Common. 'Our responsibilities,' states the head-mistress, 'are to become interested in and to care for each of the children individually, to seek and to bring out their good inborn traits.' In the primary school, Jewish Studies occupy half of the school day, and special assistance is given to pupils if required. The children are encouraged to be community-conscious by organised visits to the elderly and the disadvantaged.

The Lubavitch House Girls' Junior School is located at 105 Stamford Hill. Emphasis is placed on character development and social responsibility. The school has a gymnasium and a swimming pool. The Senior School was started with nine girls in modest premises at 113 Stamford Hill, and moved to Lubavitch House in 1964. Eleven subjects are taught to GCSE-level, and four to A-level standard, with a consistently high success rate. As a project, the pupils in the computing department set up a programme which presents an outline of the 83 *Halachot* (laws) from the *Mishneh Torah* by Maimonides.

There are over 250 families, many newly converted to Lubavitch, in London. Many more sympathise with the Lubavitch philosophy and way of life. 'We have sown a lot of seeds in the past few years,' said Rabbi Shragai Feivish Vogel, the director of Lubavitch in Britain, 'and we are now reaping a lot of benefit.'[1]

Lubavitch headquarters in Stamford Hill is their nerve centre. The extensive building-complex houses not only schools, but also a computer room, a bookshop, a library of over 7,000 volumes in Hebrew, Yiddish and English, a youth club and a synagogue. The Lubavitch Women's Organisation organises many activities for all Jewish women, irrespective of age or religious commitment. There are social and discussion groups, and *Mitzva* campaigns, promoting all aspects of Judaism, particularly *kashrut* and family purity.

There is hardly a facet of Jewish life which does not have the Lubavitch imprint. Their *tefillin* and *mezuzah* departments provide a service aimed at ensuring that the sacred texts inserted in the Tefillin and Mezuzot have not faded over the years. *Mitzva* campaigns distribute little cardboard *pushkes* (collecting boxes) to children to enhance their awareness of the need to contribute to charity with even the smallest amounts.

There are many Lubavitch teachers in part-time education in London, roughly ten per cent of the total. In some places, such as the Roding Hebrew Classes in Essex, nearly all the teachers are Lubavitch trained. Lubavitch rabbis serve United Synagogue communities in London and in provincial cities. Other Lubavitch rabbis serve in the Federation of Synagogues and the *Adath Yisrael*.[2] Their day-camps in summer reach thousands of non-Lubavitch Jews.

The founder of the Lubavitch dynasty was Rabbi Shneur Zalman (1747–1812), 'der alter Rebbe', as he was affectionately called. His teacher, Rabbi Dov Baer, the Maggid of Mezerich, encouraged him to compile a new *Shulchan Aruch* (Code of Jewish Law), and his work, the *Rav's Shulchan Aruch*, won high praise from his contemporaries. In 1773, after the death of the Maggid, he settled in Liozno. He was twice arrested and taken to St Petersburg by the Czarist authorities. He left a vast literary storehouse. His most important contribution to Jewish philosophy, however, was the *Tanya* (meaning literally 'it has been taught'), which was first printed in Slavuta in 1796 and has also been published with an English translation.

Rabbi Shneur Zalman has been described as the 'Maimonides of Chasidism'. He synthesised Lithuanian scholarship with Chasidic fervour. In his view, the intellect consists of three kindred faculties: *chochmah* (wisdom), *binah* (understanding) and *da'at* (knowledge); an acronym of the initial letters of these Hebrew words is an alternative name, *Chabad*, for Lubavitch. His son, Rabbi Dov Baer, settled in Lubavitch, White Russia, in 1814. He was known as the 'Mitteler Rebbe', i.e., the 'intermediary Rabbi'. During the benevolent paternalism of Czar Alexander I, the Rebbe strongly advocated agricultural settlements for the Jews of Russia. Like his father before him, he was unjustly imprisoned by the Russian government in 1826, on the charge that he had collected 300 roubles for the Sultan of Turkey.

He was succeeded by his son-in-law, Rabbi Menachem Mendel (1789–1866), who was known as the *Zemach Zedek* after the title of his works. He set up a special council to alleviate the sufferings of the Cantonists, the forcibly recruited Jewish child-soldiers. Special Lubavitch delegates regularly visited army groups to bring comfort and moral support to the young recruits and thus lessened the likelihood of conversion. He fought against the *Haskalah* movement, both in private and in public, and took steps to expand Lubavitch *yeshivot*. His successor, his son Rabbi Shmuel (1834–81), participated in discussions for Jewish welfare at St Petersburg and his strenuous attempts to improve the lot of his brethren resulted in his being placed under house arrest.

In the Lubavitch tradition, Rabbi Shmuel's successor, his son, Rabbi Shalom Dov Baer (1860–1920), continued to fight for equal rights for the Jewish community. He spent the years of the First World War in Rostov-on-the-Don, where he died. The educational initiatives of his son, Rabbi Joseph Isaac Schneersohn (1880–1950), aroused the suspicions of the authorities. He was imprisoned four times between 1902 and 1911. Neither the menace of the *Cheka* (secret police) nor the machinations of the *Yevsektzia* (the Jewish section of the Russian Communist Party) could discourage him. In *Sivan* 1927 he was arrested for the fifth time, confined to the Spalerno prison in St Petersburg, accused of counter-revolutionary activities, and sentenced to death. Protests were organised by world Jewry at the highest levels. A plea for clemency came from the President of the United States, Herbert Hoover. In response to international pressure, the death sentence was rescinded and, instead, he was banished to Kostroma in the Urals, and eventually, in 1928, permitted to leave Russia and to settle in Riga, Latvia.

In 1934, the Rebbe took up residence in Warsaw, and miraculously escaped the Nazi onslaught of 1939. He arrived in New York on 19 March 1940 and devoted the last decade of his life to setting up a framework for Jewish religious education. He founded the *Machne Yisroel Inc.*, and the *Merkaz L'Inyonei Chinuch*, devoted to strengthening Orthodox Judaism in America. The subsequent growth of the Lubavitch *yeshivot* in America has been truly phenomenal and quite unparallelled in the history of American Jewish education. The *Yeshivot* seek to instil into their students a readiness to put Torah and Judaism above everything else.

In the volumes of correspondence written by the Rebbe, published recently, there are a number of letters addressed to Chief Rabbi Dr Hertz.[3] In a letter dated 17 *Sivan* 1928, the Rebbe pleaded for an organisation to be set up on behalf of Russian Jewry,[4] and for an emissary to be sent to Russia.[5] He urged the proclamation of a fast day on the 22 *Elul*, on behalf of European Jewry.[6] He asked the Chief Rabbi to convey through the Russian Ambassador Maisky, the Jews' best wishes and seasonal greetings to Russian Jewry.[7]

He pleaded eloquently for the refugee children.[8] On 13 July 1944, in a telegram to the Chief Rabbi, he writes: 'I have learned from the Press reports of successful intercessions on behalf of the inmates of Bergen-Belsen. Please intercede also on behalf of the internee camp in France, among whom is the prominent rabbi Shabsai Rapoport.'[9]

RABBI MENACHEM MENDEL SCHNEERSON

When the Rebbe died on 10 *Shevat* 1950, his second son-in-law, Rabbi Menachem Mendel Schneerson, succeeded him. This Rebbe of Lubavitch was a central figure in the world of Torah and Chasidism. Born in Nikolayev on 18 April (11 *Nisan*) 1902, the son of Rabbi Levi Yitzchok and Chana Schneersohn, he was a grandson of Rabbi Menachem Mendel of Lubavitch. In 1928, the Rebbe married in Warsaw Chaya Moussia, the second daughter of Rabbi Joseph Isaac, and studied electrical engineering for a time at the University of Berlin and at the Sorbonne in Paris. After the Nazi occupation of France in the summer of 1940, he and his wife fled to Nice in the

South of France, and thence to the United States where they arrived on 23 June 1941. His father-in-law appointed him chairman of the executive committee of his newly-founded organisation *Merkaz L'Inyonei Chinuch*, the educational arm of the Lubavitch movement.

After the death of his father-in-law in 1950, Rabbi Schneerson reluctantly assumed the leadership of Lubavitch. The keyword *ufaratzta* found in the scriptual text in Genesis[10] – 'and thou shalt spread abroad to the west, to the east and to the north and to the south' – is the theme of a melody popular with Lubavitch Chasidim and became also the motto of the Rabbi. He excelled as an administrator of the Lubavitch empire no less than as a scholar. He was very attached to his aged mother and would start his day by bringing her milk, [11] spending the rest of his day in controlling and increasing the already far-flung and manifold activities of the movement. He extended its activities to north Africa, and now Chabad brings Chasidic teachings to the *Sephardim* of Casablanca, Marrakesh, Serfou and Meknes. His followers are obliged to devote themselves to 'spreading the fountain outside' by demonstrating to their fellow Jews the *mitzvot* of donning *tefillin*, kindling the Sabbath lights, pronouncing the benedictions of *Etrog* and *Lulav*, sounding the *shofar* and eating *shemura matza*.

A network of Lubavitch institutions has been established. Lubavitch disciples have organised a 'peace corps' to bring Judaism to Jews in many out-of-the-way places in the United States and elsewhere. These activities are organised as if they were a military operation with fleets of vehicles known as *mitzva* tanks. From *Merkaz L'Inyonei Chinuch* there emerges a stream of books, pamphlets and journals, designed for all age-groups, in Hebrew, Yiddish, English, French, Russian, Arabic, German and Turkish. Many volumes of the Rabbi's talks and writings have been published. Central among these are 26 volumes of *Likkutei Sichot* (collected talks). The Rebbe was forthright in his views, and very explicit on fundamentalism: 'If you can accept that God Almighty created billions and billions of atoms, why can't you accept that the Almighty created a human being?'[12] He has criticised the various scientific theories concerning the age of the world. 'The scientific speculation is actually a terminological incongruity. The discovery of fossils is not conclusive evidence of the antiquity of the earth.'[13]

Despite his advanced years and the massive heart-attack he suffered in 1978, the Rebbe used to answer the many letters he received every day. He never went outside the United States after his arrival there in 1941, nor did he ever take a vacation. Chasidim consulted him on every issue, personal or otherwise, as on marriage, health, work, relocation and other personal matters. He numbered many famous men among his followers, such as Menachem Begin, the former Prime Minister of Israel, who described the Rebbe as 'my spiritual leader'.[14] His charismatic personality was so strong that the Lubavitch Chasidim could not bear to discuss the possibility of a successor.

From his New York home the Rebbe used to intervene in many matters elsewhere, such as the Langer case: a brother and a sister by the name of Langer were declared to be *mamzerim* (children of an adulterous union) by a rabbinical court in Petach Tikvah and were not permitted to marry Jewish partners. In October 1972 Rabbi Shlomo Goren, then Chief Rabbi of Israel, declared that the Langers were not *mamzerim*. The Rebbe, in a five-hour telephone link from Brooklyn to Israel, declared Rabbi Goren's ruling to be invalid.[15] He also launched a world-wide campaign against the Israeli government's laws defining 'Who is a Jew'.[16] Judaism to him was a religion and Israel a geographical term. According to him, a secular institution like the *Knesset* cannot decide who is a Jew. That decision must be left to the experts in *Halachah*.[17]

He was opposed to all public demonstrations on behalf of Soviet Jewry, believing that they lead to 'the most terrible consequences for the countless Jews in the Soviet Union'. In his opinion, quiet diplomacy was the only means to achieve results.[18] *Chamah*, the international society to promote Jewish culture and traditions among Russian Jews, was allowed to work within the Soviet Union. In August 1990, 270 children from Chernobyl who had been exposed to life-threatening doses of radiation, following the nuclear reactor explosion in 1986, were airlifted to Israel where medical aid was provided.[19] In the Israeli general election of November 1988 the Rebbe intervened to instruct his Chasidim in Israel to vote for the *Aguda*, to the anger of many Jews everywhere.[20] He reaffirmed his view against terrritorial compromise as part of an Arab–Israeli peace settlement:

> The speculation that relinquishing of land for peace is desirable, is erroneous or naive.
>
> Any shrinking of Israel's vital borders would be mortally dangerous. It would encourage and facilitate incursions and acts of terror by uncontrollable elements, leading to loss of life and limb.[21]
>
> Today, the Jewish people demand an end to the exile. All the deadlines have already passed. It is time for the final and ultimate redemption through the Messiah. For over nineteen hundred years the Jews have

shouted '*Ad Matai*' (when will the Messiah come?). The previous Rebbe declared that 'all that was needed to prepare for the coming of the Messiah was to polish the buttons'.[22]

The Rebbe died on 3 *Tammuz* 1994.

LUBAVITCH IN ENGLAND

The beginnings of Lubavitch in England can be traced to Yochanan Moses Shapiro (1852–1915), a native of Warsaw, who, before the First World War, had a small Chabad *Minyan* at his home at 10 Raven Road, Whitechapel.[23] In the 1930s, Old Castle Street Synagogue was associated with Lubavitch and used the liturgy of Rabbi Isaac Luria. In 1933, Rabbi Abraham Rapoport (d. 1973) was its rabbi.[24] The synagogue was damaged in the war and never rebuilt. In 1945 H Chaikin was in charge of a small Chabad Synagogue at 158 Amhurst Road.[25]

Another Chabad *minyan* in London was established by Rabbi Yerachmiel Benyaminson. Known as the Zhlobiner Rav (d. 17 *Adar* 1955) he was born in Beshenkovitzy, Russia, and studied in the Lithuanian *Yeshivot*. He married the daughter of Rabbi Chayim Meir Green of Grobin, Kurland. After the death of his father-in-law, he succeeded him. In 1915 when the Jews were driven out of Kurland, he settled in Vitebsk, and was frequently arrested by the Russians for his religious activities as *mohel* and educator. From Vitebsk he moved to Zhlobin.

He arrived in London in 1935. After living in Letchworth during the war, he came to London and established a Chabad *minyan* at 112 Cazenove Road.[26] Later, on medical advice, he emigrated to Montreal, Canada. He sold his house in London to Reb Yankel Gurkov who maintained the Chabad *minyan*. When, some time later, Rabbi Benyaminson was preparing to settle in the Holy Land a motor accident aggravated his illness and he died. He was buried in New York, near the *ohel* of the Rebbe of Lubavitch in New York.

The founder of present-day Lubavitch in England was Rabbi Benzion Szemtov (d. 1975). He was a native of Warsaw who, while working for Lubavitch in Russia, was arrested in 1927 and sentenced to six years' imprisonment in Siberia. His wife joined him there. He left Russia in 1947 in the company of a number of Lubavitch Chasidim. They settled in Paris. When he was given the responsibility for extending Lubavitch activity in Britain in 1948, he settled in Cazenove Road, and turned the front room of his home into a *cheder*.[27] He sought out children who were getting no Jewish education in this country to foster Lubavitch ideology, and he established a *Talmud Torah* in Hackney.[28]

Esther Golda, his wife, initiated activities for women. After her death in 1963, Rabbi Szemtov began to travel abroad. His missions took him to the USA, Canada, South America and Israel. On his last visit to Israel, he was killed in an accident outside Kfar Chabad. Of his surviving four sons, two are engaged in Lubavitch activities in Detroit and Philadelphia.

'The Lubavitch movement took the initiative in presenting itself as a movement for the regeneration of our people, and has gone out – having adopted modern commercial methods and fashioned them for its own purpose – to sell Judaism. In that field it has proved a successful supermarket – even a mail order business,' said Sir Isaac Woolfson on 19 May 1968, on opening the London Lubavitch Centre.[29]

In 1981, Lubavitch organised four days of study and discussion of Jewish Mysticism.[30] More than 1,500 men and women of all ages and from all walks of life participated. On 29 January 1979 Lubavitch organised the second European Convention of *Neshei U'Bnot Lubavitch*. Over 900 Jewish women attended the week-long convention at the Regent Centre Hotel, London.

The Lubavitch Council for Universities and Colleges sends out emissaries who organise *shabbatonim* for the students. The first took place in Cambridge in 1966.[31] Students are also invited to spend a Sabbath with Lubavitch at Stamford Hill, in order to experience a Sabbath atmosphere. A number of Cambridge students have taken part in the 'Ivy League' programme of summer study at the 'Lubavitch *Yeshiva*' in the Catskill Mountains in New York State.

In pursuance of its policy of 'going out', Lubavitch emissaries visit the Jewish blind to enable them to hear the *Megilla* (The Book of Esther) on *Purim*, they visit hospitals on the New Year to blow the *shofar* for those unable to attend synagogue services, they distribute hand-baked *matzot* on Passover and arrange for people to recite the blessings over the *lulav* and *etrog* on the festival of Tabernacles. Similarly, the women distribute *Chanukah* gifts to children in hospitals and orphanages, and send *shalach manot* (gifts) to sick people on *Purim* and extra food for the needy on Passover.

In 1988 in Greater London, a fleet of 40 cars publicised the miracle of *Chanukah* in a strikingly dramatic way. Each vehicle carried a *menora*, and giant *menorot* were lit opposite the Hilton Hotel in Park Lane, at Edgware Station, at Golders Green station, at Tibbets Corner roundabout, on the north side of Wimbledon Common, at Redbridge round-about at Gants Hill, outside Hove Synagogue at New Church Road, and at Whitestone Pond, Hampstead.

In 1989, a £2 million appeal was launched to enable the movement to make contact with the 20,000 children in non-Jewish schools. £900,000 was raised towards this at the thirtieth annual dinner of the Friends of the Lubavitch Foundation.[32]

The Rebbe called for the establishment of Chabad Houses in as many areas as possible; these centres to serve as focal points to attract young people to a wide range of activities. 'You will not need to go and seek out each individual Jew,' said the Rebbe, 'for they will flock to the centre to pray, to study Torah or to contribute to charity.'[33]

The Chabad Centre at 372 Cranbrook Road, Ilford, was opened in 1987, in an area which has a large Jewish population. A wide range of activities are carried out and a growing number of people attend its 'Project Return', the adult education programme in which men and women can increase their knowledge of Jewish observances. Lubavitch is endeavouring to attract the youngsters who lounge about the parade of shops around Gants Hill roundabout, and who are at risk from drug-pushers and missionaries of other religions seeking converts.

There are still 6,000 Jews living in the East End of London, and a number of young people are moving back. Lubavitch has been granted a lease by the trustees of the Congregation *Kehillat Yaakov* to establish a Chabad House in the upper part of their premises at 351–3 Commercial Road, for which they are charged a nominal rent. From there Lubavitch emissaries are conducting a door-to-door campaign, endeavouring to bring back unaffiliated Jews living in the area, as well as in the newly developed Docklands region.

The latest Chabad Centre was opened in Wimbledon for the many Jews of south London who may feel cut off from Jewish communal life.

In Edgware, Lubavitch is using a converted ambulance as a new *Mitzva* Tank. At the conclusion of every Sabbath this 'Tank' may be found at Edgware station, ready to spread the Chabad message to the many young people who congregate there at that time.

In the last few decades the Lubavitch Foundation has justified its promise to provide a religious education for Jewish children of every background.[34] It does not ban fraternisation between the Orthodox and the less Orthodox, nor does it approve the erection of barriers between the various sects of the community.

20 • Belz – A Centre of Torah

The first Rebbe of Belz, Rabbi Shalom Rokeach, once promised his Chasidim that Belz would remain a centre of Chasidism, Torah and the fear of God until the advent of the Messiah. This promise has been fulfilled in the Holy Land, in New York and in London.

During the nineteenth century, Belz, a small town in the Lvov area, became the court of a famous Chasidic dynasty. What Ger was to Poland, Belz was to Galicia. 'The whole world,' the Chasidim of Belz used to say, 'journeys to Belz.' The rebbes of Belz underlined simplicity and sincerity as the fundamentals of the good life.

The founder of the dynasty, Rabbi Shalom (1803–55), devoted himself to the fight against *Haskalah*. Chasidim came to him from Galicia, from Hungary and from Poland. He refused to compromise with the reformers, categorising as heresy the slightest deviation from the traditional path. 'Days are coming,' he warned his Chasidim, 'when to rear a son in the Torah and the fear of God will be as hard to accomplish as the *Akeidat Yitzchak* [the sacrifice of Isaac].'

He was succeeded by his fifth and youngest son, Rabbi Joshua (1825–1904). The latter was the first Chasidic rebbe to engage in politics. He formed the *Machzikei Hadath* organisation in Galicia in 1879. This was the first attempt by Orthodox Jews to unite for political action to protect their traditional way of life. A bi-monthly paper *Machzikei Hadath* appeared in both Hebrew and Yiddish. Like his father, Rabbi Joshua continued building extensions to the *Beth Hamidrash* of Belz, and it became a tradition for every rebbe of Belz to enhance its structure.

The third rebbe of Belz, Rabbi Issachar Dov (1854–1924), denounced every attempt to introduce secularisation. He was kind and courteous and humane. With his blessing Sara Schenierer opened the first *Beth Yaakov* school for 20 girls in a tiny room at 1 Catachina Street in the Jewish quarter of Cracow in 1923.[1] Thus was founded a movement whose alumni were to become the upholders of Jewish tradition and the opponents of assimilationism and subversive socialism.

In 1925 Rabbi Aaron (1878–1957) succeeded his father. Like his ancestors, he was a man of many and varied interests, and his influence was far-reaching. Despite the efforts of many rabbis, he declined to support the *Aguda*. He participated, however, in a meeting called in 1930 by the rebbes of Ger and Alexander to protest against the pernicious efforts of the Polish Ministry of Education to undermine Jewish religious schools. He lived a life of self-mortification.

For four perilous years, 1940–44, the Rebbe lived precariously in Nazi Europe, moving from Przemysl to Vishnitz, to Cracow and to Budapest. He changed his name, first to Singer, then to Twersky, in order to confuse the Germans who pursued him relentlessly. His seven married children, his wife and 26 of his grandchildren all perished in the Holocaust. When his son Moses was killed, the Rebbe remarked: 'It was kind of the Almighty to have kept me alive to enable me to offer such a sacrifice.' Not one of his court of *yoshevim* (residents) remained alive. Through the intervention of Chief Rabbi I Herzog, he and his brother, Rabbi Mordechai of Bilgoraj, arrived in the Holy Land on 9 *Shevat* 1944. After a brief stay in Haifa, the Rebbe settled in Tel Aviv. His great attachment to the Land impressed all sections of the community, and his personal example stimulated a wave of Chasidic immigration from many countries.

He died on 21 *Av* 1957 at the age of 79. He was succeeded by his nephew Issachar Dov, known as Berele, who was born on 8 *Shevat* 1948, the son of Rabbi Mordechai. His father died when Berele was only two years old, and he was buried in Tiberias. Berele was educated at the *yeshiva* of Belz, and in 1965 married Sara, the daughter of Rabbi Moses Hager of Vishnitz. The wedding was attended by 30,000 people from all over the world. On his wedding day, Rabbi Berele was showered with *qvittlech* by his Chasidim.

Following his ordination and marriage, Rabbi Berele was encouraged to take over the leadership of Belz. On Shabbat *Nachamu* 1966 (the Sabbath of Comfort) when the prophetic portion begins with the words: 'Comfort ye, comfort ye, My people,'[2] Rabbi Berele became the Rebbe of Belz. From then on, he made his home in Jerusalem. Unlike his uncle, Rebbe Berele is highly organised and his religious services are held at the appointed times. Some of the older Chasidim have misgivings about him, maintaining that the countenance of Rabbi Aaron 'was like that of the sun, and that the face of [Rabbi Berele] is like that of the moon'.[3] However, Rabbi Berele has been accepted by most of the Belz Chasidim as a true heir to the crown of Belz.

He has expanded the *yeshiva* and has established a *kollel* for *baalei teshuva* from Russia, and girls' schools – *Beth Malka* – which now have over 1,500 students. Belz institutions include a number of *Talmud Torah* centres and *yeshivot.* 'We have to do it,' says the Rebbe, 'to enable our children to be reared in the spirit of Belz.' In 1984, the foundation stone of a colossal synagogue and world centre of Belz was laid in Jerusalem.

After the Second World War a number of prominent Chasidim of Belz in London, such as Elimelech Rumpler (d. 1985), a native of Vienna, Chayim Nata Katz (d. 1987) and Moshe Nachman Gross worshipped in the Shatzer *shtiebl*, because the Shatzer Rebbe himself was a Chasid of Belz, and it was out of deference to him that no Belzer *shtiebl* was established in his lifetime.

In 1957 a house was purchased at 97 Bethune Road, and, later on, the adjoining house for the establishment of a Belz centre. A compulsory purchase order by the local authority, affecting 20 houses including the Belz centre, was rescinded through the intervention of Councillor Josef Lobenstein, who was backed by letters from Chief Rabbi Brodie and the local member of Parliament, David Weitzman. In 1967 the foundation stone for the rebuilding of the Centre was laid with the participation of Dayan Padwa, Rabbi Itzikel Gewirtzman of Antwerp and Dayan I Weiss of Manchester.[4] The complex, completed in 1968, comprises dormitories for 50 students, a dining room seating 120, self-contained flats for teachers, a *matza* bakery and a *mikveh.*

The Centre houses a *Yeshiva* where the voice of Torah is heard daily from 8.30 a.m. to 9.30 p.m.; a *Talmud Torah* which caters for 200 children up to the age of eleven; an evening *kollel* that provides facilities for those who cannot attend during the day, and a place of worship that has several *minyanim* daily.

Belz, like Ger, Lubavitch and Alexander, has always followed one Rebbe. Unlike other dynasties there was no room for splinter movements, and younger sons submitted to the hegemony of the eldest. When Rabbi Berele became the Rebbe, a number of dissidents under Israel Jacob Klapholtz of Bnei Brak did not accept the Rebbe's writ. This spirit of dissension affected the Bethune Road Centre which now no longer accepts Rabbi Berele as its spiritual mentor. It gives its support to Rabbi Joshua Rokeach of Bnei Brak, the great-great-grandson of Rabbi Issachar Dov Rokeach of Belz and a descendant of the Machanovka and Chernobyl dynasties. In February 1984, Rabbi Joshua together with *Dayan* Padwa dedicated a *Sefer Torah* in the home of Elimelech Rumpler. The Centre is supported financially by Eliasz Englander.

The followers of Rabbi Berele acquired in 1972 a house at 27 Leweston Place, Stamford Hill, and began with a congregation of 30 and with a mere eight children in the *cheder*. To meet an ever-growing need, a *yeshiva* was established in the adjoining house.

In 1982, in the presence of Rabbi Berele, the headquarters of the 'new' Belz Chasidim was opened at 'Woodlands', 96–8 Clapton Common, in the heart of Jewish north London. It consists of several mansion-like houses, set in more than an acre of ground, between Craven Walk and Overlea Road. 'We should endeavour,' said the Rebbe, 'to bring up a generation of children who will not be ashamed to hasten the coming of the Messiah.'[5] The new edifice comprises a place of worship where regular discourses are given and a *Talmud Torah Machzikei Hadath* with over 300 children, divided into ten classes, where pupils are encouraged to learn chapters of the *Mishna* by heart. There is also a junior *yeshiva* and an early-morning *kollel* where study commences at 6 a.m. A girls' school, *Beth Malka*, established in 1981, now has over 200 pupils and is housed separately in Heathland Road.

The community recently acquired a large site of 30,000 square feet at Margaret's Works, Eastside, situated between Alkham Road and Margaret Road. Hackney Council has granted them permission to develop part of the former engineering works to rehouse the girls' school. The spiritual head of Belz in London is Dayan Yosef Dov Babad, the son of the late Rabbi Abraham Babad.

An offshoot of the main Belz Synagogue was established in 1991 in a converted house at 49 St Kilda's Road, Stamford Hill. The new place of worship not only has a *mikveh*, but it will also house the Belzer *Kollel* which hitherto did not have its own premises.

The children attending Belz schools, like other Chasidic school-children, are taken to and from school by minibus. Corporal punishment is not used. Jewish studies lessons are conducted in Yiddish and cover *Chumash* (Pentateuch), Mishna and Talmud. Secular studies are restricted to six hours per week, spread over five days. There is no discipline problem, no bad behaviour in class and no graffiti on the walls. There is an exceptionally high attendance record. A prize system is used to encourage the thorough acquisition of essential knowledge. There are no set fees, but parents are called upon to contribute according to their means. By the age of seven the boys are studying *Mishna* and are already familiar with Rashi's commentaries. At the age of nine, they have progressed to the study of the Talmud.

Pupils learn English as a second language, just as Welsh pupils do in Wales. Children are forbidden to watch television under the threat of expulsion from the schools.[6]

In the summer of 1981, the schools applied for registration under Section 70 of the Education Act of 1944. A four-man team of inspectors visited the schools in 1982. Their report found both school premises and instruction inadequate. The inspectors felt that the standard achieved in secular subjects was far too low for the ages and abilities of the boys in the schools. The syllabus for their non-religious education was limited to English, arithmetic, science, geography and current affairs, and there was no scope for music, the arts, imaginative writing, practical crafts and physical exercise. The inspectors stressed that the facilities at the schools and the fire precautions were poor, and complained of the hazardous surface of the playground. They advised the headmaster to increase the teaching of secular subjects to four hours for the under-eights and to six hours for the over-eights.

Based on the inspectors' report, the then Minister of Education and Science, Sir Keith Joseph, himself a Jew, issued a Notice of Complaint under section 71 of the 1944 Education Act, requiring the schools to take remedial action. It gave the governors nine months to amend the teaching programme or face closure and the removal by the Ministry of the schools from the Register of Independent Schools.

The governors of the schools challenged the power of the Ministry to intervene in its curriculum and, in April 1985, appealed to the High Court to have the Notice of Complaint quashed. The Court was told, during a two-day hearing, that the Ministry was not prepared to negotiate and that three of the four inspectors who visited the schools understood neither Yiddish nor Hebrew, the main languages of instruction at the schools. The fourth inspector, specially chosen for his expertise, failed a simple translation test in Court. Mr Justice Wolf ruled that the Court had no jurisdiction to judge the matter.[7] He took the view that a tribunal should adjudicate and he stressed that the Secretary of State must act fairly and was obliged to take reasonable steps to ascertain the facts.[8]

An independent School Tribunal, chaired by Mr Norman Turner, a former Official Solicitor, took 11 days to cover the case. The schools contended that the inspectors were not competent to judge. The counsel for the Department of Education and Science, Mr Justin Fenwick, agreed to withdraw the order of closure. The chairman made it clear that if the Department of Education and Science had not withdrawn its complaint, he would have made an order of annulment.[9]

Belz thus won an important and unprecedented legal battle against a powerful government schools inspectorate.[10] This battle cost more than £70,000 in legal fees. Subsequently, a highly qualified headmaster was appointed to be in charge of secular studies, and the Belz schools' curricula now include physical education.

21 • The Miracle of Bobow

The premises of the spacious Bobow (pronounced Bobov) Centre situated on both sides of Egerton Road, Stamford Hill, has become a hub of activity for the Chasidim of Bobow. The melodies of Bobow are heard not only on the Sabbath, but every morning on the special buses which convey children to the Centre.

Bobow has a thriving *beth hamidrash*, a *Talmud Torah*, a *yeshiva* with dormitory facilities for 35 students who come mainly from abroad, a *kollel* and a modern *mikveh*. Summer camps 'Shalva' are organised in the English countryside. So far, there is no school for girls. Bobow grants interest-free loans to its adherents to help them acquire homes and businesses.

The spiritual leader of the community since 1985 is Rabbi Benzion Blum, the son-in-law of Rabbi Shlomo Halberstam, the Rebbe of Bobow. The phenomenal rise of Bobow in London is, however, largely due to the efforts of Rabbi Leibel Stempel, who was born in Cracow in 1935. His maternal grandfather was the Rebbe of Bobow, and his paternal grandfather, Rabbi Feivish, represented the *Aguda* in the Polish Parliament from 1922 to 1927. After much hardship in a Nazi camp in Bochnia, Leibel together with his mother and sister, made his way via Hungary and Romania to the Holy Land. He came to London in 1948. From his home in Stamford Hill, Rabbi Stempel guides and supervises the Centre.

In the 1930s there were a number of Bobow Chasidim in London who prayed at the *shtiebl* of Rabbi Parnes at 86 Cazenove Road, Stamford Hill. Prominent among them were Itchele Strom (d. 1973), later the Cantor of the Hendon *Adath Yisroel* Synagogue, Mechel Lieber and Saul Bodner. After the war, Rabbi Shlomo Halberstam came to London to participate in the *Aguda* Conference (*Knessiya Mechina*). At a meeting held in the Conway Hall, London, he gave a moving address, urging British Jewry to rescue the remnant of European Jewry. It was in the home of Chayim Schlaff (1911–76) and his wife Miriam Rachel, that the Rebbe decided, albeit reluctantly, to assume the mantle of Bobow, and they were his hosts on the innumerable visits he paid to London. The first *shtiebl* of Bobow was opened in 5 Darenth Road, Stamford Hill, in 1962; another two houses were added later through the generosity of Mr O Freshwater. When the Rebbe visited London again in 1963, he asked his followers: 'Where are the *sefarim* (books)?' They pointed to the bookcase. 'No, no,' said the Rebbe, 'by *sefarim* I mean *yeshiva* students.' In 1965, the *yeshiva* commenced activities.

In 1977, Bobow acquired from the Jewish Welfare Board the Joel Emanuel Almshouses in Egerton Road, which they extensively renovated. 'We are going to establish a glorious *yeshiva*,' remarked the Rebbe. 'Torah will be studied here in a spirit of purity coupled with the love of Israel.' In 1980, the new centre was opened in the presence of the Rebbe. A decade later, Bobow bought the New Synagogue in Egerton Road, north London, from the United Synagogue for the sum of £700,000. This synagogue was originally founded in Leadenhall Street in 1761, an offshoot of the Great Synagogue. It moved to Great St Helens off Bishopsgate in 1838, and was relocated in 1915 to Egerton Road. This was the synagogue where Cantor David Goldstein and Rabbi Dr S H Lehrman officiated, where Dayan Abramsky regularly worshipped and gave discourses, and where Rabbi I Brodie was inducted as Chief Rabbi. It held pride of place among the United Synagogue houses of worship until its membership drifted to suburbia.

The sale was a two-stage agreement: the first stage was the handing over of the Marcus Samuel complex of the New Synagogue. Stage two took place in 1995 when the Synagogue itself was taken over by Bobow.

The dynasty of Bobow (Bobowa is a town in western Galicia) was founded by Rabbi Shlomo Halberstam (1847–1905), a grandson of Rabbi Chayim Halberstam of Sanz. His son Benzion succeeded him in 1905. A melodious singer as well as a noted scholar, Rabbi Benzion combined the erudition of Sanz with the music of Ropczyce. He maintained that Chasidism without a melody was like a body without a soul. 'Serve the Lord with joy,' was the Bobow slogan. Simple folk melodies became the expression for profound concepts. When the famous cantor Yosele Rosenblatt heard Rabbi Benzion sing 'By the Rivers of Babylon', he exclaimed: 'Without *ruach hakodesh* (the holy spirit) it is impossible to compose such a melody.'

Soon after he became Rebbe, Rabbi Benzion established a *yeshiva* in Bobow, and after the First World War a network of 40 such *yeshivot* with a roll of 900 students was established throughout Galicia. A special organisation called *Tomchei Oraisa* (supporters of learning) was responsible for providing the resources. Rabbi Benzion was the first Chasidic rebbe to pay special attention to the young, for whom he showed practical consideration. He urged his followers to avoid controversy and dissension, so that love and understanding would prevail among them. He based his lifestyle on Torah, service and the practice of charity. He forbade his followers to read secular and heretical literature. His charity was legendary. No one left his house empty-handed. He paid the medical bills of his poor students, and would arrange marriages for them.

The fourth of *Av* 1942 is a tragic day for the Chasidim of Bobow. It is the anniversary of the brutal murder of Rabbi Benzion, his youngest son, Rabbi Moshe Aaron, and his three sons-in-law. On that black Friday, 12,000 Jews were murdered by the Nazis. The Rebbe's grave is not known, but he lives on in the work of his son Rabbi Shlomo. After the German invasion of Russia, Rabbi Shlomo was confined to the labour camp at Bochnia, near Cracow. His wife and two children were taken to Auschwitz where they perished. The Rabbi, his mother and his sister escaped first to Grosswardein, and then to Romania. His elder son, Naftali Zevi, also survived. After the war the Rabbi made his way to Italy, and thence to London and New York. There he settled first in Manhattan, later in Crown Heights and finally in Boro Park, Brooklyn. In 1947 he remarried and he has five daughters and one son by his second wife, Freda.

The Rabbi founded a network of educational establishments. The list of his institutions is most impressive: a large *yeshiva* in Boro Park; a magnificent 50-classroom girls' school, the Miriam Locker School; *B'not Zion*, a *Talmud Torah* with almost 1,000 pupils, and a large *kollel*. The classrooms commemorate the cities of Galicia: Bobow, Cracow, Tarnow and Auschwitz. The Rebbe has also set up a career development centre where young men are trained in the use of computers. The Bobow Holiday Camp gives many children the opportunity of spending the summer vacation in a traditional atmosphere. He introduced a scheme whereby industrial training is provided in his *yeshiva* Trade School. At one time he planned to build a large housing project at Parsons Boulevard in Long Island. Because of the opposition of local residents the plan had to be abandoned.

The foundation stone of Kiryat Bobow in Bat Yam, Israel, was laid in 1958, where now many families are living. The magnificent *Yeshiva Kedushat Zion* and the Synagogue *Beth Yehoshua*, the gifts of the Rebbe's brother-in-law, Mr O Freshwater, were founded in 1963. The *yeshiva* is proud of the excellent accommodation and efficient medical services it provides for the students. 'The most effective answer to the problem [of religion in Israel] lies in education,' declared the Rebbe. Nor are the elderly forgotten. A pleasant and comfortable home *Segula* was opened for them in 1963. The full development of the *kirya* has been hindered by technical and financial problems.

There are also Bobow communities in Belgium, Montreal and Toronto. There is a Bobow *kollel* in Jerusalem, and a number of establishments in Bnei Brak.

A great supporter of Bobow institutions was the late Joshua (Osias) Freshwater, known in Chasidic circles as *hanadav hayedua* (the well-known benefactor). He was the son of Raphael, a timber merchant and Chasid of Belz. When the First World War broke out, his father was anxious for the son to emigrate to America to avoid military service. The Rebbe of Belz dissuaded him, saying: 'It is preferable to serve two years in the army than to live in America where even the stones are *trefa* (non-kosher), and it is impossible to remain a religious Jew there.' At the end of his military service, Freshwater settled in Danzig, where he worked in a bank. Danzig at that time was known as 'the Island of Tears', a stepping stone for Polish Jewish refugees in search of new havens in Canada, the USA or the Holy Land. To accommodate the large influx of Jewish refugees, the city authorities opened a transit camp for them on the island of Troyl. Together with Rabbi Y H Cymerman (later of London), Freshwater worked very hard on their behalf. At that time Danzig was already dominated by the Nazis. On 23 October 1937, they raided 300 Jewish homes. On 26 August 1939, Russia signed the Molotov–Ribbentrop Pact which made the Second World War inevitable. Freshwater left Danzig only three days before the outbreak of the war, having obtained a British visa. His wife, Clara, his children, and his brother took refuge in the home of his father-in-law Elijah Igel in Lvov. They all perished in the Holocaust.

In 1947, he married Nechama Golda Halberstam, the daughter of Rabbi Benzion of Bobow. Nechama had studied at the *Beth Yaakov* School in Cracow and had previously been married to Moses, the son of Rabbi Feivish Stempel, who had been murdered by the Nazis. She and her two children survived the war.

In London, Freshwater at first became a textile merchant and subsequently made a fortune in property. He had an amazing instinct for buying the right building at the right time. By the early 1970s he was one of London's biggest private landlords.[1] People would often consult him about their business and even their personal problems. After the war, he established at 835 Finchley Road, Golders Green, an orphanage for 50 refugee boys from Nazi Europe, in whom he took a paternal interest. He was one of the founders of the *Beth Yaakov* and *Pardes House* Schools, the Senior Vice-President of the Union of Orthodox Hebrew Congregations and President of the Mizrachi and Hapoel Hamizrachi Federation.[2] He was a generous supporter of the Bobow institutions in London, Israel and the United States.

He lived a retiring family life in his palatial mansion in West Heath Drive, Golders Green. He and his two sons, Benzion Shalom Eliezer and Shlomo Yisrael, were regular worshippers at the Sassover *shtiebl*. On the Sabbath, he dressed in a *kapote*. He would study daily the commentary of *Or HaChayim* by the Cabbalist, Rabbi Chayim Ibn Atar. It is noteworthy that Joshua Freshwater died on 15 *Tammuz* 1976 – the very anniversary of the death of Rabbi Chayim Ibn Atar. His two sons, Benzion and Shlomo, follow in his footsteps in their charitable endeavours and in their adherence to the Rebbe of Sassov. His stepdaughter Shoshanah married William Stern, a Hungarian-born Harvard graduate, who spent some of the war years in a concentration camp. He joined his father-in-law's business in the 1960s and built up a vast empire of residential property throughout London. In 1971 he set up his own Wilstar Securities company. He is now a major shareholder in a company called Dollar Land which directs American institutional investments into British property. William Stern worships at the *Beth Hamidrash* of Rabbi Chune Halpern and is a benefactor of the *Pardes House* School.

It is interesting to note that, despite the Freshwaters' great attachment to Bobow, no Bobower *shtiebl* has so far been established in north-west London. This may well be out of deference to the Rebbe of Sassov.

22 • The Importance of Ger

Unlike Satmar whose strength is in the diaspora – in New York, in London and in Antwerp – the power of Ger today is in the Holy Land. Ger is closely associated with the *Aguda* and has recognised the State of Israel, not only *de facto*, but also *de jure*. Rabbi Yitzchak Meir Levin, the brother-in-law of the late Gerer Rebbe, Rabbi Yisrael Alter, served as Minister of Social Welfare in the first Israeli provisional government until 1952.

Ger or Gura-Kalwaria (Ger in Yiddish and Gur in Hebrew), a small town near Warsaw, became the centre of the greatest Chasidic dynasty in Poland. During the inter-war years more than 100,000 Jews owed allegiance to the Rebbe of Ger, and there was hardly a town in Poland without one or two Gerer *shtieblech*. Ger controlled the *Aguda* and the *Beth Yaakov* schools. In Israel today over 4,000 families belong to Ger.

The founder of the dynasty was Rabbi Isaac Meir Rothenburg (1799– 1866), known as the *Chiddushei HaRim*, after his great work. The doc- trines of Przysucha and Kotzk were combined in Ger. There was neither emphasis on miracles nor acceptance of *pidyonot* (gifts accompanying petitions). 'Rabbi Simcha Bunem of Przysucha led his followers with love, Rabbi Menachem Mendel Morgenstern of Kotzk led them with fear, I shall lead them with Torah,' said the founder of the dynasty.

He was succeeded by his grandson, Rabbi Yehuda Aryeh Leib, known by his literary pseudonym, *Sefat Emet*, from the verse in Proverbs: 'the lips of truth shall be established for ever'.[1] His son and successor, Rabbi Abraham Mordechai Alter (1866–1948), was a diffident man, yet, in times of crisis, he acted with courage and resolution. His influence was far-reaching. A word from him could decide a communal election, and a cause he favoured was assured of success. When the Rebbe of Ger came to town, it was in the nature of a state visit, surrounded by pomp and ceremony. Rabbi Abraham Mordechai, like his grandfather before him, had a great sense of communal responsibility. At the Bad

Homburg Conference of 1909, he helped to pave the way for the founding of the *Agudat Yisrael*. He attended the three further *Aguda* conferences (*Knessiyot HaGedolot*) in Vienna and Marienbad in 1923, 1929 and 1937. 'When I will be asked in the hereafter,' he once said, 'what I have achieved in this world, I shall say, that I created the *Agudat Yisrael*.'

He endorsed the *Beth Yaakov* movement, and through the influence of the Rebbe many *Chedarim* and *Talmud Torah* Centres were combined in the Chorev School system. In 1919, he supported the establishment of the *Mesivta Yeshiva* under Rabbi Meir Dan Plotski of Ostrowiec, and he strongly supported the founding of the *Yeshivat Chachmei Lublin* and the *Daf Hayomi* (the study of a page of the Talmud daily).

The Rebbe visited the Holy Land five times in the inter-war years. When Hitler came to power in 1933, the Rebbe said: 'For 150 years our German brethren have not known the meaning of the word exile. Now they will probably find refuge in the Holy Land. I am afraid of only one thing: they will take with them their assimilated customs and will adversely influence the vitality of religious life.'

At the outbreak of the Second World War he moved to Warsaw, constantly changing his residence to evade the Nazis, who spared no effort to locate the 'wonder-rabbi'. With his wife and sons, he left Poland and, travelling through Austria and Italy, arrived in Jerusalem in *Nisan* 1940. The Rebbe died in 1948, four weeks after the establishment of the State of Israel. He was buried in the courtyard of the *Sefat Emet yeshiva* in Jerusalem, as the Mount of Olives cemetery was in the hands of the Arab Legion.

He was succeeded by his brother Rabbi Yisrael Alter (b. 1892). It was said of Rabbi Yisrael that though time was precious to him, he had time for everybody. Twice daily he would receive people in private audiences. People of all shades of religious observance sought his advice – at his home at Malchei Yisrael Street, Geula, Jerusalem – on a wide range of matters. His discourses seldom lasted longer than a few moments, but their brevity did not diminish their depth and originality. He took an active interest in the work of *Agudat Yisrael*, which he endearingly called 'the *Agudat Yisrael* of my father'. He was one of the prominent leaders of the *Moetzet Gedolei HaTorah* (the *Aguda* Council of Sages).

He expanded the *Yeshiva Sefat Emet* in Jerusalem and encouraged the building of the vast *Yeshivat Chidushei HaRim* in Tel Aviv, as well as other educational institutions. He was one of the staunchest supporters of *Chinuch Atzmai* (the religious education establishments of the *Aguda*).

The Rebbe died in 1977 and was buried on the Mount of Olives. Over 100,000 mourners attended the funeral.[2]

He was succeeded by Rabbi Simcha Bunem, the fourth son of Rabbi Mordechai Alter. He was born in Gora Kalwaria in Nisan 1889, and was named after Rabbi Simha Bunem of Przysucha. His mother was Yehudit Rada, the daughter of Noah Shahor of Biala. His father called him the 'wise one'. In 1915 in Warsaw, he married his cousin, Gita Henne, the daughter of Rabbi Nehemia Alter, the third son of the *Sefat Emet*, and *Dayan* in Lodz. The couple waited ten years for their first child, and their baby daughter, Hayyah Roda Yehudit, died at six months. After another four years, they eventually had two more children, a daughter followed by a son. Rabbi Simcha Bunem's life was full of troubles, but he never uttered a word of complaint. Together with his father-in-law, he visited the Holy Land in 1927 and stayed there for a few years. In 1934 he settled in the *Mekor Baruch* district of Jerusalem.

On returning to Poland in 1939, he lived in Lodz and then in Warsaw. As a Palestinian citizen, he was able, together with his family to leave for the Holy Land on *Chol Hamoed* Passover 1940.

For 29 years he gave his allegiance to his brother, Rabbi Yisrael, and kept out of the limelight. When his brother died intestate on 8 *Adar* 1977, he acceded to the request of ten senior Chasidim to become the fifth rebbe of Ger. He was renowned for his modesty, and carried on living in his original small apartment. He pioneered the setting-up of cost-price stores for the Chasidim. The size of an apartment, its furnishing, and the money spent on a *Bar Mitzvah*, even the cost of *etrogim* for *Sukkot*, all these were subject to detailed regulations. He was against lavish wedding celebrations. No more than 150 people in addition to the family should be invited to the wedding meal. Others may be invited to the reception after the *chupa*. He encouraged young religious couples to live outside the two main Orthodox centres of Jerusalem and Bnei Brak, and instead to settle in Arad, Ashdod and Hazor where there were opportunities for apartments at lower rentals. He led the campaign to stop El Al from flying on the Sabbath, and fought against the establishment of the Mormon University on the Mount of Olives. He encouraged the *Aguda* to join and support the coalition government.

At the sixth *Knessiya Gedolah* the rebbe instituted the study of a daily page of the *Yerushalmi* Talmud, side by side with the Babylonian Talmud. He visited London in 1954 and 1977. He was active in the leadership of the *Aguda* and was a member of the *Moetzet Gedolei HaTorah*. He supported Torah institutions and expanded the Chasidic *yeshivot* of Ger in the Holy Land. He combined an unworldly manner with worldly interests and he was renowned for his entrepreneurial skills. In 1986 his health deteriorated, and he ceased holding *tishen*, the festive Sabbath meals. He died on 7 *Tammuz* 1992 and was buried on the Mount of Olives.

He was survived by his daughter Rebecca who was married to Meir Mandel of London, but is now divorced, and by his son, Rabbi Jacob Arye, who, in *Kislev* 1960, married the daughter of Rabbi Mendel Weitz, a Rosh Yeshiva in Tel Aviv, and now lives in Bnei Brak. The Rebbe was succeeded by his half-brother, Rabbi Pinhas Menahem, son of Rabbi Abraham Mordechai Alter by his second wife, Feige Minze (daughter of Rabbi Jacob Biderman). Rabbi Pinhas Menahem married the daughter of Rabbi Moses Bezalel Alter. He is very active in the *Aguda*, writes frequently for its paper *HaModia*, and is the principal of the *Yeshiva Sefat Emet* in Jerusalem. His 27-year-old son, Rabbi Yehuda Arye Leib, who married the daughter of Rabbi Menashe Klein of New York, was killed by a car as he emerged from a ritual bath in the Romema district of Jerusalem in 1969.

In London today there are two Ger Centres, in Stamford Hill and in Golders Green. At Lampard Grove, Stamford Hill, there is a *Beth Hamidrash*, where over 100 people worship regularly. There is a *Yeshiva Beth Zevi Zeev*, named after Zevi Zeev Morgenstern, which, within a decade, has expanded from nine students to more than 60. The *yeshiva* was dedicated in 1982 by Rabbi Pinchas Menachem Alter, who also laid the foundation stone for a new and more spacious *yeshiva* on 28 January 1990. His nephew, Rabbi Jacob Arye, conveyed his father's blessing.[3] The magnificent new three-storey building, named *Lev Simcha*, in memory of the late Rebbe, was consecrated by the Rebbe of Ger on 22 November 1992. The cost of the building was two and a half million pounds.

In the 1930s a number of Chasidim of Ger were living in London, the most prominent of them being Abraham Pinchas Landau (1880–1948), a native of Ostrow-Masowiec. When he came to London in 1914, he lived at 61 Wentworth Street, East London, and had a timber yard in Bow. At first, he attended a *shtiebl* in Plumbers Row, off Fieldgate Street, a workshop converted into a *shtiebl* for the Shabbat services. Later he joined the congregation in Black Lion Yard, and then the *Machzikei Hadath*. He was popularly known as 'the Consul of Ger', because of his friendship and correspondence with Rabbi Yisrael Alter. Another Chasid of Ger at that time was Shalom Segal (1905–92), a beret manufacturer, later a coat linings merchant, who at first also worshipped at Plumbers Row, later joining the *shtieblech* of Rabbi J Spira and Rabbi B Finkelstein.

During the Second World War a number of Chasidim of Ger, originally from Antwerp, found refuge in London. Among them was the diamond merchant Hershel (Itche Meir) Morgenstern. Born in Lodz, he came to London in 1940 and attended first Hager's *shtiebl* and later the Hampstead *Adath Yisroel* Congregation, where he acted as *baal Koreh* (reader of the Law). He, too, corresponded with Rabbi Yisrael Alter. Today, his grandson is the *gabbai* (warden) of the Gerer *Beth Hamidrash* in Bridge Lane, Golders Green. Kopul Shapira, an active Chasid of Ger, lived in Golders Green and attended the Sassover *shtiebl*.

A leading Chasid of Ger was Rabbi Yaakov Henech Cymerman (1887–1965), the author of *Imrei Yaakov*, a two-volume work on the Pentateuch and *Midrash* and of the *Ethics of the Fathers*, in which he quoted many Chasidic rabbis.[4] A native of Serock, near Warsaw, he lived for some time in Ostrolenka and Danzig.

In 1929, he came to London and was appointed rabbi of the Jewish Centre synagogue, the only *Aguda* synagogue in the East End of London. He also set up the first *Beth Yaakov* school at 25 Lower Chapman Street,[5] and founded, in Jane Street, the *Merkaz Hatorah*, a hostel for young refugees from Vienna. During the years 1935 to 1939, helped by his Danzig associate, Jacob Abramovitz, he established himself as an agent for timber and veneer imports.

During the war, his *shtiebl* moved to 86 Ashford Street in the East End. He then became the rabbi of the Philpot Street *Sephardishe Shul* and was the first honorary secretary, and later the chairman, of the Federation of Synagogues' *Vaad Harabbanim*, a committee of rabbis who aimed to improve the status of the Federation rabbinate.[6]

During that time, together with Rabbi Yerucham Leiner (later of New York) and Rabbi Chayim Uri Etner (later of Los Angeles), Rabbi Cymerman worked for the *Vaad Harabbanim Hapolanim*, a committee of Polish rabbis which, together with the Federation of Polish Jews, was in constant touch with the Polish government in exile in London.

Gentle and courteous in his manner and dignified in his bearing, Rabbi Cymerman was at the same time a practical man in his dealings with problems on which he was consulted. His discourses reflected the man: large-hearted, affectionate and devoted.

Rabbi Pinchas Weitzman (1898–1960) was a native of Lodz. When his father, David Hirsch, came to London in 1929 he was left behind in

Poland to be brought up in the home of Rabbi Nechemia Alter, the brother of the Rabbi of Ger. He came to London in 1936 and became the Rabbi of the Tchechenover *shtiebl* at 18 Fieldgate Street, East London, which was founded in 1896. A kindly man, he had a warm interest in people and their problems. He and his wife, in their modest home in Heneage Street, were always able to provide Sabbath meals for poor co-religionists. In later years, he transformed part of the *shul* premises into a free kitchen for the poor. He shunned publicity and most of his charitable endeavours were known only to a small circle.[7] He was interred in the *Givat Shaul* cemetery in Jerusalem.

Rabbi Weitzman's son-in-law, Itche Meyer, the youngest son of Rabbi Y H Cymerman, was born in Serock in 1920, and studied in the *Etz Chayim Yeshiva*, London, and later, at the *Mir Yeshiva* in Poland.

He was at one time minister in Sandys Row Synagogue and proprietor of the Carmel Hotel in Bournemouth. He is very active in the *Aguda* as its senior vice-chairman, and also represents England on the executive of the World *Aguda*.

On the arrival of the first immigrants from Russia, he became chairman of RIAF (Russian Immigrant Aid Fund), an international committee established for the religious absorption of new immigrants. He also represents England on the international committee for the preservation of Jewish cemeteries in Poland. He is the chairman of the *Vaad L'Hazfotzos Daf Yomi*, the committee which is responsible for the increased popularity of the daily study of the Talmud in this country. His charitable trust, established in 1972, has substantial assets.[8] It was mainly as a result of his efforts and generosity that the new *Yeshiva* of Ger was erected.

The first *shtiebl* of Ger was opened in 1954 at 133 Bethune Road, Stamford Hill, in the home of Rabbi Simcha Bunem Lieberman. He was born in Warsaw in 1932, the son of a Chasid of Amshinov and Warka. He survived the horrors of German concentration camps and was liberated by the Russians. He came to London where he studied at the *Etz Chayim Yeshiva* in London, as well as in the Gateshead *Yeshiva*. He was ordained by Rabbi Rabinow. For a time he taught Talmud in Yiddish at the Hasmonean Grammar School, and for 14 years, until 1985, he was an instructor in rabbinics at Jews' College.[9]

For five years Rabbi Lieberman maintained a Chasidic *shtiebl* in his home, and later participated in the *Kollel Shaar Avraham* at 67 Finchley Lane, Hendon, established by Mr Freddy Greenwood in memory of his father in 1958. It was one of the first *kollelim* set up in London. Guided by Rabbi Joshua Deutsch of Katamon, Jerusalem, and later by his son R Moses, it was administered by Mr Samuel Reifer, at a cost of £2,000 per week, entirely defrayed by Mr Greenwood. More than 80 men participated in the *kollel's* morning and afternoon sessions. It was visited by Rabbi Joel Teitelbaum of Satmar, and among its notable graduates was Rabbi Friedman, now a *dayan* of the Union of Orthodox Hebrew Congregations. It enjoyed only a short existence, transferring after less than one year, in Elul 1959, to the *Csaba Kollel*, Stamford Hill. Mr Freddy Greenwood not only amassed a large number of Hebrew incunabula but also acquired some rare manuscripts of Rashi, of Menachem Recanati and of the Maharil. He also established two Talmud Torahs, one at Shirehall Lane, Hendon and one in Stamford Hill.

Rabbi Lieberman continued his educational activities, and the late Rabbi of Ger, Rabbi Simcha Bunem, stayed in his home when he spent some time in London. In 1962, Rabbi Lieberman edited *Taamei Hamitzvot* by the Italian cabbalist Menachem ben Benjamin Recanati (*c.* 1300) and a book on *shechita.*[10] In 1993, Lieberman settled in Safed, Israel.

The Chasidim of Ger orginally prayed at 55 Amhurst Park, the offices of the *Aguda,* and later at 95 Stamford Hill, on the corner of Coburg Place. It was with the help of Mr Baruch Moshe Cymerman (1915–89)[11] that 2 Lampard Grove was acquired as a Ger centre. Baruch Moshe, another son of Rabbi Y H Cymerman, was born in Ostrolenka, Poland, and studied at the Novaredok *Yeshiva.* When living in Warsaw, he worked for the *Aguda* youth movement. In 1937, he joined his father in London, and eventually became the treasurer of the Union of Orthodox Hebrew Congregations, and the London chairman of the Friends of *Chinuch Atzmai,* as well as writing for the *Jewish Tribune.* He was helped by his brother Joseph Leizer Cymerman (1913–88), who at the age of eleven had travelled to Ger to spend a Shabbat with the Rebbe. He was a vice-president of the Federation of Synagogues, and a president of the Nelson Street Sepharische Synagogue which incorporated a large number of synagogues which were closed by the decline of the once thriving Jewish East End of London. He was also honorary secretary of the Federation's own Joint *Shechita* Authority, which set up its own Kashrut Authority in 1983.[12]

A Gerer *shtiebl* was established in Golders Green in 1981 in the home of the ritual slaughterer Menachem Levinson at 15 The Drive. As he was elderly and too unwell to walk to the synagogue he was granted permission to use his home for private prayer meetings. When he died in 1984, the house was acquired by Ger. In 1986 Barnet Council and the Department of the Environment withdrew their permission to continue the *shtiebl* there.[13] In 1987, the *shtiebl* acquired a house at 98 Bridge Lane, and subsequently purchased the adjoining building. The *shtiebl* has many worshippers and follows the traditions of Ger.

After *Shacharit* (the morning service) on the Sabbath there is a *Hafsakah* (interval), the first ten minutes of which are devoted to the study of the works of the Chafetz Chaim (Rabbi Israel Meir HaKohen), the remainder of the time being devoted to Talmud study. A similar interval occurs on Friday night after the singing of the hymn *Lecha Dodi* ('Come, my beloved to meet the bride'). On the *yahrzeit* of Rabbi Yisrael Alter a special collection is made for the maintenance of the Rebbe's court in Jerusalem. New melodies are composed every year. No *Hafsofot* (additional call-ups) are made on the Sabbath, but a *misheberach* (a special prayer) is made for the Rebbe. On High Holy Days *aliyot* (honours) are sold by auction. Rabbi Chune Halpern is their honorary rebbe in London.

23 • Shtieblech *in* Stamford Hill

Stamford Hill is an area of dynamic Chasidism with over 40 *shtieblech*. After the Second World War, many Chasidic *shtieblech* were opened in London, some by well-known personalities.

One of them was Rabbi Sholom Schnitzler, the Rabbi of Csaba.[1] He was born in Pispok–Ladany, Hungary, on 20 April 1920, a descendant of Rabbi Shmelke of Nikolsburg. Sholom studied in Kalev under Rabbi Menachem Brody, and was ordained by Rabbi David Meisels of Ujhely and the *Beth Din* of Munkacz. The Rabbi spent the war years in Bergen-Belsen concentration camp. After the war, he became the rabbi in his native town, Pispok-Ladany. When his father, Shragai Shmuel, settled in Israel in 1950, Rabbi Sholom succeeded him as rabbi of Berkescaba. In 1957, after the Hungarian Revolution, he spent some time in Vienna in the refugee camp at Asten, near Linz in Austria.

He came to North London in 1959, founded the *Tiferet Sholom Kollel* in Amhurst Park in 1961 and opened a *Beth Midrash* at 37 Craven Walk. He was the author of *Shaare Sholom*, a commentary on the *Kitzur Shulchan Aruch* and of many unpublished writings on Psalms, Responsa and homiletics. He died on 21 *Adar* 1989. His son, Rabbi Baruch Yehuda, lives in Williamsburg, New York. The *shtiebl* was recently acquired by Rabbi J Meisels. Like Vishnitz-Monsey, it follows the ideology of Satmar.

An interesting personality was Rabbi Chayim Yitzchok Weingarten (1887–1970), known as the *Lieger Rov*.[2] He was the son of Rabbi Abraham Abba of Libishov, who lived in Janova, Russia. Rabbi Chayim Yitzchok's mother, Beracha, was the daughter of Rabbi Moses Safran, a descendant of Karlin and Chernobyl. He studied in Novaredok under Rabbi Joseph Shlomo Kahaneman of Ponevezh and Rabbi Aaron Kotler. He was ordained by Rabbi Yechiel Michael Epstein. During the First World War, he lived for a time in Berdichev and on his return to Wishnowitz, he established a *Yeshiva Beth Yosef* in opposition to the establishment of the *Ivrit B'Ivrit* (Hebrew speaking) school by the Tarbut Organisation. He emigrated to Belgium and through the influence of Rabbi Moses Avigdor Amiel of Antwerp, he became the Rabbi of Liege. For the rest of his life he was known as the 'Lieger Rov'. He established a Talmud Torah at Liege and a *yeshiva* at Haide, near Antwerp.

In 1940, he escaped from the Nazis by coming to London, and was befriended by the Rebbe of Shatz. During the bombing of London, he established the *Yeshiva Torat Chayim* for orthodox refugee boys who had been placed with non-Jewish foster parents in England. Its wooden hut in Bletchley was home to 70 boys. Among their teachers were Rabbis Abraham Round, Samuel Unsdorfer, Jacob Silverman, Lippa Henig, Bunim and Pesach Hirshler and Yitzhak Weiss. The *yeshiva* then moved to a small house at 3 Fairfield Avenue, near the Staines post office, and its dormitory house was along the main London Road. In April 1943 the *yeshiva* moved yet again, this time to a large mansion, Thorpe Lea House near Egham, which was surrounded by acres of ground. It had a *mikveh* and a *matza* bakery, and a nearby farm provided supervised milk. When V-bombing started in 1944, the *yeshiva* was evacuated to Manchester where it remained until the end of the war.

When Thorpe Lea was badly damaged by fire in December 1946, the *yeshiva* moved to London where it was temporarily housed in Schneider's *yeshiva*. The Trisker Rebbe offered hospitality to staff and students at his *beth hamidrash* in Cazenove Road, north London.

In the spring of 1947 the *yeshiva* returned to Egham to another even larger mansion in Clockhouse Lane, confusingly called by its original name, Thorpe Lea Hotel, and remained there until 1951. Polish Jewish ex-soldiers looked after cows, goats and chickens in the grounds of the *yeshiva*. There was also a hostel for refugees in nearby Ascot.

Rabbi Weingarten was a gifted clarinet player, and formed a band of *yeshiva* students. He urged his pupils to pray and to study aloud. 'Why did the Almighty grant you a voice and vocal cords if not to use them in His service?' he impressed upon them. The *yeshiva* produced a great number of rabbinical scholars.

Later, in 1953, he made his home in Bergholt Crescent, Stamford Hill, which was always open to those in need. He became the president of the *Yesodey Hatorah* school. He also formed the *Vaad Harabbanim VeRoshei Yeshivot* (a rabbinical organization) which gave spiritual guidance to smaller communities. He helped to establish a *mikveh* at the *Shomrei Hadath* Synagogue in Leeds. In addition to his rabbinic erudition, he was a talented painter and played the clarinet. He died at the age of 83.[3]

He was survived by a son, David, but his spiritual successor is his son-in-law, Rabbi Joshua Zeev Meisels. Rabbi Meisels is a descendant of Rabbi Dov Beirish Meisels, the Polish patriot and rabbi of Warsaw. Rabbi Joshua Meisel's ordination was endorsed by Rabbi Yoel Teitelbaum of Satmar.

In 1984, the *Kollel Mosdos Torat Chayim*, which was established in memory of Rabbi Chayim Weingarten, moved to 145–47 Upper Clapton Road. It comprises a *beth midrash*, and a *beth eshel*, a hostel for ten persons. Rabbi Meisels's son, Rabbi Shalom, is in charge of *Beth Hamidrash Zichron Shalom* in Elm Park, South Tottenham.

The *Shtiebl Birchat Yehuda*, or the *Holosh Beth Midrash*, at 47 Moundfield Road, is headed by Rabbi Menachem Mendel Lebovitz, who was born in Holosh, Hungary, in 1938. He is a descendant of Rabbi Shmelke of Nikolsburg. His father, Rabbi Baruch Yehuda, saved many Jews from the Nazis. Rabbi Menachem Mendel studied first under his father and later, for ten years, under Rabbi Yoel Teitelbaum in New York. After his father's death in 1946, his widowed mother married Rabbi Eliezer Zusya Portugal (d. 1982), who was known as the Skulener Rebbe. The latter had been imprisoned twice by the Communist authorities for his educational work in Romania. He subsequently set up 56 educational institutions, known as *Chesed L'Avraham* which included boarding schools for boys and girls in the Holy Land, in the USA, and behind the Iron Curtain. These centres rescued children from broken and deprived homes.

Rabbi Menachem Mendel in his *shtiebl* in Stamford Hill welcomes those Jews who are anxious to return to their Jewish heritage (*baalei teshuva*). He is the author of a work *Maalot Zaddikim*.[4] He imports *etrogim* (citrons), one of the four species used during the Festival of Tabernacles, from Genoa, Italy. The quality of these *etrogim* was highly esteemed already in the days of Rabbi Moshe Sofer and Rabbi Shneur Zalman of Liady. Though residing in London, Rabbi Menachem Mendel is still the official rabbi of Holosh in Hungary.

NADVORNA

'There is no town without a Rabbi of Nadvorna', is a popular Chasidic saying. There is a Rebbe of Nadvorna in Jerusalem, Bnei Brak, Chadera,

Ashdod, Petach Tikvah, Rechovot, *Kiryat Gat* and *Kfar Ata*. There is also a Nadvorna *shtiebl* in London at 45 Darenth Road, established in 1948. Its spiritual head is Rabbi Mordechai Leifer. He was born in Bregenz, near Linz, in 1950. His father is Rabbi Yissachar Baer of Boro Park, New York. He is a descendant of Rabbi Mordechai of Nadvorna (d. 1885), who was a well-known ascetic. 'I must train my body to be satisfied with whatever I eat', the latter used to say. He would prolong his prayers by many hours. 'I am sorry to keep you waiting,' he once told his followers, 'but surely you know that I was not playing cards or visiting the theatre.'

Rabbi Mordechai Leifer studied in the *yeshivot* of Bobow and Satmar in New York. When he first came to London he taught at the *Yesodey Hatorah* and *Pardes House* Schools.

RUZHIN

In 1984 a Ruzhin *shtiebl* was established at 33 Paget Road and was dedicated by Rabbi Yitzchak Friedman of Bohush (d. 1992), and often visited by Rabbi Israel Meir Erlanger, the head of the Rabinow *Kollel* and also by Rabbi David Moses Friedman (1914–88). The son of Rabbi Dov Baer and a grandson of Rabbi Israel of Czortkov, David Moses was born in Boyan and came to London from Vienna in 1939. Classified as an enemy alien, he was interned on the Isle of Man, but later released on the intervention of Dr S Schonfeld. He then served in an anti-aircraft battery. Later he obtained a B.Sc. degree in Economics from the Open University, eventually becoming a part-time civil servant for the Treasury. He refused to become a rebbe. 'My father attributed to me the quality of truthfulness. Were I to become a rebbe, I would surely lose it.' He attended the *Adath Yisroel* Synagogue, Edgware, where he acted as *Baal Makrei* (guiding the blowing of the *shofar*). He was a Talmudic scholar of repute.

Another regular visitor to the *shtiebl* was Rabbi Aaron (Fischel) Herling (1912–90), who for ten years was the rabbi of the East London Central Federation Synagogue at Nelson Street.[5] Romanian-born, he came to England in the 1950s, after escaping from the concentration camp where most of his family perished. Always seen with a smile on his face whatever the circumstances, he cheered up all who knew him. He ministered to congregations in Dublin, Grimsby, Glasgow, Whitley Bay and Tyne and Wear. He was a disciple of Rabbi Meir Shapiro of

Lublin and a Chasid of Boyan and Czorekov. His book *Beth Yisroel* has a foreword by the Chief Rabbi.

SQUARE

In 1978, the *shtiebl* of Square was established ast 22 Dunsmure Road, at one time the home of the Cabbalist, the late Rabbi Yehuda Leib Ashlag. It is guided by Rabbi Ephraim Padwa who is also the head of the *kollel*, which was established at 121 Clapton Common in 1977. There is also a *Talmud Torah Yaakov Yosef*, originally housed at Dunsmure Road in makeshift classrooms with just seven children on the roll, but now, with a roll of more than 100 children, occupying premises at 14 Heathland Road and St Kildas Road, the former home of the *Beis Shammai* Grammar School (which has since closed).

Square owed its allegiance to Rabbi David, the son of Rabbi Yaakov Yosef Twersky (d. 1968) who revived the spirit of a bygone age, the spirit of the *shtetl*. In the spring of 1956, he founded, in a village outside New York, a remarkable settlement which he named 'New Square', in memory of his birthplace. Now, many families live in the modern Cape Cod cottages, scattered over 138 acres of grassy slopes in North Hillcrest, a lonely region of Spring Valley. The Rebbe visited London in 1977, 1983 and 1989.[6]

SPINKA

In February 1988, a new *beth midrash* of Spinka was opened at 34–36 Bergholt Crescent, Stamford Hill, originally the home of the Lieger *Beth Hamidrash*. Their spiritual leader is Rabbi Menachem Mendel Kahana, who was born in Romania in 1933 and studied under Rabbi Duschinsky in Jerusalem from 1944 to 1947. His father was Rabbi Nachman Kahana of Spinka (d. 1976) who settled in Bnei Brak in 1955. Rabbi Menachem Mendel is also the director of the Getter's *cheder* in Stamford Hill.

KLAUSENBURG

At 42 Craven Walk is the *beth hamidrash* of the Chasidim of Klausenburg. There is also a *kollel* for evening and morning students. This was originally established in 1979 at 11 Darenth Road in the home of Moses

Hershkovitz. The *shtiebl* organises a *Mifal Hashas* scheme for the study of 20 pages per month of the Babylonian Talmud. At the end of each month, a written examination takes place at which points and prizes are awarded: 85–100 points earn a prize of £120; 75–80 points £96, and 65–70 points £72. No award is given to those who achieve less than 65 points.

The *shtiebl* owes allegiance to Rabbi Yekutiel Yuda Halberstam of Klausenburg, who visited London in 1956.[7] He was a descendant of Rabbi Chayim ben Leibish Halberstam.

Yekutiel Yuda was born in Rudnik in 1904 and died in Netanya, Israel, on 9 *Tammuz* 1994. He spent 20 fruitful years as rabbi in Klausenburg, gaining renown as a rabbinic authority. This period came to an abrupt and tragic end with the German 'New Order' which brought destruction to the Jews of south-eastern Europe. The Rebbe was interned in a number of labour camps during the Second World War, and for a time worked in the ruins of the Warsaw Ghetto. In 1944 he was sent to Auschwitz. In 1947, he settled in the Williamsburg section of Brooklyn. Even though he established roots in the United States, his heart was in Israel, and eventually he went to Netanya where he established the Chasidic settlement *Kiryat Sanz*. Torah institutions for every age group were set up. In 1976, the Rebbe established the Laniado Hospital which is being developed as the Sanz Medical Centre, with a current budget of over £10 million per annum, serving the 181,000 inhabitants in the Netanya area.

MUNKACS

The North London *Beth Hamidrash*, established in 1944, at 85 Cazenove Road, changed its name to *Beth Hamidrash Kehillat Chasidim Munkacs* in 1989, and Rabbi Moses Leib Rabinowicz of New York is its spiritual mentor.

BIALA BETH HAMIDRASH

A Chasidic *shtiebl*, the Biala *Beth Hamidrash Helkat Yehoshua*, was opened by Baruch Leib Rabinowicz, a grandson of the late Biala Rebbe of Jerusalem, in April 1991, on the corner of Castlewood Road and Craven Park Road, Tottenham. The *shtiebl* owes its allegiance to Rabbi Benzion

Rabinowitz who is not only the Rabbi of the Via Maderna Synagogue in Lugano, but also the Biala Rebbe.[8]

SADAGORA

Dedicated on 6 March 1994 by Rabbi Abraham Jacob Friedman, the Sadagora Rebbe of Tel Aviv, a *shtiebl* of Sadagora was opened in Golders Green Road, north-west London, which is guided by Rabbi Israel Moses Friedman, his only son. Rabbi Israel Moses married Sarah, the daughter of Chayim Moshe Feldman, and a granddaughter of Getzel Berger.[9]

More than 200 families have settled in South Tottenham during the last decade, largely representing the overspill of the Chasidic community in Stamford Hill.[10] 'Stamford Hill is no longer as pleasant as it used to be,' said Rabbi Abraham Pinter in an interview with *The Times* in October 1992.[11] It is not surprising, therefore, that in 1992, a planning application was made by the Community Group *Bayis Ne'eman* to the Hertsmere Borough Council for permission to establish a Chasidic community on a disused part of the former Shenley Psychiatric Hospital.[12] This application was turned down.

24 • Other Chasidic Centres in Britain

'I believe that the future of Judaism lies in a revival of the Chasidic spirit', declared Rabbi Dr Alexander Altmann, Communal Rav of Manchester (1938–59), at the time Professor of Jewish Philosophy at Brandeis University, and one of the present generation's most outstanding Jewish scholars.[1] 'For Chasidism holds out the promise of a renewal of Judaism from within. For it opens up a historical perspective in which Judaism reveals a plasticity and power of vision, a freshness and sense of the essential which must fill us with hope.'[2] These sentiments were echoed by him in subsequent articles.[3]

MANCHESTER

The Jewish community in Manchester is the largest and most influential community outside London. There are over 37 synagogues in the Greater Manchester area, and the Jewish population numbers more than 40,000. The 'Black Square' of Manchester is around Wellington Street, and there are 250 Chasidic families who have provided their own educational facilities to fulfil their needs. There is the Talmud Torah *Chinuch N'Orim*, now with over 100 children, founded by Samuel Krausz (d. 1988), a Chasid of Belz, in 1952. The *Keter Torah* school of the *Machzikei Hadath* and the *Bnos Yisroel* school together have a roll of approximately 400 girls, many of them from a Chasidic background. More than 100 girls continue their education at the *Beth Yaakov-Beth Soroh Schenierer* Seminary, founded in 1969 and housed in the former Jewish Old Age Home. It has set itself the task of educating a learned female laity, at the same time providing its students with training for a teaching career.

Lubavitch now has two active centres: *Machon Levi Yitzchok* (the J T Tannenbaum Centre), the cultural centre, named after Rabbi

Levi Yitzchok Schneersohn, the father of the present Rebbe. The present premises, a four-storey building, were acquired for £190,000 from ICI in 1981, formerly a training centre for engineers. It has a reading room and a lending library of cassettes, mainly American, 'to cater for everyone's taste from Chasidic Pop to *Shiurim*'.[4] The other centre accommodates the *Ohele Yosef Yitzchok* schools for boys in Upper Park Road. The girls are housed in the old *Beis Yaakov* seminary building in Singleton Road. The Lubavitch *yeshiva*, founded in 1982, shares the premises of the Lubavitch *Kahal Chasidim* Congregation in Singleton Road, Salford. In addition to local students, it attracts a number from the USA, Canada, Belgium, Holland, Switzerland and France. The *yeshiva* under Rabbi Yitzchak Klyne and Rabbi Eliezer Eidelman acquired an international reputation for excellence.

There is now a Satmar *shtiebl* under Mr Berish Weisz, and a flourishing Belzer *shtiebl*, which the Rebbe of Belz visited in 1982. The 90 families attached to these *shtieblech*, as well as a large number of the 190 families belonging to *Machzikei Hadath*, are Chasidim. Their spiritual leader is Rabbi Mendel Schneebalg, a Chasid of Vishnitz. His father, Rabbi David (d. 1968), came to England in 1947. After serving on the Manchester *Beth Din* as a *dayan* for 17 years, he retired to Bnei Brak.

By 1875 over half of Manchester Jewry were immigrants (or children of immigrants) from Poland and Russia. We have no evidence of any Chasidim settling there in the first half of the nineteenth century. There is, however, a letter, dated 1864, written by Rabbi Zadok HaKohen Rabinowicz (1823–1900) of Lublin, addressed to his former fellow-student, Dr Asher, in Manchester. To judge from the context of the letter, the possibility is that 'Asher' was the first name of a boyhood friend of Rabbi Zadok, as no other name is mentioned.

In 1890, the Ostreicher (Austrian-Galician) synagogue, using *Nusach Ari*, was established in Briddon Street. It subsequently moved to a converted church in Waterloo Road, Strangeways. A year later, the Broder *shul* was established in Cheltenham Crescent, Higher Broughton. It eventually amalgamated with the Central Synagogue, Cheetham Hill Road, which was founded in 1895. In 1889 a Romanian *shtiebl* was established in Briddon Street, also in Strangeways, where on Passover nights *Hallel* was recited in the synagogue, and the Psalm *Le'David Mizmor* after the evening service on the New Year in accordance with the Chasidic custom.[5] This synagogue was founded by Jews who had originally come from Vishnitz, Bohush and Jassy. In 1904, some worshippers formed a splinter group at 64a Waterloo Road, and others formed a new *Shtiebl Beth Yisrael* at Great Dulcie Street. Later they were reconciled and in 1914 they established in Ramsgate Street the New Romanian Shul, which, in 1954, moved to Vine Street in Kersal. In 1897, Lubavitch already had a *shtiebl* near the Victoria Railway Station, later known as Hay Shop. The *Kahal* Chasidim Synagogue was established above a row of shops at 78 Cheetham Hill Road, close to Red Bank.

The first Chasidic rebbe to make his home in Manchester was Rabbi Shmuel Meshullam Zusya Golditch, popularly known as 'Reb Zusya'.[6] He was born in Totiev, Ukraine, and traced his ancestry back to Rabbi Moshe Chayim Ephraim of Sudylkov. After serving in the Czarist army for a time, he escaped to Rymanov, Galicia, and became attached to Rabbi Joseph Cohen (d. 1912) of Rymanov. From there he went to Antwerp. After a short stay in London and Leeds, he settled in Manchester in 1919. At first, he attended the New Romanian *Shul* in Ramsgate Street. On the appointment of Rabbi Jacob Shachter as rabbi and member of the Manchester *Beth Din*, Rabbi Zusya opened a *shtiebl* at his home in Waterpark Road, Higher Broughton. He wore a *shtreimel* on *Shabbat*. He died in 1940.

His son, Rabbi Yitzchak (1907–87), a *dayan* of the Manchester *Beth Din* since 1946, displayed no Chasidic leanings, although he wore a *gartel* (special Chasidic belt). He was also the Rabbi of the Ostreicher *shtiebl* in Hightown. Yitzchak's son, Sir Philip Biron (d. 1982) adopted his mother's family name, though he retained his Hebraic and Chasidic forenames Moses Chayim Ephraim. He served as secretary of the Manchester *yeshiva* for a time, before embarking on a legal career.[7] For 30 years he served in the legal department of the Government of Tanzania, where he became a Senior Puisne Judge in 1962.

The late 1920s saw the establishment of an independent Orthodox community, the *Machzikei Hadath*, and the appointment in 1934 of Rabbi David Feldman (1885–1955) of Leipzig, as its rabbi. He was the author of a new edition of the *Kitzur Shulchan Aruch* of Rabbi Solomon Ganzfried (1804–86).[8] Rabbi Feldman came from a Chasidic background and was ordained by Rabbi Shmuel Engel. Mr Mordechai Zeev Dresner (d. 1975), a Chasid of Belz, who arrived in Manchester in 1939, greatly helped in the establishment of the *Machzikei Hadath*.

The appointment of Rabbi Yitzchak Dubov (1887–1977) to the staff of the Manchester *yeshiva* in 1929, brought another Chasidic leader to the town. Born in Penza, Russia, he studied in the Lubavitch *yeshiva Tomchei Temimim*, where he was renowned as a great *masmid* (diligent student). He was devoted to Lubavitch. In addition to his duties at the *yeshiva*, he acted as Reader at the *Adath Yisroel Shul*. He was a melodious singer, and his services on the High Holy Days were renowned. He conducted a weekly study circle on the *Tanya* of Rabbi Shneur Zalman of Liady at his home for selected students, and organised *ferbrengen* (gatherings) on Lubavitch festive days to discuss Chasidism and to recount the tales of the rebbes. Since suffering a serious illness when young, he always wore an ear-ring as a *kamea* (amulet). It was his custom not to enter the synagogue on the Sabbath prior to recitation of *Borechu* (Bless ye the Lord). His son, Zalman Joseph Alony, former *Dayan* of the Jewish communities of Ireland, was later the Head of the *Beth Din* of the Federation of Synagogues, London. Among Dubov's disciples were Dayan Isaac Lerner and Rabbi Dr Louis Jacobs. He was critical of the Anglo-Jewish establishment. 'If a Reverend is *goy*,' he would say, 'a Very Reverend is a great *goy*.'[9]

Another prominent Lubavitch personality in Manchester was dayan Yitzchak Rivkin (1869–1947). He studied under Rabbi Joseph Rozin, the Rogaczover Gaon of Dvinsk. Apart from his duties at the *Beth Din*, where he was the rabbi, he was the rabbi of the *Adath Yisroel* Synagogue from 1928.[10] He wore the *tefillin* of *Shimusha Rabba* (a type of *tefillin* only worn by the most saintly). In the inter-war years, a number of outstanding personalities such as Rabbi Meir Dan Plotzki, Rabbi Abraham Zevi Perlmutter and Rabbi Meir Shapiro visited Manchester and stayed in the home of the Belzer Chasid, Wolf Dresner. Dresner's brother, Baruch Hirsch, even made a pilgrimage to Belz.[11]

During the Second World War a number of London Chasidic rebbes went to live in Manchester. Among them were Rabbi Mechel Moskovitz, the son of the Shatzer Rebbe, who opened a *shtiebl* in Bury New Road and in 1949 emigrated to the USA; Rabbi Meshullam Ashkenazi in High Town and Rabbi Berel Rothenberg of Wlodoslav opened one in George Street.

After the death of Rabbi Y Rivkin, Rabbi Yitzchak Yaakov Weiss (1902–89) succeeded him as head of the *Beth Din*. Weiss, the son of Rabbi Joseph Yehuda (d. 1943) of Munkacz, was born in Dolina, Galicia on 8 *Adar* 1902. At the outbreak of the First World War, when he was 12 years old, the whole family moved to Munkacz, where the Rebbe of Belz lived at that time.

Weiss was ordained by Rabbi Meir Arik of Tarnow and Rabbi Shmuel Engel of Radomysl. From 1922 to 1929 he was the head of the Belzer *Yeshiva* in Munkacz. In 1929 he was appointed *dayan* of Grosswardein.

In 1943, he published his first volume of responsa, *Divrei Yitzchak*. During the Second World War, when a Ghetto was established in Grosswardein, he escaped to Romania and lived in Arad and Bucharest. In an appendix to his volume of responsa, he gives a moving account of life in Nazi-dominated Hungary and his miraculous survival.[12] His wife, Alta Rivka Lea, died in Bucharest in 1945 and a year later he married Malka (d. 1973), the daughter of Rabbi Chayim Dov Halperin (d. 1957), the Rabbi of Vaslui and a descendant of Ruzhin.

Rabbi Weiss, while waiting in Prague for an American visa, was invited by Rabbi Weingarten to his *yeshiva* in Egham, Surrey, in July 1948. On the advice of the Rebbe of Satmar, he remained in England,[13] and a year later, on 15 April 1949, was inducted by Chief Rabbi Brodie as *Rosh Beth Din* of Manchester, where he spent 21 happy years. His skill in personal relations immediately established him as a friend to rabbis and laymen alike, who flocked to him with their problems, knowing he cared for them.

When Dayan Y Abramsky left for Israel in 1951, Rabbi Weiss was offered his position at the London *Beth Din*. He agonised over the reply, but a delegation of Manchester rabbis persuaded him to remain where he was. He was highly regarded by Rabbi Yoel of Satmar. 'You do not fully appreciate,' he once told one of the Manchester Chasidim, 'whom you have in Manchester.' It was at the suggestion of the Rebbe that the *Eda Haredit* of Jerusalem appointed Rabbi Weiss to its *Beth Din* in 1970.

Although uncompromising in his rulings, he was extremely kind by disposition. He went to enormous lengths to free *agunot* for remarriage.

He was the author of responsa entitled *Minchat Yitzchak*. Nine volumes of this work appeared in print in his lifetime and a tenth volume was published posthumously.[14] During his lifetime, he always maintained contact with the Manchester community and frequently visited the city.[15] His third wife, Chana Miriam Sima (d. 1990), was the daughter of Rabbi Chayim Meir Hager of Vishnitz.

BIRMINGHAM

The Birmingham Lubavitch Centre at 95 Willows Road, a three-storey multi-faceted edifice costing £300,000, was purpose-built under the aegis of the Manpower Commission Scheme. It was consecrated by the Chief Rabbi in 1982. Its leader, Birmingham-born Rabbi Shmuel

Arkush, is deeply involved in 'Operation Judaism', a project sponsored by the Board of Deputies of British Jews and the Office of the Chief Rabbi, to counteract the increased missionary activity in Great Britain, particularly the activities of the 'Jews for Jesus' movement, the Moonies, the Divine Light Mission and the Church of Scientology, as well as the Church's Ministry among the Jews whose patron is the Archbishop of Canterbury.[16] Rabbi Arkush's activities cover the Midlands, Wolverhampton, Coventry, Nottingham, Leicester and Derby.

BOURNEMOUTH

The new *Chabad* Centre at 8 Gordon Road has dormitory facilities for weekend programmes for youths and adults.

BRIGHTON

England's fourth largest Jewish community had a Jewish day-school which closed down. The new Lubavitch primary school, situated in the grounds of the West Hove Synagogue, was warmly welcomed by the community in 1987.

CAMBRIDGE

Every Monday night the co-director of the Lubavitch University Council conducts a two-part learning evening for the Jewish students of the University.

EDINBURGH

Jews settled in Edinburgh in small numbers at the begining of the nineteenth century. The first synagogue was established in 1816. One of the early Chasidim there was Aaron ben Shneur Zalman Rabstaff (1886–1963), a native of Chernigov. He lived at first in London where he had his own *shtiebl* in Brick Lane, and was a close friend of Mendel Chaikin, the wine merchant. During the South African war, Rabstaff was encouraged by Sir Robert Glynfeld to settle in Edinburgh and to produce riding breeches for the army. Eight families soon joined him, and he established a *shtiebl* on the floor above a public house in Lothian Street. The most prominent worshipper there was Samuel Elijah Rubinstein (1919–64), who acted as *shammash* and Hebrew teacher and was an authority on Psalms. Rabbi Dr Salis Daiches, the spiritual leader of Scottish Jewry, was a man of strong will who did not brook opposition. He did not favour the *shtiebl*, nor did he like Rabbi Jacob Rabinowitz (the father of Rabbi Louis Rabinowitz), who had served in the town for some time.[17]

In 1922 the *shtiebl* engaged the services of the ritual slaughterer, Alexander Levison, who claimed to have authorisation from Rabbi A Y Kook. It eventually transpired that he was the brother of two apostates, Sir Leon Levison, first president of the International Hebrew Christian Alliance, and the Reverend Nahum Levison, a minister of the Church of Leith and an agent for the Society for the Promotion of Christianity among the Jews. Alexander Levison claimed £1,000 damages against the *Jewish Chronicle* and Dr Daiches who declared that Levison's rabbinical attestations were fraudulent. Lord Ashmore, Lord-in-Ordinary in the Court of Sessions in Edinburgh, rejected Levison's case.[18]

GLASGOW

The Jewish community in Glasgow is the largest in Scotland. Its members are mainly of Lithuanian and *Mithnaggedic* origin. There was no evidence of any Chasidim among them, but, in 1969, Rabbi Jeremy Rosen (then of Giffnock Synagogue) invited Lubavitch to Scotland to assist with Jewish education and the communal needs of the 10,000 strong Jewish community.

Rabbi Chayim Jacobs, a native of Luton, established a Lubavitch Centre on the premises of Giffnock Synagogue in 1970. This Centre is a beehive of activity: it houses a *Talmud Torah*, a mothers-and-toddlers group, a kindergarten and nursery school.

It appears that there were previously two synagogues which were attached to Chasidism dating from the early part of this century.[19] One of these was named *Nusach Ari* and was founded in 1913 in a one-room tenement flat over a public house in Oxford Street, later moving to 40 Main Street. The founders were Simon (Shiya) Felstein (d. 1943), who came from Bessarabia in 1907, and Woolf Egdoll. After the Second

World War, the *shtiebl* moved to rooms over a public house at the corner of Nicolson Street.

The other small Chasidic synagogue was *Beth Jacob*. Later both *minyanim* amalgamated, calling themselves *Beth Jacob Nusach Ari*, but generally known as just *Beth Jacob*. Their members hailed mainly from the Western Ukraine and Romania, and their attachment to Chasidism was very peripheral. When the *shtiebl* fell on hard times, its members joined another synagogue at 11 Oxford Road, taking the name *Poale Zedek*. This *shul* retained a certain Chasidic bias.

Rabbi J D Siroka (1870–1957), formerly the rabbi in Hull, came to Glasgow in 1914 when he was appointed the rabbi of the *Chevra Kadisha* Synagogue and head of the Glasgow *Beth Din*.[20] His son-in-law, the Rebbe of Kotzk, Rabbi S D Morgenstern, stayed in Glasgow for some time, and had a *Shtiebl Beth Jacob* in Abbotsford Place. The Glasgow Jewish Year Book printed a short sermon and a blessing by him.[21]

Rabbi Dr Wolf Gottlieb, who was appointed chairman of the Glasgow *Beth Din* in 1955, was also of Chasidic background. He had previously served as Assistant Education Officer of the Jewish Religious Emergency Council. He was the author of *Days of Old*.[22] He was a man of learning, a gifted orator with a lively sense of humour.

LEEDS

Leeds is now the second largest provincial Jewish centre. Though the first Leeds synagogue was not established until 1846, Jews have been living there since the middle of the eighteenth century.[23] The majority of the immigrants who settled there at the beginning of this century were involved in the tailoring industry, with a sprinkling of slipper-makers, glaziers, pedlars and shopkeepers. There is no evidence of Chasidim among the numerous *chevrot* which were first established such as the *Marienpoler, Lokever, Vilna, Polisher, Chevra Shass, Chevra Chaye Adam, Chevra Tehillim* and *Chevra Torah*.[24] This is not surprising since the majority of the immigrants came from Lithuania, where the Chasidic influence was comparatively small.

The first Chasidic congregation was the *Chevra Chasidim*, later known as the 'Chasidishe Synagogue', which was founded in Hope Street in 1890. It comprised 35 members and later moved to Bridge Street. In July 1935 it moved to a purpose-built synagogue (now used as a mosque) at 46 Spencer Place and by 1958 it still had 260 members.[25] Its claim to be called Chasidic was based entirely on its use of the liturgy of *Nusach Ari*. The Synagogue never had a full-time rabbi, but would often host rabbis from other Leeds congregations. During the Second World War, Rabbi B Finkelstein officiated there, and Rabbi B Szemtov paid the synagogue a visit in 1954.[26] For 20 years Mr Joseph Rapoport (1889–1984) was the president of the Synagogue.[27] Today, it is accommodated in a room of the *Talmud Torah* at 2 Sandhill Lane, and has about 130 members.

Lubavitch activities began in Leeds in 1975. In 1987 they established a small post-graduate *kollel*, organised businessmen's luncheons, began to carry out Chanukah and Purim campaigns, and distributed a monthly newsletter. Another of their important contributions to religious life in the community was the establishment of a day-school, the *Menora*, which has grown from 20 pupils in 1986 to more than 70 today.

LIVERPOOL

There is no evidence that the private *minyanim*, such as *Chevra Torah* or *Chevra Tehillim* which met in rooms in Gill Street in 1888 were Chasidic. The first reference to Chasidic ritual is found in a deed of appointment of new trustees, dated 20 July 1908. It records that the property of the new *beth hamidrash* was 'vested for and on behalf of a new Congregation entitled the "Hasidim, worshipping according to the ritual and liturgy of *Nusach Ari*."'[28]

On 11 September 1927 two small *minyanim*, *Nusach Sephard* of Russell Street, and *Nusach Ari* of Grove Street joined forces and were subsequently known as the Great Synagogue *Nusach Sephard*. They later moved to 55a Crown Street. The consecration of the imposing new premises took place on 24 March 1929. In 1937, the Reverend Shlomo Baron, a descendant of Rabbi Moses Chayim Ephraim of Sudlykov, officiated there as reader. Their *baal koreh* from his earliest youth was Reverend Moses Yitzchak Aaron (d. 1976).[29] The Trisker Rebbe from London would occasionally pay a visit to the *shtiebl* and conduct *tisch* there. In the course of the following 50 years, numbers dwindled, and the congregation moved, first to the *yeshiva* premises at 18 Church Road. It later moved to 2 Dovedale Road. The congregation ceased to exist in 1990.

The *Rosh Hashochtim* (chief supervisor of the ritual slaughterers) of Liverpool, Samuel Asher Lachs (1903–60), lived there from 1930, and conducted *shiurim* at various synagogues.[30] Another notable resident was Rabbi Israel Aryeh Leib Schneersohn, the son of Rabbi Levi Yitzchak, a brother of the renowned Rebbe of Lubavitch. He died on 13 *Iyar* 1958, and was interred in the Holy Land.

OXFORD

Established in 1988 and located at 75 Cowley Road on the corner of Alma Place is the Lubavitch Alec and Eileen Coleman Centre, known as the *L'Chaim* Society which hopes to cater for the 900 to 1,300 Jewish students who annually study in Oxford. This centre was generously endowed by the financier Alec Coleman. The annual cost of running the centre is over £200,000. Its present membership totals 980, and its founding senior members are the Pro-Vice Chancellor of Oxford University and the Provost of Oriel College, Sir Zelman Cowen, the former Governor-General of Australia.

Twice weekly the Society hosts educational and social activities. Seminars on topics ranging from evolution to economics are given by leading figures in these fields. Such notable personalities as Elie Wiesel, Adin Steinsalz, Simon Wiesenthal, Yitzchak Shamir, Mikhail Gorbachev, Bob Hawke, the former Australian Prime Minister, Christian Barnard, Perez de Cuellar, Henry Kissinger, and Branko Lustig, one of the producers of 'Schindler's List', have participated.

Each Friday night the Society plays host to students for the Sabbath dinner. For most it serves as their first introduction to the Sabbath. Discussion groups on contemporary issues are held regularly. The themes range from 'surrogate motherhood', 'drug abuse', 'euthanasia', 'organ transplants' to 'contraceptives' and 'artificial insemination'.

Recently ex-President Ronald Reagan launched a Jewish Studies Programme at the newly established Oxford Maimonides Institute. Among the celebrated speakers were Lord Young, a former member of Mrs Thatcher's Cabinet, and Godfrey Bradman, a leading British property developer.

The Centre's controversial founder and director, Rabbi Shmuel Boteach (popularly known as Shmulie), born in 1967, comes from Miami, Florida, USA. His parents were divorced and from the age of ten he regularly attended Lubavitch summer camps. Educated at *Torat Emet Yeshiva* in Jerusalem and in Sydney, Australia, as well as the Central Lubavitch *Yeshiva* in New York, he was ordained at the age of

21 and is a prolific writer. He is the author of *The Wolf shall lie with the Lamb – the Messiah in Chasidic Thought,* based on the teachings of Rabbi Menachem Mendel Schneerson. In this work he evokes with insight Judaism's view of the Messiah. He maintains that the belief in the coming of the Messiah is more central to Judaism than even the observance of the Sabbath and the Day of Atonement. He has also published recently *Moses of Oxford* and *The Jewish Guide to Adultery.*

There were great reservations[31] by some members of the local Jewish community, fearing that his activities would undermine the Jewish establishment in Oxford. In September 1994 Rabbi Boteach invited the Israeli Prime Minister Yitzhak Rabin to address his Society. This invitation was strongly opposed by Rabbi Shragai Feivish Vogel, the director of the Lubavitch Foundation in Britain, who felt that Rabin's 'peace accord' with Yassir Arafat was contrary to the wishes of the late Rabbi of Lubavitch.

Rabbi Boteach was suspended and later resigned. He is now trying to establish his Society as an independent and registered charity. 'My aim,' he stated, 'is to make Oxford into more of a Jewish city. I like to make the world more aware, and it is a good idea to start here in Oxford, in what is a cradle of civilization. Students think of Judaism as passive and lacking in intellectual energy. At Chabad House we present a challenging and dynamic experience of Jewish life.'

25 • The Chasidic Community

The Chasidim who lived in east and north-east London before the First World War and in the inter-war years fully integrated into the Anglo-Jewish community within two generations. They no longer felt insecure and had no desire to transplant the East European *shtetl* to their new home, nor did they publicly proclaim their Orthodoxy. They strove for integration not isolation. Apart from their rebbes, few wore the distinctive garments of the Chasidim nor was there a *kipa* to be seen in the streets of London. Most men were clean shaven. There were no facilities at that time for their children to continue in the Chasidic way of life, and, therefore, they permitted them to receive their education at local County Council schools or the Jews' Free School where they became Anglicised. Their Jewish religious education became merely a supplement to their secular education. The children received their Hebrew education after school hours in local *chedarim*, where the language of instruction was Yiddish, and was geared towards preparing them for their *bar mitzvah*, generally stopping shortly thereafter. Many of them studied for the professions, becoming doctors, lawyers and accountants.

The offspring of the Chasidim fully participated in the Anglo-Jewish synagogal organisations, in the United Synagogue,[1] in the Federation of Synagogues,[2] and communal and national bodies.[3] They were well represented in the Anglo-Jewish ministry and in science.[4] Many assimilated to the host culture. Sir Isaiah Berlin, the well-known philosopher and former President of Wolfson College, Oxford, is, through his mother, descended from Rabbi Dov Baer of Lubavitch, whose *tefillin* he still cherishes. Sir Yehudi Menuhin traces his ancestry to Rabbi Shneur Zalman of Liady.[5] Abraham Israel Richtiger (d. 1973), the former chairman of the *Poale Zion* in London, came of Chasidic background.

An 'open door' policy of allowing immigrants into Britain was maintained by the government for ten years following the end of the

Second World War. This enabled many Chasidim from war-torn Europe to enter this country.

Slum clearance, bombing and redevelopment had made Jewish Orthodox life in the East End of London difficult, and the 1950s saw a shift of the Jewish population to Stamford Hill in north London, where there now live more than 20,000 Jews. Walking through Stamford Hill today is like stepping back into a pre-1939 European ghetto. To the Chasidim, Stamford Hill is the Jerusalem of England where they continue to live in the style of the *shtetl*.[6] Unlike the Chasidic immigrants of the inter-war years, they reject completely any compromise with modernity. They are opposed to any social integration with non-Chasidim. They have established their own *glatt* kosher butcher shops, kosher bakeries and grocers, *shaatnes* laboratories, innumerable *shtieblech* representing most known Chasidic dynasties, kindergartens, *chedarim*, boys' and girls' schools, seminaries, *yeshivot*, *kollelim* and *mikvaot*.

Many Chasidim still dress in their distinctive Polish or Hungarian garb: they wear a *kaftan* or *kapote*, a kind of long black coat, and a sable- or beaver-trimmed circular hat, known as a *shreimel* (after a corruption of the Polish word *stroj*, meaning costume). There is a verse in Isaiah which says 'righteousness shall be the girdle of his loins, and faithfulness the girdle of his reins',[7] so Chasidim of all dynasties wear a twisted silken girdle around their waists at prayer to distinguish between man's upper and lower parts.

The Chasidim are content to remain in their present surroundings, as the thought of changing their environment is traumatic for them, and they are, therefore, rebuilding and extending their homes to accommodate their growing families. It is a static community, with Stamford Hill becoming another Williamsburg or Boro Park. There are naturally great divisions and disagreements among the Chasidim, but they now realise that they must exercise a measure of tolerance to those with different ideas.

How influential is contemporary Chasidism? Can the movement that once rejuvenated Jewry renew the Jews of our jaded world? What is the numerical strength of the traditionalists? There are no accurate statistics. There is a wide diversity of conflicting estimates. It seems probable that there are some 2,000 Chasidic families in the London Borough of Hackney: Satmar is the largest group, followed by Belz. Though Lubavitch is the most dynamic section, it is surprisingly not the most numerous.

Before the Second World War, north London formed the heartland of the United Synagogue with large synagogue buildings in Islington, Dalston, Stoke Newington and Stamford Hill. Now nearly all these have been closed. The Synagogue *Adath Yisroel* of the Union of Orthodox Hebrew Congregations in Stoke Newington is declining in numbers, some of its members having moved to Tottenham, where a branch synagogue has been established. Stamford Hill with its environs has now become the centre of Chasidic London, although it is a multi-racial borough. It is a place of some danger for identifiable Jews, because muggings, burglaries, nuisance attacks of wig-snatching, and racial attacks are common. Chasidic mothers are often propositioned by curb-crawlers. Graffiti with the words 'Jews out' and swastika daubings are not unknown. Used injection needles and condoms are often thrown into Jewish school playgrounds during the night.[8]

Nevertheless, when a little lad scarcely higher than your knee rushes up to you with shining eyes and shoulder-long sidelocks, and implores you to give him money 'for his *yeshiva*', your heart as well as your pocket is touched and you know that you have arrived in Stamford Hill. A scraggy grey-bearded grocer like Sholem Aleichem's character Tevye, the dairyman, unloads dairy produce. A patriarchal baker with white hair moves majestically around his products.

The majority of the Chasidim are naturally affiliated to the right wing of the Orthodox spectrum. Their aim is to live around the centres of learning which they have built, and this leads to great competition for available local property. It is a world in miniature, a reproduction of the mediaeval *shtetl* in modern surroundings. The younger generation fit themselves willingly and enthusiastically into the old traditions. Each group provides for its own needs. It is said that in a single street in Stamford Hill there is more Torah learning going on than in the whole of the rest of Britain.

The Anglo-Jewish community is estimated to number 330,000, 0.6 per cent of the general population, with an annual decline of 3,000. A low birthrate, intermarriage and emigration to Israel are the causes of this decline. Not so in the Chasidic world where the birthrate is very high, families with eight, nine or even ten children being quite common, making five children per family the average.

The relief of poverty has long been regarded as a great *mitzva* by the Chasidim. They have a strong spirit of solidarity and provide help for the less fortunate among them, the better-off caring for those who are materially disadvantaged. No section of the community spends so much on charity to maintain some hundred needy families. There are no two nations, no growing bitterness or resentment towards the better off. There is a variety of funds to help those who are unable to earn a living wage.

Two Chasidim of Satmar collect annually over £100,000 which ensures a twice-annual distribution of food to the needy – at Passover and at the New Year. The Passover package contains wine, *matzot*, potatoes, eggs and fruit, all in sufficient quantity for a large family. No other Chasidic group in England matches their charitable endeavours. These charitable ventures do not cater exclusively for any particular Chasidic group. On the contrary, they often pride themselves that they provide philanthropic services to all sections of Jewry. Hence, the Satmar *Bikkur Cholim* is renowned for its work among the sick, irrespective of the Chasidic affiliation of those who are helped. 'I do not like Satmar,' a Chasid once said, 'but if I were to be sick, I would like to be in their midst.'

Emissaries from Israeli *yeshivot* and Torah Institutions regularly visit London. A week without a *meshullach* or a Rebbe is a very rare event. Special 'car services' take them to Jewish homes throughout London. Special lists of names and addresses of donors are issued monthly. The *Shomer Shabbos* north London and north-west London telephone directories, giving names, addresses and telephone numbers, are the *vade mecum* of the *meshullach*.

Often there may be as many as 20 *meshullachim*, mainly from Israel, visiting London. Mr Jackie (Yankel) Levinson of Craven Walk (a former partner of Zalman Margulies) offers them free board and lodging. The length of stay varies from a day to several weeks. Few are ever turned away. A *meshullach* once asked his host, mistaking him for a fellow-*meshullach*, 'How long can one stay here?' and was told, 'I have not yet been thrown out!'

'Callers' are a regular event in Stamford Hill. Several visits per night are not uncommon. Few leave empty-handed. The affluent and the not so well-off give donations according to their means. The Society of Friends of the Torah was established to take advantage of existing tax regulations for the distribution of monetary gifts to charities. Bobow, Belz and Vishnitz patronise their own institutions and supply their own charity vouchers. The more affluent families have established charitable trusts, such as S & W Berisford, the Berger Family Trust, the Cymerman Trust Limited whose avowed aim is 'to advance religion in accordance with Orthodox faith'; all invest capital through their trustees for charitable purposes. A number of donors have 'open house' once a week for 'callers'.[9]

More than six million pounds are spent annually on education alone. Latterly, economic success has made it possible to establish many and varied Torah institutions. Only two schools are state-aided.[10]

Yiddish is not a dead language in Stamford Hill. As Yiddish was the language of the millions of martyrs of Eastern Europe, they feel that they must maintain it as their means of communication,[11] and it is therefore the first language of their children. It is spoken in the home, in the synagogue, in the school, in the *yeshiva* and in the *kollel*, yet it is not taught as a language. It is taken for granted that boys and girls are able to read and speak Yiddish without any formal instruction. They affirm that *A Yid redt Yiddish* (a Jew speaks Yiddish). No attention is paid to spelling or sentence structure. Modern Hebrew is not taught in Chasidic schools, for it has too many associations with secular nationalism and Zionist ideology.

Rabbi Samson Raphael Hirsch's ideal of *Torah Im Derech Eretz* (the study of the Torah combined with secular education) has been utterly rejected by the Chasidim. They reject secular academic learning, and they do not regard it an asset. They adopt an anti-intellectual approach. Secular studies in schools are merely tolerated. They maintain that the acquisition of alien cultural values does not enrich the Jewish personality. To Chasidic children secular subjects are *Goyishe* (non-Jewish) subjects, and both parents and children regard them as a burden and as a concession to the secular authorities' requirements. As soon as the child learns to talk, he learns the basic prayers. At five, sometimes even earlier, he goes to *cheder*. No Chasidic child goes to a State school.

Girls are prevented from acquiring too much secular knowledge. For them to embark on further education would delay their early marriages, and expose them to alien influences. Study in religious seminaries (teacher training college for girls) is their ideal. Girls who do not qualify as teachers become office workers in religious organisations.

Before the First World War some 10,000 students studied in the *yeshivot* of Eastern Europe. The Chasidim subscribe to the view of Rabbi Meir Shapiro that 'the main purpose of a *yeshiva* is not to produce rabbis or *roshei yeshivot* (principals), but rather to produce learned *baalei batim* (laymen)'. They utterly reject the concept of *Torah U'Mada*, an academic programme based on a fusion of secular knowledge with a traditional *yeshiva* curriculum. Philosophy, theology and the humanities are forbidden territories. Vocational training is not part of a *yeshiva* curriculum in England. The Chasidim do not regard the Yeshiva University of New York and the Bar-Ilan University in Israel as Torah-true

217

institutions. It is felt that in this age of widespread Jewish ignorance, the study of the Torah *lishmo* (for its own sake) is the ideal. Most of their rabbis and rebbes have no secular high school education, and generally adopt a narrow intellectual approach. Only Lubavitch *yeshiva* students are encouraged to mix with the wider community. To pursue knowledge is the chief recreation even of laymen.

Kollelim have become very popular in the Chasidic world. The purpose of a *kollel* is to provide an opportunity for advanced research in all aspects of Torah study. It is generally accepted that high standards in science and industry can only be maintained by means of advanced research. This applies equally to Torah study. It was Rabbi Israel Salanter who said:

> Though I admire the method of Austritt of Rabbi Samson Raphael Hirsch who opposed the Reform Movement, I would suggest a better way. In every town where there is a Reform community, ten rabbinical scholars should be maintained to sit in the Beth Hamidrash and to dedicate themselves to the study of the Torah. They will have an automatic influence upon the whole community and stop the community from going over to the Reform and assimilationists.[12]

Higher criticism is naturally regarded as heresy. Chasidims believe in a personal Messiah, in the restoration of the sacrificial system, and in traditional rabbinic eschatology.

Although all Chasidim love Zion, they do not approve of Zionism. They do not celebrate *Yom Atzmaut* (Israel's Independence Day), or *Yom Yerushalayim* (the annual commemoration of the liberation of Jerusalem). Their teachers and spiritual leaders are openly anti-Zionist. On the questions of ritualism and ethical standards, many of their leaders stress that the minutiae of ritual observance should be linked with high ethical standards and that the *glatt kosher* syndrome should not be a substitute for the Commandments governing *mitzvot shebein adam lachavero* (the *mitzvot* governing the relationships between man and man).

26 • The Chasidic Way of Life

In pre-war Eastern Europe it was customary for a son-in-law to live with his wife's parents – *eidem oif kest*.[1] Today's Chasidic son-in-law does not live with his in-laws, but expects to be maintained in a home of his own.

A large percentage of those who study in the *kollelim* receive financial support from the *kollel*. Amounts vary; some even provide subsidised housing for their students. The aim of most students is to become either a *maggid shiur* (a teacher of Talmud) or a principal of a *yeshiva* or a *kollel*. Others become rabbis, teachers, scribes, kosher meat slaughterers and supervisors, and a few become computer programmers or businessmen.

Girls between the ages of 16 and 18 are encouraged to attend a teachers' seminary. There is in London a *Beth Yaakov* Seminary which was established in 1946. Its two-year syllabus includes the teaching of Pentateuch, rabbinic commentaries, the Book of Samuel and the Ethics of the Fathers, Jewish history and the practice and psychology of education. The language of instruction is English. Eighty per cent of the students come from Chasidic homes. Satmar has its own seminary where the language of instruction is Yiddish. The Pentateuch is studied orally and not textually.

Some girls study in the Jewish Teachers' Training College (*Beth Midrash Lemorot*) in Gateshead, which provides a thorough training for girls who intend to become teachers in Jewish primary and secondary schools.

Other places of higher education are the Seminary in Lucerne, Switzerland, and the Massoret Institute in Golders Green, which provides advanced education for women. There are prohibitions against reading novels, just as there is a serious objection to frivolous talk. Places of entertainment such as the cinema, the theatre and concert-hall are not to be patronised. Radio is tolerated, but videos are banned. In a letter to his community Rabbi Padwa writes: 'There is no estimating the danger caused to Godliness and to the education of boys and girls by having a video recorder in the home. This is an opening for sinning and the destruction of humility and modesty.' He also forbade his followers to make video recordings of wedding parties.[1]

The Jewish woman 'was given complete equality in the emotional, mystical, religious life of Beshtian Chasidism,' S A Horodezky wrote uncritically half a century ago.[2] Radical feminism and the Women's Rights Movement are regarded as part of non-Jewish and secular ideology. Chasidic women have no desire for professional pursuits or careers. Marriage and propagation are to them positive religious obligations, and they devote themselves exclusively to the time-honoured spheres of family and home. Despite their total exclusion from synagogal management and communal affairs, they do not regard themselves as second-class citizens or battery-hens. Though they live in a male-dominated society, Chasidic women have a loving relationship with their husband and children. Married women generally work as long as they can before having children, their earnings supplementing the family income and thus allowing their young husbands to continue full-time study. Portraits of rebbes are prominently displayed around the house. Those who can afford it have two sinks and two dishwashers, so as to keep meat and dairy dishes and crockery separately. Some even have special Passover kitchens. Chasidic women are not generally expected to attend synagogue regularly on the Sabbath, but pray at home and recite special *techinot* (supplications).

Lubavitch encourages girls over the age of three to light candles on the eve of the Sabbath and its women to participate in communal life. One Lubavitch woman was recently co-opted on to the Hackney Social Services Committee to represent women's needs.

The ideal age for marriage is 18 for boys and 17 for girls. Dating is unknown. There are no professional matchmakers (*shadchanim*) but everybody is a *shadchan*. Often the *rosh yeshiva* or the teacher recommends matches (*rett shidduchim*). The main consideration is a good family background, and if possible, the same Chasidic affiliation. The suitability of the families and the compatibility of their social standing are given high priority. No betrothal takes place without the rebbe's blessing. A girl and her intended mother-in-law, and a boy and his intended father-in-law, should preferably not have the same first names. Marriages are frequently arranged with sons and daughters of families from Antwerp, Strasbourg, New York, Israel and Switzerland.

Courtship is very limited. The young couple, however, are given the opportunity 'to talk' together in the presence of a member of the family to make sure that they are compatible. Romantic love is associated with sin and lustfulness. The sexual act is holy and has nothing to do with passion or lust. The marriage of a poor or orphaned girl is the concern of the whole community. Special funds are available to provide her with a dowry and a trousseau.

On the Sabbath preceding the wedding ceremony, the bridegroom is called up to the Reading of the Law (*Aufruf*), and nuts and sweets are thrown over him as a symbol of fertility. All Chasidic marriages in London take place under the auspices of the *Adath Yisrael*. The wedding ceremony (*chupa*) is held in the open, either in the courtyard of the synagogue or outside the banqueting hall. Holding the ceremony within a synagogue is regarded as an Anglicised custom. The bride is led around the bridegroom seven times; no address is delivered during the ceremony. At the wedding banquet, the sexes are segregated, with the bride in the woman's part of the hall, and the bridegroom in the men's. Elaborate screens divide the two sections, and the women, present but unseen by the men, are frequently banished to the back of the hall. Between courses, there is dancing, men with men and women with women. One by one, fragile elders, bent beneath the dual weight of age and erudition, come forward to dance the *mitzva tanz* (handkerchief dance) with the bride.

Eyes closed and faces uplifted, expressions ecstatic, shoulder to shoulder, and arm in arm, linked by common joy and uncommon camaraderie, they form a wide and winding chain around the hall. The sparks fly from the flushed cheeks of the little *kapote*-coated boys and the flying boots of their grey-beared elders. And as they sway, the band plays on and on, vigorous, vibrant, half-hypnotic in exotic and unceasing rhythm, so, in tireless, timeless steps they dance away the night.

Even the poorest provides a festive meal. There are some caterers who will undertake to provide the festive meal for a needy bride at cost price or below. Among many Chasidic groups it is customary to cut off the bride's hair even before the ceremony, and for her to wear a wig from that time on.

Birth control, unless there are serious medical complications, is strictly forbidden, and abortion is akin to murder. The rabbinic maxim, 'He who gives life will also sustain life' is the motto of the Chasidim. Parents who put financial considerations first and the procreation of children second are regarded as having misplaced values. Children are regarded as the deepest source of happiness; nothing can compensate for childlessness, adoption is not regarded as a suitable substitute. In the words of the Rebbe of Lubavitch: 'Statistical evidence tells us that, parallel to the reduction in the size of families, has gone an alarming increase of marital discord, separation, divorce and mental breakdown.'[3] Women bear, nurse and rear a houseful of children, cook meals, clean, wash and shop, yet rarely complain or consider themselves exploited. Many also work in a part-time capacity to help with the family budget.

Lack of preparation for marriage, economic hardship, the growing acceptance of divorce, the loneliness of young wives who have come from abroad, all these may lead to marital breakdown. The comparative incidence of divorce in Stamford Hill was so high in the 1960s that the rabbinate of the Union of Orthodox Congregations contemplated proclaiming a public fast.[4] Today divorce in Chasidic circles is still much below the national average, but higher than it was years ago. Infidelity, child neglect or abuse are inconceiveable to the true Chasid. Traditional practices go unchallenged. Parents are still in a position of authority and children are aware of their duties. Mental illness is no longer regarded a stigma (*shanda*) or an embarrassment. Psychiatry is no longer ignored, but used where it is considered helpful.

'A close neighbour is better than a distant relative' applies to the community. All are involved. They lend to, and borrow from, one another. No one needs to feel isolated. A wedding, an engagement, a *bar mitzvah* or a circumcision creates a joyous mood, funerals evoke a general sadness. The laws of *yichud* and *negia* (physical contact) are strictly observed. Mixed activities such as swimming are not allowed, social functions are held entirely separately (or at least the seating is separate). The laws of family purity (*taharat hamishpacha*) are strictly observed.

Unlike the situation in Jerusalem, or even in Vienna, there is no specific Chasidic *shechita* in London. The five *shochetim* employed by the *Adath* are all Chasidim and so are most of the *mashgichim* (supervisors). Most of the Chasidim are affiliated to the *Adath Yisroel* Burial Society, and pay an annual contribution of £35 per family, if under 49 years of age. Ger, Ruzhin and some other groups are not officially affiliated, and must pay £1,000 to the Burial Society when a death takes place. The Society allows three charity funerals per year. The Chasidim fully participate in the *Chevra Kadisha* (the volunteer society which looks after the burial and the rites connected with it).

In the election of the 23-man executive of the Union of Orthodox Congregations, held in July 1990, Satmar Chasidim gained the positions of the vice-presidencies and one of the treasurers.[5]

Though Belz and Bobow style their spiritual leaders '*dayan*', they do not, in any way, infringe on the status of the *Beth Din* of the Union of Orthodox Hebrew Congregations under the leadership of Rabbi Chanoch Dov Padwa, a Chasid of the late Rabbi of Belz. Rabbi Padwa, who was appointed principal rabbinical authority in 1955, was born in Bobruisk, Poland in 1914 and studied in the Hungarian *yeshivot*. He was interned by the Austrian authorities, and after his release made his way to the Holy Land in 1940, where he became a member of the *Beth Din* of the *Eda Charedit*.[6] He exhorted his community to 'act modestly' when holding family celebrations. He suggested that no more than 80–100 couples be invited to a festive meal, and that the cost of the meal 'excluding supervision costs' should be no more than £24 per couple.[7]

The community is not generally bellicose, believes in *sha shtil* ('keep quiet' mentality) and very rarely hits the headlines. An exception to the rule occurred in 1991. Some Chasidim were angered when an Orthodox non-Chasidic Jewish couple reported to the police and social workers that their youthful baby-sitter had indecently assaulted their daughter, aged five. The offender was sentenced to six months' youth custody, later reduced by the Court of Appeal to one year's probation. The family was stigmatised as *mosrim* (informers) and a number of Chasidic zealots took the law into their own hands and so harassed the family that they had to be moved to a safe house. Rabbi Padwa issued a conciliatory statement, describing the incident as a *chillul haShem* (profanation of God's name) and condemned the demonstrations.[8]

Rabbi C Halpern and Dayan S Friedman (a son-in-law of Rabbi Padwa) are members of the *Beth Din* which meets every Thursday morning. Of its seven members, three are Chasidim. They deal with divorce (five or six per year). Proselytisation and *chalitza* are not dealt with.

The Chasidim support *Kedassia*, the Joint Kashrut Committee of the Union under the guidance of the Chasid I Kohn. It supervises butcher shops, bakeries, grocers, caterers and hotels. Strictly kosher meals under *Kedassia* supervision are now available in 250 hospitals in the London area, and on airplanes on request.

The Chasidim are law-abiding citizens, Jewish Stamford Hill having the lowest crime rate in London. There is a total absence of alcoholism and drug-taking, there is filial respect, no marital infidelity and no suicide. Traffic offences are normally the only misdemeanours. They are mindful of the words of the Rabbi of Satmar who told his followers that, in view of the fact that Jews today are not barred from normal activities, they have no reason to engage in illegal dealings.[9]

The Chasidic community is not wealthy. There are several reasons why this is so. Its members are mostly wages-earners or run small family businesses and the father is generally the sole wage-earner. The cost of kosher food is higher than that of non-kosher products, and education takes place in private schools, for which fees must be paid. Strict Sabbath observance, especially in the winter, when the Sabbath begins early on Friday afternoon, limits employment prospects and lack of professional training and their distinctive clothing make the securing of employment difficult for young Chasidic men. Nevertheless, Chasidim can be found in a variety of professions: there are Chasidic kitchen designers, textile manufacturers, computer programmers. A number of Chasidim are in the diamond trade.

On 26 April 1990, over one thousand people participated in the *Aguda* celebrations of the completion of the ninth cycle of Talmud study at the Great Hall, Picketts Lock Lane, London. The guest of honour was Rabbi Levi Yitzchok Horowitz, the Bostoner Rebbe, now of Har Nof, Jerusalem.[10]

Though London has no Chasidic court, rebbes from the United States and Israel frequently visit London, and each visit is a festive occasion. Many a rebbe has used the large hall of the *Yesodey Hatorah* School to address his Chasidim on the Sabbath. The Chasidic community, except for Satmar (Monsey) and Belz, supports the *Aguda*, which publishes the *Jewish Tribune*. From March 1977 it has appeared weekly, whereas for the previous 15 years it was published fortnightly. It is the successor to the *Jewish Weekly*, established on 31 January 1936 and edited by H A Goodman until his death in 1961.

The *Tribune's* first editor was Simcha Bunem Unsdorfer (1925–67), who was born in Bratislava, Czechoslovakia, and educated at the *yeshivot* of Bratislava and Nitra. He was imprisoned in the concentration camps of Auschwitz and Buchenwald. On his arrival in England after the war, he studied at the Staines and Manchester *yeshivot*. In 1953, he was appointed secretary of the *Aguda* and the editor of the English section of the *Jewish Tribune*. He also wrote a successful book, *The Yellow Star*, describing his personal experience and his reaction as a deeply religious Jew to the terrors of Nazism.[11]

He was succeeded as editor by Elchanan Liff (d. 1966). Born in Russia, Liff settled, after studying at various *yeshivot*, in Riga, the capital of Latvia, where he worked with the Agudist Mordecai Dubin, and acted as the editor of the *Haint*. He spent the war-years in Siberia, and in the post-war period lived for a time in France. In 1950 he came to

London where he edited the Yiddish section of the *Jewish Tribune*. His co-worker was Shabse Schonfeld (1898–1986), known as a man of wit and wisdom. A Chasid of Ger, he was active in pre-war Vienna, later in London, where for two decades he was the general secretary of the *Agudat Yisroel* World Organisation.[12] Satmar Chasidim patronise the New York Yiddish paper *Der Yid*, and those of Belz, the *Machne HaChareda* of Jerusalem or *Dos Yiddishe Vort*, published by the *Aguda* in New York. Non-Chasidic Yiddish papers and even the Anglo-Jewish press are called 'Sabbath-desecrating papers'.

The beginnings of the *Aguda* movement in this country go back to the time when Rabbi Meir Dan Plotski, Rabbi of Warta and Rabbi Joseph Lew, later Rabbi of Bow, visited London in 1920.[13] It has had very active leaders here. For over 40 years, Harry Goodman was in charge of the political activities of extreme Orthodox Jewry, missing no opportunity to represent its members at national and international level. A man of eloquence, vision, courage, energy and acute intelligence, he spoke in favour of uncompromising Orthodoxy, continually asserting that neither the World Jewish Congress nor the World Zionist Organisation nor any other international body could represent the Orthodox community.[14] At the Third Convention of World *Aguda*, he declared: 'We must put an end to the criminal monopoly of the Zionists.'[15]

Bezalel (Sigi) Stern (1899–1990) was a vice-president and member of the executive of the British *Aguda*. He organised a youth movement in Vienna which encouraged the Jewish youngsters in the Austrian capital to remain steadfast to their Jewishness. During the war he found refuge in London and directed the *Beth Hamidrash Etz Chayim* at 69 Lordship Road, which was under the spiritual leadership of his cousin, Rabbi Shlomo Baumgarten.[16]

Today the *Aguda* serves the wider community. It has an advice centre which deals with a variety of problems, an employment agency, a housing association, a crèche and adult education classes. In 1990 the *Aguda*, together with *Yad Voezer* – a committee founded in Stamford Hill in 1975 to help handicapped children and adults – opened a residential home for young women. They acquired a number of houses for homeless families and are now developing, with the Federation of Jewish Family Services, an Orthodox township on the site of the former Bearsted Memorial Hospital. The nine-acre site now comprises not only 36 sheltered flats, but also a 30-room well-equipped home for the elderly,[17] which has two dairy and two meat kitchens, as well as a Passover kitchen.

Rabbi Abraham Pinter represented the Northfield Ward for Labour between 1982 and 1990, and Councillor Abraham Lew of Satmar now represents the Labour Ward. Councillor Joe Lobenstein (b. 1927), a native of Hanover, who came to London in 1933, and has served for 30 years as Councillor on the Hackney Borough Council, is now leader of the Council's Conservative Opposition. He writes regularly for the *Jewish Tribune* under the pseudonym of *Ben Yitzhok* and is very active in the *Aguda*. Hackney Borough Council now has a number of Orthodox Jews with voting rights on its various committees.

The London Borough of Hackney is one of the most deprived areas in this country. It has the largest concentration of working-class Jews in England, and they comprise 30 per cent of the Borough's population.[18] So far it has not allocated any of its houses to homeless Chasidic families. However, it does employ home-helps who are fully trained in the laws of Kashrut, and has given grants for other projects.

Nearly 4,000 children from Chasidic and Orthodox homes are educated in 40 strictly Orthodox schools. Yet of Hackney's £93 million budget for education, it only spends £1,123,000 on the Orthodox community. After the abolition of the Inner London Education Authority, Hackney promised to increase financial support for Orthodox Jewish education and, in its 1991 budget, it allocated £473,000 for nursery education.[19] The money will be allocated to the 14 Orthodox schools which cater for the nearly 1,000 under-fives in Hackney.

The 300 strictly Orthodox children with special learning needs are given scant special teaching and therapy in a Jewish environment. A proposal to create a unit for them in the New River School attached to the state-aided Avigdor Primary School in Clissold Road has been rejected.[20]

27 • The Literary Horizon

Schechter and Zangwill were among the first Anglo-Jewish writers to present Chasidism in a favourable light. It took some time, however, before their 'revisionist' efforts were emulated. A number of English authors, both academic and popular, have written on Chasidism. They include non-Jews, and Jews of differing commitments: Orthodox, liberal and agnostic.

Outlines of Jewish History by Lady Katie Magnus (1844–1924), dealing with the history of the Jews from biblical times to the present day, was published in 1888.[1] Her style was poetic, emotional and sensitive, and her book became a recognised textbook on Jewish history. She made the past live again.

She followed faithfully in the footsteps of Graetz who had described the Cabbala as

> a fungous growth which, since the 13th century, crept over the body of the Law and of tradition. This Cabbala is a weed of Eastern planting, but amongst Western scholars, in waste places, it got some space to grow. It is a strange combination of faith and philosophy and its mystical character facilitated the introduction of all sorts of unJewish beliefs and super- stitions under the name of Cabbala. Thus we have a quantity of so-called Cabbalistic literature, containing a superstitious agglomeration of signs and wonders, which would lead its students to credulous musings on evil spirits and false prophets and spurious Messiahs instead of to earnest belief in the one true God and His servant Moses.[2]

She devoted a whole section to Moses Mendelssohn,[3] but not one word to Rabbi Israel Baal Shem Tov. In a subsequent book, *Jewish Portraits*, she still does not mention him.[4] In a revised edition, however, the editors gave a sympathetic description of the Chasidic movement, stating that 'this conception of the hereditary transmission of a spiritual dignity was an idea entirely foreign to Jewish tradition; but it was widely accepted, and it is astonishing that the charlatans were few and the number of pious and respected leaders were many in these dynasties.'[5]

David Cassel's (1810–93) book, *Manual of Jewish History and Literature*, was translated from German into English by Mrs Alice Lucas.[6] In this work Chasidism is censured. Cassel writes:[7]

> Another very unfortunte circumstance is the spread of the so-called 'Chasidism' among the Jews of Poland, Galicia and Russia. This tendency connected with the teachings of the Cabbala and supposed to originate with 'Israel Baal Shem', is not only hostile to the Talmud, but to every kind of intellectual progress; while, on the other hand, it encourages superstition and many other un-Jewish views. The belief in the prophetic gift and miraculous powers of some rabbi or 'Zaddik' brings thousands of sufferers and large sums of money to the supposed miracle-worker. Greed of gain on the one hand and blind superstition on the other, constantly increase the evil, against which the energy of Elias Wilna and, in later times, the satire of Isaac Erter, have vigorously exerted themselves.[8]

A keen student of Jewish mysticism, to which he devoted many years of research, was Welsh-born Rabbi Joshua Abelson (1873–1941), the author of a doctoral thesis 'The Immanence of God in Rabbinical Literature' and 'Jewish Mysticism'.[9] He also wrote an introduction to the Soncino Edition of the Zohar. In an essay on 'Chasidic Ideas of Prayer', he writes: 'Chasidic prayer holds the true secret of what Jewish prayer should be and what it was primordially intended to be. Shorn of its obsolete naivete, its exaggerated and uncomely eccentricity, it contains elements of perennial value and significance to us.'[10] 'The Chasidim,' he stated, 'are the true successors of the old Psalmists in their power of soul-cultivation, in their ability to reach the Traces of Divine in even the lowliest phenomenon of everyday life.'[11]

Rabbi Dr Israel Weinstock (1909–80), a descendant of Ruzhin, was the rabbi of the Hampstead Garden Synagogue in London during the war. He was the author of *Studies in Jewish Philosophy and Mysticism* (*Be'Maagale HaNigla VeHaNistar*)[12] and was the editor of the Hebrew periodical *Temirin*, studies and texts in Cabbala and Chasidism.

Professor Gershom Scholem, a towering figure in the world of Jewish mysticism, delivered lectures in London on the *Historical Baal Shem*[13] and on cognate subjects.[14] 'It must be clear,' said Scholem in his reference to the Besht,

> that he had read old books with the mind of a mystic, infusing new meanings and frequently surprising depths into simple sayings which, in their original texts, were anything but mystic. There was a great spiritual

richness and a peculiar effervescence in the way in which he used the old adage as a vehicle of his own. It must not be forgotten that while Chasidism brought an unheard-of intensity and intimacy of religious life, it had to pay dearly for its success. It conquered in the realm of inwardness but it abdicated in the realm of Messianism.

The Hebraist and translator Maurice Simon (1874–1955) in his *Jewish Religious Conflicts* devotes a chapter to *Chasidism and Mithnaggedim*.[15] He maintains that the Besht was entirely devoid of arrogance or of envy.[16] He felt that Chasidism, even in its degeneracy – nor was it everywhere degenerate – preserved intact two of the most precious qualities of its founder: the feelings of brotherly affection towards fellow-Jews and cheerfulness in adversity, based on a living faith. In the merit of these qualities it succeeded in retaining a strong hold on Polish Jewry almost to the present day.[17] 'Rabbi Israel,' in Simon's view, 'did not proclaim himself as a *zaddik* . . . Certainly if there was one man more than any other in the Jewish people who deserved the title, it was the Besht.' In his booklet *Israel Baal Shem*[18] Simon states that the Baal Shem kindled a new interest in, and an attachment to, Judaism in many who, but for him, might have been seduced from it either by the Jesuits, or by heresies like those of Jacob Frank.[19] The Baal Shem's Judaism, like that of Luria, was based essentially on the Cabbala rather than on the Talmud.[20]

Victor Gollancz (1894–1967), publisher, author and public campaigner, described himself as a 'heretical Jew',[21] and Rabbi Israel Baal Shem Tov 'as the only religious teacher in the history of the world or, at any rate, in the west who has never caused a moment of unhappiness'.[22] He regarded him as one of the world's greatest geniuses[23] and Chasidim as 'exceptional if not unique among the religious teachers, for their use of paradoxes, dry humour and every day familiarity of their intercourse with God'.[24] In his other books, he also makes extensive use of Chasidic teachings and maxims.[25]

Dr Cecil Roth (1899–1970), the distinguished Anglo-Jewish historian, gives a succinct but sympathetic view on Chasidism. 'The new leader,' he writes, 'a tender-hearted mystic of rare personal magnetism, taught that piety was superior to scholarship, and that it was the prerogative of any man, however ignorant and however poor, to attain communion with his God.'[26] He further pointed out that 'its advent (Chasidism), nevertheless, had made an enduring difference to Judaism, the poetical element which it had reinforced: while its hold among the lower, more impressionable classes, who felt the need for some mystical constituent in their daily life, was enduringly strengthened.'[27]

Similarly, James Parks, one of the leading Christian scholars, regarded Chasidism 'as a new type of Judaism which brought an undiluted relief to the poverty-stricken ghettoes deep in the mud, gloom and isolation of the Polish market town and countryside'.[28]

One of the foremost researchers and interpreters of Chasidism, Dr Joseph G Weiss, who died in London at the age of 51 in 1969, was a lecturer in Jewish Studies at University College, London.[29] He was the author of *Mecharim BaChasidut Bratslav* (Studies in Bratslav Chasidism)[30] and *Studies in Eastern European Jewish Mysticism*, a collection of sixteen studies which was published posthumously.[31] His works on Chasidism were marked by meticulousness and sensitivity. The originality of his research is remarkable. He fully explored the writings of Rabbi Nachman of Bratslav whom he regarded as an extraordinary and paradoxical thinker and poet, who believed that 'the Chasid is like any other Jew, but does everything with passion'.[32] Weiss stated that 'even the most impartial historian cannot help wondering whether an heretical blood-transfusion, such as occurred in Chasidism, did not put new life into the dying body of eighteenth-century Judaism'.[33] He maintained that Chasidism, like any other revivalist movement, always aims at the total mobilisation of emotions, and Chasidism wherever it spread, brought in its wake emotional intensification in Jewish life, somewhat akin to the religious upheaval in seventeenth-century England.[34]

At a *HaPoel Hamizrachi* symposium, Dr Weiss stated that the Jewish mystic accepted the whole literature of Jewish tradition – both the *Halacha* and the *Aggada*. Indeed, Jewish mysticism had produced a new theory of the performance of religious commandments which became a real force when, later, its thought-modes spread among wide sections of the Jewish people.[35]

Rabbi Dr Louis Jacobs, the rabbi of the New London Synagogue, has devoted several studies to Cabbala and Chasidism. He translated Moses Cordovero's book on the imitation of God in Cabbalistic thought, *Tomer Devora* (under the English title of *The Palm Tree of Deborah*).[36] With profound reverence and exotic imagery, Cordovero illumines the central doctrines of Cabbala.

In his book *A Jewish Theology*[37] Dr Jacobs states: 'For Chasidim there is a divine providence over everything; nothing moves without direct control, no stone lies where it does unless God wills it so. This is a natural consequence of the Chasidic emphasis that the creation exists within God.'[38]

'In Chasidic monotheism it is God alone who embraces all and is in all, so that, in fact, from His point of view, He is the all and there is none else.'[39] The love of God receives the greatest possible emphasis in the writings of the movement,[40] and Chasidism stresses joy in God's service as an integral part of the love of God.[41] In Chasidism, the ideal of *devekut* (cleaving to God) is a personal aim capable of realisation even without the advent of the Messiah.[42] Dr Jacobs' latest book, *Holy Living – Saints and Saintliness in Judaism*, is an original study of Chasidism and the pattern of saintly behaviour.[43]

David Goldstein (1933–87), Curator of the Hebrew Section of the Department of Oriental Manuscripts and Printed Books of the British Library, was a most profound, sensitive and talented writer. He translated Isaiah Tishby's Hebrew work under the title *The Wisdom of the Zohar*, an anthology of extracts from the Zohar arranged according to topics with extensive annotations and introductory material.[44]

Jeanette Kupferman, anthropologist and daughter of a Chasid of Sassov, wrote a thesis for the M.Phil. degree of the University of London on 'The Lubavitch Chasidim of Stamford Hill'.[45]

An expert on Chasidism is the Israeli-born Dr Ada Rapaport-Albert, whose mentor was Dr J G Weiss. She is the author of many studies and articles on Chasidism.[46]

Dr Naftali Loewenthal, head of the sixth form and history teacher at Lubavitch House Senior School, obtained his doctorate from the University of London for a thesis on 'The Concept of *Mesirat Nefesh* (self-sacrifice) in the Teachings of Rabbi Dov Baer of Lubavitch (1772–1827)'. He is the author of several erudite articles and his latest book *Communicating the Infinite, the Emergence of the Chabad School* is an authoritative analysis of Chabad philosophy.[47]

Chief Rabbi Dr Jonathan Sacks has translated a number of the Lubavitcher Rebbe's talks (*sichot*), which were then published in 1986 as *Torah Studies* by the Lubavitch Foundation. He views Chasidism in a very sympathetic light. Writing about the late Rebbe of Lubavitch, whom he visited, he stated: 'his leadership, rare, almost to the point of uniqueness in the present day, consists in self-effacement. Its power is precisely what it effaces itself towards – the sense of irreplaceability of each and every Jew.'[48]

Among the many publications of the Lubavitch Foundation in England is *Challenge – an Encounter with Lubavitch Chabad*, which offers both to the friends of Lubavitch and to those who have not yet encountered it, an introduction to its history, philosophy and activities.[49] It has also published another volume of *Challenge – an Encounter with Lubavitch Chabad in Israel*, dealing with the activities of Chabad in Jerusalem, Hebron and Safed, places of learning in the Land of Israel which are supported by the leaders of Chabad.[50] It stresses that Chabad has at all times maintained an unbroken chain of association with the Promised Land.

Morris Myer published in 1942 a book in Yiddish on *Israel Baal Shem Tov*.[51] His book is generally a blend of research and lively writing. He points out that Chasidic stories are part not only of Jewish heritage but also of world culture.

Mr Joshua (Shaya) Tiger (1898–1960), a native of Galicia, came to England in 1937, and wrote regularly for the London Yiddish daily *Die Zeit*. He was the author of a Yiddish work, *Der Tsadik un der Bal-Tshuve oder der shvartser Bishof* (The Saint and the Renegade). His story, written in beautiful Yiddish, is woven around the legend of the Black Bishop of the Russian Orthodox Church who was a Jewish renegade. One day the Bishop visited a town at the same time as the Besht, under whose influence he returned to Judaism.[52] The journalist Charles C Klinger (b. 1905) settled in London and was the author of *Lekuved des Besht Akademye* on the occasion of the anniversary of Israel Baal Shem Tov's death.[53]

Avrohom Nochum Stencl (1897–1983), the Yiddish writer and poet, came to London in 1936. He was a familiar figure in London's East End, and he regarded Whitechapel as his beloved *shtetl*. He was a prolific writer, and though not Orthodox himself, he was friendly with all the Chasidic rebbes, and his periodical *Loshn un Lebn* which he edited from 1937 until his death is replete with Chasidic themes. He felt particularly drawn to *Amcho* – the common people – and to Chasidism. In this, he follows in the footsteps of Y L Peretz.[54]

The contemporary writer, well-known journalist and author, Paul Johnson, in his *History of the Jews*, deals very sympathetically with Chasidism. 'The Zaddik,' he writes, 'in Baal Shem Tov's teaching, was not a Messiah, but not quite an ordinary human being either – somewhere between the two. Moreover, since the Zaddik did not claim a messianic role, there could be many of them. Thus a new kind of religious personality arose, to perpetuate and spread the movement.'[55]

Similarly, Stephen Brook in his book *The Club* avers that 'Chasidism was essentially a life-affirming movement, infused with joy and enthusiasm', and those elements are still strikingly present today.[56] The book is informative and up-to-date and provides illuminating portraits of a number of Chasidic personalities.

The popularity of Chasidism today cannot be denied. It still lives and has added a revitalising dimension to traditionalism. It has not abrogated Orthodox practices as was feared by its opponents in the eighteenth century. It aims rather at giving greater meaning, and inspiring greater commitment, to the belief and practices of Judaism.

Chasidism has also received publicity on radio, film, television and other media.[57]

The destruction of the great centres of European Chasidism during the Second World War was an unprecedented catastrophe with far-reaching repercussions. It places a heavy burden and responsibility on the Chasidic community of today which recognises that the deep void created then will take many generations to fill.

Notes

The following abbreviations are used in the Notes.

Preface, pp. xiii–xv

1. 'Unknown documents relating to the history of Chasidism', Yivo Bletter, Vol. 136 (New York, 1952), p. 113.

1 The Chasidic Movement, pp. 1–13

1. M S Lew, The Jews of Poland (London: E Goldston, 1944), p. 82.
2. R A Mahler, A History of Modern Jewry (London: Vallentine Mitchell, 1971), p. 436.
3. S H Dresner, The Zaddik (London: Abelard-Schuman, 1960), pp. 104, 107.
4. 'Miedzyboz and Rabbi Israel Baal Shem Tov (Besht)', Zion, Vol. 52 (Jerusalem, 1987), pp. 178–89.
5. Chaim Weizman, Trial and Error (London: East and West Library, 1950), p. 398.
6. Stephen Sharot, 'Hasidism in Modern Society' in Gershon David Hundert (ed.), Essential Papers on Hasidism (New York University Press, 1991), pp. 511–33.
7. First published at the end of Porat Yosef (Korzec, 1781), and in Keter Shem Tov (Zolkiev, 1794); see also S A Horodetsky, HaChasidut VeHaChasidim (Berlin: Dvir, 1922), Part 1, pp. 54–6.

2 Winds of Change, pp. 14–21

1. H Graetz, History of the Jews (Philadelphia: JPSA, 1941), Vol. 5, pp. 375–96.
2. S Maimon, Autobiography (London: East and West Library, 1954), p. 70.
3. I M Jost, Geschichte der Israeliten (Berlin: Schlesinger, 1820–47).
4. M McCaul, Sketches of Judaism and the Jews (London: B Wertheim, 1838), pp. 17 and 18.
5. H Adams, History of the Jews (Boston: John Eliot, 1812), 2 Vols.

6. Adams, *History of the Jews*, pp. 281, 282, 285. A similar view is expressed by the Reverend W Ayerst of St. John's College, Cambridge, in his book *The Jews of the 19th Century* (London: London Society House, 1848), pp. 100–5; and by G F Abbott in his book *Israel in Europe* (London: Macmillan, 1907), p. 322, where he writes: 'Today the Chasidim, though numbering in Roumania, Poland, and South-Western Russia about a million of adherents, are scorned by the orthodox as a mob of fanatics, redeemed by genuine faith, but deluded and exploited by leaders, who are no longer saints.'

7. *JC*, 16 July 1880, p. 12.

8. Dr L Loewe (ed.), *The Diaries of Sir Moses and Lady Montefiore* (London: Griffith Farran Okeden & Welsh, 1890), Vol. 1, p. 162; see also Samuel Klein, *Toldot HaYishuv HaYehudi B'Eretz Yisrael* (Tel Aviv: Mizphah, 1935), p. 271.

9. Loewe, op. cit., p. 162.

10. A Schischa, *Pi Yemale Tehilothecha* (London: private publisher, 1984), p. 8.

11. Loewe, op. cit., p. 324: 'A special delegate arrived from Poland'.

12. Ibid., pp. 354–5.

13. *JC*, 12 June 1846, p. 153.

14. *Megillat Esther* 2:21.

15. *JC*, 28 Sept. 1866, p. 6; see also H M Hillman, *Beth Rebbe* (Berdichev, 1903; reprinted in Jerusalem, 1953), p. 189.

16. Yitzchak Ewen, *Funm rebbens hoif* (New York: 1922, reprinted New York: L A Frankel, 1970), pp. 122–6, 164–5, 266–70, quoted by Lucy S Davidowicz, *The Golden Tradition* (London: Vallentine Mitchell, 1967), p. 197.

17. *Blackwood Magazine*, Edinburgh, 1883, Vol. 130, pp. 641–3.

18. *JC*, 19 Oct. 1883, p. 11.

19. Ibid., 3 Nov. 1882, p. 4; on Oliphant see A Taylor, *Laurence Oliphant* (Oxford: University Press, 1982), P Anderson, *Life of Laurence Oliphant* (London: R Hale, 1956), and A M Hyamson, *The British Projects for the Restoration of the Jews to Palestine* (New York: Publications of the American Jewish Historical Society, 1917), Vol. 26.

20. *Sefer Hazichronos* (Memoirs of Rabbi Joseph I Schneersohn), translated into Yiddish by D L Mekler (New York: Kehot Publication Society, 1988), Vol. 2, pp. 274–6. The literary activities referred to by the Rebbe have eluded biographers. It is very unlikely that the memorial sermon on David ben Loeb of Berlin and Joseph of Brody by Moses ben Judah Loeb, *Shaarei Dima*, printed in London, 1771, can be attributed to (Rabbi) Moshe. Cecil Roth, *Magna Bibliotheca Anglo-Judaica* (London: JHS, 1937), p. 235, No. 25.

21. Chayim Lieberman, 'Reb Nachman Bratzlaver und di Umaner Maskilim', *Yivo Bletter*, Vol. 29 (New York: 1947). English translation in *Yivo Annual of Jewish Social Studies*, Vol. 6 (New York: 1951); also reprinted in Lieberman's *Ohel Rochel* (New York: Express, 1980), part 2, pp. 161–99; see also Arthur Green, *The Tormented Master* (Alabama: University Press, 1976), pp. 153–8.

22. Beth-Zion Lask Abrahams, 'Sanislav Hoga – Apostate and Penitent' in *TJHSE* (London: Edward Goldston, 1946), Vol. 15, pp. 121–51; see also E N Frank, *Meshumodim in Poland* (Warsaw, 1923); M Walden, *Ohel HaRabbi* (Piotrokov, 1913), part 3, p. 15. Hoga's grave in Highgate is Number 10092.

23. Norman Bentwich, *Solomon Schechter* (Philadelphia: JPSA, 1938), pp. 237 and 238.

24. *JC*, 18 Nov. 1887, pp. 9, 14–16; 25 Nov. 1887, pp. 14–15; 2 Dec. 1887, pp. 14–16.

25. S Schechter, *Studies in Judaism* (London: Adam & Charles Black, 1896), pp. 1–56, reprinted by the Jewish Publication Society (Philadelphia, 1945). It was also published in German as *Die Chasidim: Eine Studie über Judische Mystik* (Berlin:

Judischer Verlag, 1904), p. 93; also published in Romanian, see Alexander Marx, *Studies in Jewish History and Booklore* (New York: The Jewish Theological Seminary of America, 1944), p. 381.

26. Schechter, *Studies in Judaism*, p. 2.
27. *HaShachar* (ed. Peretz Smolenskin), Vol. 7, Vienna, 1876, pp. 383–90. See also Vol. 8, pp. 324–7, 416–9, 460–83.
28. Ibid., Vol. 8, Vienna, 1877, p. 417.
29. Ibid., p. 460.
30. Ibid.; see also A Oko, *Solomon Schechter – A Biography* (Cambridge: University Press, 1938); Alexander Marx, *Essays in Jewish Biography* (Philadelphia, 1947), p. 234; I Davidson, *Parody in Jewish Literature* (New York: Columbia University Press, 1907), pp. 74–6.
31. Mattisyahu Gutmann, *Rabbi Dov MiLeove* (Tel Aviv: Netzah, 1952).
32. Schechter, *Studies*, p. 18.
33. Ibid., p. 32.
34. Ibid.
35. Op. cit., p. 40.
36. He is referring here to Rabbi Dov Baer, the *Maggid* of Mezerich (d. 1773), the successor of the Besht.
37. Schechter, *Studies*, p. 38.
38. He is referring to Rabbi Shneur Zalman of Liady (1747–1812), the founder of *Chabad*.
39. Rabbi Menachem Mendel of Vitebsk, a disciple of the *Maggid* of Mezerich. He settled in the Holy Land in 1773, and died in Tiberias in 1788.
40. Schechter, *Studies*, p. 43.
41. Ibid., p. 47.
42. Ibid., p. 18.
43. Ibid., p. 42.
44. Ibid., p. 54.
45. Ibid., p. 2.
46. *JC*, 18 Nov. 1887, p. 9.
47. Ibid.
48. Ibid.
49. Norman Bentwich, *Solomon Schechter*, p. 71.
50. F Adler (1851–1933) was the founder, leader and philosopher of the Ethical Culture Movement.
51. N Bentwich, *Schechter*, p. 183.
52. Shalom Chayim Porush, *Encyclopaedia of Chasidism*, Vol. 1 (Jerusalem: Mosad Harav Kook, 1980).

3 *In the Footsteps of the Master*, pp. 22–30

1. J Leftwich, *Israel Zangwill* (London: James Clarke, 1957), pp. 75–7; see also M Wohlgelernter, *Israel Zangwill* (New York: Columbia University Press, 1964).
2. N Bentwich, 'The Wanderers and Other Jewish Scholars of my Youth', *TJHSE* (1959–61) (London, 1964), Vol. 20, pp. 51–63.
3. M Simon (ed.), *Speeches, Articles and Letters of Israel Zangwill* (London: Soncino, 1957), p. 68.
4. Ibid., p. 67.
5. Preface to I Zangwill, *Dreamers of the Ghetto* (London: William Heinemann, 1898), p. xviii (reprinted Philadelphia: JPSA, 1948).

6. Bentwich, *Solomon Schechter*, pp. 58–9.
7. See M Simon, *Speeches*, p. 18.
8. I Zangwill, *Children of the Ghetto* (London: Globe Publishing Co., 1925), p. 204.
9. Ibid.
10. London: McClure & Co., 1893.
11. Joseph H Udelson, *Dreamer of the Ghetto* (University of Alabama Press, 1990), pp. 115–17.
12. See note 5.
13. *The Dreamers of the Ghetto*, p. 224.
14. M Wohlgelernter, *Israel Zangwill*, p. 109.
15. Zangwill, *Dreamers*, p. 280; Wohlgelernter, op. cit., p. 111.
16. Zangwill, op. cit., p. 270.
17. Ibid., p. 281.
18. Ibid., p. 279.
19. Ibid., p. 286.
20. Ibid.
21. Ibid., p. 287.
22. Ibid., p. 279.
23. Ibid., pp. 285–6.
24. I Zangwill, *The Voice of Jerusalem* (London: Heinemann, 1920), p.300.
25. E Levene, 'Essays in memory of E. N. Adler' in *Miscellanies* of the *TJHSE*, part V (London, 1945), p. 119.
26. Samuel Pepys, *Diaries of Samuel Pepys* (London: Everyman Library, 1906), Vol. II, p. 46.
27. E N Adler, *Jews in Many Lands* (Philadelphia: JPSA, 1905), pp. 50–6.
28. Ibid., p. 56.
29. *JC*, 18 Nov. 1887, p. 9.
30. *TJHSE*, Vol. 7, Session 1911–14, p. 305.
31. *Leaders of Hasidism*, translated by Maria Horodezky-Magasanik (London: 'Hasefer' Agency for Literature, 1928).
32. Ibid., in Foreword, pp. IX and XII.
33. Ibid., p. XIII.
34. Ibid.
35. Mss. 1342–59.
36. Ms. 1351; see H Rabinowicz, *Treasures of Judaica* (New York: T Yoseloff, 1971), p. 162.
37. J H Hertz, *Sermons, Addresses and Studies*, 3 vols. (London: The Soncino Press, 1938), Vol. 1, p. 86.
38. Ibid., Vol. 3, *Studies*, pp. 316–17.
39. Ibid., p. 318.
40. 'Jewish Mystics', *JC Supplement*, February 1929; J H Hertz, op. cit., Vol. 3, p. 316.
41. Chief Rabbi's Files, Greater London Record Office.
42. *JC*, 13 July 1990, p. 22.
43. Ibid.
44. Isidore Epstein, *Judaism* (London: Penguin Books, 1939), p. 270.

4 *Early Chasidim in England*, pp. 31–35

1. D'Blossiers Tovey, *Anglia-Judaica – A History of the Jews in England* (1738, recently reprinted: London: Weidenfeld & Nicolson, 1990), p. 302.

2. V D Lipman, *Social History of the Jews in England, 1850–1950* (London: Watts & Co., 1954), p. 7.
3. 23 Oct. 1854, *Letter Book of the Chief Rabbi*, Vol. 3; *Records of the Office of the Chief Rabbi*, quoted by Steven Singer in *Orthodox Judaism in Early Victorian London, 1840–1858*, PhD thesis (New York: Yeshiva University, 1981), pp. 31–2.
4. Solomon Sofer, *Iggerot Soferim*, Vol. 4, p. 85 (Tel Aviv: Sinai, 1970), quoted by Singer in op. cit., p. 31.
5. *JC*, 15 June 1888, p. 9.
6. W J Fishman, *East End 1888* (London: Duckworth, 1988), p. 153.
7. Ibid., p. 153.
8. J Jung, *Champions of Orthodoxy* (London, privately printed, 1974), p. 112.
9. Israel Meir Kagan, *Nidchei Yisrael* (Warsaw, 1893), quoted by Lloyd P Gartner, *The Jewish Immigrant in England, 1870–1914* (London and Detroit: Simon, 1960), p. 30.
10. *Hamelitz* (Odessa), Vol. XXVIII, p. 287 (30 Dec. 1888 to 1 Jan. 1889); Gartner, op. cit., p. 24; also *HaMaggid* (Lyck), Vol. XXXIII, 5 Jan. 1889.
11. I Finestein, 'The New Community in 1880–1918' in V Lipman (ed.), *Three Centuries of Anglo-Jewish History* (Cambridge: W Heffer, 1961), p. 114.
12. Lipman, *Social History of the Jews in England, 1850–1950*, pp. 13 and 71.
13. C Roth, 'The lesser London Synagogues of the 18th century', *TJHSE*, Misc., Part 3 (London), 1937, p. 5; also see *JC*, 23 Sept. 1870, p. 3. In 1870 there were also *shtieblech* in Carter Street, Mansell Street and Parliament Court.
14. P Abrahams, 'Abraham Sussman – from Berdichev to Bevis Marks', *TJHSE*, Vol. 21 (London, 1968), pp. 243–61.
15. Ibid., p. 252.
16. Ibid., p. 245.
17. Ibid., p. 257 and A Sussman, *Banim miBanim* (Vilna: J Rom, 1869), pp. 97–8.
18. P Abrahams, *TJHSE*, Vol. 21, p. 257.
19. A Sussman, *Sefer Millel Avraham* (London, 1872), p. 38.
20. A Sussman, *WaYosef Avraham* (A commentary on *Yemin Mosheh* by Moses ben Joseph Ventura) (Lvov, 1860); Phyllis Abrahams, op. cit., p. 259.
21. A Sussman, *Vaya'as Avraham* (Vilna, 1871), p. 57.
22. Ibid., p. 118.
23. Ibid., pp. 12–14.
24. L P Gartner, op. cit., p. 49.
25. Lipman, *Social History*, pp. 89–90.
26. Zangwill, *The Children of the Ghetto*, p. 204.
27. B Homa, *A Fortress in Anglo-Jewry* (London: Shapiro Vallentine, 1953), p. 76.
28. Ibid.
29. *JC*, 25 Feb. 1955, Supplement, p. 14.
30. S Oberman, *In my Days* (London: Narod Press, 1947), pp. 108 and 132; *JC*, 4 Dec. 1953, p. 28.
31. Homa, *A Fortress in Anglo-Jewry*, p. 33.
32. Ibid., p. 27; *JC*, 4 June 1911.
33. Jung, *Champions of Orthodoxy*, p. 183.
34. Ibid., p. 196.
35. A I Bromberg, *Migdolei HaChasidut – Belz* (Jerusalem: Machon L'Chasidut, 1953), p. 134.
36. Jung, *Champions*, pp. 194 and 197.
37. A Bauminger (ed.), *Sefer Cracow* (Jerusalem: Mosad Harav Kook, 1959), p. 125.
38. Jung, *Champions*, p. 225.
39. D Cesarani (ed.), *The Making of Modern Anglo-Jewry* (London: Blackwell, 1990), p. 143.

5 *East End Chasidic Shtieblech*, pp. 36–52

1. Ps. 126:16.
2. Ps. 35:10.
3. *JC*, 3 Feb. 1942, p. 18.
4. Ibid., 14 Nov. 1975.
5. Pinkas of the Dzikover Shtiebl, p. 124 (in the author's possession).
6. Ibid., p. 164.
7. *Die Zeit*, 23 Jan. 1936, p. 3.
8. *JC*, 24 Jan. 1936, p. 34.
9. *Die Zeit*, 11 Feb. 1936, p. 3.
10. *JC*, 29 Jan. 1937, pp. 22–3.
11. Ibid., 17 June 1948, p. 139; see also Agenda of Meeting of the Federation of Synagogues, 26 Oct. 1949.
12. *JC*, 5 May 1954.
13. Following the death of Mr A Kesselman in 1972, the members of the Dzikover Shtiebl were transferred to other Federation synagogues.
14. A B Levy, 'In search of the East End', *JC*, 26 April 1938, p. 10.
15. B. Homa, *A Fortress in Anglo-Jewry*, p. 75.
16. Ibid., p. 76.
17. Ibid., pp. 88–9.
18. B Homa, *Footprints in the Sands of Time* (London: B. Homa, 1990), p. 92.
19. J Cooper, 'The Bloomstein and the Isenberg families', in A Newman (ed.), *The Jewish East End, 1840–1939* (THSE, 1981), pp. 59–75; see also *Die Zeit*, 10 Oct. 1925, p. 5; 1 Nov. 1925, p. 3; 6 Nov. 1925, p. 4.
20. *JC*, 20 Dec. 1957, Supplement p. 2.
21. The *Tekanot* are in the possession of Mr Ivor Golker, Kibbutz HaEmek, Israel.
22. *Die Zeit*, 10 Oct. 1925, p. 5; 1 Nov. 1925, p. 3; 6 Nov. 1925, p. 4.
23. *JYB* (London: *JC*, 1957), p. 103.
24. Ibid. (London: Greenberg & Co., 1896), p. 39.
25. Ibid., 1904, p. 48.
26. *Die Zeit*, 21 Jan. 1914.
27. Pinkas of *Agudat Achim Kehal Chabad*, p. 29.
28. *Apologie des Juifs*, 'Etude historique et litéraire sur l'état politique et social des Juifs depuis la chute de Jerusalem jusqu'à 1306' (Paris: P Vieweg, 1887); *Sepher Kelalei Haposkim* (London: *Express*, 1923); *Sepher Tziyon Rashi* (London: *Express*, 1923).
29. J Jung, *HaMaor*, Organ of the Federation of Synagogues, London, July 1968.
30. Hertz, *Sermons*, Vol. 3, p. 113.
31. *Die Zeit*, 27 Aug. 1937.
32. *Hamaor*, Dec. 1973, p. 23.
33. *JC*, 12 Oct. 1973, p. 38.
34. The Swardishe Dunk Street Shul; the Swardish Fashion Street; Beth Haknesset Kalish Ubnei Pultava, Alie Street; Sons of Britcham Synagogue, 25 Bromehead Street; Poltava Synagogue, 10 Spital Square; the Romanian Shul, 6–7 Matilda Street, off Christian Street.

6 *Controversial Rebbes*, pp. 53–66

1. A I Bromberg, *Admorei Neskhiz* (Jerusalem: Hazaot Hamachon L'Chasidut, 1963).

2. Przemysl, 1879, reprinted in Cracow in 1891 and in Jerusalem in 1927.
3. S Kaizer, *Sefer Toldot Chen* (London: Hebrew Book and Gift Centre, 1979), p. 12.
4. *JC*, 25 Jan. 1895, p. 9.
5. *Netivot Chen* (London: E Z Rabbinowitch, 1895).
6. Kaizer, *Sefer Toldot Chen*.
7. *Sunhedrin* 56a, 105a and *Chulin* 92a.
8. *JC*, 3 Sept. 1920, p. 18.
9. Kaizer, op. cit., pp. 74a, 75.
10. *JC*, 3 Sept. 1920, p. 18; *Die Zeit*, 26 Aug. 1920, p. 1; see also Greenwood, *Hatzofe L'Chochmat Yisrael* (Budapest, 1921–31), No. 5, p. 281; Y Alfasi, *Ha-Chasidut* (Tel Aviv: *Maariv*, 1977), pp. 168–70.
11. *Die Zeit*, 27 Dec. 1929. His visit to Glasgow: ibid., 14 Feb. 1936; 1 Jan. 1937, p. 5.
12. *JC*, 12 July 1985, p. 26.
13. *Chicago Sun Times*, 10 April 1989.
14. B A Sochachewsky, *Joseph Shapotshnick* (London, 1927).
15. 1914: 16 Fieldgate Street; 1916: 16 Pelham Street; 1918: 28 Hanbury Street; 1921: 37 Chicksand Street; 1925: 62 Fieldgate Stret; 1928: 7 Frostic Place (off Old Montague Street); 1932: 18 Black Lion Yard.
16. *Die Zeit*, 7 March 1928.
17. The work was printed in Berlin: Druck von Itzkowski, 1913.
18. London, 1915, 32 pages.
19. *The World Doctor*, London, 1 Feb. 1934.
20. Ibid.
21. *Die Zeit*, 8 Jan. 1914, p. 7.
22. Ibid., 12 July 1914, p. 7.
23. Ibid., 19 Jan. 1915, p. 5; 12 Feb. 1915, p. 5.
24. Ibid., 26 March 1915, p. 5.
25. Ibid., 25 March 1920, p. 3; 29 March 1920, p. 3.
26. Ibid., 29 March 1920, p. 3; 21 March 1920, p. 3; 1 April 1920, p. 3.
27. See Bibliography under Shapotshnick.
28. *Die Zeit*, 31 March 1932, p. 3.
29. *Chasidut der Nayer Sort* (London: 1921), available at British Library, WP 6804.
30. Ibid., p. 3.
31. Ibid., p. 7.
32. Rabbi David Twersky of Talno (1808–82).
33. Shapotshnik, *Chasidut*, pp. 7–8.
34. Ibid.
35. *Die Zeit*, 6 July 1916, p. 3; 9 July 1916, p. 3.
36. Ibid., 31 Aug. 1916, p. 3. He also delivered an eulogy for Chaim Soloveitchik at 44 Dunk Street, see *Die Zeit*, 30 Aug. 1918, p. 3.
37. Ibid., 22 July 1918, p. 3.
38. Ibid., 10 Oct. 1918, p. 3.
39. Ibid., 22 Oct. 1918, p. 3; 23 Oct. 1918, p. 3; 24 Oct. 1918, p. 3.
40. Ibid., 21 June 1919, p. 4; 18 Aug. 1918, p. 3; 19 Aug. 1918, p. 3.
41. Ibid., 12 Sept. 1918, p. 3; 8 Oct. 1918, p. 3.
42. Ibid., 8 May 1920, p. 3.
43. Ibid., 2 Oct. 1925, p. 4; 13 March 1926, p. 6; 15 March 1925, p. 2.
44. Ibid., 8 Feb. 1925, p. 3.
45. Ibid., 6 Feb. 1925, p. 6.
46. *The World Doctor*, 24 Jan. 1933, p. 1.
47. *JC*, 28 Nov. 1930, p. 29.
48. L M Epstein, *The Jewish Marriage Contract* (New York: Jewish Theological

Seminary, 1927); *Le-Sheelat HaAgunah* (New York: published by L M Epstein, 1940); Joel Sussman Hodes, *Leda'ath Hakahal Be'Inyan* (London: Narodiczky, 1936).

49. *Die Zeit*, 11 Dec. 1927, p. 2.
50. Ibid., 3 Feb. 1928.
51. Ibid.
52. Ibid.
53. *Wyd Zwiaszku Rabinow Rzezpos Polskiej* (Warsaw: 1929); *Kislev, Kuntres Macha Geluya neged Shapotshnick*.
54. Ibid., p. 7.
55. Ibid., p. 14.
56. Ibid.
57. Ibid., pp. 17 and 18.
58. *Jewish Post*, London, 14 *Shevat* 1928.
59. M Adler, *Sefer Mareh Kohen, Mahadura Tanina* (Piotrokov: 1931), p. 341.
60. *Die Zeit*, 20 March 1932, p. 3; 23 March 1932, p. 3; 1 April 1932, p. 5; 7 April 1932, p. 3; 8 April 1932, p. 5; 14 April 1932, p. 3.
61. Ibid., 11 March 1932, p. 1.
62. *Minutes of the London Board of Shechitah*, 18 Oct. 1934.
63. *Evening Standard*, London, 28 Oct. 1937.
64. *JC*, 30 July 1937, p. 15; *Minutes of the London Board of Shechitah*, 1 March 1937; *JC*, 1 Jan. 1937, pp. 18–19; Court Case Report, *Evening Standard*, 28 Oct. 1937, p. 5; *Jewish Weekly*, 16 Jan. 1937.
65. *Die Zeit*, 12 Feb. 1937; *JC*, 12 Feb. 1937, p. 26; *Wochenzeitung* (London), 1 Feb. 1937.
66. File of the Chief Rabbi, Greater London Record Office Library. The *Dayanim* were: Asher Feldman, Y Abramsky, H M Lazarus and M Gollop.
67. Photostat copies of the Hebrew letters in the possession of the family.
68. Files of the Chief Rabbi's Office, at present housed at Greater London Record Office Library.
69. *JC*, 29 Oct. 1937, p. 9; also p. 13; *Die Zeit*, 24 Oct. 1937, p. 3.
70. Block B8, No. 1; *Die Zeit*, 26 Oct. 1937, p. 1; *News Chronicle*, 26 Oct. 1937; *The Star*, 25 Oct. 1937; *The City and East London Observer*, 30 Oct. 1937.
71. *JC*, 24 May 1946, p. 14.
72. *Die Zeit*, 26 Oct. 1937, p. 1.
73. *JC*, 29 Oct. 1937, p. 15.
74. Ibid., 12 Aug. 1949, p. 19.
75. *AJYB* (London: *Jewish Chronicle*, 1939), p. 121.

7 The Inter-War Years, pp. 67–77

1. Lipman, *A Social History*, p. 75.
2. *Die Zeit*, 31 Jan. 1936, p. 5.
3. *JC*, 4 Nov. 1954, p. 26. After Myer's death, his son Harry continued the paper until it ceased publication in 1950.
4. Ibid., 2 Sept. 1949, p. 9.
5. *Die Zeit*, 18 April 1930; 20 June 1929; 16 May 1930.
6. M Myer, *Rabbi Yisrael Baal Shem Tov* (London: *Jewish Times*, 1942).
7. *Die Zeit*, 26 Dec. 1913, p. 3.
8. Ibid., 1 Dec. 1914, p. 2.
9. Ibid. Published under the pseudonym 'Baal Madrega' in 1914 on 8 May, p. 4;

13 May, p. 6; 20 May, p. 4; 15 June, p. 4; 25 June, p. 4; 2 July, p. 4.
10. Ibid. A series of articles were published in 1936 on: 4 Oct., p. 3; 5 Oct., p. 2; 12 Oct., p. 2; 13 Oct., p. 2; 15 Oct., p. 2; 16 Oct., p. 2; 23 Oct., p. 4; 28 Oct., p. 4; 30 Oct., p. 4; 1 Nov., p. 3; 2 Nov., p. 3.
11. Ibid., 3 Oct. 1935, p. 2.
12. Ibid., 22 Oct. 1935, p. 2; 23 Oct. 1935, p. 2.
13. Ibid., 30 Oct. 1935, p. 2.
14. Ibid., 6 May 1937, p. 3.
15. Ibid. A series of articles by 'Historicus' were published in 1936 on: 20 Dec., p. 3; 21 Dec., p. 3; 22 Dec., p. 2; 24 Dec., p. 2; 25 Dec., p. 2; 28 Dec., p. 2.
16. Ibid., 17 March 1936, p. 2.
17. Ibid., 10 Feb. 1936, p. 2.
18. The serialisation began on 12 December 1936 and continued through 1937.
19. Ibid., 23 Jan. 1928.
20. See Bibliography.
21. *JC*, 15 May 1964, p. 43.
22. Ibid., 18 April 1947, p. 13.
23. I J Lew, *Yalkut Yosef* (London: Narodiczky, 1942), Introduction, p. 1.
24. *JC*, 13 April 1951, p. 15.
25. Myer S Lew, *The Jews of Poland* (London: Edward Goldston, 1944).
26. London, 1939, but printed in Bilgoraj, Poland.
27. *JC*, 17 May 1968, p. 43.
28. Ibid., 20 Aug. 1954, p. 16.
29. A I Kon, *Siach Tefilla* (Jerusalem: Mechon L'Hozaot Sefarim, 1964). Translated into English under the title *Prayer* (London: Soncino Press, 1971).
30. This work was edited by Reverend Yitzchak Dov Feld (London: Hamadfis, 1960).
31. Printed by Narodiczki, London, 1944.
32. Judge Leonard Gerber 'Reb Elia and Etz Chaim Yeshiva' in *JT*, 13 July 1989, p. 8.
33. *Die Zeit*, 15 Feb. 1924, p. 6.
34. Rabbi Greenspan was the author of *Melechet Machshevet* (London, 1955).
35. Morris Myer, *Yiddish Theatre in London* (London: *JT*, 1942), p. 148.
36. Ibid., p. 169.
37. Victor Schonfeld, *Life's Purpose* (London: *Jewish Post* Publications, 1956).
38. Ibid.
39. The Avigdor Secondary School (Grammar School) was augmented by the establishment of the Avigdor Primary School, the Preparatory School, the Hasmonean Grammar School for Boys and for Girls, the Hasmonean Primary School, and the Menora Primary School.
40. *Die Zeit*, 3 Feb. 1919, p. 3.
41. Ibid., 16 Sept. 1924.
42. Ibid., 23 Jan. 1931.
43. Ibid., 26 Aug. 1927; ibid., 7 Sept. 1923; ibid., 29 March 1937; 1 April 1937, p. 5.
44. S Kling, *Nachum Sokolow – Servant of His People* (New York, Herzl Press, 1960), pp. 35 and 77.
45. A I Bromberg, *R Yehuda Leib Alter MiGur – Sefat Emet* (Jerusalem: Machon L'Chasidut, 1957), p. 108.
46. *Die Zeit*, 7 Feb. 1928, p. 3.
47. S Kling, *Nachum Sokolow*, p. 158. On 19 May 1936 *Die Zeit* announced that he was working on a history of Chasidism.
48. S Oberman, *In my Days*, p. 107.

8 *The Sassover Rebbe,* pp. 78–82

1. These are *Alfei Menashe,* a dissertation on Caro's *Chosen Mishpat* (Przemysl, 1895); *Matei Menashe* on Torah and Festivals (Munkacz, 1927); *Torah HaAshom* (Podgorze, 1905).
2. *Die Zeit,* 1 Sept. 1928.
3. Ibid., 10 Feb. 1929.
4. Ibid., 27 June 1936.
5. *JC,* 24 Jan. 1936, p. 10.
6. *Die Zeit,* 16 April 1938, p. 5.
7. Ibid., 21 Sept. 1945, p. 3.
8. Ibid., 5 Jan. 1946.
9. Monty Modlyn in *JC,* 29 Jan. 1988, *London Extra,* p. 2.
10. *JT,* 6 June 1972.
11. Ibid.
12. Ibid., 2 Oct. 1986.
13. Ibid., 30 March 1989, p. 3.
14. Ibid., 6 June 1972.
15. Ibid., 5 May 1988.
16. Ibid., 5 May 1988; 28 Sept. 1989, p. 10; 4 July 1991, p. 9.
17. Ibid., 17 Aug. 1985, p. 5.
18. Ibid., 4 July 1991, p. 9.
19. Ibid., 5 May 1988; 17 Aug. 1985, p. 5.
20. Ibid., 12 Sept. 1987, p. 5.
21. Ibid., 12 Sept. 1987, p. 5; 6 July 1989, p. 8; 6 Sept. 1990, p. 5.
22. Ibid., 6 Sept. 1990, p. 5.
23. Ibid., 22 Nov. 1990, p. 8.
24. *JC,* 19 Nov. 1971, p. 19; 26 Nov. 1971, p. 6; 26 May 1972, p. 16.
25. *JT,* 24 Jan. 1991, p. 9.
26. Ibid., 14 March 1991, p. 9.
27. *JC,* 2 Aug. 1991, p. 1; *The Times,* 31 July 1991, p. 21; The *Hendon Times,* 8 Aug. 1991, p. 3.

9 *The Trisker Rebbe,* pp. 83–89

1. *Shabbat* 127a.
2. *Mishna, Pirkei Abot* 1:4.
3. *Die Zeit,* 18 April 1930, p. 4.
4. Joel Cang, *The Silent Millions* (London: Rapp-Whiting, 1969), p. 60.
5. *Die Zeit,* 1 Sept. 1923.
6. Ibid., 19 Aug. 1923.
7. Ibid., 18 Jan. 1924, p. 4.
8. Ibid., 19 July 1929; 3 July 1932, p. 1; *Jewish Post and Express,* 28 April 1927.
9. *JT,* 20 Sept. 1929, p. 3.
10. I Brot, *Tal Hashamayim* (London: Narod, 1929).
11. *Die Zeit,* 4 July 1933, p. 4.
12. *JT,* 20 Sept. 1991, p. 3.
13. *Die Zeit,* 2 Nov. 1932; see also 15 March 1936.
14. Ibid., 11 Dec. 1936.
15. Die Zeit, 23 March 1945.
16. The letters are available at the home of his son, Jack Lass, London.

17. *Die Zeit*, 14 Dec. 1930.
18. Ibid., 9 March 1950.
19. Ibid., 15 Nov. 1967; 30 July 1971; 23 June 1973; 14 May 1976; 8 June 1979; see also *JC*, 26 Oct. 1979, p. 31.
20. *Die Zeit*, 14 March 1946.
21. Ibid., 17 Oct. 1924, p. 6.
22. *JC*, 15 Dec. 1950, p. 13; 18 April 1958, p. 18; 17 June 1983, p. 12.
23. *Die Zeit*, 26 Feb. 1926.
24. Ibid., 28 Aug. 1927.
25. J Spira, *Mille De Hespedah*, published by M. Spira, 33 Greenfield Street, London, 1927, and printed by B A Sochachewsky.
26. J Spira, *Maamar Hayashar V'Hatov*, published in London by S & B Spira, Booksellers, but printed in Przemysl.

10 *The Biala Rebbe*, pp. 90–100

1. He edited *Yishrei Lev* (on the Sabbath) (Lublin, 1906), *Divrei Binah* (commentaries on the Torah) (Lublin, 1909, 1913 and Piotrokov, 1929), as well as commentaries on the *Ethics of the Fathers* (Lublin, 1928 and reprinted in Jerusalem, 1983).
2. Tzvi Rabinowicz, *Chassidic Rebbes* (New York: Targum/Feldheim, 1990), pp. 289–97, see also *JC*, 13 Jan. 1933, p. 12.
3. Ibid., 19 Dec. 1919, p. 12.
4. *Report by Sir Stuart Samuel on his Mission to Poland*, Comd. 674, Miscellaneous No. 10 (London: His Majesty's Stationery Office, 1920), pp. 6 and 8.
5. Ibid., p. 16.
6. Ibid.
7. *JC*, 30 Dec. 1932, p. 8.
8. Jer. 5:7.
9. *Die Zeit*, 20 Dec. 1935.
10. Ibid., 11 Jan. 1937, p. 3; 7 Feb. 1937, p. 3.
11. *Hamaor*, Sept. 1974, p. 44.
12. *JC*, 20 April 1951, p. 21.
13. Genesis, 29:10.

11 *The Biala Traditions*, pp. 101–109

1. *Die Zeit*, 22 Jan. 1937; *JC*, 15 Aug. 1975, p. 27.
2. *Sefer Shaarei HaMitzvot* (London: Narodiczky, 1954); see also *Hamaor*, Sept. 1975, p. 34.
3. *JC*, 8 Jan. 1954, p. 6; he was the author of *Michtov M'Eliyahu*, edited by Ariel Carmel, Alter Halpern and Chayim Friedlander, 3 Vols. (London: 1985). Also printed in English under the title *Strive for Truth* (New York: Feldheim, 1978); see also *JT*, 27 Feb. 1970, p. 5.
4. A Committee of pupils published his novella *Divrei Shir* (London, printed privately, 1959).
5. *Rosh Hashanah*, 32b.
6. Psalms 51:13; *Die Zeit*, 29 Oct. 1947.
7. N D Rabinowicz, *The Will and Testament*, edited by H Rabinowicz (London: Narod Press, 1948), p. 13.

8. Inscription can be found in the Warsaw Jewish Cemetery.
9. N D Rabinowicz, *The Will and Testament*, p. 9.
10. Ibid., p. 16.
11. Ibid., pp. 13–14.
12. Ibid., p. 14.
13. *Die Zeit*, 1 Nov. 1949; *Jewish Weekly*, 4 Nov. 1949; *Jewish Voice*, 17 Oct. 1958; *JC*, 4 Nov. 1949; 17 Oct. 1952; 26 Dec. 1952; 12 Nov. 1954, p. 27; 14 Oct. 1955; 17 Oct. 1958, p. 8.
14. N D Rabinowicz, *The Will and Testament*, pp. 14–15.
15. *JC*, 26 Feb. 1960, p. 19; 11 Aug. 1961, p. 15; 20 April 1962; 6 May 1963, p. 21; 6 May 1966.
16. Rachel Anne Rabinowicz, *The Land and People of Israel* (London: A & C Black, 1959).
17. *The Feast of Freedom* (New York: American Rabbinical Assembly, 1982); *JC*, 9 April 1982, p. 9.
18. *New York Times*, 30 March 1988.

12 *The Premishlaner Rebbe*, pp. 110–116

1. His discourses are to be found in *Divrei Meir* (Bartfield, 1909); *Or HaMeir* (Przemysl, 1913); *Marganita de Rabbi Meir* (Lvov, 1926).
2. Among his works were: *Beth Ephraim* (Lvov, 1809); *Rosh Ephraim* (Lvov, 1809); *Shem Ephraim* on Rashi's commentaries to the Pentateuch and *Haftorot* (Ostrog, 1826); *Maalot HaYachasin* on Genealogy (Lvov, 1809).
3. The author of *Or HaYashar* (Amsterdam, 1709); *Meorei Or* (Frankfurt, 1709).
4. The author of *Degel Machnei Ephraim* (Korzec, 1810).
5. He wrote a commentary on *Sefer Mitzvot Gadol*, (Kapust, 1807).
6. Told by his brother, Alexander Margulies.
7. Genesis 33:18.
8. *Sefer Shimon Dubnow* (London/Jerusalem/Waltham, MA: Ararat, 1954).
9. The publication was supervised by Alexander Margulies and his nephew, William, the son of Benzion.
10. *Theodor Herzl, A Biography* (London: Ararat, 1946); *Dubnow, Herzl, Achad Ha'am* (London: Ararat, 1967).
11. *Independent*, London, 19 May 1991, p. 16.
12. *Die Zeit*, 28 Feb. 1930.
13. Ibid., 16 Dec. 1927.
14. *JC*, 30 Dec. 1938, p. 28.
15. Ibid., 25 April 1969, p. 30.
16. *Jewish Post*, 23 July 1954.
17. *JC*, 21 Jan. 1955, p. 11.
18. Ibid.
19. Ibid., 3 May 1985; 3 April 1987, p. 30; 19 Oct. 1990, p. 44.

13 *The Progeny of the Premishlaner*, pp. 117–123

1. Dr Isaac Levin (ed.), *Elle Ezkera* (New York: Research Institute of Religious Jewry, 1959), Vol. 3, p. 146.
2. *JT*, 23 March 1936.
3. David Kranzler and Gertrude Hirschler (eds), *Solomon Schonfeld: His Page in*

History (New York: Judaica Press, 1982), pp. 39, 89; *JC*, 8 Oct. 1937, p. 36; ibid., 18 Nov. 1938, p. 45.
4. A Levy, *History of the Sunderland Jewish Community 1755–1955* (London: Macdonald, 1956), pp. 206–7; *JC*, 18 April 1947, p. 18.
5. *JC*, 11 April 1947, p. 13.
6. *Jewish Post*, 3 Sept. 1954, p. 2.
7. Ibid., 20 July 1956; see also *JT*, 2 April 1971, p. 9 and 23 April 1986, p. 6.
8. A M Babad, *Imrei Tava* (Bnei Brak, published by the family, 1981), p. 17.
9. *JT*, 2 Dec. 1949; see also I Grunfeld, *JT*, 23 April 1971; ibid., 28 March 1991, pp. 9 and 15.
10. Babad, *Imrei Tava*, p. 62.
11. *JC*, 2 Aug. 1991, p. 7.
12. *Die Zeit*, 11 Feb. 1924, p. 6.
13. *Jewish Post*, 15 Sept. 1950.
14. *JC*, 20 Dec. 1957 (Supplement, p. 1).
15. Ibid.
16. Ibid., 12 Aug. 1983, p. 26; *Der Yid* (London edition), 29 July 1983.

14 Rabbi Shulim Moskowitz – The Rebbe of Shatz, pp. 124–130

1. *Die Zeit*, 20 June 1929.
2. Ibid., 6 June 1937, p. 3.
3. Deuteronomy, 1:17.
4. V D Lipman, *A History of the Jews of Britain since 1958* (Leicester: University Press, 1990), p. 113, Note 8 quotes S A Sharot, 'Religious change in native Orthodoxy in London, 1870–1914', *Jewish Journal of Sociology*, London, XV, June 1973; see also Lipman, 'Jewish Settlement in the East End of London' in A Newman (ed.), *Jewish East End, 1840–1939*, p. 50, note 4.
5. Lev. 14:45.
6. The Will is printed at the end of *Mayyim Rabbim* by Rabbi Yechiel Michael of Zloczow, and was published by Rabbi Joseph Moskowitz in Brooklyn in 1979 and also printed by M Deutsch in a Passover Haggadah (London: Deutsch, 1990), pp. 210–25. The translation is by L Jacobs, *Helping with Inquiries* (London: Vallentine Mitchell, 1989), pp. 127–8.
7. Jacobs, *Helping with Inquiries*, p. 128.
8. *JT*, 7 Jan. 1983, p. 7; *Jerusalem Post*, 18 Oct. 1976.
9. *Die Zeit*, 20 Sept. 1976; *Jerusalem Post*, 22 Sept. 1976.
10. See Rabbi S Moskowitz, *Ethical Will*.
11. *JC*, 17 Jan. 1958, p. 23; C. Halpern (ed.), *Yagdil Torah* (London: 1958), p. 16.
12. *Die Zeit*, 17 Jan. 1930.
13. *JC*, 26 Oct. 1979, p. 31.
14. C Halpern, *Yagdil Torah*, p. 16.

15 Chasidic Personalities, pp. 131–143

1. *Shabbat*, 118a.
2. B Susser, 'Questionnaire of 1845', in A Newman (ed.), *Provincial Jewry in Victorian Britain* (London: JHSE, 1975) and Lipman, *A History*, p. 28.
3. *JYB*, 1936, p. 74.
4. *Die Zeit*, 26 May 1946; *JC*, 18 April 1947, p. 3.

5. *JC*, 24 Jan. 1947, p. 4; ibid., 18 April 1947, p. 3.
6. Numbers 15:38.
7. Y Leiner, *Tiferet Yerucham* (Brooklyn: published by his son Mordechai Joseph, 1968), p. 178.
8. *Die Zeit*, 26 April 1935; see also *JC*, 2 Feb. 1940, p. 21. A Reich was the President, H Sternfield, the Warden, and Reverend Shalom Coleman, later Minister of Perth Hebrew Congregation, was the Secretary.
9. *JC*, 17 Dec. 1943, p. 14. The Revised Edition of the Prayer Book with Commentary was published in London in 1942.
10. *JC*, 21 March 1947, p. 13.
11. New York, 1956.
12. Ecclesiastes 1:5.
13. *JC*, 18 April 1947.
14. Ibid., 29 Aug. 1947, p. 12.
15. Ibid., 26 Feb. 1960, p. 20.
16. Ibid., 11 July 1958, p. 27.
17. *JC*, 5 Sept. 1947, p. 20; ibid., 12 Sept. 1947, p. 5; ibid., 15 July 1955, p. 6.
18. Ibid., 12 Jan. 1940, p. 20.
19. Ibid., 8 Aug. 1969, p. 9.
20. Ibid., 8 Oct. 1954, p. 18.
21. Ibid., 7 Jan. 1955, p. 20.
22. Ibid., 29 Oct. 1954, p. 22.
23. Ibid., 13 Dec. 1957, p. 28.
24. Ibid., 10 Feb. 1957, p. 6.
25. Ibid., 6 April 1956, p. 16.
26. Ibid., 27 April 1956, p. 23.
27. Ibid., 7 Oct. 1977, p. 24.
28. Ibid., 30 Oct. 1987; see also ibid., article by Trevor Bell, 24 June 1977, p. 23.
29. A J Heschel and S H Dresner (eds), *The Circle of the Baal Shem Tov* (Chicago: University Press, 1985), p. XXIX.
30. Ibid., p. XXX.
31. *JC*, 28 March 1947, p. 18.
32. N M Friedman, *Discourses on Festivals* (Jerusalem: privately published, 1964).
33. J Fraenkel (ed.), *The Jews of Austria* (London: Vallentine Mitchell, 1967), pp. 347–61.
34. *Hamaor*, Vol. 1, No. 4, Dec. 1962; Vol. 2, No. 1, April 1962; Vol. 2, No. 3, July 1963; Vol. 3, No. 13, Dec. 1964; Vol. 4, No. 14, April 1965; see also *JC*, 27 May 1955, p. 17; 17 Aug. 1951, p. 17.
35. *JC*, 8 Jan. 1971, p. 35.
36. Ibid., 2 Feb. 1940, p. 21.
37. Arieh Handler, *The Zionist Year Book, 1981–82* (London: Zionist Federation Educational Trust, 1981), pp. 248–9; *JC*, 7 Dec. 1979, p. 25.
38. *Jewish Review*, 24 Dec. 1954, p. 2.
39. *Nasa*.
40. Satmar, 1940; reprinted Jerusalem, 1965.
41. Miriam Sperber, *Misipurei Hasabta* (Jerusalem: Imrei Sefer, 1986), p. 187.
42. *Die Zeit*, 31 Oct. 1934.
43. *Chayenu*, Organ of Jewish Religious Labour, London, published by British Chalutz Datiim, Vol. 5, No. 12, Dec. 1942.
44. S Sperber, *Maamarot* (Jerusalem: Mosad HaRav Kook, 1978).
45. *JC*, 13 Feb. 1953, p. 23.
46. Ibid., 31 Aug. 1984, p. 20.

47. *Die Zeit*, 3 April 1936; 10 Nov. 1937; 11 Sept. 1936; 28 Feb. 1936.
48. *JC*, 19 Dec. 1930, p. 29; also 18 Dec. 1931, p. 21.
49. Ibid., 9 Oct. 1925, p. 5; 26 Feb. 1936, p. 5; 28 Feb. 1936, p. 7.

16 *The North-west Passage*, pp. 144–151

1. *JC*, 10 May 1991, *LE*, p. 1.
2. Ibid., 27 July 1990, *LE*, p. 1.
3. *JT*, 22 March 1990, p. 3; ibid., 7 March 1991, p. 6.
4. Cyril Domb, 'Rav Mordechai Knoblewicz', in *L'Eylah*, a Journal of Judaism today (London: Jews' College, Passover, 1991), pp. 36–41.
5. *Divrei Baruch* on the Ethics of the Fathers, *Zera Baruch* on the Pentateuch, and *Otzar HaChayim* on the Talmud (New York, 1959), originally printed in Lvov in 1911.
6. Proverbs 3:4.
7. *JT*, 3 Nov. 1988.
8. *JC*, 9 June 1950, p. 8.
9. *Baba Bathra*, 21a.

17 *The Jerusalem of England*, pp. 152–157

1. *JC*, 23 Jan. 1987, *LE*, p. 2.
2. Ibid., 18 Jan. 1991, *LE*, p. 9.
3. Ibid., 17 Jan. 1947, p. 6; he also visited London in January 1958; *JC*, 17 Jan. 1958, p. 1.
4. *JT*, 29 May 1990, p. 11.
5. *Gilyoni Mahari* in *Zecher Zaddik Livrucha*, published in Israel by his disciples in 1990.
6. Ibid., pp. 187–211.
7. Author of *Imrot Tohorot* (Lvov, 1911).

18 *The Power of Satmar*, pp. 158–166

1. N Laski, *Jewish Rights and Jewish Wrongs* (London: Soncino Press, 1939), p. 73.
2. *JC*, 21 July 1989, *LE*, p. 1.
3. Ibid., 27 Sept. 1985, *LE*, p. 1.
4. *JT*, 16 May 1991, p. 3; 27 June 1991, p. 3.
5. *JC*, 6 Sept. 1952, p. 29.
6. Ibid., *LE*, 27 Jan. 1984, p. 2; 9 March 1973, p. 15; 14 Oct. 1983, *LE*, p. 1; *Sunday Times*, 15 Sept. 1977, p. 2; *JC*, 15 July 1988; *The Daily Express*, 22 Sept. 1977, p. 7.
7. See *All England Law Reports* (London, 1989), pp. 591–604; *JC*, 5 Aug. 1988, p.19.
8. New York, 1952 (second edition, New York, 1957).
9. *Kethubot*, 111a.
10. *JC*, *LE*, 27 Jan. 1984, p. 3.
11. *New York Times*, 9 Aug. 1979.
12. I Domb, *The Transformation* (London: Hamadfis, 1958), pp. 31, 137.
13. *Megillat Esther*, 3:2.
14. *Jewish Post*, 8 Feb. 1957, p. 3.
15. *JC*, 18 July 1969, p. 14; 14 Aug. 1981, p. 36; 14 Aug. 1981, p. 36. They also

protested against lewd posters advertising swimwear (*JC*, 13 June 1986), *LE*, p. 1.
16. *Jewish Post*, 15 Aug. 1952; *JC*, 15 Sept. 1952.
17. Ibid., 22 Aug. 1952.
18. Ibid., 17 June 1955, p. 11; 26 June 1959, p. 9; ibid., 24 June 1955, p. 37.
19. Ibid., 24 Aug. 1979, p. 3.
20. Sighet (1927–34).
21. *Atzei Chayim* on Festivals (Sighet, 1934); on *Mikvaot*, (Sighet, 1939); on *Gittin* (Sighet, 1939), and *Responsa*, in two parts (1939).
22. *JC*, 6 July 1990, p. 12.

19 *Lubavitch – A Global Challenge*, pp. 167–175

1. *JC*, 4 Sept. 1987, p. 23.
2. S Levin in South Hampstead; Eli Suffrin, Chigwell; Aryeh Suffrin, Redbridge; Zevi Lieberman, formerly of Kingston, now of the *Adath Yisroel* Synagogue, Edgware; Zevi Telsner, Finchley Central Synagogue; Yitzchok Shochet, Mill Hill (*JC*, 18 Jan. 1993); Hershel Rader, formerly at Solihull, now at Woodside Park, London; Gershon Overlander, Sale Hebrew Congregation (*JC*, 17 Jan. 1992, p. 11); Rachman Goodman, New Synagogue, Birmingham; Fishel Cohen, Chaplain to the Midland Regional Universities; Rabbi Y Angyalfi, Etz Chaim and New Central Vilna Synagogue, Leeds; Yonoson Golomb, Sheffield Hebrew Congregation (*JC*, 24 Jan. 1992, p. 13); Herschel Gluck, Minister of the independent Walford Road Synagogue, London (*JC*, 13 March 1991), *LE*, p. 1); Menachem Junik, Richmond Synagogue (*JC*, 4 Oct. 1991, p. 8); Leo Sunderland, Rabbi of Belfast (*JC*, 18 June 1989); Rabbi Yehudah Pink, Solihull, Manchester (*JC*, 14 Jan. 1994, p. 11); Yitzchak Suffrin, Highgate Synagogue, London (*JT*, 28 April 1994, p. 3).
3. *Igrois Koidesh Kvoid Kedushat Admur Shlite, 1928–1938* (New York: Kehot, 1989).
4. Ibid., p. 84.
5. Ibid., Vol. 5, p. 446.
6. Ibid., p. 460; see also p. 465 (7 Sept. 1941).
7. Ibid., p. 481 (20 Sept. 1941); see also p. 216.
8. Ibid., Vol. 7, p. 312; see also p. 777.
9. Ibid., p. 349. There is no record in the Chief Rabbi's files of the replies to the Rebbe.
10. Genesis 28:14.
11. *New York Times*, 27 March 1972.
12. *JC*, 16 April 1982, p. 21.
13. *New York Times*, 2 March 1962.
14. *JC*, 22 June 1977, p. 2.
15. Ibid., 19 Jan. 1973; see also 26 Jan. 1978, p. 14.
16. Ibid., 4 Aug. 1972, p. 16.
17. Ibid., 26 Jan. 1978, p. 14.
18. Ibid., 28 Feb. 1971.
19. Ibid., 30 Nov. 1990, p. 27.
20. Ibid., 20 April 1990, p. 2.
21. Ibid., 27 April 1990, p. 48.
22. Ibid., 30 Nov. 1990, p. 27.
23. *Die Zeit*, 2 Feb. 1915, p. 3.
24. *JT*, 26 Oct. 1973.
25. *Die Zeit*, 7 Feb. 1936, p. 5; see *AJYB* (1939), p. 118.

26. *Jewish Post*, 11 March 1955; *JC*, 4 March 1955, p. 4; *AJYB* (1952), p. 109.
27. *Challenge: an Encounter with Lubavitch-Chabad* (London: Lubavitch Foundation of Great Britain, 1970), p. 68; *JC*, 20 June 1975, p. 12.
28. *Challenge*, p. 69.
29. Ibid., p. 82.
30. *JC*, Supplement, 8 May 1981.
31. *JC*, 18 Feb. 1966, p. 31.
32. Ibid., 7 July 1989, p. 40.
33. Ibid., 4 Sept. 1987, p. 23.
34. Ibid., 21 April 1961, p. 10.

20 Belz – A Centre of Torah, pp. 176–181

1. Judith Grunfeld-Rosenbaum, 'Sara Schenierer', in Leo Jung (ed.), *Jewish Leaders (1750–1940)* (New York: Black Publishing Co., 1953), p. 414.
2. Isaiah 40:1.
3. *Baba Bathra*, 75a.
4. *JT*, 1 Dec. 1967.
5. Ibid., 24 Jan. 1982; *JC*, 12 Feb. 1982, *LE*, p. 1.
6. *The Guardian*, 4 Nov. 1985.
7. *JC*, 30 Aug. 1985, 6 Sept. and 13 Sept. 1985, p. 6.
8. Ibid., 12 April 1985, *LE*, p. 1; *JT*, 18 April 1985.
9. *Times Educational Supplement*, 13 Sept. 1985; *JC*, 27 Dec. 1985, *LF*, p. 2.
10. *Daily Telegraph*, 11 Sept. 1985, *JT*, 12 Sept. 1985; see also *The Guardian*, 4 Nov. 1985; *Jerusalem Post*, 27 Sept. 1985.

21 The Miracle of Bobow, pp. 182–186

1. *JC*, 19 Nov. 1971, p. 19; 26 Nov. 1971, p. 6; 26 May 1972, p. 16; *Sunday Times Magazine*, 14 April 1991, p. 3; Philip Beresford, *The Sunday Times Book of the Rich* (London: Penguin Books, 1990), p. 173.
2. *JC*, 16 July 1976, p. 35.

22 The Importance of Ger, pp. 187–194

1. Proverbs 12:19. On Ger see Eleonora Bergman, 'Gora Kalwaria: The Impact of a Hasidic Cult on the Urban Landscape of a Small Polish Town' in *Polin – A Journal of Polish Jewish Studies*, Vol. 5, pp. 3–23 (Oxford: Basil Blackwell for the Institute for Polish Jewish Studies, 1990).
2. *JC*, Feb. 1977.
3. *JT*, 1 Feb. 1990, p. 1; *JC*, 24 Sept. 1982, pp. 43–6.
4. Imrei Yaakov, *Commentaries and Essays* (London: Narodiczky & Sons, 1944); *Ethics of the Fathers* (London: Hachinuch L. Honig, 1955).
5. *JC*, 11 Dec. 1931, p. 29.
6. Ibid., 24 Sept. 1965.
7. Ibid., 22 April 1960, p. 27; 6 May 1960, p. 25.
8. *Directory of Grant-Making Trusts* (London: Charities Aid Foundation, 1989), pp. 497–8.

9. *JC*, 22 Feb. 1985, 19 April 1985, 5 July 1985; *Hendon Times*, 5 May 1985.
10. Published in Israel in 1990.
11. *JC*, 7 July 1989, p. 24.
12. Ibid., 30 Sept. 1988, p. 29.
13. Ibid., 7 Feb. 1986, *LE*, p. 1; ibid., 18 April 1986, *LE*, p.1.

23 *Shtieblech in Stamford Hill*, pp. 195–201

1. *JT*, 2 March 1989; *JC*, 10 March 1989, p. 32.
2. *JT*, 2 March 1989, 13 Nov. 1970, p. 7.
3. *JT*, 30 Oct. 1970; 15 Oct. 1971.
4. New York: published by the author, 1970.
5. *JT*, 25 Jan. 1990, p. 1; 1 Feb. 1990; *JC*, 26 Jan. 1990, p. 15.
6. *JT*, 11 May 1989.
7. *Jewish Post*, 20 July 1956, p. 1.
8. *JT*, 11 April 1991, p. 3.
9. *JT*, 3 March 1994, p. 1.
10. *JC*, 15 June 1984, *LE*, p. 6.
11. *The Times*, 29 Oct. 1992, p. 12; *JC*, 30 Oct. 1992.
12. Ibid., and *JC*, 30 Oct. 1992.

24 *Other Chasidic Centres in Britain*, pp. 202–212

1. *JC*, 7 Nov. 1952, p. 10.
2. Ibid., 20 May 1960, p. 23.
3. *Jewish Review*, 18 Sept. 1953, p. 3; 30 Sept. 1953, p. 3.
4. *JC*, 9 Jan. 1987, p. 23.
5. Psalm 24.
6. L Jacobs, *Helping with Inquiries*, p. 21. I am indebted to Mr L Reich of Manchester for his help. See *JT*, 28 Sept. 1989, p. 9.
7. *JC*, 22 May 1987, p. 18; 8 Jan. 1982, p. 10.
8. Ibid., 13 May 1955, p. 117; ibid., 29 July 1977, p. 20; L Jacobs, op. cit., pp. 32 and 34.
9. L Jacobs, op. cit., p. 32.
10. *AJYB* (London: *Jewish Chronicle*, 1935), pp. 190 and 478.
11. L Jacobs, op. cit., p. 32.
12. J I Weiss, *Sefer Sheelot Uteshuvot Minchat Yitzchak* (Israel: Kefar Chabad, 1969); *Pirsumei Nisa*; Preface to the tenth volume *Minchat Yitzchak*, Jerusalem, 1990, p. 7; also see *JT*, 15 June 1989; *JC*, 23 June 1989, p. 18.
13. *JT*, 29 Oct. 1971.
14. *Minchat Yitzchak*, Part 2, Jerusalem, 1990.
15. *JC*, 23 June 1989, p. 18; *JT*, 22 June 1989.
16. *The Times*, 27 Dec. 1990, p. 5.
17. He published his father's glosses under the title *Hilchot Eretz Yisrael* by Jacob ben Asher, London, 1900.
18. K E Collins, *Aspects of Scottish Jewry* (Glasgow: Glasgow Jewish Representative Council, 1987), pp. 43–4; *JC*, 7 Nov. 1924, p. 5; *Glasgow Herald*, 1 Nov. 1924 and Frederick Levison, *Christian and Jew, Leon Levison* (Edinburgh: The Pentland Press, 1989).

19. K E Collins, *Second City Jewry* (Glasgow: Scottish Jewish Archives, 1990), pp. 140–41.
20. *JC*, 26 April 1957, p. 9.
21. *Glasgow Jewish Year Book, 1938–1939*.
22. W Gottlieb, *From Days of Old* (London: Central Council for Jewish Education, 1948).
23. E Krausz, *Leeds Jewry* (Cambridge: JHSE and W Heffer, 1964), p. 9.
24. Murray Freedman, *Annual Demographic Reports for 1989–1991 on Leeds Community* (Leeds: self-published, Jan. 1992).
25. Krausz, *Leeds Jewry*, pp. 9 and 43; *AJYB*, 1904, p. 167.
26. *JC*, 10 Oct. 1954, p. 19.
27. Ibid., 3 Feb. 1984, p. 22.
28. B B Benas, 'Later Records of the Jews in Liverpool', in *Transactions of the Historic Society of Lancashire and Cheshire* (London: Frome, 1929), pp. 9–15.
29. *JC*, 23 July 1976, p. 16.
30. Ibid., 29 Jan. 1960, p. 15.
31. *Sunday Times*, 22 May 1994, Section 9, p. 12; see also *Lubavitch UK* (London: published by Lubavitch Foundation, Dec. 1989), pp. 4–5.

25 *The Chasidic Community*, pp. 213–218

1. Asher Wingate (d. 1969), son of the Chasid S Winegarten was Vice-President of the United Synagogue, Treasurer of its Burial Society, and Warden of the Willesden Synagogue; Jack Cinna, Warden of the Willesden Synagogue was an Elder of the United Synagogue; Norman Charles Oster, was a Warden of the Wembley Synagogue and of the *Machzikei Hadath*; Hyman Gerstler (d. 1969) and his brother Leon were Wardens of the Cricklewood and Marble Arch Synagogues respectively; Cyril Gertler, son of a Chasid of Ostrowiec was Warden of Dollis Hill Synagogue; I Josephs, a Chasid of Biala, Warden of Finsbury Park Synagogue; Jack Steinhart, Warden of Hendon (1969–72); Ben Waller, son of a Chasid of Bobow, Sam Greenspan (1961–70), a Chasid of Biala (Financial Representative, and from 1977–79 Warden), and Freddie Fisher, son of a Chasid of Boyan (Warden, 1970–93) were Honorary Officers of the Finchley Synagogue; Jonathan Lew (b. 1937), Chief Executive of the United Synagogue, is a grandson of Rabbi J Lew; Jack Lass (b. 1916), Warden of Brondesbury Synagogue. L Stern, Warden of St. Johns Wood Synagogue (1953); Hyman Schiff (d. 1948), the son of M C Schiff, was Warden of the New Synagogue. Wolfie Schiff (d. 1965) was the Warden of Grove Lane Synagogue, and his son-in-law, Henry Gross (d. 1953) was the Warden of Stoke Newington Synagogue.
2. Abraham Bernard Olivestone, Elder of the Federation of Synagogues, Life President of the Yeshurun Synagogue, was the son of Hanoch Olivestone (1882–1953), a Chasid of Ger who served as a *shochet* and Minister from 1914 onwards at the *Adath Yisroel* Synagogue, Green Lanes, London, successively at Ebbw Vale, Tredegar (South Wales), Blackpool, Portsmouth and finally at the Walthamstow and Leyton Synagogue, London. Morris Lederman, a native of Mezerich, whose father was a *Chasid* of Radzyn, was for 30 years the President of the Federation of Synagogues and is now its Honorary President; Maurice Caplin, son of a Bialer Chasid, past President of Sinai Synagogue and past Treasurer of the Federation of Synagogues; Hershel Steinhart (of Dzikov) was the *gabbai* of the *Chevra Kadisha*; Joseph Waller (d. 1968), son of a Chasid of

Bobow, and Elchanan Chanan (d. 1975) were Vice-Presidents of the Federation and Wardens of the Ohel Shem Synagogue for 20 years (*JC*, 14 Feb. 1975, p. 39); Avigdor Shakovitch (1883–1975), was an Elder of the Federation as well as the President of the Sidney Street Synagogue. Mr J L Cymerman (1911–88), of Cannon Street Synagogue, chairman of the Federation Kashrut Authority and a leading light of the Federation of Synagogues which he served in several capacities, finally becoming vice-chairman (*JC*, 30 Sept. 1988, p. 16). Rabbi Myer Frydman (1909–1994), a son of a Chasid of Amshinov, also served for many years as an Honorary Officer and Vice-President of the Federation of Synagogues and the Mizrachi Movement. Simon Arthur (Jimmy) Schiff, founder member of the Kosher Meals Service and for 20 years a member of the Board of Management of the Cricklewood Synagogue (*JC*, 4 July 1980, p. 33).

3. One of the founders of the New London Synagogue was Alfred Wolkovitch (d. 1963), the son of a Chasid of Alexander; S J Frankfurt, President of the Board of Shechita; Judge Henry Lazarus Lachs, Circuit Judge of Liverpool.

4. M Spira in Willesden; Lipa Naftali Baum (1920–90) (brought up in the *shtiebl* of Dzikov) served in Pollockshields, Glasgow, Luton, South Hampstead and Woodside Park; Dayan A Rapoport (d. 1973) was a member of the London *Beth Din*; Dayan D Berger, a descendant of Rab Elimelech of Lejask, was a member of the London *Beth Din* until 1994; Reverend Simon Hass, former Reader of the Central Synagogue, son of a Chasid of Bobow, studied in the Belz *yeshiva* in Tarnow and regularly visited the Rebbe of Belz (*JC*, *LE* 1 March 1991); Reverend Maurice Dubiner was Reader of the Brondesbury and the Western Synagogues; Reverend Michael Lionel Plaskow, Reader of the Woodside Park Synagogue since 1956, is a grandson-in-law of Mr B Weisfogel; Rabbi Ephraim Levy Gastwirth (b. 1920) held rabbinical posts at Sale, Manchester, Blackpool and South Hampstead, and was principal of the Judith Lady Montefiore College; Dayan Ivan Binstock in Golders Green; Reverend Ephraim Rosenberg (d. 1978) was the reader of the *Shomrei Hadath* Synagogue, 1947–49 (*JC*, 21 Feb. 1978, p. 19); Rabbi S Halstuk in South Tottenham; Rabbi Simon Winegarten, Bridge Lane; Reverend Malcolm Weisman, Recorder SE Circuit, Religious Adviser to Small Communities, grandson of a Chasid; Chayim Abramovitz, Reader at St. Johns Wood Synagogue and the late Abraham Schechter of Cricklewood, both sons of Gerer Chasidim. A grandson of the Chasid Abraham Dombrowsky is Professor Cyril Domb who held the chair of Theoretical Physics at King's College, London. Dr Norman Dombrowski was a Lecturer in Chemical Engineering at Imperial College, London. Dr Gerald Davis and Mr Sydney Davis were well-known lecturers in Physics. Jonathan Winegarten, Vice-President of the Federation of Synagogues, was appointed Master of the Supreme Court, Chancery Division (*JT*, 13 Sept. 1991, p. 6).

5. *JC*, 13 July 1990, p. 1.

6. Ibid., 20 April 1990, p. 14.

7. Isaiah 11:5.

8. *JC*, 15 March 1991, p. 4.

9. Among them are Berish Berger, Zalman Margulies, Rabbi Meisels and William Stern.

10. Simon Marks Primary School and Avigdor Primary School.

11. S Poll, 'The Role of Yiddish in American Ultra-Orthodox and Chasidic Communities' in Joshua A Fishman (ed.), *Never Say Die* (The Hague, Paris and New York: Mouton Publishers, 1981), p. 208.

12. *Hamaor*, Vol. 4, No. 20, Sept. 1966, pp. 14–15.

26 The Chasidic Way of Life, pp. 219–226

1. *JC*, 21 Dec. 1990, p. 321.
2. Horodezky, *HaChasidut Ve HaChasidim*, Vol. 4, p. 10.
3. *JC*, 16 April 1982, p. 20.
4. Ibid., 12 March 1976, *Supplement*, p. iv.
5. Ibid., 3 Aug. 1990, p. 36.
6. Ibid., 2 Sept. 1955, p. 6.
7. Ibid., 18 Jan. 1991, *LE*, p. 7.
8. *JT*, 8 Aug. 1991, p. 1; *JC*, 9 Aug. 1991, p. 14 and p. 36.
9. I Rubin, *Satmar – An Island in the City* (Chicago: Quadrangle Books, 1972), p. 259, note 5; in May 1986 two brothers were jailed for a tax fraud: *JC*, 9 May 1986, *LE*, p. 1.
10. *JT*, 26 April 1990, p. 1.
11. *JC*, 8 Dec., 1967, p. 39; he was also the author of *Stories of Simcha* (London, New York: Thomas Yoseloff, 1961).
12. *JT*, 22 Aug. 1986; *JC*, 26 Aug. 1986, p. 10.
13. *Die Zeit*, 7 Dec. 1920, p. 3.
14. *Jewish Post*, 20 Oct. 1961.
15. *JC*, 27 Aug. 1937, p. 19.
16. *JT*, 26 April 1990, p. 10; ibid., 11 April 1991, p. 3.
17. *JC*, 12 July 1991, p. 10.
18. Ibid., 8 March 1991, *LE*, p. 1.
19. Ibid., 15 Nov. 1990; ibid., 31 Jan. 1991, p 1; *JC*, 1 Feb. 1991, *LE*, p. 4; ibid., 5 Feb. 1991, *LE*, p. 1.
20. Ibid., 3 Nov., *LE*, p. 2; ibid., 21 Dec. 1990, *LE*, p. 1.

27 The Literary Horizon, pp. 227–233

1. Lady Magnus was the daughter of Alderman E Emanuel (1807–88), Mayor of Portsmouth. She married a cousin of the Reverend (later Sir) Philip Magnus (1842–1933), Minister of the West London Reform Synagogue in 1870.
2. H Graetz, *History of the Jews* (Philadelphia: Jewish Publication Society of America, 1946), Vol. 5, pp. 383–5, 473 and 611.
3. Lady Magnus, *Outlines of Jewish History* (London: Vallentine Mitchell, 1963), pp. 173 ff., 186, 188.
4. Lady Magnus, *Jewish Portraits* (London: Unwin, 1888, reprinted in London: Myers, 1905 and 1925).
5. Lady Magnus' book *The Outline of Jewish History* was originally printed by Kegan Paul in 1879, but was frequently reprinted and revised, first by M Friedlander (London: Longman, 1886, 1888) and by the Jewish War Memorial Council in 1928. In 1931, Dr Cecil Roth added further chapters. The American Publications Society added chapters for the American scene. Vallentine Mitchell reprinted it in 1958 and in 1963.
6. D Cassel, *The Manual of Jewish History and Literature*, published in 1879 and then printed in London by Macmillan in 1905.
7. Ibid., p. 222.
8. Ibid.
9. *JC*, 3 Jan. 1941, p. 17.
10. Ibid., 26 Feb. 1932, p. 8.
11. Ibid., Dec. 1935, *Supplement*, p. 5.

12. Jerusalem: *Mosad Harav Kook*, 1969; *JC*, 7 Nov. 1980, p. 2.
13. Ibid., 7 May 1954, p. 10. The Annual Lawrence Kostoris Lecture at the Institute of Jewish Studies, *JC*, 23 June 1961, p. 12.
14. He gave lectures on Buber in 1961 and in 1970; ibid., 27 March 1970, p. 21.
15. M Simon, *Jewish Religious Conflicts* (London: Hutchinson University Library, 1950), pp. 77–85.
16. Ibid., p. 79.
17. Ibid., pp. 85–6.
18. M Simon, *Israel Baalshem His Life and Times* (London: Jewish Religious Educational Establishment, 1953).
19. Ibid., p. 26.
20. Ibid., p. 19.
21. V Gollancz, *Reminiscences of Affection* (London: Victor Gollancz, 1968), p. 24.
22. Ibid., p. 123.
23. Barbara Greene and V Gollancz, *God of a Hundred Names* (Hodder & Stoughton, 1962), p. 281.
24. *JC*, 22 Sept. 1958, p. 8.
25. Greene and Gollancz, op. cit., p. 75; see op. cit., pp. 179, 185 and 232; V Gollancz, *My Dear Timothy – An Autobiographal Letter to His Grandson* (London: Victor Gollancz, 1952), pp. 119, 336; Gollancz, *Year of Grace*, pp. 8, 11, 34, 57, 95, 130, 138, 169, 179, 180, 183, 184, 186, 249, 276, 289, 340, 361 and 389.
26. Cecil Roth, *A Short History of the Jewish People* (London: East and West Library, 1953), p. 334.
27. Ibid., p. 335.
28. James Parkes, *A History of the Jewish People* (London: East and West Library, 1969), p. 107.
29. *JC*, 12 Sept. 1969, p. 84.
30. Jerusalem: Bialik Institute, 1974.
31. Ed. David Goldstein.
32. *JC*, 23 June 1978, p. 6.
33. Ibid., 20 May 1960, p. 23.
34. Ibid., 19 March 1965, p. 9.
35. *Jewish Review*, 6 March 1953, p. 3.
36. L Jacobs, *Palm Tree of Deborah* (London: Vallentine Mitchell, 1960).
37. L Jacobs, *A Jewish Theology* (London: Darton, Longman and Todd, 1973).
38. Ibid., p. 115.
39. Ibid., p. 35.
40. Ibid., p. 166.
41. Ibid., p. 167.
42. Ibid., p. 297.
43. L Jacobs, *Holy Living* (New York: Jason Aronson, 1990).
44. Oxford: Littman Library, 1990; *JC*, 31 July 1987, p. 25.
45. J Kupferman, *The Lubavitch Chasidim of Stamford Hill*, London: M.Phil., University College, unpublished.
46. See, for example, Rapaport-Albert, Doctoral Thesis, in Bibliography.
47. See Bibliography.
48. *JC*, 30 Nov. 1990, p. 27; *Forty Years Light, Joy and Unity* (New York: Merkos L'Inyonei Chinuch, 1990), p. 11.
49. Published by Lubavitch Foundation of Great Britain, London, 1970.
50. Published by Lubavitch Foundation of Great Britain, London, 1973.
51. London, *Jewish Times*, 1942.
52. Joshua Tiger, *The Tsaddik un der Baal Tshuva* (London: Hamadfis, 1960), 243

pages. On J Tiger see *JC*, 16 Dec. 1960 (Obituary); ibid., 5 Feb. 1960, p. 24.

53. C Klinger, *Lekuved des Besht Akademye* (London: 1961).

54. *Loshn un Lebn*, 'Rab Mendele Kotzker', 'Rab Nachman leint a Qvittl', Aug. to Sept. 1958; 'Der Koshinitzer fiert Tish in Whitechapel', Nov./Dec. 1958; 'Rab Sishe', May/July 1976; 'Rab Yecheskele un Beis Chesed L'Avrohom', Feb./May 1977; 'Die ershte Slichos in Kotzk', June/Sept. 1977; 'Der Baal Shem, der Choize Mi'Lublin, Rebbe Rab Hershel', Dec. 1978 (also printed in *Die Zeit*, 6 Sept. 1937, p. 3); 'Tiferet Shloimo', April 1980; 'Die Mizritcher Chavrisa', June 1981; see also, *Whitechapel Shtetl d'Britain*, London, *Loshn un Lebn*, 1961, pp. 68 and 77; *JC*, 28 Jan. 1983, p. 22.

55. P Johnson, *A History of the Jews* (London: Weidenfeld & Nicolson, 1987), p. 296.

56. S Brook, *The Club* (London: Constable, 1989), p. 53.

57. *JC*, 2 Sept. 1955, p. 19; ibid., 23 Dec. 1949, p. 13; ibid., 11 April 1980, p. 21; 27 Sept. 1974, p. 14; 14 Sept. 1990, p. 62; *Volvo City*, by Roy Ackerman, directed by Susanna White, a UK 1991 portrait of Chasidism in Stamford Hill, London, was shown on Channel 4 Television on 4 Nov. 1991 at 9 pm.

Glossary

Adar: The twelfth month of the Jewish calendar.

Adar Sheni: The extra month in a leap year.

Admor: Title given to a Chasidic rabbi.

Aggadah: Ethical or homiletical portions of rabbinic literature.

Agudat Yisrael: World Orthodox Jewish movement founded in 1912.

Agunah: Woman unable to remarry according to Jewish Law because of desertion by her husband.

Aliyah: (Lit. 'Going up'). Being called up to the Reading of the Law.

Am HaAretz: An ignorant man.

Amidah: The main daily prayer which consists of Eighteen Blessings (*Shemoneh Esray*).

Arba kanfot: The four corners of a ritual undergarment. It has an opening for the head in the centre of an oblong piece of cloth with the minimum of the required fringes on the four corners.

Ashkenazim: Term applied to Jews of Germany, west, central and east European Jews in contrast to Sephardi Jews.

Av: The fifth month of the Jewish calendar.

Av Beth Din: President of the Jewish Court of Law.

Baal koreh: Reader of the Law.

Baal makrei: One who announces the 'sounds' of the *shofar*.

Baal shem: 'Master of the Name'. A name given to a man who works miracles.

Baal Shem Tov: (Lit. 'Master of the Good Name'). The name given to Rabbi Israel ben Eliezer, the founder of Chasidism.

Baal tefillah: One who leads the prayers.

Baal tekiah: One who blows the *shofar*.

Baal teshuvah: A penitent.

Backesha: Long winter coat, half-lined with fur.

Bar mitzvah: (Lit. 'Son of Commandment'). A boy attaining the age of 13.

Besht: The popular name by which Rabbi Israel Baal Shem Tov is known. It is an acronym formed from the name Baal Shem Tov.

Beth Din: House of Law or judgment. A gathering of three or more learned men acting as a Jewish Court of Law.

Beth Hamidrash: House of Study.

Bima: The platform in a synagogue on which the Torah is read.

Bochur: *Yeshiva* student.

Borechu: 'Bless ye the Lord'. The invocation to prayer with which the public service now opens.

Cabbala: Jewish Mysticism.

Chabad: An acronym of *chochmah*, *binah*, and *daat*, wisdom, understanding and knowledge. Another name for the Lubavitch movement founded by Rabbi Shneur Zalman of Liady.

Chalitzah: Ritual conducted at *Beth Din* by which the childless widow becomes liberated from Levirate marriage.

Challa: Special soft bread, often in braided shape, eaten on the Sabbath and festivals.

Chanukah: An eight-day festival, commencing on 25 *Kislev*, in celebration of the victory of the Maccabees in the year 161 BCE.

Chaye Adam: (Lit. 'the Lifetime of a Man'). *Chevra Chaye Adam* was a group who studied a book of Laws called *Chaye Adam*.

Chazan: Cantor.

Cheder, plural *chedarim*: (Lit. 'a room'). A traditional Jewish school.

Chevra, plural *chevrot*: A small congregation of traditional Jews, an association for specific or ritual purposes.

Chevra Kadisha: (Lit. 'Holy Society'). A society whose members look after burials.

Chevra Shass: A society for studying the Talmud.

Chinuch: Jewish education.

Chol Hamoed: The intermediate days of festivals of Passover and Tabernacles.

Chukat hagoy: Aping the ways of the Gentiles.

Chumash: Pentateuch.

Chupa: A canopy under which the bride and bridegroom stand during the marriage ceremony; the marriage ceremony itself.

Daf Yomi: The study of a page of the Talmud daily.

Dayan: A judge in a Rabbinical Court.

Devekut: 'Cleaving' to the Divine.

Din: A law.

Dybbuk: A restless soul of a dead sinner which attaches itself to a living body.

Ein Yaakov: A popular anthology of the narrative material in the Talmud, collected by Rabbi Jacob Ibn Chabib in the sixeenth century.

Elul: Sixth month of the Jewish calendar.

Eretz Yisrael: The Land of Israel.

Etrog, plural *etrogim*: A citron. One of the 'four kinds of plants' used during the Festival of *Sukkot*.

Frum: (Yiddish) Religious.

Gabbai, plural *gabbaim*: Honorary Official of the congregation.

Galut: Exile. Dispersion of the Jewish People after the conquest of Palestine by the Romans in 70 A.C.E.

Gan Eden: Paradise.

Gaon: Plural *Geonim*. The title of the heads of the Rabbinical Academy in Babylon.

Gartel: Belt worn during prayer.

Gemara: The portion of the Talmud which discusses the Laws in the Mishnah.

Gilgul: Transmigration of souls.

Glatt kosher: Unquestionably kosher. The most rigorous standard of *kashrut*. It indicates that the meat or meat products are Kosher without any shadow of doubt.

Goy, plural *Goyim*: Gentiles.

Hafsakah: Interval.

Hallel: Hymns of praise, consisting of a number of psalms.

Haskalah: Jewish Enlightenment. A movement promoting secularization and modern European culture among the Jews in Germany in the eighteenth and nineteenth centuries.

Hitlahavut: (Lit. 'inflamed'). Spiritual enthusiasm in prayer and other religious activities.

Hoif: A Chasidic court.

Illui: An outstandingly brilliant young Talmudist.

Iyyar: The second month of the Jewish calendar.

Kaddish, plural *kaddishim*. Holy or sacred. Refers to the doxology recited in the Synagogue by mourners during the period of mourning and on the anniversary of a death.

Kapote: Long black coat, fastened with a girdle, worn by Chasidim.

Kavanah: Concentration and deliberation in the performing of sacred tasks.

Kiddush: (Lit. 'sanctified'). A benediction recited to inaugurate the Sabbath and festivals, usually over a cup of wine before the meal.

Kiddush Hashem: Sanctification of God's name. The Jews' readiness to suffer martyrdom.

Kipa: A skull cap.

Kislev: The ninth month of the Jewish calendar.

Kittel: White overgarment worn by officiants and Orthodox Jews during the New Year and the Day of Atonement.

Knesset: Israeli Parliament.

Kollel: A *yeshiva* for married men to continue Torah study after marriage.

Kollel avreichim: A *kollel* for young men.

Kollel boker: Morning study.

Kollel erev: Evening study.

Kol Nidrei: The Evening Service on the Day of Atonement is preceded by the chanting of *Kol Nidrei* – 'all vows'.

Kosher: Food suitable for consumption by religious Jews.

Lag B'Omer: The thirty-third day of the counting of the *Omer* corresponding to 18 *Iyyar*. The Scholar's Feast. It is observed as a minor holiday.

Lulav: Palm branch, used on festival of *Sukkot*.

Maariv: The Evening Prayer.

Maftir: (Lit. 'concluding'.) The last portion of the *Sidra* is known as *Maftir*.

Maggid: Popular preacher, usually speaking in Yiddish.

Mashgiach: A religious supervisor of *kashrut*. Also a supervisor of the religious welfare of young men at a *yeshiva*.

Maskil, plural *Maskilim*: A follower of the *Haskalah* (Enlightenment) movement. A man versed in western culture.

Matza: The unleavened bread eaten on Passover.

Mazal: (Lit. 'constellation'.) A term used to mean luck.

Mechutanim: Relatives by marriage.

Megilla: (Lit. 'scroll'.) A term commonly applied to the five short books: The Song of Songs, Ruth, Lamentations, Ecclesiastes and Esther. The Book of Esther is generally referred to as the *Megilla*.

Melave malka: (Lit. 'escorting the Queen'.) It applies to the meal after the termination of the Sabbath and is accompanied by community singing and a discourse from the Rebbe. This meal achieved great prominence among the Chasidim.

Menora: The seven-branched lamp used in the Temple, and the eight-branched candelabrum used on Chanukah.

Meshullach, plural *meshullachim*: Emissary sent to conduct propaganda or to raise funds for rabbinical or charitable institutions.

Mesirat nefesh: Self-sacrifice.

Mezuzah: Contains religious texts and is attached to a doorpost. (See Deut. 6:4–9 and 11, 13–21)

Midrash, plural *Midrashim*: Expositions. Homiletical interpretations of the Scriptures. A general term applied to a very important section of Jewish literature.

Mikveh, plural *mikvaot*: An indoor ritual bath required for Jewish ritual purification.

Mincha: The Afternoon Service.

Minhag: Custom, rite.

Minyan: A quorum of ten men above the age of thirteen required for prayer.

MiSheberach: It is usual for a blessing to be invoked upon the one who is called to the Reading of the Law. As a rule such a blessing is accompanied by an offering to the congregation or towards some charitable cause.

Mishna: (Lit. 'Repetition'.) The collection of the statements, discussions and biblical interpretations of the *Tannaim* edited by Rabbi Judah the Patriarch (135–220). English translation by H Danby (Oxford, 1933).

Mithnagged, plural *Mithnaggedim*: (Lit. 'Opponent'.) Those who opposed Chasidism.

Mitzva: Obligation or duty ordained either by God or the rabbis. A good deed.

Moetzet Gedolei HaTorah: Council of Torah Sages.

Mohel: A person who performs the religious rite of circumcision.

Musaf: Additional prayers on the Sabbath, Holidays and *Rosh Chodesh*.

Musar: Ethical movement developed in the latter part of the nineteenth century and founded by Israel Lipkin (Salanter).

Negiah: (Lit. 'touch'.) Prohibition of a man being touched by a woman other than his wife.

Neilah: Concluding Service on the Day of Atonement.

Niddah: A menstruating woman who is forbidden to have intercourse with her husband.

Nisan: First month in the Jewish calendar.

Nusach Ari: Prayer Book and liturgical custom according to Rabbi Isaac Luria.

Nusach Sephard: Prayer Book text of the *Sephardim*.

Ohel: Sepulchre on the grave of a *zaddik* where candles are lit and people can pray.

Olam Haba: The World to Come.

Passover: The Festival commemorating the liberation of the Jews from their bondage in Egypt. The Festival is kept for eight days from 15 *Nisan* to 22 (or 21 *Nisan* in Israel).

Payot: Earlocks, see Lev. 19:27.

Pidyon: (Lit. 'Redemption'). Money followers give to a Rebbe when visiting him.

Pidyon HaBen: Redemption of the first-born son. This is a ceremony held on the thirty-first day after the birth.

Piyutim: Liturgical poetry for Sabbath and festivals.

Pruve Tisch: (Lit. 'table'.) A Chasidic Rebbe conducting the Sabbath meal.

Purim: (Lit. 'lots'.) The Festival is celebrated on the 14th of *Adar* in commemoration of the deliverance of the Jews in Persia from the hands of Haman as described in the Scroll of Esther.

Qvittlech: Written petitions given to the Rebbe by the Chasidim.

Rashi: Acronym of Rabbi Solomon ben Isaac (1040–1105), the great commentator of the Bible and Talmud.

Rav: Rabbi. A man who has received *Semicha* (Ordination).

Reb: Honorary title or mode of address equivalent to 'Mr'.

Rebbe: Yiddish form of Rabbi, usually applied to a Chasidic master.

Rebbetzin: A Rabbi's wife.

Responsa: Written replies (*teshuvot*) given to questions on all aspects of Jewish Law by qualified authorities from the time of the late *Geonim* to the present day.

Reverend: A minister. A title used for Jewish clergy who have not been ordained.

Rosh: Head.

Rosh Chodesh: New Moon. The beginning of the Jewish month.

Rosh Hashanah: New Year, the 1st and 2nd days of *Tishri*, beginning of the Civil Jewish Year, usually in September.

Rosh Hashochtim: Chief supervisor of slaughterers.

Rosh Yeshiva: The Dean of a Talmudical School.

Ruach: Spirit. An aspect of the soul.

Ruach HaKodesh: The Holy Spirit. A form of prophecy.

Sandek: The one who holds the baby on his knees during circumcision.

Seder: The order of the home service on Passover.

Sefer Torah: The Book of the Law. The handwritten scroll of the Torah from which readings are made.

Selichot: Pentimential prayers, recited on certain days of the Jewish calendar.

Semicha: Rabbinical ordination. Conferring the title Rabbi.

Sephardi, plural *Sephardim*: Jews of Spain and Portugal and their descendants.

Seudah: Festive Meal.

Seudah shlishit or *Shaloh seudot*: (Hebrew: third meal). The third of the three traditional meals eaten on Sabbath. A setting for Chasidic teachings or the telling of tales.

Seudat mitzva: (Lit. 'meal of commandment'.) A meal in honour of a religious occasion.

Shaatnes: It is forbidden to wear garments which contain any interwoven fibres of wool and linen (Deut. 22:11). Orthodox Jews have developed methods of testing fabrics in a special laboratory.

Shabbat HaGadol: Name given to the Sabbath before Passover.

Shabbaton: A festive Sabbath gathering.

Shacharit: Morning Prayer recited daily.

Shadchan: Matchmaker.

Shammash: (Hebrew: 'servant'). A synagogue beadle.

Shavuot: Pentecost or the Feast of Weeks celebrated on 6 and 7 *Sivan*, commemorating the Giving of the Torah and the Ingathering of the Harvest.

Shechinah: Divine presence.

Shechita: The traditional manner of killing animals for food.

Sheitl: Wig worn by Orthodox married women.

Shelach manot: Interchanging of gifts on *Purim* between friends and neighbours.

Shemini Atzeret: The Feast of the Eighth Day or the Eighth Day of Solemn Assembly (Numbers 30:35).

Shemura matza: Matza which is specially prepared for Passover, the wheat having been 'guarded' from becoming unleavened.

Sheva Berachot: Seven blessings recited during wedding celebrations.

Shevat: The eleventh month of the Jewish calendar.

Shidduch: Arranged marriage.

Shimusha rabba: A type of *tefillin* worn only by the most saintly. The order of the parchments differs from that of normal *tefillin*.

Shirayim: Remnants left from the meal of a *zaddik*.

Shiur: A Talmudical discourse.

Shochet: One who slaughters animals or fowl according to Jewish ritual. He must have a certificate (*cabbala*) from a rabbi.

Shofar: A ram's horn used in the Service of *Rosh Hashanah*, at the conclusion of the Day of Atonement, and other special occasions.

Shomer: (Lit. 'guard'.) One who supervises the cooking, selling and manufacture of Kosher food.

Shtetl: Yiddish for a small town or village in Eastern Europe.

Shtiebl, plural *shtieblech*: A small room used as a Chasidic place of worship.

Shtreimel: A wide-brimmed fur hat worn by Chasidim.

Shul: Yiddish for Synagogue.

Shulchan Aruch: (Lit. 'Prepared Table'.) A Code of Jewish Law by Rabbi Joseph Caro (1488–1575) and first published in 1565.

Shushan Purim: The day succeeding *Purim*. Referred to in Esther 9:18 as that on which the Jews of Shushan (Susa) celebrated their triumph, i.e. 15 *Adar* and regarded as a minor festival.

Sidra: Weekly Torah portion.

Siddur: The Prayer Book of the Jews.

Simcha: A joyous occasion.

Simchat Torah: Rejoicing of the Law. The Festival immediately after *Shemini Atzeret*.

Sivan: Ninth month of the Jewish calendar.

Siyum: (Lit. 'completion'.) When a course of study is completed, the occasion is marked by a celebratory meal.

Sukkah: Tabernacle or booth erected for the festival of *Sukkot* (Leviticus 23:34).

Sukkot: The festival of Tabernacles commemorates the wanderings of the children of Israel in the wilderness and is observed from 15 to 23 *Tishri*.

Tabernacles: See *Sukkot*.

Tachanun: (Lit. 'supplications'.) Prayers recited between the *Amidah* and the Conclusion of the Morning Service.

Taharat Hamishpacha: Family purity.

Tallit: The four-cornered prayer shawl with fringes at each corner worn by males at Morning Services.

Talmud: It is commonly used to mean the comments and the discussions (*Gemara*) on the text of the *Mishnah* by Palestinian and Babylonian scholars from the third to the fifth centuries of the Common Era, comprising the Palestinian Talmud and the Babylonian Talmud.

Talmud Torah: A traditional Jewish religious public school.

Tammuz: The fourth month of the Jewish calendar.

Targum: Aramaic translation of the Bible.

Tashlich: Ceremony of the symbolic casting away of one's sins on the afternoon of the first day of *Rosh Hashanah*.

Tefillah: Prayer.

Tefillin: Phylacteries. Small leather cases containing passages from the Scriptures and affixed to the forehead and left arm during the recital of Morning Prayers.

Tekia: Blast of the *shofar*.

Tevet: Tenth month of the Jewish calendar.

Tikkun Chatzot: A Cabbalistic prayer recited at midnight, expressing mourning for the exile of the *Shechinah*.

Tisch: (Lit. 'table'.) Communal meal at the Rebbe's table.

Tisha B'Av: The Fast of the 9th of *Av*, commemorating the destruction of both the First and Second Temples (586 BCE and 70 CE).

Tishri: The seventh month of the Jewish calendar.

Torah: Hebrew word meaning teaching, instruction or guidance. Torah represents the whole body of Jewish teaching from the commencement of the Bible right down to our own day.

Tosafot: Critical glosses on the Talmud mainly by French rabbis of the twelfth and thirteenth centuries. Printed together with Rashi in all standard editions of the Talmud.

Trefah: Food that is not Kosher.

Tzitzit: The Biblical name of the fringes that are attached to each of the four corners of the garment (Numbers 14:38).

Vaad HaChinuch: Education committee.

Wissenschaft des Judentums: 'Science of Judaism', a movement for the scientific study of Jewish history and literature.

Yahrzeit: Anniversary of a person's death.

Yarmulka: Skull cap.

Yeshiva: Jewish traditional academy devoted to the study of rabbinic literature.

Yeshiva Gedola: Advanced *yeshiva*.

Yichud: (Lit. 'privacy'). The prohibition instituted by the rabbis against the private association of the sexes.

Yiddish: Jewish language based on old German with a strong mixture of Hebrew and Slavonic words.

Yiddishkeit: Jewishness. The essence of Orthodox life. The observance of the Mitzvot and Torah Study.

Yishuv: Jewish settlement in Israel.

Yom Kippur: The Day of Atonement.

Yom Tov: A good day. Generally applied to holidays and festivals.

Yoreh Deah: Second part of the *Shulchan Aruch*. Deals mainly with dietary and ritual laws, including mourning.

Yoshevim: Permanent resident in a Chasidic master's court.

Zaddick, plural *zaddikim*: (Lit. 'the righteous one'.) A person outstanding for his faith and piety. The leader of a Chasidic group.

Zeddaka: Charity.

Zemirot: Sabbath table songs. Many of the hymns were composed by the Cabbalists.

Zohar: Title of the mystical work introduced into Spain by Moses de Leon at the end of the thirteenth century and attributed to Rabbi Simeon bar Yochai of the second century. It was first published in Mantua, 1558–60. English translation edited by M Simon, 5 volumes (London: Soncino Press, 1932).

Bibliography

ADAMS, Hannah, *The History of the Jews from the destruction of Jerusalem to the 19th century* (Boston: John Eliot, Jr., 1812)

ADLER, E N *Jews in Many Lands* (Philadelphia: JPSA, 1905)

ALDERMAN, Geoffrey, *The Federation of Synagogues, 1887–1987* (London: Federation of Synagogues, 1987)

ANDERSON, Philip, *The Life of Laurence Oliphant* (London: R. Hale, 1956)

ARIS, Stephen, *The Jew in Business* (London: Cape, 1970)

BAUMINGER, Aryeh, *Sefer Karako* (Jerusalem: Mosad Harav Kook, 1959)

BENTWICH, Norman, *Solomon Schechter* (Philadelphia: JPSA, 1938)

BERNSTEIN, Saul, *The Renaissance of the Torah Jew* (New Jersey: Ktav, 1985)

BLACK, Eugene C, *The Social Politics of Anglo-Jewry, 1880–1920* (Oxford: Basil Blackwell, 1989)

BROMBERG, Abraham Isaac, *Migdolei HaChasidut - Belz* (Jerusalem: Mechon L'Chasidut, 1953)

—, *Sefat Emet* (Jerusalem: Mechon L'Chasidut, 1957)

BROOK, Stephen, *The Club – The Jews of Modern Britain* (London: Constable, 1989)

BROT, I, *Tal Hashamayim* (London: Narodiczky, 1929)

CANG, Joel, *The Silent Millions* (London: Rapp-Whiting, 1969)

CESARANI, David (ed.), *The Making of Modern Anglo-Jewry* (London: Blackwell, 1990)

COLLINS, Kenneth E, *Second City Jewry* (Glasgow: Scottish Jewish Archives, 1990)

DAVIDSON, Israel, *Parody in Jewish Literature* (New York: Columbia University Press, 1907)

DAVIDOWICZ, Lucy S, *The Golden Tradition* (London: Vallentine Mitchell, 1967)

DOMB, I, *The Transformation* (London: Hamadfis, 1958)

ELBOGEN, Ismar, *A Century of Jewish Life* (Philadelphia: JPSA, 1953)

ENDELMAN, Todd M, *Radical Assimilation in English Jewish History, 1656–1945* (Indiana: University Press, 1990)

EPSTEIN, L M, *The Jewish Marriage Contract* (New York: The Jewish Theological Seminary, 1927)

ETTINGER, Philip, *'Hope Place' in Liverpool Jewry* (Liverpool: T Lyons, 1930)

FEDERBUSH, Simon (ed.), *HaChasidut VeZion* (New York: Moriah, 1963)

FELDMAN, David, *Kitzur Shulchan Aruch* (Israel: 1971)

FISHMAN, William J, *East End Jewish Radicals* (London: Duckworth, 1975)

—, *East End 1888* (London: Duckworth, 1988)

GARTNER, L P, *The Jewish Immigrant in England 1870–1914* (London and Detroit: Simon, 1960)

GOLLANCZ, Victor, *From Darkness to Light* (London: Victor Gollancz, 1950)

—, *Year of Grace* (London: Victor Gollancz, 1950)

—, *My Dear Timothy* (London: Victor Gollancz, 1952)

—, and Barbara Greene, *God of a Hundred Names* (London: Hodder & Stoughton, 1962)

—, *Reminiscences of Affection* (London: Victor Gollancz, 1968)

GOTLIEB, Wolf, *From Days of Old* (London: Council of Jewish Education, 1948)

GRAETZ, Heinrich, *History of the Jews* (Philadelphia: JPSA, 1946)

GREEN, Arthur, *The Tormented Master* (Alabama: University Press, 1976)

GUTMANN, Mathathias Ezekiel, *MiGibore HaChasidut: Rabbi Dov Baer of Leove* (Tel Aviv: Sifria Nezach, 1952)

HALEVY, Shoshana, *The Printed Hebrew Books in Jerusalem during the first half century, 1841–1891* (Jerusalem: The Ben Zvi Institute, 1963)

HELMREICH, William B, *The World of the Yeshiva – An Intimate Portrait of America's Orthodox Jewry* (New York: The Free Press, 1982)

HERTZ, J H, *Sermons, Addresses and Studies* (London: The Soncino Press, 1938)

HESCHEL, Abraham Joshua, *The Circle of the Baal Shem Tov*, ed. Samuel H Dresner (Chicago and London: University of Chicago Press, 1985)

HOMA, Bernard, *A Fortress in Anglo-Jewry: The Story of the Machzike Hadath* (London: Shapiro, Vallentine, 1953)

—, *Footprints in the Sands of Time* (London: published by the author, 1990)

HORODETSKY, Samuel A, *The Leaders of Chasidism*, translated by Maria Horodezky-Magasanik (London: Hasefer Agency for Literature, 1928)

—, *HaChasidut Ve HaChasidim* (Tel Aviv: Dwir, 1944)

HYAMSON, A M, *British Project for the Restoration of Jews to Palestine* (New York: American Jewish Historical Society, 1917)

JACOBS, Louis, *Palm Tree of Deborah* (London: Vallentine Mitchell, 1960)

—, *Tract on Ecstasy* (London: Vallentine Mitchell, 1963)

—, *Seekers of Unity* (London: Vallentine Mitchell, 1966)

—, *Hasidic Prayer* (London: Routledge & Kegan Paul (Littman Library), 1972)

—, *A Jewish Theology* (London: Darton, Longman & Todd, 1973)

—, *Jewish Mystical Testimony* (New York: Schocken, 1977)

—, *Helping with Inquiries – An Autobiography* (London: Vallentine Mitchell, 1989)

—, *Holy Living* (New York: Jason Aronson, 1990)

JAKOBOVITS, Immanuel, 'Torah Im Derech Eretz today', in *L'Eylah*, journal published by Jews College, London: New Year, 1986

JOHNSON, Paul, *A History of the Jews* (London: Weidenfeld & Nicolson, 1987)

JOST, Isaac Marcus, *Allgemeine Geschichte des Israelitischen Volkes* (Berlin: Carl Friedrich Amelung, 1832)

JUNG, J, *Champions of Orthodoxy* (London: privately printed, 1974)

JUNG, Leo, *Jewish Leaders (1750–1940)* (New York: Black Publicity Company, 1953)

KAISER, Israel David Solomon Hakohen, *Sefer Toldot Chen* (London: Hebrew Book and Gift Centre, 1979)

KLEIN, S, *Toldot HaYishuv HaYehudi B'Eretz Yisrael* (Tel Aviv: Mizpah, 1933)

KLEINBAUM, Jacob Moses, *Haskamah to Torah Or* (Piotrokov, 1925)

KLING, Simcha, *Nachum Sokolow – Servant of his People* (New York: Herzl Press, 1960)

KRANZLER, George, *Williamsburg, A Jewish Community in Transition* (New York: Philip Feldheim, 1961)

KRAUSZ, Ernest, *Leeds Jewry* (Cambridge: JHSE and W. Heffer, 1964)

KUPFERMAN, Jeanette Ann, 'The Lubavitch Hasidim of Stamford Hill' (London: M. Phil, University College, 1975, unpublished)

LAMM, Norman, *Torah Lishmah* (Jerusalem: Mosad Harav Kook, 1972)

LASKI, N, *Jewish Rights and Jewish Wrongs* (London: Soncino Press, 1939)

LEFTWICH, Joseph, *Israel Zangwill* (London: James Clarke, 1957)

LEVY, Arnold, *History of the Sunderland Jewish Community, 1755–1955* (London: Macdonald, 1956)

LIPMAN, Vivian David, *Social History of the Jews in England, 1850–1950* (London: Watts & Co, 1954)

—, (ed.) *Three Centuries of Anglo-Jewish History* (Cambridge: W. Heffer, 1961)

—, (ed.) *Sir Moses Montefiore* (Oxford: Centre for Post-Graduate Studies, 1962)

—, (ed.) *The Century of Moses Montefiore* (Oxford: University Press (The Littman Library), 1985)

—, *A History of the Jews in Britain since 1958* (Leicester: University Press, 1990)

LOEWENTHAL, Naftali, *Communicating the Infinite* (Chicago: University Press, 1990)

LUBAVITCH FOUNDATION, *Challenge: An Encounter with Lubavitch-Chabad* (London: Lubavitch Foundation, 1970)

MAGNUS, Lady, *Outlines of Jewish History* (London: Vallentine Mitchell, 1963)

MALACHI, A R, *Letoldot Beth HaAriga Shel Montefiore B'Yerushalayim* in *Abraham Weiss Jubilee Volume* (New York: 1964), pp. 441–59

—, *Toldot ha-Yishuv Hayashan* (Tel Aviv: University Press, 1987), pp. 150–67

MARX, Alexander, *Studies in Jewish History and Booklore* (New York: The Jewish Theological Seminary of America, 1944)

—, *Essays in Jewish Biography* (Philadelphia: Jewish Publications Society of America, 1947)

MONTEFIORE, Moses, *Diaries of Sir Moses and Lady Montefiore*, ed. L Loewe (London: Griffith Farran Okeden & Welsh, 2 vols., 1890; reprinted by the JHSE, 1983)

MYER, Morris, *Rabbi Yisrael Baal Shem Tov* (London: *Jewish Times*, 1942)

NEWMAN, A, *The Jewish East End 1840–1939* (London: Jewish Historical Society of England, 1981)

OBERMAN, S, *In mayne Teg* (*In my days*) (London: Narod Press, 1947)

OLSOVER, Lewis, *The Jewish Communities of North-East England, 1755–1980* (Gateshead: Ashley Mark Publishing Co., 1980)

PARKS, James, *A History of the Jewish People* (London: East & West Library, 1969)

POLL, Solomon, *The Hasidic Community of Williamsburg* (New York: Schocken Press, 1969)

PORUSH, Shalom Chayim, *Encyclopaedia of Chasidism* (Heb.) (Jerusalem: Mosad Harav Kook, 1980)

PRAGER, Leonard, *Yiddish Culture in Britain* (Frankfurt am Main: Verlag Peter Lang, 1990)

RABINOV, Samuel Joseph, *Divrei Shir* (London: published privately, 1959)

RABINOWICZ, Harry M, *Guide to Chasidism* (New York and London: T Yoseloff, 1960)

—, 'Yeshivot in Poland in the Interwar Years', *Jewish Life*, New York, March/April 1964, pp. 53–9

—, *The Legacy of Polish Jewry* (New York and London: T Yoseloff, 1965)

—, *The World of Hasidism* (London: Vallentine Mitchell, 1970)

—, *Treasures of Judaica* (New York and London: T Yoseloff, 1971)

—, *Hasidism and the State of Israel* (London and Toronto: Associated University Presses, 1982)

—, *Chasidic Rebbes* (New York: Targum/Feldheim, 1990)

—, *Hasidism: The Movement and its Masters* (New Jersey: Jason Aronson, 1988)

RABINOWICZ, Nathan David, *The Will and Testament* (London: Narod Press, 1948)

RAPAPORT-ALBERT, Ada, 'The Problem of Succession in the Hasidic Leadership, with special reference to the Circle of R Nahman of Bratslav', doctoral thesis, University of London, 1974

—, *Hasidism: Reappraisal* (Oxford: Littman Library, 1994)

ROTH, Cecil, *Magna Biblioteca Anglo-Judaica* (London: JHSE, 1937)

—, 'The Lesser London Synagogues of the 18th Century' in TJHSE, Miscellanies, Part III (London: Purnell & Sons, 1937)

— *A History of the Jews in England* (Oxford: Clarendon Press, 1941)

—, *History of the Great Synagogue 1690–1946* (London: Edward Goldston, 1950)

—, *A Short History of the Jewish People* (London: East & West Library, 1953)

RUBIN, Israel, *Satmar – An Island in the City* (Chicago: Quadrangle Books, 1972)

SANDERS, Moshe, *Jewish Books in Whitechapel* (London: Duckworth, 1991)

SCHECHTER, Solomon, *Studies in Judaism* (London: Adam & Charles Black, 1896)

SCHISCHA, Abraham, *Pi Yemale Tehilothecha* (London: privately published, 1984) 11 pages

SCHNEERSOHN, Yosef Yitzchak, *Lubavitcher Rabbi's Memoirs* (Brooklyn: Kehot, 1956)

—, *Iggrois Koidesh*, 12 vols (Brooklyn: Kehot, 1982–85)

SCHOLEM, Gershom, *Origins of the Kabbalah* (Philadelphia: JPSA and Princeton University, 1897)

SHAPOTCHNICK, Joseph, *Midrasch Josef – Randglossen und Indices zum Talmud* (Berlin: H Itzakowski, 1913)

—, *Birchat Yosef* (Odessa: Abba Duchna, 1902; second edition: London: B Weinberg, Gibraltar Press, 1917), 32 pages

—, *Tekuphah Chadashah B'Yisrael*,
Part 1 (London: R Mazin, Misan 1914), 20 pages
Part 2 (London: Express, Iyar 1914), 41 pages
Part 3 (London: Express, Tammuz 1914), 64 pages
—, *Roshei Alphei Yisrael*, periodical: Parts 1 to 17 published in London between 1915 and 1919
—, *Shulchan Hagoboah Shulchan Aruch*, Parts 2, 3, 4 and 5 translated by R C Cohen (London: Express, 1916), 96 pages
—, *Kol Kallah* (London: Express, 1917), 48 pages
—, *Chinuch Hayelodim*, Part 2 of *Kol Kallah*, translated into English by R C Cohen (London: R Cohen, 1917), 14 pages
—, *Sefer Kedushat Hashem* (6 tracts), Part 1, translated by R C Cohen (London: 1918), 53 pages
—, *Passhegn Ksav Hadas*, a religious monthly, Nos 1 and 2 (London: 1918)
—, *Talmud Bavli* (London: 1921)
—, *Shar HaKallah* (London: 1921)
—, *Shas HaKollel* (London: M M Shernitzky, 1921), 68 pages
—, *Chevrat Hakololit Mefitzei Torah* (London: Narodiczky, 1921), 8 pages
—, *Chasidut, der Nayer Sort* (On the new Orthodox movement) in Yiddish (London: 1921), 8 pages
—, *Zeraim-Berachot* in Yiddish (London: 1922)
—, *Shas Hamasbir-Berachot*, Commentary on Tractate Berachot (London: 1923), 100 pages
—, *The London Jewish Free Press* (London: E Shernitzky, 1924)
No. 1 – 11 July 1924
No. 2 – 18 July 1924
No. 3 – 29 Aug. 1924
No. 4 – 26 Oct. 1924
—, *Mephise Torah* (London: 1935), 8 pages
—, *Farvos Veren Iden Gestroft* (London: 1925), 3 pages
—, *Dos Iddisher Vort* (London: 15 May 1925)
—, *Talmud Zeraim* in Yiddish, (London: 1925)
—, *Maaseket Shabbat Mishas Hamasbir* (London: 1925)
—, *Der Iddisher Geist – A Plan Vegen dos Shafn a Iddishe Academye in Eretz Yisrael* (London: 1926), 9 pages
—, *HeAtid HaKarov* (London: 1926), 8 pages
—, *Farshtet Zich Zelbst – 50 Lekties Vegen Menshlicher Psychologye* (London: 1926), 8 pages
—, *Shas Arikat Ner* (London: T B Moet, 1926)
—, *Shas HaMashpia*, Commentaries (London: 1926–8)
—, *Do you know thyself – a Study on Human Psychology in All its Stages.* (London: A B Sochachevsky, 1927), 96 pages
—, *The London Folkszeitung* (People's Paper), London:
No. 1 – April 1927
No. 2 – 4 Oct. 1927
No. 4 – 7 Oct. 1927
No. 5 – 27 Oct. 1927

No. 6 – 25 Nov. 1927
No. 7 – 25 Dec. 1927
No. 8 – 20 Jan. 1928
No. 9 – 21 Feb. 1928
No. 10 – 6 March 1928
No. 11 – 30 March 1928
—, *Dos Eibige Licht* (Perpetual Light) (London: 24 Aug. 1928), 4 pages
—, *Oifn Ekonomishen Krizis* – plea for the establishment of a new Hebrew Printing Press (London: 1928), 8 pages
—, *Untervegens Shas* – *Masechta Gerim* with punctuation (London: Shernitsky, 1927), 32 pages
—, *Likro LaAssurim D'Ror* on halachic questions (London: 1927-8)
—, *Motzi Asirim* – Part 3 (London: 1927), 240 pages
—, *Jewish Observer*, (in English) London: printed by the *Jewish Observer*, No. 1, December and January 1928/29, 4 pages
No. 1 – April 1928
No. 2 – July 1928
—, *Gut Morgen* (*Good Morning*), No. 1 – 18 May 1928 (London: 1928), 4 pages
—, *A New Beth Din* (London: 1928), 10 pages
—, *Cherut Olam* – on the problems of the *Agunah* (56 pages) (London: Express, 1928)
—, *Siddur Revid HaZahav* (London: 1929), 112 pages
—, *Revid HaZahav Sefer Tehillim* (London: Narodiczky, 1930)
—, *Der Yom Hadin* (London: Superior Printers, 5 Sept. 1930), 4 pages
—, *Der Emes* (London: 7 June 1931)
—, *Tikkun Eruv L'Shabbat* (London: 1932), 8 pages
—, *Shulchan Aruch Limmudei HaShem* (London: 1932), 26 pages
—, *The London Free Press* (London: Express, 4 April 1933), 4 pages
—, *The Morning Star* (London: 25 June 1933), 4 pages
—, *The World Doctor*, in English and Yiddish, London:
24 Nov. 1933
2 Feb. 1934
24 Nov. 1936
—, *The Jews Amongst the Nations* – *in Defence of the Talmud* (London: 1934), 15 pages
—, *Matter and Spirit* – *The Four Principles of the Universe* (London: Express Printers, 1935), 8 pages
—, *The Talmud* – *Brachot* (Abridged) part 1 – Commentary and Interpretation, in English (London: M M Shernitzky, second edition 1936), 32 pages
—, *Hamaor SheBe'Talmud* – the Talmud abridged with commentaries (London: Express, 1936), 16 pages
—, *The Soul of the Bible*, Genesis Chapter 1, verses 1–9 (London: 1936)
—, *The New Prospect for World Peace* – *The World Doctor* – extra special edition (London: 29 May 1936), 4 pages
—, *In Memory of our beloved King George V* (London: 1936)
—, *Jewish Tutor for Home Study* (London: Express Printers, 1937), 32 pages

271

—, *To our Sovereign Lord, King George VI and to our Gracious Queen Elizabeth on the occasion of their Majesties accession to the throne* (London: 1937)
—, *Folks Zeitung* (London: Nisan 1937)
—, *A Nayer Beth Din* (News Sheet) (London: 1937)
    No. 1 – 15 Jan. 1937
    No. 2 – 22 Jan. 1937
    No. 3 – 29 Jan. 1937
    No. 4 – 12 Feb. 1937
    No. 5 – 19 Feb. 1937
    No. 6 – 5 March 1937
    No. 7 – 30 April 1937
    No. 8 – 28 May 1937
    No. 9 – 4 June 1937
—, *The Talmud with New Commentary – Baba Kama* (London: June 1937), 18 pages
—, *The Talmud with New Commentary – Baba Bathra* (London: 1937)
—, *The Talmud with New Commentary – Avodah Zarah* (London: 1937)
—, *The Free Press* (London: 30 September 1937), 4 pages
—, *The Talmud – Pirkei Avot*, Commentary and Interpretation (London: 1937), 16 pages
—, *The Jewish Tribune*, by the circle of 'Rabbi Shapotchnick, Bnei Brith', ed. Levi Shapotchnik (London: Express, 1937), 4 pages
SHEMIAN, Zelig (ed.), *Dos Londoner Yiddishe Vort* (polemics against Shapotchnick) (London: B. Weinberg, 1928)
SIMON, Maurice, *Jewish Religious Conflicts* (London: Hutchinson University Library, 1950)
—, *Israel Baalshem, His Life and Times – Leading Figure in Jewish History* (London: Jewish Religious Educational Establishment, 1953)
SINGER, Steven, 'Orthodox Judaism in Early Victorian London, 1840–1858' (PhD thesis, New York: Yeshiva University, 1981)
SOCHACHEWSKY, B A, *Joseph Shapotchnick: A Biography* (London: Ben A Sochachewsky, 1927), 30 pages
SOKOLIC, Leonard Barry, 'Change and Transition in a Religious Immigrant Group in the East End of London, 1881–1940', PhD thesis, 1984 (London: Jews' College, unpublished)
SPERBER, Miriam, *Misipurei Hasabta* (Jerusalem: Imrei Sefer, 1986)
—, *Grandmother's Tales* (Jerusalem: Imrei Sefer, 1990)
SPIRA, Jacob Joseph, *Mille D'Hespeda*, Eulogy on Rabbi Issachar Dov Rokeach of Belz (London: privately published, 1927)
SZPETMAN, Joshua, *Chevlei Haneshama Umusar Hayahadut* (Warsaw, 1938)
—, *Kuntres Ha-Emes, Aleph*, London: May 1942, 15 pages;
    Bet, London, Sept. 1942, 16 pages
    Gimel, London Nov. 1942, 16 pages
    Daled, London, Dec. 1942, 32 pages
    Hey, London, Jan. 1943, 32 pages
—, *Der polisher Yid* (London: Narodiczky, 1944), 32 pages
—, *Mimamakim Halev, Harzige Verter zu unser Folk* (London, 1951), 20 pages

—, *BeigilofinFergangene Velten* (Past Worlds – about Chasidim and Folklore) (London: Superior Printers, 1951), 96 pages

—, *Teshuva un Geula Momenten* (Moments of Repentance) (London: 1952), 24 pages

—, *Lekoved Pesach* (London: 1952), 20 pages; (another edition: London, 1953), 24 pages

—, *Lekoved Yomim Noroim* (London: *Rosh Hashana* 1953), 24 pages

—, *Chag HaPesach, Eliyahu Hanovi* (London: Nisan 1953/54), 24 pages

—, *Lekoved Pesach, Lag B'Omer, Shavuoth* (London: Superior Printers, April 1955), 31 pages

—, *Lekoved Rosh Hashana . . . Simchat Torah* (London: 1955), 31 pages

—, *Pesach, Shavuoth* (London: Superior Printers, March 1956), 43 pages

—, *Rosh Hashana . . . Chanuka* (London: September 1956), 47 pages

—, *Lekoved Pesach* (London: April 1957), 48 pages

—, *Lekoved Rosh Hashana* (London: September 1957), 48 pages

—, *15 Years since the Uprising in the Warsaw Ghetto* (London: Superior Printers, April 1958), 48 pages

—, *Rosh Hashana* (London: Superior Printers, 1958), 48 pages

—, *Kuntres Cheshbon Hanefesh* (London: September 1959), 56 pages

TAYLOR, Anne, *Laurence Oliphant* (Oxford: University Press, 1982)

TEITELBAUM, A, *Der Emes un Shecker*, translated by J Stone (London: Razor Printers, 1916), 20 pages

UDELSON, Joseph H, *Dreamer of the Ghetto* (Tuscaloosa and London: University of Alabama Press, 1990)

UNSDORFER, Simcha, *The Yellow Star* (New York: Yoseloff, 1961)

WEISS, J G, *Studies in Eastern European Jewish Mystiscism*, ed. David Goldstein (Oxford: University Press (Littman Library), 1985)

WEIZMANN, Chaim, *Trial and Error* (London: East and West Library, 1950)

WOHLGELERNTER, Maurice, *Israel Zangwill* (New York: Columbia University Press, 1964)

ZANGWILL, Israel, *Children of the Ghetto* (London: The Globe Publishing Co, 1921)

—, *Dreamers of the Ghetto* (London: William Heinemann, 1898)

—, *Speeches, Articles and Letters of Israel Zangwill*, ed. Mauric Simon (London: Soncino, 1957)

ZINBERG, Israel, *A History of Jewish Literature*, translated and edited by Bernard Martin, 12 vols (New York: Ktav, 1978)

Index